DISCOVERING MOSCOW

The flag on the front cover and at the head of each page is Moscow's
coat-of-arms: St George Fighting the Dragon.

DISCOVERING MOSCOW

The Complete Companion Guide

Helen Boldyreff Semler

St. Martin's Press
New York

In memory of our daughter
Tasha Semler
and for all those who
love Moscow and struggle to preserve
its cultural and historical heritage

Library of Congress Cataloging-in-Publication Data

Semler, Helen Boldyreff.
    Discovering Moscow : the complete companion guide / Helen
Boldyreff Semler.
        p.   cm.
    Updated ed.: New York : Hippocrene, c1987.
    Includes index.
    ISBN 0-312-05076-3
    1. Art, Russian—Russian S.F.S.R.—Moscow—Guide-books.   2. Moscow
(R.S.F.S.R.)—Description—Guide-books.   I. Title.
N6997.M7S47   1990
    914′31204854—dc20   90-36142
                                                                    CIP

First published in the United States by Hippocrene Books.

10   9   8   7   6   5   4   3   2   1

CONTENTS

ACKNOWLEDGEMENTS

*T*he author gratefully acknowledges the editorial assistance of Nadiezda Kizenko, Nicholas and Ruth Daniloff, Tatiana Pouschine, Helen v. T. Semler, Peter Semler, Robert L. Krattli, as well as contributions from Nicholas Daniloff, Dorothy Fels Alquier, Madeleine Kirk, Professor Dmitry Pospielovsky (who edited the chapters on the clergy), and my own father, Professor Constantin W. Boldyreff, who reviewed the book for its historical content.

Writing and editing credits: Nick Daniloff did much of the writing and major editing on the Introduction and Moscow of the Tsars. Nadiezda Kizenko edited Excursions 1 and 5. Mrs Dorothy Alquier wrote the French version of the Pushkin Museum and Metro section, which Mrs Patricia Legras translated into English. Ruth Daniloff, Robert Krattli, Susan Yost, and Elizabeth Kirk also helped with editing the text. Martin Fowkes and Jean Farrow helped with research. Nathalia N. Chernishova did the final proofreading and editing. The index was compiled by Kate Chapman.

Typing credits and special thanks: Anita Taylor, Connie Voegele, Bobbie Brooks, Cecilia Angelsberg, Susan Yost, Caren Laughlin, Terry Hiener, Fiona Bignell, and Edna Rey. Also many thanks to all the Russian consultants who wish to remain anonymous, but without whose help this book would never have happened. And a special word of gratitude to my husband Peter and my daughters Tania and Helen who either edited or wrote parts of this book, and who stood by me (more or less enthusiastically) during the twenty years it took me to produce this volume.

Photography credits: Mrs Evelyn Musser, Mr Jack Morgan, Mrs Katja Kuchinke, Aleksei Aleksandrovich Alexandrov, Mr Tom Spencer, and Mr Jack Tracy.

My deep appreciation also to Michael Cox, my editor, for the care and painstaking attention which he devoted to the book.

Note: Most of the Excursions that follow are preceded by an Excursion Plan. References to the appropriate plan are by means of ringed numbers in the text, thus ㉑. Ⓜ on the Excursion Plans signifies Metro stations.

THE FACE AND SPIRIT OF MOSCOW

*M*ore than eight hundred years have gone into the making of Moscow. Today it is an industrial metropolis of eight million people, the capital of both the Russian Federation (RSFSR) and the Soviet Union (USSR). It remains, however, the embodiment of the Russian character.

For centuries, Moscow has been the political capital of the Russian state, the holy city of Russian Orthodoxy, and the traditional heart of Russian culture. To understand Moscow, one must recall the sweep of Russian history. Only then does the city reveal its face and disclose its secrets — why it grew in concentric circles about the Kremlin's battlements, why fortified monasteries ring its outer limits, why small houses alternate with brightly painted churches and imposing palaces.

Today, as in pre-revolutionary times, the Western visitor to Russia feels more at home in the European architecture and traditions of Leningrad (the former St Petersburg). Moscow is different and elusive. Foreigners used to return from a visit to Moscow with tales of open-air markets and long rides to the Yar Restaurant at night to hear gypsy music. They delighted in the symphony of onion domes rising about the city and the pleasant confusion of narrow twisting streets, punctuated by the surprise of ancient churches, the quaint wooden houses, and the city-village character of central Moscow. Even the mammoth new railroad stations sought in their architecture to capture the variety and colour of the Russian hinterland, while the new department stores retained some of the flavour of the oriental bazaar. For the visitor, this exotica co-existed with the familiar reassurance of international-style hotels, with their European orchestras, and with the cultural sophistication of the well-travelled Muscovite élite.

These contrasts persist to this day. Even after nearly a century of concentrated official socialism, Moscow remains a Russian city. It is the product neither of Communist ideology nor of the Westernized philosophy that shaped St Petersburg. Beneath the surface, an unconquerable spirit has helped Moscow to endure hardships. Moscow proudly suffered the ignominy of Peter the Great's transfer of the capital to St Petersburg at the beginning of the eighteenth century, relegating Moscow to provincial status until Lenin returned it as the seat of government in March 1918. It survived the incursions of Napoleon and Hitler as it had the Tartars in earlier centuries. Even Stalin's facelifts, the severest crippling a city suffered at the hands of one of its own since Nero burned Rome, failed to break Moscow's spirit. For those willing to discover it, the beautiful old face of the city smiles a welcome from under its modern overlay as if from behind a Greek mask.

PART I

MOSCOW OF THE TSARS

INTRODUCTION

*I*van III (*r*. 1462–1505), the ambitious Grand Prince of Moscow was the first to use the title of 'tsar', a Russified version of the word Caesar. The title was formally assumed by his grandson **Ivan IV,** who in 1547 crowned himself tsar and adopted the double-headed eagle of Byzantium as the new Russian emblem. The transformation of the rulers of Moscow from grand dukes (see Excursion 1, p. 18) into imperial autocrats was triggered by the fall of Constantinople in 1453. Seeing the capital of Eastern Orthodoxy overrun by the infidel Turks, Ivan III proclaimed himself the protector of the true faith and the rightful successor to the Roman and Byzantine Caesars.

Ivan III's new obligation added yet another dimension to the 'sacred' duty which he inherited from his predecessors: to unify the dismembered Russian state under the Moscow banner. (Kiev, the first capital, was gutted by the Tartars in 1240, and its successor, the Grand Duchy of Vladimir, disintegrated as a result of feuds among the princes.) The sacred task which now fell upon Ivan III was to liberate Kievan lands still under foreign rule, to safeguard Russian Orthodoxy, whose Holy See settled in Moscow (see Excursion 1, p. 19) in 1326, after the fall of Vladimir, and to establish once and for all that he was the true heir of the grand princes of Kiev and Vladimir.

In doing so Ivan III, like his forerunners, laid claim to all the symbols that served Moscow's cause: the crown jewels of Kiev, the legacy of Byzantium, the best painters of the cities which escaped sacking by the Tartars, and the sacred icons of the Russian principalities, including the icon of *Our Lady of Vladimir*, the most sacred possession of Russia and the palladium (protector) of the previous capitals. Whether taken by force or given freely, all the treasures and venerated icons eventually ended up in Moscow — more specifically in the Kremlin.

After the fall of Constantinople, the rulers of Moscow adopted the Byzantine conception of *symphonia*, the essential unity of Church and State, with the ruler as the representative of God and the true faith on earth. The intellects and talents of the tsars were far from equal, but they all sensed the weight of the Crown of Monomach* (the fur-trimmed cap with which tsars were crowned), of their roles as anointed tsars, inescapably answerable to God.

In theory, all authority belonged to the Russian autocrats, who had the state apparatus as the powerful agent of their will. In practice, many factors

* The imperial regalia was allegedly the gift of the Byzantine Emperor Constantine Monomach to the Kievan Prince Vladimir.

INTRODUCTION

restrained the tsars and the emperors from the arbitrary exercise of their status: their allegiance to the Christian faith, the opinions of their advisors, and the laws of the land. Even Ivan IV (r. 1533–84), who at the age of 17 was crowned the Tsar of all the Russias, could not escape being tormented by the transgressions of the darkest years of his reign.

Because of Ivan's excesses, many Western historians rendered his Russian epithet *Groznyi* into 'the Terrible', when in fact *Groznyi* means 'awe-inspiring'. Ivan IV indeed shared this appellation with his illustrious grandfather, Ivan III.

Ivan was only three when his father, **Basil III,** died in 1533. The cruelty of the ranking boyars towards the orphaned youth caused him to grow suspicious of the nobles, a suspicion which, following the death of Ivan's wife **Anastasia** in 1560, turned into an obsession.

During Ivan the Terrible's 'benevolent' period, however, Russia made great strides; the tsar expanded the borders, opened new trade routes, subdued the Tartars, and established contacts with the West. He patronized the arts and introduced many administrative, legal, and military reforms. The repressions which intensified after 1560 were directed mainly against the landed boyars, whom Ivan accused of treason and whom he strove to replace with a service class drafted from the lower gentry.

The pious, gentle **Fedor I,** Ivan the Terrible's oldest surviving son, ruled in name only. The actual power was wielded by **Boris Godunov**, whose sister Irina was married to Fedor. In 1598, upon Fedor's death, the National Assembly elected Boris to the Russian throne. A shrewd and capable ruler, Boris was haunted by calumnies and palace intrigues, whilst rumour accused him of murdering Prince Dmitry, Ivan the Terrible's youngest son and potential rival to the throne.

After the death of Boris Godunov in 1605, the Time of Troubles was upon Russia, bringing political disorder, social revolution, and foreign invasion. The Kremlin was captured by the Poles. This period ended in 1613 with the election of **Michael Romanov** (r. 1613–45), the founder of the Romanov dynasty, which ruled until 1917.

Michael's son, **Alexis,** became tsar in 1645. He was succeeded by his son **Fedor III** in 1676, a weak-legged lad of fifteen who suffered from scurvy and immediately found himself in a vicious family feud. His sister **Sofia**, a well-educated and ambitious spinster, led one faction that represented the Miloslavskys, her mother's family; Natalia Naryshkina, the second wife of Tsar Alexis and the mother of **Peter,** directed the other. Once the ailing monarch died in 1682, the feud broke out into the open. Fedor had had no sons, so the choice of a successor was left to a National Assembly, who had to decide between the nine-year-old Peter and his sixteen-year-old half-brother, Ivan, who was partially blind and mentally retarded. Peter was proclaimed tsar, but Sofia instigated a coup aided by the musketeers, who stormed the Kremlin and massacred Peter's uncle and his mother's closest advisors as the young Peter watched the carnage. His hatred of Sofia, of the fickle musketeers, and above all of the Moscow Kremlin stemmed from that day. Sofia emerged

Tsar Fedor III, son of Alexis Romanov.

victorious from the coup with the title of regent and had Ivan proclaimed senior tsar with Peter as junior tsar. Sofia ended her days at Novodevichiy Convent after being deposed by Peter in 1689. Ivan died in 1696 and Peter became the sole ruler.

In 1712, Peter the Great did the extraordinary thing that Nikolai Gogol described as putting the capital of Russia 'at the end of the world'. Peter moved the Russian capital out of the Kremlin and transported it four hundred miles north-west, to the mouth of the Neva River. There, on the marshy banks of the Gulf of Finland, rose the new Westernized capital of St Petersburg. Its ruler, the 41-year-old Tsar Peter, the last Moscow ruler to be crowned with the sable-fringed Crown of Monomach, would formally assume the title of 'Father of the Country, Emperor and Great', although he would also stage a formal coronation ceremony for himself and his wife, **Catherine I.** The traditional rite took place at the Uspensky Cathedral in Moscow in 1724.

But despite its reduced status, Moscow remained the heart of Russia, and the Kremlin the keeper of traditions. Imperial heads continued to be crowned in Uspensky Cathedral.

Peter's daughter, **Elizabeth** (r. 1741–61), defined the St Petersburg–Moscow relationship: national policy and major architecture were executed in St Petersburg, but homage was still paid to Moscow. Moscow's architectural monuments were no longer made to order but became the cast-offs from Petersburg's Italian Baroque palaces of Elizabeth or the classical monuments of **Empress Catherine II,** the Great.

This German-born empress, who overthrew her husband **Peter III** during a palace coup in 1762, became the true successor to Peter the Great's reforms and aspirations. She fulfilled his dream of creating a strong Russian empire by bringing under Russian control the right bank of the Dniepr River, the North-western Ukraine, Lithuania, and Courland. In doing so, she also realized the sacred mission of the Moscow tsars: Russia had at last reclaimed all of its Kievan heritage.

The wars which Catherine II waged against Turkey secured for Russia the access to the Black Sea and legitimatized the annexation of the Crimea.

A cultivated woman, who corresponded with the leading intellectuals of her time, Catherine fostered knowledge and patronized arts. Her building enthusiasm, however, nearly caused the Kremlin's demise.

Deciding that Russia's imperial grandeur should be commemorated by an imposing Kremlin palace, she entrusted **Vasily Bazhenov** with this task. Bazhenov conceived the palace as an enormous triangular-shaped edifice which would have displaced and destroyed most of the Kremlin's historic buildings except for three cathedrals and two monasteries.

The southern wall of the Kremlin was dismantled so that the palace would face directly on the Moscow River below. When Catherine ordered the work stopped in 1772, mostly because of the heavy expenditure of the Russo-Turkish War, the remainder of the Kremlin was saved.

Napoleon's invasion of Russia in 1812 brought Moscow's importance back into the limelight. The victorious Grand Army had surged across the central plains and reached the city gates by September. When Napoleon entered the Borovitskaya Gates of the Kremlin, however, a disastrous blaze broke out, destroying two-thirds of Moscow.

Overcome by fire and famine, Napoleon was forced to abandon Moscow, but not before ordering it blown up and plundering the Kremlin churches. The demolition was executed only in part, sparing the greater part of the historic fortress, but the Uspensky Cathedral was virtually cleaned out by the retreating troops. Some five tons of silver and 288 kilos of gold were stripped from the interior and the icons carried away.

On 19 March 1814 it was the turn of **Alexander I** (1801–25) to march into the capital of his opponent. Paris, unlike Moscow, offered its conqueror a thunderous ovation.

Moscow, however, was not to share in the grandeur that Alexander brought to Russia. While the majestic Palace Square and the semicircular building of the Russian General Staff ushered in the 'Empire' style in St Petersburg, the Kremlin was left to lick its wounds.

Also abandoned were Alexander's earlier promises to liberate the serfs and grant Russia a constitutional monarchy. When the Emperor died unexpectedly in 1825, a handful of reform-minded guard officers challenged the ascent of his brother **Nicholas I** to the throne. On 14 December the organizers, known as the Decembrists, staged a hastily hatched coup in St Petersburg. Nicholas quelled the revolt, but the conspirators were treated mildly in comparison with twentieth-century totalitarian regimes. Of the 121 Decembrists brought to trial, thirty six were sentenced to death, but only five were executed due to Emperor Nicholas's personal intercession.

Known as the 'Gendarme of Europe', Nicholas I (r. 1825–55) censured criticism and punished dissent. This did not, however, prevent intellectual thought from flourishing, nor Russia from celebrating its golden age of literature.

Alexander II (r. 1855–81) was remembered in Russian history as Tsar the Liberator and the ruler who strove to grant Russia a constitutional monarchy. He freed peasants from serfdom and the Slavonic people in the Balkans from their Turkish overlords. Alexander also introduced major legal and self-governing reforms which contributed to Moscow's cultural and economic development.

On 1 March 1881, after seven attempts, a group of revolutionary terrorists assassinated the tsar. His son **Alexander III** (r. 1881–94) sharply curtailed the pro-constitutional movement in Russia. **Nicholas II,** who next ascended the throne, continued the reactionary policies of his father. Contributing to his fall was the unsuccessful war with Japan, the Revolution of 1905, the struggle against the newly created Duma, the murder in 1911 of Prime Minister and reformer Stolypin, and finally the devastating First World War.

On 25 February 1917 the Revolution flared up in St Petersburg. Nicholas was forced to abdicate in favour of his brother **Michael,** who, in turn turned over the power to a democratic Provisional Government. Fourteen months later, Nicholas II with his wife, four daughters, and the sick male heir, who had been taken prisoners by the Bolsheviks, were brutally murdered by agents of the Soviet government. During the difficult war years and internal turmoil, the shaky Provisional Government only had time to prepare general election to the Constituent Assembly. On 7 November 1917 Bolsheviks overthrew the Kerensky government. On 19 January 1918 **Lenin** disbanded the lawfully elected Constituent Assembly and thus *de facto* established the Soviet government. Lenin died in 1924. The power was assumed by **Stalin,** who soon established his dictatorship.

In the Soviet period red stars replaced the double-headed eagles on the towers of the Kremlin, and red flags the imperial standards. The monarch is gone, but the ambitions and the defeats, the joys and the sorrows of the tsars and tsarinas are still mirrored in the Kremlin's art work and stone. The tsars have come and gone, but the venerable monuments of the Kremlin complex record their proud passage and their contribution to the evolution of Moscow from a backward principality to the capital of a powerful empire.

INTRODUCTION

Excursion Plan 1
The Kremlin

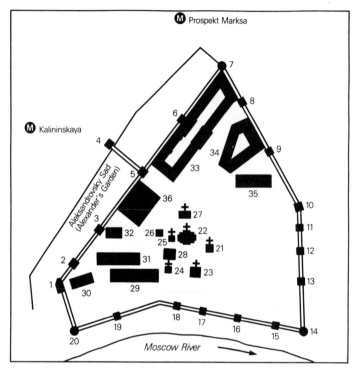

The Kremlin Walls and Towers

1. The Borovitskaya Tower
2. The Armoury Tower
3. The Kommendantskaya Tower
4. The Kutafya Tower
5. The Trinity Tower
6. The Arsenal Tower
7. The Sobakina Tower
8. The Nikolskaya Tower
9. The Senate Tower
10. The Saviour's Tower
11. The Tsar's Tower
12. The Alarm Tower
13. SS. Constantine and Helen Tower
14. Beklemishev Tower
15. Petrovskaya Tower
16–17. Nameless Towers
18. The Tower of the Secrets
19. The Annunciation Tower
20. The Water Tower

Inside the Kremlin

21. The Bell Tower of Ivan the Great
22. Uspensky (The Dormition Cathedral)
23. Arkhangelsky (Cathedral of Archangel Michael)
24. Blagoveshchensky (The Cathedral of the Annunciation)
25. Church of the Deposition of the Virgin's Robe
26. The Upper Saviour's Cathedral
27. The Church of the Twelve Apostles
28. The Granovitaya Palace (Palace of the Facets)
29. The Great Kremlin Palace
30. The Armoury Museum
31. The Terem Palace
32. The Amusement Palace
33. The Arsenal
34. The Senate Building
35. Presidium of the Supreme Soviet of the USSR
36. The Kremlin Palace of Congresses

THE KREMLIN

Uspensky Cathedral — Annunciation Cathedral — Arkhangelsky Cathedral — Palace of the Facets — Golden Hall of the Tsarianas — Bell Tower of Ivan the Great — Tsar's Bell — Tsar's Cannon — Armoury Museum — Terem Palace — Upper Saviour's Cathedral — Church of the Deposition of the Virgin's Robe — Church of the Twelve Apostles — Amusement Palace — Arsenal — Senate — Great Kremlin Palace — Kremlin Palace of Congresses.

Access to the Kremlin is by the Trinity (Troitskaya) Gate at the centre of its northern wall. Check with Intourist to see which buildings are open to visitors and make arrangements for the Armoury Museum, the Diamond Collection, and Lenin's Apartment, all of which require organized tours. No special permission is necessary for the following buildings: Uspensky (Dormition) Cathedral, Blagoveshchensky (Annunciation) Cathedral, Arkhangelsky (Archangel Michael's) Cathedral, the Bell Tower of Ivan the Great, the former Palace of Patriarch Nikon, and the Church of the Deposition of the Robe, adjoining it. The former churches are now state-run museums; tickets are available at the kiosk at the foot of the Bell Tower of Ivan the Great.

*T*he Kremlin, a panorama of golden domes above red crenellated walls, is the focal point of Moscow and the heart of Russia. Seen from the air, the walls of the fortress form an irregular triangle, enclosing an area of some sixty-nine acres. Twenty towers, six of them lofty gates surmounted by tent-shaped steeples and red stars, once guarded the Kremlin from its marauders — Tartars, Poles, Swedes, Lithuanians, and the French. In 1917 the ancient churches looked down on another bloody battle, as a detachment of Red Guards seized the fortress from volunteers loyal to the Provisional Government. Five months later, in March 1918, the former citadel of the tsars and the See of the Orthodox faith became the seat of the Soviet government.

The growth and embellishment of the Kremlin have reflected the major events which shaped the destiny of Moscow. As Moscow's status changed from that of a military outpost securing the south-western boundary of the Vladimir-Suzdal principality to the capital of a centralized Russian state, the Kremlin also evolved from a wooden fortress into a magnificent architectural ensemble with cathedrals, towers, and palaces. Struck by the majesty of its panorama, the poet Lermontov exclaimed, 'What can be compared with the Kremlin surrounded by its spiked walls, priding itself in the beauty of its golden domes, as it rests upon the mountain like the crown on the brow of a mighty ruler? . . . Neither the Kremlin, nor its turreted walls, its dark passages, or magnificent palaces, lends itself to description: one must see it and listen with an open heart to the feelings it inspires.'

The first time the Kremlin is mentioned in the Russian chronicles two themes that recur throughout the rest of the history of Muscovy emerge: hospitality and political intrigue. The two have often gone hand in hand. The founder of Moscow, Prince Yuriy of Suzdal, gave a 'mighty banquet' for his ally, Prince Sviatoslav of Chernigov, in 1147. Two years later, assured of the latter's support, Yuriy seized the senior throne of Kiev, earning himself the nickname of 'Dolgoruky', meaning 'he of the long hand'. Transforming a primitive village into a sturdy fortress (kremlin), Prince Yuriy Dolgoruky created a protected trading centre and set the course of Moscow history into motion.

Even more important than trade in Moscow's development was the emergence of a ruling dynasty of Moscow princes who, having given up the claim to the throne of Kiev, settled in the Kremlin permanently. **Daniel** (r. 1276–1303), the youngest son of the great statesman and military leader, Prince Aleksandr Nevsky of Novgorod, founded the dynasty when he arrived with a retinue of nobles to take up residence in the Kremlin in 1272. He transformed the transient quarters of the Suzdal princes into the capital of a new city-state, which he later enlarged by annexing the cities of Kolomna and Pereslavl-Zalessky. To reinforce the Kremlin and to protect the new merchant settlement, Daniel ordered a number of fortified monasteries built around Moscow. The first of these buttressed cloisters, named **Danilovsky** in honour of the prince's patron saint, went up on the road leading to the Tartar headquarters. A settlement grew up around the monastery, establishing a sequence that would repeat itself time and again: new monasteries and settlements sprang up along the periphery of Moscow, while new walled suburbs spread outward from the Kremlin. The suburbs and the monastery settlements eventually converged to form a unified city, and Moscow came to resemble a giant spiderweb cut through by roads which all came together at the Kremlin.

Under Daniel's son, **Ivan** (r. 1325–41), known as 'Kalita' (moneybags) for the efficient management of money that earned him the right to act as the Tartar agent for collecting tribute from the Russians, Moscow emerged as the most powerful of several Russian city-states. Ivan expanded the territory of Moscow by buying or subjugating neighbouring principalities. In 1328 the Tartar Khan gave him the *yarlyk*, or title of Grand Prince, which established his seniority over the other Russian princes. Ivan's descendants retained the Tartar-derived seniority.

Ivan's efforts to consolidate the dismembered Russian principalities into a united state did not go unnoticed by **Metropolitan Peter,** the head of the Russian Orthodox Church. To assist Ivan in his task and to enhance Moscow's political prestige, the metropolitan engineered the move of the Holy See from Vladimir, where it had settled after the fall of Kiev in 1240, to Moscow in 1326. Moscow's secular authority was thus strengthened by its new status as the religious capital of Russia. The Kremlin, the seat of government, also became the centre of ecclesiastical power.

The value of Church support for the Russian autocracy was clearly demonstrated when **Prince Dmitry** inherited the Russian throne in 1359 as an eight-year-old boy. The cause of Russian unity and the difficult negotiations with the Golden Horde were conducted on his behalf by **Metropolitan Alexis.** After the death of Alexis his close friend, **Sergei of Radonezh,** founder of the **Trinity Sergius Monastery,** rallied the Russian princes around Dmitry, enabling him to challenge the Tartar supremacy for the first time at the battle at Kulikovo Field in 1380. This battle on the upper Don gave Dmitry the surname 'Donskoy' and assured his place in Russian history. Under him, Moscow began to eclipse Vladimir, the former Russian capital in the north-east, as a national and cultural centre.

Under **Ivan III** (*r.* 1462–1505), known as the 'Gatherer of the Russian Lands', Moscow stopped paying tribute to the Tartars and its frontiers expanded toward the Ural Mountains in the east and as far as the Arctic Sea in the north. With Ivan's annexation of the merchant republic of Novgorod, Russia finally gained access to the sea.

It was not, however, Moscow's geographical expansion that changed the course of Russian history but the fall of Constantinople to the Turks in 1453. Moscow came to regard itself as the Third Rome and the new centre of Eastern Orthodoxy, while Ivan III announced himself the rightful successor to the Byzantine emperors. To reinforce his claim, he married Zoe Palaelogue, the niece of the last Byzantine emperor, and was the first grand prince to call himself tsar.

It was also Ivan who gave the fourteenth-century Cathedral Square its present appearance. In place of three earlier cathedrals and the golden-roofed palace of Dmitry Donskoy, he commissioned splendid new buildings from Italian Renaissance architects summoned for this task. A palace and three new cathedrals rose in rapid succession around the Cathedral Square, while sturdy walls and towers replaced the old crumbling fortifications between 1485 and 1516.

Embellished and enlarged, Cathedral Square now matched its role as the stage for the royal ceremonies of the Third Rome. Each of the new buildings served a specific need: the tsars were crowned in the Uspensky Cathedral, baptized and wed in the Blagoveshchensky, and, when they died, buried in the Arkhangelsky Cathedral. The Bell Tower of Ivan the Great served as the Kremlin's focal point, while the Granovitaya Palace provided formal quarters for royal receptions.

(Uspensky Sobor) ㉒

Uspensky (Dormition) Cathedral

The rectangular, five-domed cathdral built by the Bolognese architect Aristotle Fioravanti between 1475 and 1479 is austere, majestic, and beautifully proportioned. It represents a feat of architectural diplomacy: Fioravanti struck a perfect balance between the prototypes of the cathedrals in Vladimir, Novgorod, and Pskov, which he had been dispatched to study, and the innovative features of the Italian Renaissance.

Ivan III had wanted exactly that: a national shrine embodying the concept of Russian 'unity' expressed via frescoes, icons, and architectural prototypes from all Russia but built, for lack of experienced native know-how, with the

EXCURSION 1

best available technology from abroad. Here the tsars and the metropolitans would jointly invoke the name of the Lord: the metropolitans as they crowned the tsars, and the tsars as they invested the newly elected heads of the Church.

Fioravanti combined Italian workmanship and Byzantine tradition to make the Uspensky Cathedral an architectural jewel.

Architecture

It took Fioravanti four years to complete the Uspensky Cathedral. Following the directions to model it after the Uspensky Cathedral in Vladimir, Fioravanti made the Kremlin church roughly the same size as its prototype but lengthened it by adding a loggia. He placed the Uspensky on a tall socle and divided its stout walls by flat pilaster strips with capitals. To soften the severity of the facade, he used the Suzdal and Vladimir method of adding a belt of decorative arcades around the walls at mid-height. He opened up the interior to light by fitting window embrasures in the small niches formed by the arcades and placed larger and taller windows in the semicircular arches crowning the walls. The narrow windows in the drums of the cathedral's five domes became Uspensky's third and most important source of light.

While respecting Russian church-building traditions, Fioravanti made use of his Renaissance training as well. Designing five apses instead of the usual three, he equalized the height of the semicircular *zakomar* arches and levelled them off under a common roof. Inside, four rounded pillars supported the light drums and the raised cross-vaulting, while two square pillars were hidden behind the altar division. The thickness of the pillars and the walls, in relation to the height of the interior, was such that the eye could take in the entire expanse at a glance. Fioravanti's combination of Italian workmanship and Byzantine tradition created an architectural jewel where, in the words of the Moscow chronicles, the circular pillars 'seemed like slender trees reaching towards Heaven'.

Art

While Ivan III had of necessity searched for an architect abroad, he could entrust the interior decorations of his cathedrals to Russian artists. In 1481, Dionysius, the priest Timofei, Yarets, and Kon were charged with the delicate task of decorating the church, weaving together two central themes: unity between the terrestrial and heavenly Church and unity between Russia's principalities and their Moscow ruler, the successor to the Byzantine emperors. The frescoes and the icons of the Uspensky Cathedral were thus to provide the official illustration of religious dogma for the national shrine of the Third Rome.

In executing their task the painters relied on Byzantine and Kievan traditions. The narration of themes, for example, begins at the ceilings and upper sections and progresses downward, telling the story of Christendom from Creation through the earthly cycle of Jesus Christ.

The largest cycles of **frescoes** is devoted to the glorification of the Virgin Mary. Illustrated chants from the *Acathistos*, a series of odes to the Mother of God, occupy most of the northern and southern walls. Their presence in the Uspensky is explained by the dedication of this Moscow church to the feast of *Uspenie*, the Virgin's *Dormition* and *Assumption* to Heaven. This was a marked departure from the Byzantine tradition of consecrating the main cathedral to St Sofia, or the Wisdom of God, as was the case in Constantinople, Kiev, and Novgorod. Not fully identifying with the concept of St Sofia as a victorious, imperial Orthodox Church reigning on earth, the princes of Vladimir searched for a simpler depiction of God's wisdom when it came to their turn to inaugurate a new cathedral. They finally chose to portray it with the vehicle through which wisdom became manifest: the Mother of God, and her Assumption to heaven in the arms of her son as mankind's highest moment of redemption and triumph.

Seven compositions showing the Ecumenical Councils, gathering of bishops summoned by the Byzantine emperors to elaborate Church dogma and to affirm the veneration of the Virgin Mary, complete the cycle of religious frescoes. They are shown below those dedicated to Mary's glorification on the northern and southern walls.

Another cycle of frescoes is imbued with political meaning, often veiled in symbolic language. In using the rounded pillars of Uspensky to depict canonized warriors and martyrs, the artists not only reinforced the Byzantine idea of saints as the 'pillars of Orthodoxy' but, by portraying Russian saints side by side with saints recognized by the Greek mother Church, also conveyed the message that Uspensky Cathedral was supported by the combined forces of all Christendom.

EXCURSION 1

The same theme is further accentuated by the four strategically located frescoes intended to remind the onlooker of this historical parallel of the mother-and-son teams introducing Christianity to their respective countries. *Empress Helen* and her son, *Constantine*, who brought Christianity to Byzantium, appear over the southern portals, while their tenth-century Kievan counterparts from the north, *Princess Olga* and her grandson *Prince Vladimir*, are painted over the northern portals.

Uspensky's greatest treasure is its icons, particularly those in the bottom, or local, tier of the **iconostasis** (altar screen). The four upper rows are contemporaries of the iconostasis made by the monks of the Trinity Sergius Monastery in the seventeenth century, later covered by a silver gilt frame. A quick glance at the icons of the local tier shows that they differ in style, size, and age and were not specifically commissioned for the Uspensky's iconostasis. There is a reason for the discrepancy: each time the grand princes of Moscow annexed a new principality, its icon was carried away as a trophy and mounted in the icon screen of the Uspensky Cathedral.

The *Saviour Enthroned*, to the right of the royal gates, for example, used to hang in Novgorod's St Sofia Cathedral. Legend has it that the Byzantine Emperor Manuel had an innocent priest wounded. Dreaming that similar wounds appeared on his own body, he woke in pain to see that the stern Christ on the icon was pointing not to the Bible but to his hand. As it happened, the accusing finger of the Lord came to point at Novgorod's inhabitants. In 1477, Ivan III discovered a treaty authorizing the Lithuanians to aid Novgorod against Moscow. The nobles of Novgorod were promptly executed and its treasures, such as the bell used to summon citizens to meetings of the Novgorod Assembly, were added to the Moscow collection. The early twelfth-century icon of *St George the Warrior*, another Novgorod icon hanging to the right of the royal gates, shows a robust, broad-shouldered young man, the embodiment of the Russian ideal of military virtue celebrated in the medieval epics and tales.

The thirteenth-century icon of *Archangel Michael* and that of the *Redeemer of the Golden Hair*, both from Vladimir, tell a different story.

The greatest treasures of the Uspensky Cathedral are its icons. This view of the main nave shows that even the pillars are covered with frescoes.

Unlike the merchant republic of Novgorod, which enjoyed relative calm and prosperity, Vladimir, the former seat of the Russian grand princes, was constantly under Tartar attack. The deliberate effort of the Vladimir artist to render his saint warlike and severe is clearly expressed by the militant figure of Archangel Michael, depicted as the leader of heavenly forces with sword drawn, ready to strike. The diminutive figure of Joshua kneeling at his feet creates an optical illusion of the Archangel's monumental stature, despite the small size of the icon.

The craftsmanship of the *Redeemer of the Golden Hair* makes it one of the best examples of the Vladimir-Suzdal school of painting. The stern expression on the face of the Redeemer was meant to intimidate the enemy. The Saviour's locks illuminate the dark green background, while the sombre tones of his cloak bring out the bright ochres of his face and the pink of his tunic.

One icon of the Virgin has served throughout all of Russian history as the country's sacred protectress and a source of artistic inspiration. The *Virgin of Vladimir*, a copy of which hangs immediately left of the royal gates, was painted by a Byzantine artist and appeared in Kiev in 1136, a century and a half after the city had adopted Christianity from Byzantium. Each of the three cities where the icon came to rest — Kiev, Vladimir, and Moscow — became in turn the religious and political capital of Russia. The presence of the icon in each capital almost seemed to constitute proof of its claim to primacy. When Basil I placed the *Virgin of Vladimir* in the Kremlin's Uspensky Cathedral in 1395, Moscow could claim to have become the centre of the Russian heritage. As soon as Lenin came to power, he ordered the Kremlin churches closed and the icon of the Vladimir Virgin removed to a museum. Russia's most venerated icon now occupies its place in the Tretyakov Gallery. A fifteenth-century copy hangs in the Uspensky Cathedral.

The *Virgin of Vladimir* portrays a tender and accessible Mary and infant Jesus. The snub-nosed child presses

his cheek against his mother's, while his arm encircles her neck. Even as the face of the Virgin displays unmistakably Byzantine features — long nose, tiny mouth, narrow, pointed eyes — her expression is warm and human. Gazing directly at the onlooker as if to reproach him for the future suffering of her son, she is not the austere and regal Virgin of the Greek school of painting but humble and gentle. Russia came to call this image of Mary *Umilenie*, or the Virgin of Tenderness. The source of inspiration in hard times and the companion of troops in battle, *Our Lady of Vladimir* was also the matrix

Lady of Vladimir *dates from twelfth century and is Russia's t revered icon. It is now ibited at the Tretyakov Art ery.*

23

from which developed the Russian school of icon painting.

Icons commissioned specifically for the Uspensky Cathedral in the fourteenth century include the *Trinity*, the *Saviour of the Stern Eye* and the *King of Kings*. The influence of the Vladimir-Suzdal style is obvious, particularly in the menacing expression of the Saviour, the aristocratic traits of the left-handed Trinity angel, and the regal countenance of the Virgin and enthroned Christ.

The fifteenth-century icon *In Thee Rejoiceth*, inspired by a religious ode to the Virgin, was also painted for Uspensky and is to the left of the royal gates. Attributed to the Moscow iconographer Dionysius, it conveys spaciousness, majesty of composition, and abundance of light. Earth and heaven are united in a single luminous design, in the centre of which sits a tall, graceful Virgin with Child. Golden-haired angels support the blue-green sphere around the throne. A third larger concentric belt encompasses the heavenly kingdom depicting a translucent green church with trees and plants flowering in the Garden of Eden. The lower horizontal section groups the people of the earth together, regardless of rank, in common adoration of the Heavenly Queen.

The story of the Virgin's death and her assumption is beautifully told in a fifteenth-century icon, *Dormition of the Virgin*, fixed to the iconstasis to the left of the royal gates. Against the golden background of the sky, a flotilla-like formation rushes towards the dying Virgin. These are the Apostles, summoned by angels, who have gathered from the ends of the earth to bid her farewell. Below, their grief is shared by bishops, angels, and the faithful of Jerusalem. In contrast to the mourners who are bent over the funeral bier, the figure of Christ rises calmly in the centre of the blue oval. In his arms he holds the soul of Mary, swaddled as a newborn child. This is the moment of the Virgin's earthly death.

Directly above, the artist portrayed her assumption: four winged angels carry the sphere which encloses the enthroned Mother of God. A small figure in the foreground represents the episode of Anthonios: an avenging angel is severing the hand of a blasphemer who tried to upset the stretcher of the Virgin, serving to remind the worshipper that the mystery of the Church must not be profaned.

Uspensky Cathedral has two **side chapels** that have retained late fifteenth-/early sixteenth-century frescoes. The northern, or left, chapel restates the theme of the *Adoration of the Virgin* through a well-preserved mural. The southern chapel honours *SS. Peter and Paul*, the patron saints of Metropolitan Peter, the co-founder of the Uspensky Cathedral. Save for a few fragments depicting the life of St Peter, many of the original murals of this chapel have been lost. One remaining fragment is above the metropolitan's metal crypt and shows the saint bending over an ailing man reclining on an elongated and slightly curved couch.

There is an evident parallel between this fresco and Dionysius' icon of *Metropolitan Peter* (above Patriarch Iov's tomb), where the cleric, cloaked in green vestments, is framed with eighteen border scenes illustrating important events from his life. In the lowest border, the circular grouping of people around a couch repeats the composition of the fresco and recalls the miracles which are supposed to have taken place around the tomb of the Church Father, Dionysius, who portrayed Peter in the traditional white headgear of the Moscow Metropolitans, may have painted the fresco as well.

Part of the wall with a section of the monumental fresco of the *Forty Martyrs of Sebaste* which separated the chapel from the main altar has been removed, and so only twenty-four of the half-naked figures grouped in the waters of the lake are still visible. The double row of crowns above their heads represents their coming martyrdom. The bodies of Metropolitan Peter and his successor, Theognostus, who finalized the transfer of the Holy See to Moscow in 1326, lie buried in the chapel.

The other Russian metropolitans and patriarchs (with the exception of St Alexis) rest in underground **crypts** and along the frescoed walls of the Uspensky's **nave**. Special mausoleums mark the remains of Patriarch Germogen, canonized for his martyrdom during the Time of Troubles, and those of Metropolitan Iov.

The tsars and the metropolitans worshipped side by side in the Uspensky. Each had a special seat provided for him in the church: the stone elevation decorated with carved flowers for the clergymen, a tent-roofed throne for the tsars.

Ivan the Terrible's Throne is the seat which Ivan the Terrible commissioned for himself in 1551. It stands in the right-hand corner of the cathedral and is known as the Throne of the Monomachs. The elaborately carved decorations of the throne relate the story of the Kievan Prince Vladimir Monomach (*r.* 1113–25) receiving the insignia of imperial power from the Byzantine Emperor Constantine Monomach and other events stressing the Russian-Byzantine link. The third seat in the Uspensky Church, a gilded wooden throne, was intended for the tsarina.

A terrifying icon, *The Last Judgement*, on the northern wall and the monumental composition above the cathedral's western portal depict the final judgement by Christ. The icon, which bears Dionysius' signature, is a more complex version of Isaiah's vision of the final judgement than the fresco. In its various scenes it confronts the viewer with visions of the calamities which can befall the human race. An image of the final reckoning was deliberately placed above the western portals to remind the tsar and the metropolitan that even they were mortal.

Cathedral of the Annunciation

Blagoveshchensky Sobor ㉔

The scaffolding had barely been removed from the inside of the Uspensky Cathedral when Ivan III initiated work on the Annunciation (Blagoveshchensky) Cathedral to replace an earlier church by the same name at the western edge of the Cathedral Square. He summoned goldsmiths, jewellers, enamellers, icon painters, and architects to the Kremlin in 1484.

Ivan decided that Russian masters from Pskov should work on his second cathedral rather than inviting foreign architects from abroad as had been the

EXCURSION 1

case with the Uspensky Cathedral. The reason was simple enough: the Annunciation Cathedral was to serve as the private chapel of the tsars, where no alien influences were to be tolerated. Moreover, the Pskov builders, having assisted Fioravanti, had acquired sufficient skill to tackle a smaller church.

Only the tsars and their families would kneel before its great icon screen; only they would be married or their children baptized there. The Blagoveshchensky's most treasured icons painted by the greatest artist of that time were for their worship alone.

Architecture

The nine-domed Annunciation Cathedral started out as a small brick church with three domes, surrounded by a gallery on three sides and incorporating architectural features of earlier Russian churches. The Pskov builders adopted from their native churches belts of patterned bricks to encircle the drums of the cathedral domes and used corbelled arches arranged in receding tiers. They also introduced an innovation in the pointed, spade-shaped arches which became known as *kokoshniki* to mark the transition from the walls to the drums. These arches became a standard feature of sixteenth- and seventeenth-century Moscow churches.

While both the Annunciation and Uspensky cathedrals were copies of the Vladimir cathedral, they exhibit a marked difference in style. In the Uspensky, Fioravanti had produced a rectangular, symmetrical, and supremely logical adaptation of the Vladimir church. Even as the Russian builders of the Annunciation retained certain Vladimir features — four tiers, three apses, entrances on three sides — their rendition was less restrained than that of Fioravanti. To make entry to the royal living quarters easier, the builders placed the church on a tall foundation, which rose to the level of the second storey of the royal palace. Of great beauty, and typical of the old Moscow style, was the southern portal with its sheaf-like capitals and beaded columns.

In the sixteenth century, the cathedral was aggrandized at the insistence of Ivan the Terrible. Four small chapels, each surmounted with a cross and a cupola, were added to the exterior terrace. As these additions upset the previous balance, it was decided to add two more domes. After Ivan the Terrible, the Annunciation Cathedral had nine golden domes and festive northern and western portals.

The transgressions of Ivan the Terrible necessitated other additions. The Russian Orthodox Church forbids its faithful to marry more than three times. When Ivan took a fourth wife, he was accordingly banned from entering the church. The rebuilding of the southern part of the gallery and the addition of a second porch with a carved staircase in 1572 allowed him to follow the liturgy from a position outside the building rather than from the usual place for the tsar at the choirs.

Art

Portraits of Russian princes depicted on the walls of the outside gallery form a reception line greeting visitors at the door and leading them inside the church. A sharp eye can pick out the figures of *Ivan III* and *Basil III* on the eastern wall of the western gallery: the builder of the Annunciation Cathedral and his son are the first to welcome their guests.

The paintings of the gallery are less homogeneous than those in the cathedral proper. Because of fires and subsequent alterations, most of the original murals were replaced by nineteenth-century frescoes repeating the same themes. Among the surviving mid-sixteenth- and seventeeth century frescoes of interest are the figures of *Greek writers and philosophers* on the pilasters of the gallery. Their location in the entry to the church, rather than in the church itself, is symbolic: although the writings of the Hellenistic philosophers foretold the coming glory of God, the Russian Church Fathers rate their wisdom lower than Christian teaching.

Among the restored paintings, note the *Miracle of the Prophet Jonah* on the wall of the northern gallery, as well as the deep shadowed entries, which, combining Russian beading and band ornament with Italian Renaissance motifs, are masterpieces in themselves. The sixteenth-century northern doors display the *Annunciation of the Virgin* and *Old Testament prophecies* symbolically foreshadowing the event in gold relief. The southern portal is the oldest, restored in 1950 from fragments of the earlier entry.

The interior of the Annunciation Cathedral appears small in comparison with Uspensky's. Four pillars carrying the tiered vaults of the tall dome take up most of the standing room below. The royal family watched the service from the balcony, access to which is by a spiral staircase built into the thickness of the northern wall. The beautiful floor is made of red jasper and Persian agate.

The most remarkable aspect of the Annunciation Cathedral, and its greatest treasure, are the early fifteenth-century icons of the gilded **icon screen.** An entry in the Russian chronicles for 1405 notes that Theophanes the Greek, Prokhor the Elder, and Andrei Rublev executed icons and frescoes for the original Annunciation Cathedral started by Basil I in 1397 and completed in 1425. The frescoes perished during the reconstruction of the church by Ivan III, but the icons were incorporated into the iconostasis of the new church. For a long time it was believed that these icons, revered a full century before the enthronement of Ivan the Terrible, had perished in the fire of 1547. In removing oil-paint overlays from the images of the *Saviour, Mary,* and *John the Baptist* in the second and third rows of the icon screen, however, twentieth-century restorers uncovered the original works of Theophanes, Prokhor, and Rublev.

The discovery not only enriched the treasury of Russian art but also confirmed the collaboration between Russia's two greatest icon painters: the shy and fair Andrei Rublev, a monk from the Trinity Sergius Monastery at Zagorsk, and the wordly, sophisticated layman, Theophanes, a dark and temperamental representative of Byzantium's Renaissance. When he began work on the cathedral in 1405, Theophanes was in his sixties and at the zenith of his career, having securely established a name for himself in Novgorod. Rublev, half his age, was known only for the frescoes he had done at the Trinity Sergius Monastery.

EXCURSION 1

27

As senior artist, Theophanes was in charge of the deisus (meaning 'supplication') tier (second from the bottom) of the icon screen. The figures of the *Virgin* and *John the Baptist* represent the apex of his genius. Theophanes conveyed their mood of prayer and trepidation before Christ Pantocrator by careful selection of colour. The grey-greens of St John's tunic and the blue of the Virgin's robe focus the viewer's attention on the Majesty of the Saviour and the luminosity of his golden vestments. Theophanes achieved this effect by placing the figure of Christ against a scarlet rectangle inscribed into a greenish oval.

The Virgin, *from the deisus tier in the Annunciation Cathedral, dates from 1405. Theophanes the Greek.*

Next to *St John* and the *Archangel Gabriel*, the figure of the *Apostle Paul* radiates strength and maturity. The powerful proportions of his body are balanced by a small, delicately shaped head with a thoughtful face and piercing eyes.

The magnetic personality of Theophanes had a strong effect on his Moscow colleagues. Even as Rublev learned the art of composition from the Greek master and admired his technique, he could not identify with the feeling of turmoil in his teacher's work. Rublev replaced the harshness of Theophanes' pictorial movement with rounded lines, the asymmetry by nearly parallel silhouettes, dark tones by joyful colours, and the pessimism of watching Constantinople's decline with optimism in Russia's anticipated liberation from the Tartars. The rounded face of *St Peter* and the soft expression of his eyes, for example, disclose Rublev's authorship, as does the luminous silhouette of *Archangel Michael*.

Icons of the holiday tier (third from the ground) were executed by Rublev and Prokhor of Gorodets, who represents the midpoint between Theophanes and Rublev. While the works of Rublev — the *Annunciation*, the *Nativity of Christ*, the *Presentation*, the *Entry into Jerusalem*, the *Transfiguration*, and the *Resurrection of Lazarus* — are lyrical, rounded, and joyful in colour, Prokhor's *Last Supper, Pentecost*, the *Laying into the Tomb*, the *Descent into Limbo, Ascension and Dormition of the Virgin* display a dramatic and temperamental style closer to that of Theophanes. The disparity is best illustrated in Prokhov's *Laying into the Tomb*: contrasting colours intensify the drama of Christ's death while a towering black cross dramatically heightens the scene's emotion.

Besides the masterpieces of the middle tiers, two other treasures are found in the local (bottom) tier of the icon screen: the stern-faced *Saviour Enthroned*, painted in 1337 for Grand Prince Ivan Kalita, and the seventeenth-century copy of the famous *Annunciation of the Virgin of Ustiug*. The original Annunciation, to which Muscovites ascribed miracles, was painted in Novgorod between 1119 and 1130. In the middle of the sixteenth century, Ivan the Terrible removed Novgorod's sacred panel and brought it to Moscow for the icon screen of the Uspensky Cathedral. The lyrical quality of Mary's thoughtful face and the serenity of the round-faced Archangel Gabriel rank the icon among the earliest masterpieces of Russia. The original is on display at the Tretyakov Gallery.

The remaining icons of the lower tier are primarily of historical interest. As was the case in Uspensky Cathedral, these icons were brought to Moscow from the various Russian principalities, while those of the fourth tier were commissioned in the sixteenth century by Ivan the Terrible.

The distribution and symbolism of frescoes in the Annunciation Cathedral differs from Uspensky both because of limited space and its function as the tsar's private chapel. The wall decorations survived the fire of 1547 remarkably well; ever since the oil overlays were removed, visitors have been able to savour the elegant works painted by Theodosius, the son of Dionysius, in 1508. The murals are light, with refined shades of azure and gold and elongated figures of saints appearing to float in the air.

The frescoes on the southern wall, intended to make the tsar and his family ponder what would happen to them in the next life, stress the concept of fate and illustrate its possibilities. Each member of the royal house could wonder whether he or she would be among the chosen few entering the Garden of Eden with *St Peter* (south-west corner), would enjoy the bliss of *Abraham's repose*, or would be cast before the naked *Lucifer*, riding atop a double-headed dog.

The scenes from the Apocalypse are hardly more reassuring. The cities painted on the eastern arches of the choirs appear bare and forbidding. A representation of *Death*, mounted on horseback, rides in search of victims, while angels hide from the sight of men. This and other visions of the final day are revealed to the *Evangelist John* by a sword-bearing angel as he reads the fortunes of mankind in an open book.

Besides their preoccupation with the end of the world, the fifteenth-century frescoes carried a political message to Russia's leaders: they tried to illustrate that dissension among Russian princes was to be feared almost as much as the end of the world. The figure of the *Saviour-Warrior on His White Mount* (beneath the choirs) dispensing justice reminded the grand princes of Moscow that their appointed task was to create unity and justice in Russia.

The paintings on the church pillars reveal another aspect of the message: princes of Russia and Byzantium stand in pairs, expressing both the conventional concept of lending support to the structure of the Church and Moscow's inheritance of divine right from Byzantium through Kiev and its saints.

Cathedral of Archangel Michael

(Arkhangelsky Sobor) (23)

Immediately before his death in 1505, Ivan III decided to rebuild the fourteenth-century Cathedral of Archangel Michael, or Arkhangelsky Cathedral, which occupied the eastern edge of Cathedral Square. Having completed the Uspensky and Annunciation cathedrals, the ageing grand prince wished to create a suitable burial place for the Moscow tsars. He again summoned an architect from abroad, a Venetian named Alevisio, whom the Russians dubbed Alevisio Novy — 'the new' — to distinguish him from an earlier Italian and who, as did his predecessor, received the same command from the tsar: go to Vladimir and study before you start.

The Renaissance features of the Arkhangelsky Cathedral fired the imagination of Russian architects. Designed by Alevisio, it influenced many later Russian churches.

30

Architecture

The five-domed cathedral that Alevisio raised on a tall socle and decorated with white stone bands was finished in 1508. Like Fioravanti, Alevisio added elements of Venetian architecture to the characteristics of the Vladimir Cathedral model. He shifted the domes toward the east but stressed breadth rather than depth. While the thickness of Arkhangelsky's walls matches that of Uspensky's, it is not offset by the height of the building.

Alevisio excelled in the exterior decorations of the facade, where he incorporated forms of the late Italian Renaissance, proving to many experts that he was as good (or better) a decorator as an architect. An imaginative distribution of pilasters, panels, arches, and sculptured ornaments creates the illusion of a two-storey building.

Several of Alevisio's decorative innovations fired the imagination of Russian architects. From the sixteenth century on, his bold horizontal cornice became a popular element in Russian churches and was frequently used by other designers. They also adopted his graceful shells and the practice of using contrasting materials as means of highlighting sculptural details: in the sixteenth and the seventeenth centuries, Moscow builders would emulate Aleviso by making lavish use of white stone cornices, capitals, arches, and shells to enliven the red brick churches.

Art

Forty-six metal **tombs** line the walls or adjoin the cathedral's faceted pillars: a host of grand princes, tsars, and military leaders from Moscow and other parts of Russia repose beneath their frescoed likenesses. Gathering the remains of the Russian leaders, particularly those martyred or venerated outside of Moscow, in Arkhangelsky served the same purpose as collecting sacred icons from all of Russia in Uspensky: it stressed that even in death Russian princes were united, while at the same time it reaffirmed the Christian dogma of life eternal.

The sarcophagi, which were encased in bronze in 1903, all carry Slavonic inscriptions carved into the white stone. The first prince so buried was Ivan Kalita (r. 1325–41), who built the original church to give thanks for the end of a famine. From Grand Prince Ivan II until Peter the Great moved Russia's capital to St Petersburg, all but a few grand princes of the Rurik dynasty and all of the Romanovs were buried in this cathedral. The exceptions were Prince Daniel, who preferred to be buried in the Danilovsky Monastery in Moscow; Tsar Boris Godunov, whose body was unceremoniously disinterred by the False Dmitry and transported to the Trinity Sergius Lavra; and Peter II, who died during the 1730 outbreak of smallpox.

The six-faceted pillars, the high vaulted ceiling with the drums of the domes, and every other inch of Arkhangelsky's walls are covered with **frescoes** painted between 1652 and 1666, replacing the sixteenth-century originals. They were executed by a team of Russian artists, such as Yakov Kazantsev, Stepan Rezanets,

Above *Icon of the* Archangel Michael, *fifteenth century.*

Right *These frescoes on the western walls of the Arkhangelsky are a pictorial rendition of the Creed.*

and Simon Ushakov, and follow the traditional distribution of frescoes in Russian churches. The enthroned *Lord Sabbaoth* is in the central drum with *Jesus and the Holy Spirit*, the forefathers and floating angels are between the windows and the drums, with the *Sons of Jacob* below them. The main events of the New Testament represent the fulfilment of Old Testament prophecies.

One notable exception among the biblical figures are the many frescoes appearing on the pillars and the southern wall which depict the Russian princes and tsars buried in Arkhangelsky. The likenesses of *Ivan III* and his son, *Basil III*, the founders of the church, appear on the southern wall above their tombs, which occupy the place of honour, the right side of the church adjoining the altar screen. Another portrait of Basil III appears on the first pillar to the left as one enters the church.

Here, all of the major Russian princes of the principalities which joined Moscow are gathered together. On the south-eastern pillar, the portrait of *Grand Prince Andrei Bogoliubsky*, who represents the Grand Duchy of Vladimir, recalls his death at the hands of political enemies. *Aleksandr Nevksy*, by contrast, evokes his victories over the invading Swedes and Teutonic knights. *Prince Dmitry*, another victim of political intrigue, is near the front in a tomb marked by a carved white stone canopy, as is *Tsar Vasily Shuisky*, who brought the remains of the young heir of Ivan the Terrible to Moscow to prove the prince's death and to dispel the rumour that he was alive.

The artists who executed the drawing of Dmitry and the other princes showed little concern for physical resemblance. Instead, they sought to emphasize the rank of their subject by reproducing their garb in minute detail, showing the fabric design, jewels, and trimmings. Princes with bare heads are buried in the cathedral; princes who were martyred, tortured, or tonsured are depicted as monks.

The dedication of the church to the Archangel Michael and the many frescoes celebrating his military victories stem from his renown as the captain of the heavenly host, defending creation against the spirits of darkness, and the patron saint of the grand princes of Russia. As they spent most of their time defending the principalities against the Tartar hordes and western invaders, the princes invoked Michael throughout their reigns.

Much stress is laid on the military achievements of *Archangel Michael* in the biographical frescoes. On the northern wall, the winged archangel annihilates, in a single swoop, the army of the Assyrians. The Roman Emperor *Constantine I*, seated on a throne, is clearly impressed by this defeat and points upwards to the cross in the sky.

On the southern wall there are other examples of military prowess. In a fresco on the upper central section of the wall, *Abraham*, with the help of the archangel, defeats his enemies. Below it, there is a portrayal of the *Siege of Jericho*. In another series, *Archangel Michael* strikes one blow after another at the retreating Midianites, as *Gideon*, at the head of the army, looks on.

The present **iconostasis**, built and decorated by Fedor Zubov and Dorofei Zolotarev between 1680 and 1681, replaced the low altar screen originally designed for Arkhangelsky Cathedral. The oldest and finest icon depicts *Archangel Michael*. It is believed that Evdokia, the wife of Dmitry Donskoy, commissioned the icon to celebrate his victory over Khan Mamai at Kulikovo Field.

The icon presents a striking portrait: the archangel stands out against the background of his red cloak, wings outstretched in the pose of a relentless warrior. His sword, pointing downwards, suggests that he is resting after a victory. The style of the fifteenth-century artist who executed the central panel and the eighteen border scenes reflects the influence of both Theophanes the Greek and Rublev.

The **sacristy** was a part of the altar until the middle of the sixteenth century. Then, in 1561, Ivan the Terrible ordered a thick wall raised between the two, for shortly after his coronation in 1547 he had decided to build himself a special burial shrine, rejecting interment with his ancestors in the central part of the church.

Upon entering the sacristy south of the altar, one notices a marked change in the style of frescoes: the composition becomes laconic and condensed, and decorative detail disappears. The restained gestures of the saints and the simple backgrounds against which they are portrayed convey emotion, not action. These frescoes differ from those of the church proper because they are the only surviving sixteenth-century murals in Arkhangelsky. Their discovery created a sensation, allowing art critics to fix their dates at 1564-5.

The frescoes of the sacristy disclose an insight into the character of Ivan the Terrible. Ivan was born in 1530; his father, Grand Prince Basil III, died when he was three. The fresco on the eastern wall of the chapel portrays the grief-stricken family gathered around the bed of the dying prince: the young Ivan and Helen Glinska, holding Ivan's young brother, Yuriry, stand to the right of the couch supporting Basil III.

Five years later, Ivan's mother was poisoned and later his devoted nurse was imprisoned. During his minority, the boyars seized land and plundered treasure. One of them went so far as to lie on the bed of Ivan's father. Ivan, only thirteen, punished the offender by having him bound in animal skins and thrown to the wolfhounds. The recollections of these early years were still fresh in the mind of the 34-year-old Ivan when, in a message of 1564 to the Muscovites, he compared himself to a 'poor orphan', claiming that he

EXCURSION 1

was oppressed by the rich boyars whom he accused of being traitors, embezzlers, and grafters.

This accusation may be reflected in another fresco on the eastern wall, near the dying scene. It shows an unjust trial presided over by a boyar. Nearby, Death is preparing to strike the offender. Ivan wanted to illustrate what was awaiting the hateful boyars.

The unprecedented elaboration of the biblical account of *Lazarus* occupying almost half of the northern wall of the sacristy may also stem from Ivan's hatred of the boyars. In this series of frescoes, the artist contrasts the terrestrial life of the sinful rich man and the virtuous pauper Lazarus. The roles are reversed after death: the soul of the rich man is mercilessly speared by an angel and cast into the flames of Hell, while solicitous angels bend over Lazarus to ease his suffering.

The remaining sections of the southern and western walls concern episodes from the life of *St John* (in Russian, Ivan, the tsar's namesake) and those of *St Varus*. The portrayal of their deeds in the tsar's burial chapel underscores Ivan's wish to be accepted as a member of the heavenly army.

One leaves the church struck by the anomaly presented by the western wall, usually reserved in Russian churches for the scene of the Last Judgement. By analysing the sequence of frescoes on the western wall, it is clear that what the visitor perceives is a pictorial rendition of the Creed. The narration starts with the first part of the Creed ('I believe in one God') in the south-western corner of the ceiling and continues on the western wall.

The last parts of the Creed, which deal with confession, resurrection of the dead, and the Lord's judgement, are combined to form the central unit of the western wall. As a result, the scene of the final reckoning, so often forbidding and monumental, is discreetly incorporated into the Creed and given an optimistic turn.

Palace of the Facets

(Granovitaya Palata) (28)

The two-storey Renaissance palace adjoining the Annunciation Cathedral, built of the bevelled stones that gave it its name, is the least Russian-looking building in the Kremlin and Ivan III's secular contribution to the Kremlin of the Third Rome. The Palace of the Facets was to provide the stage for the increasingly elaborate ceremonies of the Russian tsars and their grand receptions, such as the 1552 celebration of Ivan the Terrible's victory over the Tartars of Kazan. In this hall, foreign envoys were received, metropolitans were nominated, and national assemblies were convened.

Architecture

Since no Russian precedent existed for such a building, Ivan III gave free reign to two Italian builders. Unlike their predecessor-countrymen, Marco Ruffo and Pietro Solari did not have to comply religiously with Russian models. With a rusticated façade and eighteen windows, the flat-roofed palace they erected is reminiscent of the Renaissance palaces in Ferrara and Bologna. The lower storey was for administrative purposes; the upper chamber was the tsar's throne room. A single pillar supporting four cross vaults dominates the beautifully proportioned throne room, which measures four hundred and ninety-five square metres and is nine metres high.

The frescoes of the Palace of the Facets executed on a background of pure gold are imbued with political meaning.

The Palace of the Facets originally opened onto a terrace which linked it with the Annunciation Cathedral: three wide staircases led from Cathedral Square to the terrace. Over the years the palace has undergone various alterations. The lavishly carved and gilded stone portals and the central pillar restored in 1968 are all that remain of the original decor. In the seventeenth century, the original double-arched windows were widened and received the present opulent, pillared frames. In the nineteenth century, the palace was joined to the Great Kremlin Palace, whose Vladimir Hall now provides the only access to the former throne room. The famous **Red Porch** was dismantled in the 1930s. Today the palace is still used for formal state occasions.

Art

The colourful frescoes executed on a background of pure gold are of great artistic merit and political content. What is visible today is the work of late nineteenth-century artists from Palekh who skilfully recreated the original sixteenth-century decorations. Tsar Alexis Romanov (r. 1645–76) is responsible for preserving the original sixteenth-century frescoes: when he instructed the celebrated painter Simon Ushakov to redecorate the throne room, he had him follow the originals to the most minute detail. In 1881 the Palekh restorers used Ushakov's drawings for both the Holy Vestibule and the Hall of Facets.

The frescoes of the **Holy Vestibule** were designed to impress on the waiting visitors that God grants victory to those who serve his cause, especially to the Russian tsars protecting the true faith. There are, for example, portrayals of *Emperor Constantine's vision* of a cross bearing the words 'Thou Shalt Conquer', *Prince Dmitry Donskoy* being blessed on the eve of his victory over the Tartars in 1380, and the *Appearance of the angel to Joshua* before the walls of Jericho.

While the frescoes of the antechamber stressed the holy and invincible character of Moscow, the decorations of the **Hall of Facets** were a pictorial statement of the official 'Moscow as Third Rome' ideology and of the political absolutism which matured under Ivan the Terrible. This concept of Russian tsars as heirs to Roman and Byzantine emperors, as well as Kievan Grand Princes, underlies the sacred themes depicted on the vaulted ceiling and the scenes frescoed on the chamber's walls.

Two parallel scenes illustrate Ivan's claim to his link with the Roman Emperor Augustus: a group of three men seated at a table represent *Caesar Augustus dividing his realm among his two brothers*, and another trio depicts *Rurik partitioning his land between Igor and Sviatoslav*. The Kievan Grand Prince *Vladimir Monomach* (r. 1113–25), who supplied the crucial link to Byzantium, is shown receiving the coronation 'cap' from his maternal ancestor, *Emperor Constantine Monomachus*.

The early, benevolent period (1547–60) of Ivan's reign must have inspired the artists to portray him as 'The Just Knight'. The young tsar is shown as a righteous judge, protector of the poor, and fearless defender of Orthodoxy. In 1552, Russians had every reason to praise the 22-year-old leader, who had just triumphed over the Tartars of Kazan, one of the last remaining bastions of the disintegrating Mongol empire.

As the Muscovites rejoiced over the victory in the streets, Ivan the Terrible celebrated with unprecedented pomp in the Hall of Facets. According to the chronicles, the banquet lasted for three days and three nights.

It was also in this hall that Ivan fêted Sir Richard Chancellor's English trading delegation, which led to the conclusion of a commercial treaty with England and an offer for Queen Elizabeth to become Ivan's tsarina. Ivan's last triumph, coming shortly before his death, was another occasion for a Granovitaya banquet. On 26 October 1582, the Cossack leader Ermak Timofeyevich annexed western Siberia after defeating the powerful Siberian Tartar, Khan Kuchum.

The second series of frescoes in the Palace of Facets, drawn from the life of *Joseph*, had more to do with the ambitions of Boris Godunov than the wishes of the soft-spoken Tsar Fedor, who had commissioned the murals. Boris, who had himself portrayed at Fedor's right (wearing long-sleeved, fur-trimmed vestments), intended to compare his role at Fedor's court to that of St Joseph at the Pharaoh's.

The Imperial Sofia (Zoe) Paleologue insisted on being present in the Hall of Facets whenever his husband, Ivan III, received foreign visitors, but Russian

tsarinas who succeeded Sofia were barred from state ceremonies, having to content themselves from watching the proceedings from a specially built hiding place, a **'look-out' room** above the western wall. The tsars, too, would occasionally conceal themselves there to listen to preliminary deliberations between the visiting foreigners and the boyars.

(Zolotaya Tsaritsina Palata)

Golden Hall of the Tsarinas

The Golden Hall of the Tsarinas adjoins the Palace of the Facets from the northeast and is closed to visitors. It is a striking building with two intersecting arches supporting the vaulted ceiling that carries the weight of seventeenth-century churches superimposed above. The hall is notable for its windows with their carved polychrome frames and for its elaborate frescoes painted on a gold background. Dated 1526, it was rebuilt in the 1580s during the regency of Boris Godunov.

Art

Seeking to enhance the political image of his sister Irina, the wife of Tsar Fedor I, Boris Gudunov provided her with the lavishly decorated Tsarina's Hall where she could receive the leading ladies of the realm, the patriarch, or her husband. If the sickly Fedor were to die (as he soon did), the strongest contender for the throne would be Prince Dmitry, Ivan the Terrible's son from his marriage to Maria Nagaia, who was a foe of the Godunovs. To maintain his own status and power, Boris sought to advance the candidacy of Irina for the throne in the dynastic struggle that would ensue.

The best way to achieve this goal, Boris felt, was to stress the role imperial women played in the past and their contributions in upholding the Christian faith. As a result, the frescoes which Boris commissioned in the 1580s depict scenes from the lives of Byzantine and Russian women who were acclaimed for their piety and wisdom.

Two propagators of Christianity are particularly prominent: *Empress Helen of Byzantium* is shown raising the True Cross she reputedly discovered, and *Princess Olga*, Regent of Kiev, journeys to Constantinople to be baptized. Near these two women is *St Irina*, the patroness of Irina Godunova. Another fresco of note portrays *Queen Dinara*, daughter of the Georgian Tsar Alexander, greeted by victorious troops returning to announce the defeat of their Persian adversaries.

The frescoes thus served a dual purpose: they recognized the contributions of famous women and stressed Irina's direct link to her famous Byzantine and Kievan predecessors.

Then on 15 May 1591, the unforeseen occurred. The nine-year-old Dmitry was found with his throat slashed. A commission of high-ranking boyars was sent to investigate and declared that Prince Dmitry was not murdered but died during a fit of epilepsy while playing with a knife; but in the halls the

EXCURSION 1

37

boyars whispered that Boris Godunov had killed the child.

Fedor died seven years after the scandal involved in Prince Dmitry's death. The Russian throne was offered to Irina, who refused it, choosing instead to became a nun at the Novodevichiy Convent. A few months later Boris was crowned tsar.

Bell Tower of Ivan the Great

(Kolokolnya 'Ivan Veliky') (21)

The snow-white Bell Tower of Ivan the Great stands 270 feet tall in the centre of Cathedral Square. The belfry owes the epithet 'Veliky', meaning 'great' or 'tall', to its size and its name of Ivan to St Ivan of the Ladder (John Climacus), the patron saint of Ivan Kalita, who commissioned it. The original tower-church was built in 1329 and rebuilt between 1505–8.

It was said that the work Tsar Boris Godunov initiated in 1600 to increase the height of the great tower was his act of atonement for murdering Prince Dmitry. Despite the fact that the Russian National Assembly elected Boris to the throne, in the eyes of many Russians he was a usurper. The reconstruction of the bell tower was a paradox: the taller it grew, the shakier became the foundations of Boris's power.

The tower of Ivan provides the Kremlin with a focal point. As it reaches upward, the tower narrows. The first three tiers, one slightly recessed above the other, are un-

The Bell Tower of Ivan the Great provides the Kremlin with a focal point and houses twenty-one bells.

adorned octagons, each with a terrace and a gallery for bells. At the point where a band of spade-shaped gables encircles the top section, the octagonal towers fuse into a cylindrical drum which, in turn, is surmounted by a cupola. Marking this transition is an inscription in Old Slavonic script:

> By the Grace of the Holy Trinity and by order of the Tsar and Grand Prince Boris Fedorovich, Autocrat of all Russia, this temple was finished and gilded in the second year of their reign.

The reason the inscription carried the word 'finished' instead of 'built' is that Boris did not build the tower from the ground up but rather extended the two existing lower sections which had formed a combination building known as Ivan's Tower.

The Bell Tower of Ivan the Great houses twenty-one bells. The most important of these is the giant *Uspensky*, also known as the *Holiday Bell*, weighing sixty-four tons and recast from earlier bells in the nineteenth century. It was traditionally the first to announce the coming of a Church holiday or a state ceremony, tolling three times for the death of a tsar.

Two of the Kremlin's curiosities are located near the Bell tower: a royal bell that never rang and a royal cannon that never fired.

Tsar's Bell
(Tsar Kolokol)

At the foot of Patriarch Nikon's Palace is the Tsar's Bell, the largest bell in the world. All bell-casters, including such great masters as Ivan Motorin and his son Mikhail, who created this 200-ton bell, were superstitious. The bell never rang, they claimed, because Empress Anna Ivanovna (r. 1730–40), the granddaughter of Tsar Alexis Romanov, had no right to the Russian throne. Whatever the cause, in executing Anne's commission the Motorin father-and-son team did run into problems from the start: it took two years to prepare a mould and, when it was finally finished, molten copper gushed from the furnace and started a fire. The mould had to be recast, but another fire destroyed the supports on which the bell was resting. The bell fell into the casting hole and cracked. Only in 1836 was the damaged bell raised and set on a stone pedestal. The great fissure separating the portrait of Tsar Alexis from that of Empress Anna perhaps symbolizes the gulf that divided this authentically Russian monarch from his Germanized granddaughter.

Tsar's Cannon
(Tsar Pushka)

The awesome cannon (weighing forty tons) was cast in bronze by Andrei Chokhov at the Moscow Cannon Yard. It was designed to fire crushed stone at the enemy trying to cross the Moscow River and stood near the Spasskaya (or Saviour's) Tower Gate on Red Square. The cannon was commissioned by peace-loving Tsar Fedor (son of Ivan the Terrible), which explains why his likeness appears on its surface. The decorative gun carriage was added in 1835.

Armoury Museum
(Oruzheinaya Palata) ㉚

The present nineteenth-century building, an attempt by the architect Konstantin Thon at neo-Russian revival, started as a storage safe for Kremlin treasures in the fourteenth century. By 1485 the number of valuables had grown so enormously as to warrant the construction of a special stone building. Grand Prince Basil III, son of Ivan III, created the post of supervisor of the Armoury Chamber, who was also to oversee the workshops of the tsars, producing many of the items on exhibit today. The workshops, created primarily

EXCURSION 1

to manufacture battle gear and ceremonial weapons, gradually diversified as jewellers, enamellers, metal-workers, embroiderers, and icon painters joined the royal master's ranks. Boyar Khitrovo, whom Tsar Alexis Romanov appointed supervisor of the Armoury Chamber in the mid seventeenth century, turned it into a veritable academy of arts. Peter the Great closed the royal workshops and converted the building into a museum.

The Armoury Museum provides a fascinating insight into the changing moods of the Kremlin rulers. The earlier princes' preoccupations with consolidating Moscow as a political and religious centre is reflected in armour and jewel-studded icon covers. The prosperity of the sixteenth and particularly the seventeenth centuries manifests itself in the splendour of the royal vestments, the crowns, the thrones, saddles, and exquisite objects of gold and silver. Finally, carriages, porcelain, and other luxury items bespeak the Westernized tastes of the later rulers.

Hall I: Arms and Armour of the 13th and 18th Centuries

On Stand 1 of special note is the helmet which belonged to the father of Aleksandr Nevsky. The name of the owner is inscribed on the front of this helmet covered in embossed silver. Also on show is the helmet of Prince Ivan, who was killed by his own father, Ivan the Terrible, in 1581. On the same stand are examples of old Russian armour, the breastplates of Michael and Alexis Romanov, battle-axes, maces, and other arms.

On Stand 2 are mostly harquebuses, both foreign and Russian, from the sixteenth and seventeenth centuries.

Of the ceremonial armour and sabres displayed on Stand 3, note the sabres of Prince Pozharsky and Kuzma Minin, who liberated the Kremlin from the Poles in 1612.

Stand 4 shows seventeenth-century armour and weapons. The golden mace with golden crests was the present of Shah Abbas II of Persia to Tsar Alexis Romanov.

Included among the trophies on Stand 5 from the Northern War (1700–2) is a bas-relief of Peter the Great by the sculptor Bartolomeo Rastrelli.

The equestrian armour in the centre of Stand 6 was the gift of the Polish King Stefan Batory to Tsar Fedor (1584).

Hall II: Russian gold and silver of the 12th and 17th Centuries

The treasures include silver chalices, including a twelfth-century chalice which belonged to Yuriy Dolgoruky (founder of Moscow), necklaces, gospels (the decorative gospel studded with gems and picked out with enamel was presented by Ivan the Terrible to the Uspensky Cathedral in 1571), drinking vessels, round bowls, and goblets for pouring drinks. Two watches are of particular interest: Ivan the Terrible's, made from gilded copper in the form of a book, and a wooden Russian watch dating from the last century.

Hall III: Silver and jewellery of the 18th to 20th Centuries

Of special interest among the many exquisite items on display is the collection of *snuff-boxes*, many of which are decorated with portraits and precious stones. Osipov, one of the first Russian Miniaturists, is believed to have painted the portrait of Peter the Great which adorns one of the snuff-boxes, while the one with a bas-relief portrait of the Empress Elizabeth is believed to have been made by Posier, one of the outstanding craftsman of the nineteenth century. Fabergé, the most famous of the Russian jewellers, is represented by his Easter eggs, many of which contain miniature models made from precious stones and metals. One contains a gold model of a Trans-Siberian express train with crystal windows that actually works. Other models inside the eggs include the palace at Pushkin outside Leningrad and the royal yacht set in a sea of rock crystal.

Hall IV: Vestments

The vestments in this hall belonged to the royal family and Church leaders. Since neither silk nor brocade was manufactured in Russia before the eighteenth century, the cloth for many of the early exhibits was originally imported from the Middle East or western Europe; the oldest vestment is the robe of Peter, the first Metropolitan of Moscow, made in 1322. Several of the robes are decorated with portraits of rulers or religious leaders of the time. By the seventeenth and eighteenth centuries, vestments were heavily embellished with precious stones and other decorative features. The velvet robe of Metropolitan Platon of Moscow, which Catherine II presented to him in 1770, has more than 150,000 precious stones embroidered inside.

Hall V: Western gold and silver of the 13th to 19th Centuries

Many of the exhibits were originally gifts to the tsars from ambassadors, including a goblet which is believed to have been presented to Ivan the Terrible by an English merchant. The largest section, gifts from Sweden, dates from the seventeenth century. The silver service on display is but part of a service consisting of more than 3,000 pieces which Catherine II presented to Count Orlov in 1772. The Sèvres service was presented to Alexander I by Napoleon after the signing of the Treaty of Tilsit.

Hall VI: Regalia of the Royal House

The earliest throne, made in western Europe and decorated in ivory, belonged to Ivan the Terrible. The second throne, finished in gold leaf with more than 2,000 precious stones, was presented to Boris Godunov in 1604 by the Persian Shah Abbas I. The most famous throne is known as the *Diamond Throne*. It was the gift of an Armenian trading company from Persia to Alexis Romanov. It features 900 diamonds and was used at coronations by Russian empresses in the nineteenth century.

The *Cap of Monomach* was made by Eastern craftsmen in the thirteenth or fourteenth century and is said to have been copied from the gift of the Byzantine Emperor Constantine to Grand Prince Monomach of Kiev. It is made of gold lace and is edged with a sable band.

The *Kazan Cap* was made to celebrate Ivan the Terrible's capture of Kazan. Among the caftans (loose gowns) on display is one reputed to have belonged

EXCURSION 1

41

to Peter the Great. The hall ends with exhibits of jewellery, including a collection of earrings, which Russian men wore until the reign of Peter the Great, but only in one ear.

Hall VII: Harnesses

The saddles displayed were mostly gifts to Russian tsars from foreign ambassadors, often from Poland. The oldest saddle, its velvet embroidered with golden eagles, was made during the reign of Ivan the Terrible. Tsar Michael's saddle, made in 1637, is fashioned of gold and studded with gems.

The brocade saddle of Ivan the Terrible (sixteenth century), stamped with gold, silver, and semi-precious stones, is on display in the Armoury.

Hall VIII: Carriages

Elizabeth I of England is supposed to have presented the young Boris Godunov with the oldest carriage. Some of the most lavish coaches, such as the gift of Count Razumovsky (made in Paris in 1757), are those presented to Empress Elizabeth.

Diamond fund exhibit of the USSR

Unique precious stones and crown jewels are displayed in this second famous collection of the Armoury, located on the ground floor of the building. Included are more than 100 rare unset diamonds, many of which are known by proper names, such as *The Star of Yakutia* (232 carats). The fabulous *Orlov Diamond* (189.62 carats) leads the parade of grand set stones. This diamond, a seventeenth-century, 300-carat stone from India, served as the eye of a god in the Shehringan Temple. In 1774 Count Orlov bought it from the Armenian merchant Lazarev for his beloved Catherine the Great, who mounted the diamond into the imperial sceptre. The *Shah Diamond* was Shah Mirza's present to Tsar Nicholas I in atonement for the murder of his envoy.

The *grand crown* made for the coronation of Catherine the Great by Posier in 1762 is considered the greatest art work of the collection. Finding that 4,936 diamonds alone were not enough, Posier spruced up the crown with a generous sprinkling of perfect pearls.

(Teremnoi Dvorets)
③①

Terem Palace

If one stands between the Uspensky and Annunciation cathedrals with one's back to the Bell Tower of Ivan the Great, one can catch a glimpse of this colourful seventeenth-century palace with its crested roof painted like a chess board.

The palace with its fairytale golden *terem* was built on the model of the old Russian dwellings. A *terem* is a garret, or belvedere, which housed the children and the female relatives of a tsar or a nobleman. It was usually the upper tier of a Russian house. One originally entered the Terem through the Upper Saviour's Porch, but both were later incorporated into the Great Kremlin Palace. Access now is only through the Hall of St Vladimir in the Great Kremlin Palace.

The **Upper Saviour's Porch**, once an open terrace, was reconstructed in the seventeenth century along with the upper floors of Tsar Michael's Terem Palace by four Russian masters: Bazhen Ogurtsov, Trephil Shaturin, Larion Ushakov, and Antip Konstantinov, who drew on their knowledge of Russian timber architecture in creating stone masterpieces. Laying brick as they would lay logs, they broke the palace up into self-contained units: each set of chambers had its vestibule, porch, staircase, and landing linked to one another by open terraces and covered galleries. The builders also added chapels and eleven drums surmounted by cupolas on top of the palace roof.

When the palace was completed, with the golden garret for the royal children, the architects began to work on the interiors. The rooms reflected the Russian preference for compactness and warmth, the qualities they most cherished in wood. Carved lace work appeared on the window architraves, portals, entablatures, and even floors. The bas-reliefs closely resembled the motifs used in timber carving, with mythical animals and birds frolicking in bright gardens of flowering plants. Delicately tinted ceramic tile stoves heated the cosy rooms.

The most elaborate part of the Terem Palace are the five chambers on the fourth floor which were the **private apartments** first of Michael and later of his son Alexis Romanov. Except for major state occasions in the Hall of Facets, most state affairs were conducted in the Terem Palace. Alexis believed in elaborate court ceremony and never missed an opportunity to impress foreigners with the magnificence of tsardom. This robust and impulsive man is remembered in Russian history for being closest to the ideal of *batushka* — the tsar-father figure — as an example of piety, order, and paternalism, devoted to his two wives and all of his children.

The first of the five royal chambers was the **vestibule**. Beneath the vaulted ceiling decorated with frescoes of the *Saviour surrounded by Evangelists* and archangels, the boyars waited for the tsar's levee. At the appointed moment they would be summoned into an adjoining anteroom, the **Hall of the Cross**, a chamber of quiet dignity. Flowers of geometric design decorate the walls of this green room, and three double windows are set in mica panes. Frescoes of the Russian saints looked down on the boyars as they awaited the tsar, seated on a throne, to reach and announce his decision. The decree which had proclaimed the election of Tsar Michael Romanov and the charter in creating the Russian patriarchate are also kept here.

The third of the tsar's rooms, the **Golden Throne Room**, served as his private study. There he reviewed state papers and the petitions brought to him from the petition box, which served as an unusual method of communication with the common people. It was regularly lowered from the middle window (decorated with pillars and the royal emblem of the double-headed eagle) to the street where the people would gather to submit petitions.

Few people other than the tsarina, the tsar's personal confessor, and the blind storytellers entered the last two rooms, the **tsar's bedroom** and the **royal chapel**. Daybreak would usually find Tsar Alexis kneeling before the pulpit; he would sometimes pray for six hours a day. Near the Golden Throne

The Throne Room of the Terem Palace was the private study of Tsar Michael Romanov.

Room a spiral staircase leads downstairs to the tsar's zinc-lined bath and upstairs to the **Golden Garret**, the most magnificent room of the Terem Palace. It was added in 1637 as a playroom for Alexis and Ivan, Tsar Michael's children, and accounts for the palace's name.

(Verkhospassky Sobor)

㉖

The Golden Gates are just one example of the lacy detailing of mythical animals and plants everywhere in the Terem Palace.

Upper Saviour's Cathedral

In the same deliberate manner that marked everything he did, Tsar Fedor began renovating the Terem Palace churches. The Cathedral of the Saviour, dating from the original construction of the Terem Palace, required the most urgent attention. This church is on the third floor directly above the Golden Hall of the Tsarinas.

Because of a copper grating built in 1670, the church was renamed the **Church Behind the Golden Grill**. Ironically, this grill, intended for the protection of the tsar, was forged from copper coins withdrawn from circulation after the Copper Mutiny of 1662.

Fedor spared no money in redecorating the Saviour's Cathedral. He commissioned a new silver-sheathed iconostasis as a sign of his devotion.

The cathedral's seventeenth-century icons are remarkable for ornamental details, most particularly in the gold and black decorations on the tunic of *St Theodore*, patron saint of the tsar.

Other Churches

Fedor also renovated the **Resurrection Church**, which today contains an eighteenth-century iconostasis of gilt wood inset with oval icons, and expanded it by adding the **Church of the Crucifixion** (1681). Both churches are on the fourth floor of the Terem Palace. The **Church of St Catherine** was built in stone as early as 1627 and the **Church of the Nativity** served as the private chapel of the royal women.

The small square **Church of Lazarus**, directly beneath the Nativity Church, is an authentic example of the fourteenth-century Moscow style of architecture and the only one left standing.

The Chuch of the Resurrection has n 18th-century iconostasis of gilt wood insert with oval icons.

The cleanly hewn lines of the four pillars, the vaulted ceiling, and the ogee-shaped portals reflect its close link with the Vladimir style of architecture and display a high degree of sophistication on the part of the Moscow masons.

Fedor did nothing to improve this church; he never even suspected that it existed. It was walled up during the sixteenth century and was re-discovered only in the nineteenth, when the construction of the Grand Kremlin Palace was begun. Sealed off for so long, its style, unlike its fourteenth-century contemporaries, survived the ages.

(Tserkov Rizpolozheniya) ㉕

Church of the Deposition of the Virgin's Robe

In 1480, Grand Prince Ivan III clashed with Metropolitan Geronty over an issue of scarcely world-shattering importance: should a Church procession move with or against the sun? When the prince dared accuse the metropolitan, who believed that the process should move in the direction of the rising sun, of error, Geronty responded to what he perceived as a transgression against his religious authority by announcing that he would divest himself of his position as head of the Russian Orthodox Church unless the prince gave in. Ivan did.

Architecture

Geronty celebrated his reconciliation with Ivan by ordering work on the Deposition Church, which was to become his private chapel. Distrustful of the Italians whom Ivan had brought in to work on the Kremlin cathedrals, he kept a close watch over the Pskov architects whom he hired for the job to see that the Western innovations they learned from the Italians did not sully his place of worship.

Built between the Uspensky Cathedral and the Palace of the Facets, the

EXCURSION 1

church combines early Moscow styles with some new features from Pskov. In one example of the combination, a Moscow-type ornamental frieze, placed on the walls at mid-height, forms a direct line with the cornice of the altar apsides, lowered in the style of Pskov. Another such mixture of old and new is the juxtaposition of the old-fashioned ogee arches with Pskovian brick trim under the cupola drum. The staircases and open terraces also reflect the heritage of Old Russian timber architecture. Other notable innovations include the sheaf-like mass of thin semicolumns in the corbel table and deep-shadowed portals.

The church, completed in 1486, was dedicated to the Deposition of the Virgin's Robe.

Art

The interior of the church, altered in subsequent reconstructions, retains the ingenious arrangement of corner windows that was later replicated in

the Church of the Ascension at Kolomenskoye. The frescoes, restored between 1955 and 1956, were painted in 1644 by the same masters who decorated the Uspensky Cathedral.

The icons date from 1627, as does the four-tier iconostasis. The precise composition of the icons and their refined colouring suggest the craftsmanship of Nazary Istomin, a renowned seventeenth-century painter from the metropolitan's own workshops. Despite their elegance the icons lack the spiritual refinement and purity on which Geronty had insisted when he commissioned the church some two centuries earlier. As was the custom under Geronty's successors, the icons are encased in delicately chiselled silver covers. The icon of the *Deposition of the Virgin's Robe*, which the church honours, is immediately to the right of the royal gates. Geronty's attempt at a pure little church is now a Museum of Russian Folk Art.

Church of the Twelve Apostles

(Tserkov Dvenadsati Apostolov)
㉗

The four-storey **Patriarch's Palace** incorporating the Church of the Twelve Apostles (marked by five helmet-shaped cupolas at its eastern end) delineates the boundary between Cathedral Square and Troitskaya Place farther to the

north. The reason for the palace's location at the northern edge of Cathedral Square was its proximity to both the Uspensky Cathedral and the Trinity Gates, which the upper-ranked Russian clergy used for staging their formal entries to the Kremlin.

Patriarch Nikon initiated the construction of the Apostles' Church, having decided that the modest and severe exterior of the Church of the Deposition was unworthy of his rank and that the existing metropolitan's residence occupied a subservient role in the architectural ensemble of the Kremlin.

The four-storey ochre palace and the Church of the Twelve Apostles form an architectural unit emphasized by the thin arcature of a purely Vladimir-Suzdal style, which creates a common decorative belt on the facades of both buildings.

e builders of the Church of the
elve Apostles borrowed a
ature from each of the other
emlin cathedrals.

The church reflects Nikon's views on religious architecture. Having condemned tent-type roofs, Nikon ordered the architects to revert to the Byzantine-inspired early Moscow style. The builders borrowed something from each of the Kremlin cathedrals: the mass from Annunciation, the elongation and treatment of the drums from Arkhangelsky, and the rounded *zakomars* and the five-dome arrangement from Uspensky. A feature unique to the Church of the Twelve Apostles is the raised, arcaded foundation which provided access

EXCURSION 1

47

from the central Kremlin to the patriarch's property in the northern section of the fortress.

The vaulted **Hall of the Cross** is the most striking feature of the palace and the church. It made architectural history in Russia because of its great vault without a single support. Like the tsars, Nikon wanted a formal hall where he could hold church councils or receive visitors, including the tsar.

After the secularization of the church by Peter the Great in 1721, the palace was turned over to the ecclesiastical council, known as the Holy Synod. Under the Communists it became a museum. Of special interest is the vessel for preparing myrrh, the oil used for anointing in the Russian Orthodox Church. It is in the Hall of the Cross, to the right of the entry, along with other clerical regalia.

(Poteshny Dvorets)

Amusement Palace

The Amusement Palace, where Tsar Alexis staged theatrical performances, stands parallel to the Kremlin's northern wall, behind the Palace of the Congresses.

Built in 1652 as the residence of Ilia Miloslavsky, the father-in-law of Tsar Alexis, the palace was turned into a theatre after Miloslavsky's death.

The building was reconstructed in the nineteenth century but retained some of its seventeenth-century features, including carved frames around the windows of the second storey, a richly ornamented entry with a pediment and stout half-columns, and a turret chamber as in the Terem Palace. Of special note is the projecting, cantilevered balcony which was constructed to support a house chapel. According to the rules of the Church, such a chapel could not be located directly above the living quarters.

One anecdote provides an insight into the conflicting tensions of the prevailing conservatism of Moscow and Alexis' attraction to 'Westernizing'. It is said that after the tsar attended a play, a Western innovation, he would return to the Terem Palace to take a sauna followed by a traditionally lengthy prayer session as a final spiritual purification.

③③ # The Arsenal

The yellow two-storey building directly across from the Palace of the Congresses stands sixty-five metres high and is built around a spacious inner court. The building was meant to serve as a storehouse for weapons, but Peter the Great, after his military successes against the Swedes, decided to turn it into a trophy museum. Victorious Russian rulers have displayed the spoils of war — enemy banners, guns, and cannons — there ever since. Stucco mouldings on the wall portray these victories, as do the 875 cannons captured from Napoleon in 1812, some of which are displayed in front of the Arsenal. Although Peter the Great took considerable interest in the Arsenal and frequently visited the construction site, the building was finished only after his death in 1736.

The Arsenal was a trophy museum for Peter the Great.

The Senate Building

The severely classical Senate building which Matvei Kazakov executed for Catherine the Great in 1787 is now used by the Soviet Council of Ministers. The building's shape, resembling a truncated triangle, was dictated by the topography of the site — Kremlin walls to the east, the now destroyed Chudov Monastery to the south, and the Arsenal to the west.

The Senate building is three storeys high and rests on a tall basement. The façade of the second and third storeys is broken by an alternating rhythm of windows and pilasters. A triumphal arch with two Ionic columns on either side supports a great pediment leading to a central court.

In the centre of the building a spacious dome tops one of the finest circular halls in Russia. The hall is seventy-eight feet wide and ninety-five feet high. It is decorated with eighteen columns and stucco bas-reliefs that depict the Russian grand princes and the tsars. In the niches between the columns stand eighteen high reliefs which portray, in allegorical form, the ideals of Catherine's Russia: Enlightenment, Justice, and the Rule of Law.

On the third floor of the eastern wing is the study which Lenin used from 1918 until December 1922. His desk is still covered with his favourite objects and gifts, including the famous statue of a monkey given to him by Armand Hammer in 1921. Nearby is Lenin's telephone book.

One of the three doors of the study leads to a modestly furnished four-room apartment which Lenin shared with his wife and his younger sister.

Bolshoi Kremlevsky Dvorets)

Great Kremlin Palace

Russian national pride awakened by the victory over Napoleon finally produced a monument designed specifically for the Kremlin on the orders of Emperor Nicholas I.

The Great Kremlin Palace, executed by Konstantin Thon, became a testimonial to Nicholas's principles of 'Orthodoxy, Autocracy, and Nationality'. Recalling the Kremlin's seventeenth-century palaces, it was placed in the very heart of the Kremlin to symbolize the unity and integrity of the Russian Empire; the same concept is illustrated by the five halls which constitute the formal reception rooms of the palace.

Access to the palace is from the southern façade. Sixteen steps lead to the

EXCURSION 1

state vestibule, a white marble hall with four imposing columns of grey granite topped with Doric capitals. Rich deposits of marble and semi-precious stones, which were being mined in Siberia and elsewhere in Russia, were used in the interior to demonstrate the all-Russian character of the building.

A formal staircase with five landings leads to the official apartments and ceremonial rooms. At one time there were five reception halls on the second floor, corresponding to the most prestigious military orders: St George, St Alexander, St Andrew, St Catherine, and St Vladimir. Two of these, the halls of St Alexander and St Andrew, were united to form a single meeting hall of the Supreme Soviet (parliament).

The **meeting hall of the Supreme Soviet** occupies most of the southern wing of the palace. It is well proportioned and decorated in white. Windows at the second storey overlook the Moscow River. A renovation in 1934 provided enough room for 2,500 people.

Adjoining the meeting hall is an anteroom decorated in blue and white stucco work which opens onto a long hall of white and gold. This is the **Hall of St George**, a saint whom Russians revere as the personification of military valour. The Russian Order of St George, created in 1769, was awarded 'For Service and Courage' and was, in its day, the highest military honour.

The decorations of the hall follow the theme of victory. Statues with shields proclaiming triumph surmount the capitals of the twisting white columns lining the walls, each shield marked with the arms of the conquered kingdoms and provinces and the date of their annexation to the Russian Empire. The names of the knights of the Order of St George and of the victorious Russian regiments are carved on the marble plaques riveted to the walls. A bronze clock portraying St George and the Dragon rests on the mantlepiece. The reception for Yuriy Gagarin, the world's first astronaut, was celebrated here in April 1961.

Next the Hall of St George, the **Hall of St Vladimir** opens out onto Cathedral Square. Of all the new reception rooms, it has the highest ceiling, shaped into an octahedral dome. The walls and pilaster strips of this octagonal hall are faced with pink marble. The sculptured bas-reliefs of the vaults and cornices depict the cross of St Vladimir, the Grand Duke of Kiev, being awarded to civil servants for 'service, honour, and glory'.

In the west wing of the Great Kremlin Palace is the white and gold **Hall of St Catherine**, which served as the empress's throne room and conveys a feminine presence. The hall honours the order of St Catherine, founded by Peter the Great in 1714 to commemorate his release on 24 November 1711 from Turkish captivity during the Pruth Campaign. Each of the noble ladies on whom the order was conferred considered it a duty 'to set free one Christian from barbaric slavery, ransoming him with her own money'. When there were no more Christians to be freed, the women wore their silver and red decorations for other services performed 'for love and the Fatherland'.

The doors leading to this hall are decorated with golden ornaments and floral medallions set on a silver background. The exquisite floor lamp of gold

*Kremlevsky Dvorets
Syezdov)*
㊱

Kremlin Palace of Congresses

Nikita Khrushchev inaugurated this gigantic steel and glass structure in October 1961 just in time for the twenty-second Congress of the Soviet Communist Party. The 'palace' was built in sixteen months and designed by Mikhail Posokhin.

When there are no congresses or other state-sponsored meetings, the 5,600-square-metre auditorium is used for opera or ballet performances. There are earphones by each of the 6,000 seats and a simultaneous translation system for twenty-nine languages.

The palace occupies 400,000 cubic feet of space and was sunk 15 metres into the ground to keep it from towering over the rest of the Kremlin structures.

EXCURSION 1

Excursion Plan 2
The Secrets of the
Kremlin Towers

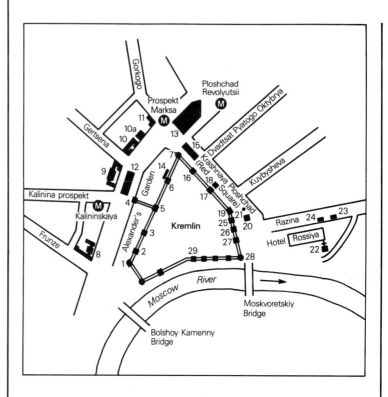

1. Borovitskaya Tower Gates
2. Arsenal Tower
3. Kommendatskaya Tower
4. Kutafya Tower
5. Trinity Gate-Tower
6. Arsenal Tower
7. Sobakina Tower
8. Pashkov House (Lenin Library Annex)
9. Moscow University (New Building)
10. Moscow University (Old Building)
10a. Intourist Headquarters
11. Hotel Natsional
12. Manège
13. Hotel Moskva
14. Alexander's Garden and the Tomb of the Unknown Soldier
15. Historical Museum
16. Nikolskaya Tower
17. Senate Tower
18. Lenin Mausoleum
19. The Saviour's Gate-Tower
20. St Basil's
21. The Statue of Minin and Pozharsky
22. Church of the Inception of St Anne
23. House of the Boyars Romanov
24. Znamensky Convent
25. Tsar's Tower
26. Alarm Tower
27. SS. Constantine and Helen Tower
28. Beklemishev Tower
29. Tower of the Secrets

Excursion 2

THE SECRETS OF THE KREMLIN TOWERS

A walk round the Kremlin fortress, beginning with the Beklemishev Tower, nearest the Morskvoretskiy Bridge over the Moscow River, and ending on Red Square. Also included are the 'Old' University, Manège, and Alexander's Gardens.

*N*early every tower of the Kremlin fortress and even the newer buildings are surrounded by legends. It is said, for example, that the network of underground passages beneath the Kremlin and the area surrounding it is far more intricate than the street plan on the surface. In times of siege these secret passages provided an escape route for the beleaguered rulers. Muscovites also claim that the towers of the Kremlin's southern wall were once linked with underwater tunnels that led to the opposite side of the Moscow River.

The Kremlin's southern wall, which follows the banks of the Moscow River, is the oldest part of the fortress. It was built in 1485 to ward off the attacks of the Tartars, then the principal enemy of the Moscow state. In the decade that followed, the Kremlin's outside fortifications were completed. The walls, enclosing an area shaped like a five-sided polygon, are 2,235 metres long. Their thickness varies from 3.5 to 6.5 metres and their height ranges from 5 to 19 metres depending on the terrain. Twenty towers rise above the walls, five of which double up as gate houses and are connected to each other by a protected rampart running atop the walls.

The corner towers and gate houses tend to be taller and more festively decorated than the intermediary towers along the wall. The latter are smaller and sturdier, their purpose being strictly defensive and their distance from each other dictated by the range of the fifteenth-century firearms.

The round tower at the south-eastern corner of the Kremlin wall is known as the **Beklemishev (Beklemishevskaya) Tower** ㉘. It is believed to be haunted by the ghost of Ivan Bersenev-Beklemishev, whose ancestral home adjoined the tower in the sixteenth century and gave it its name. Slightly over 46 metres tall, the Beklemishev Tower occupies a pivotal location, guarding what used to be the most vulnerable access to Moscow. When the Italian architect Marco Ruffo erected the tower in 1487, he designed it to withstand the full force of an enemy's assault. Its elegant walls are thicker than most of the other towers and contain a well and a secret chamber.

Of the seven towers that dominate the southern wall, the one which has provoked the greatest interest in the past three centuries is the **Tower of the Secrets (Tainitskaya)** ㉙. This sober, unadorned tower, fourth from corner, is the Kremlin's oldest (1485) and most mysterious. In addition to housing an underground passage to the Moscow River, it was also believed to be the hiding place of Ivan the Terrible's fabled library, started by Sofia Paleologue (his grandmother) who brought many rare ancient manuscripts to Moscow. The existence of the library was confirmed by German scholars and in 1934 a Soviet archaeologist, Ignaty Streletsky, thought he located it in the Arsenal

Every tower of the Kremlin is surrounded by legends. The two shown here are part of the southern wall and are known as the Nameless Towers.

Tower, but his search was stopped short by Stalin.

At the corner nearest the Kamennyi Bridge is the round **Water-Drawing Tower**, used to raise water from the river and convey it along an aqueduct to the Kremlin palaces and gardens. It was destroyed in 1812 and restored in 1819.

The next tower to the right is the **Borovitskaya Tower** ①, one of the two Kremlin accesses that Stalin allowed to remain open. The gates and the 50-metre-high tower above them were built in 1490 to replace the wooden guardhouse protecting the south-western corner of the ducal settlement on the Kremlin hill. The Borovitskaya Gates took their name from the thick pine forest, or 'bor', covering the heights. The tower itself is shaped like a pyramid: its arrangement of four superimposed cubes narrows as the tower rises toward an arcaded octagon that is topped by a tent-roofed steeple dating from the end of the seventeenth century. The keyhole openings above the gates recall that chains were slung through these slots to raise and lower the drawbridge.

Until the nineteenth century the Borovitskaya Gates served as the service entrance and a back door to the fortress. When the Moscow rulers wished to slip unnoticed into the Kremlin they passed through these gates. Grand Prince Basil III, on one occasion, had himself carried through the gates so that foreign emissaries at the Kremlin would not discover that he was ailing. Today the Borovitskaya Gates are reserved for the cars of high government officials.

The **Trinity (Troitskaya) Tower** ⑤ at the centre of the northern wall is the only access to the Kremlin open to general public. The tower which surmounts the gate is the tallest in the Kremlin, measuring 76.35 metres. It takes its name from the Trinity Sergius Monastery, whose representational buildings once adjoined the gates. A bridge links the Trinity Gate to the **Kutafya Watchtower** ④, which once stood on the other side of the Neglinnaya River now flowing underground alongside the Kremlin wall. This festive tower was unjustly named 'Kutafya', which in Old Russian meant a clumsy, poorly dressed peasant woman.

Because of their proximity to the quarters occupied by the Moscow high clergy in the Kremlin, the Kutafya and the Trinity gates were the site of formal religious processions. Here, too, the Moscow metropolitans and patriarchs would greet the tsars on their return from hunting expeditions, pilgrimages, or victories. Napoleon's Grand Army filed victoriously through the Trinity Gate and retreated ignominiously through it a month later.

*e Trinity Tower is the only
ess to the Kremlin open to the
eral public.*

*Manège was once a riding
a for the tsars but has also
used for military exercises,
phony concerts, and dinner
es.*

The **Manège** ⑫, the former riding arena of the tsars opposite the Trinity Gate, is a remarkable structure from the point of view of aesthetics and engineering. It was begun in 1817 by A. A. Betancourt, a military engineer, and completed between 1824 and 1825 in the Empire style by Osip Bove. The roof is a piece of technical wizardry, measuring 95 metres from wall to wall without a single intermediate support.

The Manège was large enough to hold military exercises, symphony concerts, and even dinner parties for emperors. After the Bolshevik Revolution, the building became a large garage but was eventually reconstructed in 1957 and is now the Central Exhibition Hall where large art exhibitions are often held.

In the mid-1960s Ilya Glazunov, then an unknown painter, opened his highly publicized show here. Despite government opposition, a million visitors saw paintings depicting Russian churches, historical scenes, and illustrations to Dostoyevsky's works. Glazunov's show ushered in a neo-Russian revival and led to the creation of the All-Russian Society for the Preservation of Historical and Cultural Monuments which marked the beginning of an open struggle against further disfiguration of the city.

The two elegant yellow buildings occupying both sides of Gertsena Street and fronting on Prospekt Marksa belong to the 'old' **Moscow University**. Empress Elizabeth signed the university project by Ivan Shuvalov on 12 January 1755, the day commemorating St Tatiana. From then on St Tatiana became the patron of the students and 'Tatiana's day' came to be regarded as a major holiday on which student pranks enjoyed full immunity from the tsarist police.

The Soviets abolished the feast day of St Tatiana and turned the Church of St Tatiana into a students' club. The rounded projections of the church can still be discerned on the eastern extremity of the 'new' university building (nearest to the Manège), which was built by architect Tiurin between 1833 and 1836.

The **'old' University Building** ⑩, slightly receding from Prospekt Marksa on the right side of Gertsena Street, bears the unmistakable signature of the architect Matvei Kazakov. Completed in 1793, the building suffered extensive fire damage in 1812 and was restored seven years later by the architect Domenico Gilliardi. Since its foundation, the university has been a centre of Russian thought and culture. The main university complex is now on Lenin Hills.

The headquarters of **Intourist** ⑩ₐ, the Soviet agency which controls all travel by foreigners in the USSR, is located at No. 16 Prospekt Marksa. A well-known neoclassical creation of I. V. Zholtovsky, Stalin's pet architect, the building occupies the site of the sixteenth-century Church of St George, razed for that purpose in 1930. It once housed the American Embassy.

Hotel Natsional ⑪, at the corner of Prospekt Marksa and Gorkogo Street, was built in 1903 by architect A. I. Ivanov. It is six storeys high, contains 208 rooms, and still boasts one of the best restaurants in Moscow. Only VIPs rate suite No. 107 because, when the Soviet government moved to Moscow in 1918, Lenin lived in this suite before he moved into the Kremlin.

Hotel Moskva ⑬, which faces into October Square, sports two different wings because of an error in Stalin's plans. Presented with the plans in which the architect purposely drew two different versions of the wings to give him a choice, Stalin approved the drawing as it was. When the architect brought to Stalin's attention the differences in the wings, Stalin supposedly glared at the architect and snapped: 'Build it as it is.' They did.

In the 1970s the hotel was enlarged and its capacity expanded to 1,033 rooms. It has several restaurants, including one on the fifteenth floor from which a beautiful view opens on the Kremlin.

On the opposite side of October Square from Hotel Natsional are **Alexander's Gardens (Aleksandrovsky Sad)** ⑭, hugging the north-western wall of the Kremlin. The garden was created by Osip Bove between 1819 and 1822 shortly after the mischievous Neglinnaya River was put underground. The iron gates and fence separating October Square from the gardens commemorate the victory over Napoleon. The grotto 'Ruin' near the **Middle Arsenal Tower** was also the work of Osip Bove. In 1913 an obelisk was erected in the gardens to celebrate the 300th anniversary of the House of Romanov tsars.

In more recent years, the **Tomb of the Unknown Soldier** was erected to honour the Soviet soldiers who lost their lives during the Second World

War. Their ashes were transferred from a common grave on the outskirts of Moscow and re-interred under the Kremlin wall. The memorial was unveiled on 8 May 1967, the anniversary of the victory over the Nazis. The eternal flame lights up the inscription 'Your name is unknown, your feat is immortal'.

Turning south at the **Corner Arsenal Tower (Sobakina)** ⑦, the neo-Gothic **Nikolskaya Tower** ⑯ and farther down the famous **Saviour's (Spasskaya) Gate-Tower** ⑲ are seen. Both face Red Square.

The towers were named after the icons which once hung above the gates: *St Nicholas* on Nikolskaya and that of the *Saviour* above the Spasskaya gates. The icons were removed shortly after Lenin moved the capital to Moscow but survived in the Church of St John the Warrior on the opposite shore of the Moscow River.

The **Saviour's Tower**, rising above Red Square to its lofty height of 67.3 metres, is the most handsome of the Kremlin's twenty towers. The gates located at the base of the ten-storey tower were used for the formal entries of the tsar and all the major processions to and from the Kremlin. A Latin inscription carved into the tower names Pietro-Antonio Solari as its original builder and gives the construction date as 1491. In its early years, the gateway was known as Florovskaya and was half its present size and lacked ornamentation. Access to the tower was by a bridge spanning the moat then dividing the Kremlin from Red Square.

...iour's Tower is often judged to ...he most handsome of the ...mlin towers.

The tower's present multi-tiered appearance, with red brick arches, turrets, and pinnacles outlined in white, reflects Gothic and Renaissance influences and dates from 1625. The reconstruction was carried out by Christopher Galloway, an Englishman, and Russian architect Bazhen Ogurtsev. The builders used the first storey with its *porte-cochère* as a base for the second rectangular tower, facing the brick with white stone work and adding a covered gallery. Above, an octagonally shaped tower was surrounded by an open terrace and a battlemented parapet. The tower also received a tall brick steeple. A large red star replaced the old double eagle of the tsar at the top of the steeple in 1935.

Christopher Galloway mounted a clock in the tower which lasted until the end of the seventeenth century. The present clock dates from 1918.

The chimes of the Saviour's Tower, like Big Ben's in London, are broadcast by Moscow radio around the world and mark the beginning and end of every day.

The beauty of the tower inspired a famous legend which explains why the Florovskaya Gates were renamed Spasskaya, or Saviour's Gates.

In the early sixteenth century, shortly before Grand Prince Basil III divorced his wife Solomonia for failing to produce an heir, a nun from the Kremlin's Voznesensky Convent reported a vision: she saw St Peter, St Alexis, and St Jonas, the three canonized Moscow metropolitans, leaving the Florovskaya Gates carrying away the icon of the Virgin of Vladimir.

Approaching the metropolitans from the opposite direction were two revered saints, St Sergius, the founder of the Trinity Sergius Monastery, and St Varlaam, the abbot of the Preobrazhensky Monastery in Novgorod, who stopped the metropolitans and asked them why they were leaving the city and removing its most sacred icon. The metropolitans replied that the prince of Moscow and his people had disobeyed the commandments of the Lord and were about to suffer punishment (referring to Basil III's divorce, which the Church condemned, as well as his shaving his beard). At that, St Sergius and St Varlaam fell to their knees and begged the Lord to forgive the sinful Muscovites. Moved by their prayers, the metropolitans returned to the Kremlin and restored the *Virgin of Vladimir* to its place in the Uspensky Cathedral.

Tsar Alexis Romanov was so moved by the legend that, in 1648, he commissioned an artist to paint an icon of the *Saviour* flanked by the kneeling figures of *St Sergius* and *St Varlaam*. The icon was mounted above the entrance to the Kremlin's Florovskaya Gates and was illuminated by a gilded lantern day and night; the gates were renamed the Saviour's Gates in honour of the occasion.

The icon made the Muscovites regard the Saviour's Gates with special reverence. Even tsars bared their heads as they entered the historic gateway; for failure to remove their hats, transgressors — Russian and foreign alike — were punished on the spot. With the advent of the Revolution the icon was removed and the gates closed to the general public.

The **Tsar's (Tsarkaya) Tower** ㉕ is the nearest to St Basil's Cathedral. The tower allegedly owes its name to Ivan the Terrible. Tradition has it that the tsar liked to observe the ceremonies on Red Square from a secluded wooden tower, which the present one replaced in 1680.

The present tower, or more precisely a stone turret perched atop the wall, looks like something out of a Russian fairy tale. Its green, cone-shaped roof, surmounted by a gold-plated weathervane, rests on four tublike posts decorated with stone bands and pinnacles.

Continuing clockwise, the **Alarm (Nabatnaya) Tower** ㉖, farther south on Red Square, once housed a tocsin to warn the Muscovites of approaching danger. The alarm bell cast in 1714 by Ivan Motorin, Russia's foremost craftsman, was silenced by Catherine the Great. The empress, with a degree of venom, ordered the 'tongue pulled from the seditious bell' which sounded the alarm during Pugachev's uprising in 1773. The bell is now on display at the Kremlin's

Armoury Museum. Thirty-eight metres high, the lookout tower features brick half-columns with white stone bands and capitals.

The next tower, honouring **St Constantine** and **St Helen (Konstantino-Elenenskaya)** ㉗, has a sinister reputation: Muscovites claim that its thick walls, built in 1490 by Pietro-Antonio Solari, conceal torture chambers which were especially equipped for interrogating traitors. The earlier gateway which the tower replaced recalls a major victory: in 1380, Prince Dmitry Donskoy passed through this gate when he rode out to challenge the Tartars at the Kulikovo battlefield. Here, too, the Muscovites greeted their victorious grand prince upon his return to the city. In 1680 a steeple was added to the tower, extending its height to 36.8 metres.

Excursion Plan 3
The Out-of-Town
Estates of the Tsars

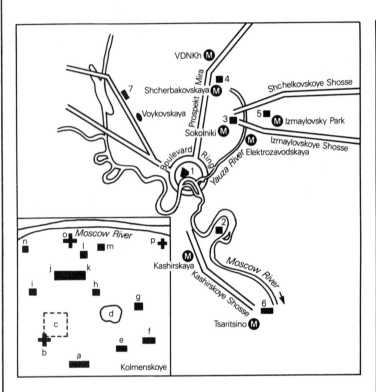

1. Kremlin
2. Kolomenskoye
3. Rubtsevo
4. Alekseyevskoye

5. Izmaylovo
6. Tsaritsino
7. Petrovsky Palace

Kolomenskoye:

a. Back gates
b. Church of Our Lady of Kazan
c. Location of Tsar Alexis's
   Timber Palace
d. Oaks planted by Peter the
   Great
e. Peter's House
f. Prison Tower from Bratsk
g. Watchtower from Korelsk
h–k. Museum incorporating the
   Colonel's quarters, the
   administrative and Sitnyi
   chambers, and the mead
   brewery

l. St George's Church
   (bell-tower)
m. The Falcon or Water Tower
n. Pavilion of the former palace
   (1825)
o. Church of the Ascension
p. Church of the Decapitation of
   St John the Baptist in Diakovo

Excursion 3

THE OUT-OF-TOWN
ESTATES OF THE TSARS

A tour to the out-of-town estates of the tsars that includes Kolomenskoye (Museum of Russian timber architecture and folk crafts) — Izmaylovo (an amusement park) — Tsaritsino Palace — Petrovsky Palace (Zhukovsky Aero-Engineering Academy).

*K*remlin life in the seventeenth century, with its frequent state and religious ceremonies, was strenuous, even for the most robust of tsars. It was equally taxing for the royal family. They looked forward to the summer months when they could forsake the crowded and noisy fortress for the open stretches of their summer estates.

Kolomenskoye ② (on the southern outskirts of Moscow) and **Izmaylovo** ⑤ (on the north-eastern outskirts) were two such estates, much prized and frequently visited by Tsar Alexis. These residences were important both for the relaxation they afforded and because they served as 'royal farms', supplying the tsar's household with meat, grain, fruit, vegetables, and flax. Tsar Alexis took special interest in their agriculture and hardly missed a chance to attend the grain harvest.

Falconry was another attraction. Alexis had a boundless enthusiasm for hunting and, according to the Russian historian Vasily Kliuchevsky, kept over 300 hawks, falcons, and other birds of prey which were trapped, reared, and trained by more than 200 hawkers and falconers. More than 100,000 doves were kept to feed the birds of prey, and about 600 bailiffs, grooms, hostlers, and saddlers were required to look after 4,000 horses.

② | # Kolomenskoye

Kololenskoye, situated on a steep hill overlooking the Moscow River, was a favourite retreat of Moscow rulers from the early fourteenth century. Its first mention in the chronicles is in 1339, in connection with the last will of Prince Ivan Kalita, who, fearing death at the hands of the Tartars, left the estate to his youngest son, Andrei. Since then, every grand prince and tsar has either visited or embellished the estate. Basil III (r. 1505–33) and Tsar Alexis Romanov (r. 1645–76) left the greatest number of monuments.

Kolomenskoye witnessed some of the greatest joys to befall the Russian rulers as well as their darkest hours. From its earliest days in the thirteenth century, it was sacked by Tartars, besieged in 1606 by the peasant troops of the runaway serf Ivan Bolotnikov, and threatened by rebellious musketeers in 1682. In periods of peace, Kolomenskoye provided the tsars with an escape from the cares of state.

Since the 1930s, Kolomenskoye has become a museum of Russian timber architecture and folk crafts. Beyond the entry gates, with their recently restored double-barrelled roofs, one sees wooden buildings which were brought here from different parts of Russia. The sturdy tent-roofed towers, one a **prison tower from Bratsk** ⓔ built in 1652 and the other a **lookout tower from Karelsk** ⓕ built in 1690, interesting as examples of timber fortifications, provide a visual link of how secular timber architecture influenced sixteenth-century masonry construction — more specifically, that of the towering **Church of the Ascension** overlooking the Moscow River.

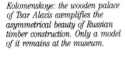

Kolomenskoye: the wooden palace of Tsar Alexis exemplifies the asymmetrical beauty of Russian timber construction. Only a model of it remains at the museum.

Exhibitions of wood-carving, metalwork, ceramics, as well as documents pertaining to the historical events which took place in Kolomenskoye, are housed in the seventeenth-century **front gateway** adjoining the service quarters, which divide the estate into two parts.

What is now the entry to Kolomenskoye was originally the estate's backyard, famous for its four orchards containing apple and cherry trees, berry bushes, flowers, and medicinal plants. Peter the Great planted several **oaks** ⓓ in the seventeenth century which have now grown into enormous trees. The wooden **four-room hut** ⓔ in which Peter the Great lived in Arkhangelsk on the White Sea is located nearby and includes the bedroom, dining room, and attendants' quarters furnished with articles which were in wide use during the end of the seventeenth century.

Presaging the coming of the ornamental Moscow Baroque, the **Church of Our Lady of Kazan** ⓑ is a massive square set upon an arcaded foundation which supports a narrower cube. Five rounded drums topped by blue, onion-shaped domes with golden stars rise above a flat green roof. The tent-roofed entrance with a covered staircase, inspired by similar features of timber construction, provides a contrast with the rectangular body of the church, as does the pointed bell tower to the north, also connected by a roofed passage. The church, started by Michael Romanov, was finished by his son Alexis in the 1660s and is a working church today.

The beautiful seventeenth-century icon of *Our Lady of Kazan*, mounted into the carved icon screen to the left of royal gates, represents a variation on the theme of 'Tenderness' (Eleusa). The image of *Our Lady of Kazan* was recovered seventeen years after Ivan the Terrible captured the Kazan fortress from the Tartars in 1552.

...e Church of Our Lady of Kazan ...s a green roof and blue domes ...th gold stars.

The Romanovs's decision to dedicate this church to the Kazan Virgin was influenced by the role the icon played during the tumultuous Time of Troubles. During the siege of the Kremlin in 1612, Russians carried the icon with them, as did the liberation troops of Prince Pozharsky and Burgher Minin, who ousted the Poles from Moscow and restored the monarchy.

The southern, or right-hand, chapel is dedicated to St Demetrius of Salonica, possibly in memory of Prince Dmitry Donskoy, who stopped in Kolomenskoye after his victory over the Tartars in 1380. Note the icon of *St George* on the choir screen near the altar. The icon was moved from the Church of St George, which was destroyed during the restoration works of the 1930s.

The northern chapel in the left part of the church honours St Averky, who preached the gospel in Syria and Asia Minor in the second century AD. A rare wooden sculpture of *Christ in Prison* can be seen there behind a glass enclosure.

Until the late eighteenth century, the Church of Our Lady of Kazan was connected with a large four-storey **timber palace** ⓒ built by Alexis Romanov in 1667. A laboriously detailed model which Catherine the Great ordered of the dilapidated palace before tearing it down is now on display in the museum. The turrets, barrel-shaped roofs, domes, spires, double-headed eagles, cocks, and other marvels of timber carving earned Alexis Romanov's palace the reputation of being the 'eighth wonder of the world'.

The two administrative buildings, the **Prikaznaya** and the **Sitnyi Chambers** ⓗ-ⓚ, on either side of the front gates, have been fully restored

EXCURSION 3

and serve as an extension of the Moscow Historical Museum. The Prikaznaya Chamber museum houses a typical seventeenth-century interior, including a long table covered with a red cloth, reversible benches, and the so-called red, or festive, corner with icons. In the wooden bookcases are documents relating to the Copper Rebellion of 1662, which started at Kolomenskoye when a crowd of 5,000 angry Muscovites protested against the minting of new copper coins.

The eight rooms of the Sitnyi Chamber house an exhibition of Russian decorative arts. The rooms contain carved gates and delicate window frames of the sort which used to grace the peasant houses of the period. There are colourful stoves made from the tiles baked by the ceramists of Moscow and a display of Russian clock mechanisms, including one by Petr Vyssotsky, craftsman of the tsar's roaring mechanical lions.

Kolomenskoye's most valuable buildings stand between the front tower gates housing the museum and the Moscow River. To the right of the gateway is the round **Bell-Tower of the Church of St George** Ⓛ, a remnant from this destroyed sixteenth-century church, and next to it is a sturdy red turret with a round gateway known alternately as the **Water Tower** or **Falcon Tower** Ⓜ. This tower, which dates from 1627, formed a part of the front gates, with its first storey designed as a guard room, its second as the waiting room for the falconers on duty, and its third as housing for the birds.

Rising between the Bell-Tower of St George, on the left, and Falcon Tower, on the right, is Kolomenskoye's most important building, the tent-roofed Church of the Ascension.

The towering **Church of the Ascension** Ⓞ, built by Grand Prince Basil III in 1532 to celebrate the birth of his son Ivan (the Terrible) after twenty-five years of ardent prayers, is one of Moscow's architectural rarities. The oldest surviving monument at Kolomenskoye, it is a triumph of Russian skill in translating the traditions of wooden architecture into stone. Unlike the Byzantine-styled Uspensky Cathedral in the Kremlin, this church is patterned on the tent-roofed churches and defence towers of native Russian architecture.

The absence of rounded domes and altar apses endow the church with a secular character. Only the cross at the top of the tower reminds the onlooker of its religious function. This building also served as a lookout tower.

The light which streams into the church through cleverly positioned windows illuminates the four-tiered iconostasis, a wooden canopy, and the royal throne from the city of Kostroma, brought to Kolomenskoye during the eighteenth century. All are outstanding examples of Russian wood carving. Another throne, made of white stone, is located outside the church on the eastern section of the circular terrace gallery. Tsar Alexis used it after church services to review petitions from his subjects.

It is interesting to compare the Ascension Church to the **Church of the Decapitation of St John the Baptist** ⓟ, rising on the crest of the hill farther south in Diakovo Village.

This church was built by Ivan the Terrible to celebrate his coronation in 1547 as the first 'tsar' of Russia and was dedicated to his patron saint. The auxiliary chapels commemorate the saints whose intercession his parents sought in praying for an heir.

The architect of St John's Church was probably Barma, one of the builders of the Church of St Basil the Blessed on Red Square. In both cases there is a grouping of small and separate tower-like chapels around the large, central chapel. In Diakovo, the cluster consists of five octagonal chapels raised on a high square terrace and crowned with a single, depressed dome. This contrasts with the eight onion-shaped domes which surround the central chapel of St Basil the Blessed.

Both represent a compromise between the traditional Byzantine five-domed plan and the tower-shaped chapels which were adopted from Russian timber architecture. The octagonal towers and five Byzantine domes symbolize Orthodoxy, which the Russian tsars championed after the fall of Constantinople.

(Restoration Studios of the Ministry of Culture of the RSFSR)
⑤

Izmaylovo

Izmaylovo, the former royal residence located in the old hunting reserve of the tsars, is now a park of some 2,950 acres with an amusement park, an open-air theatre, and several cafés.

In 1663, Tsar Alexis Romanov began to experiment here with animal husbandry, plant cultivation, and a range of cottage industries. To accomplish his purpose, Alexis transferred some seven hundred families to Izmaylovo and engaged foreign experts to supervise the work and act as advisors.

Their first task was to create a system of thirty-seven ponds (each with a special function) by damming the numerous rivers and brooks that crossed the estate. After that, choice trees, shrubs, flowers, medicinal herbs, and food cultures were imported from different parts of Russia or from abroad. By seventeenth-

...lovo is a former royal ...ce and now has an ...ment park, theatre, and ...rants. Its open-air art ...s attract many visitors.

65

century standards, Izmaylovo, with its glass factories, ponds stocked with medicinal leeches, flax hills, and grain fields, was a remarkably productive estate.

Izmaylovo reflected the attitude of Tsar Alexis toward modernization. He welcomed Western ideas and experts, believing that the modernization of Izmaylovo and Russia must evolve naturally, without upsetting the deeply rooted traditions of Muscovy.

During one of his visits to Izmaylovo, Alexis' son, Peter (the Great), came across a small wooden boat, which may have been a gift from Queen Elizabeth I of England to Ivan the Terrible. Delighted, Peter repaired the boat and fitted it out with a new mast so he could sail on the estate's ponds. In years to come, when Peter began building ships at Lake Pereslavl near Moscow, this English boat, nicknamed the 'grandfather of the Russian navy', was transported there, where it is still kept in a local museum.

According to seventeenth-century visitors to the estate, the palace and the two palace churches were surrounded by a thick wall with an imposing entrance connecting to a white stone bridge and several watch towers. Nearly a hundred buildings, half stone, half wood, provided storage space and were used to service the palace, which was a popular excursion site for members of the royal family.

Major parts of the Izmaylovo palace have been destroyed over the years: only the festive **Triple Gates** (1682), which once led to the palace, and one of the two bridge towers have survived. The turreted and much-copied Triple Gates are noteworthy for their sculptured decorations and balustrade.

The heavy squat **Bridge Tower** (1671), by contrast, is an outgrowth of Russian timber architecture typical for its receding tiers and tent-type roof. Only belts of patterned brick, thin columns, and ceramic inlays relieve the severity of its facade.

The Triple Gates provide an attractive setting for the estate's five-domed **Cathedral of Pokrov** (1671–72), which commemorated Tsar Alexis' victory over Poland in the Ukraine. While distinctly reminiscent of its model, the Uspensky Cathedral of the Kremlin, the large elongated windows, the magnificent ceramic decorations of the facade, and the five onion-shaped domes, however, are examples of the cathedral's distinctive features. The tapestry-like ornamentation of the *zakomars* and the three semicircular arches crowning the walls were the work of Russia's leading ceramist, Stepan Polubes.

⑥ Tsaritsino Palace

In 1775, Catherine the Great purchased Tsaritsino, Irina Godunova's former estate, and commissioned architect Vasily Bazhenov to build her a summer palace. He created an English park with pleasure buildings, bridges, grottos, and artificial ruins. The park was to serve as the site for two identical rectangular palaces with tall pavilions.

The architectural style, a complete departure from Bazhenov's earlier work, was a curious mixture of Moorish, Gothic, and Old-Russian styles. The red brick used in the palaces and the white stone details represented an effort

— *Out-of-Town Estates of the Tsars* —

*he gates to the Tsaritsino Palace
ombine a curious mixture of
tyles.*

to recapture Russian building traditions. The palaces were ready for Catherine's inspection in 1785. The empress praised the gates of the entrance and the graceful opera house but frowned at the sight of the neighbouring palaces and ordered them torn down and replaced. She chose Matvei Kazakov to resume her work at Tsaritsino, but he redesigned the ill-fated palace as a central block with towerlike corner pavilions using Bazhenov's pattern of brick with white ornaments.

The half-ruined palace was never finished because of subsequent financial difficulties during Catherine's reign; work was stopped on her death in 1796.

⑦ Petrovsky Palace

Kazakov was more successful with the Petrovsky Palace on the outskirts of Moscow, which he began in 1776 and which was finished in 1782. It was completed, with Catherine's approval, three years before the unsatisfactory events at Tsaritsino. The palace features red bricks and white trim in a combination of Moorish, Gothic, and Old-Russian styles. The semicircular court, which the palace faces, and the central rotunda of the palace recall the palace of Bazhenov in Pavlosk. This is yet another demonstration of the architect's considerable influence on Russian architecture. In 1840 the Petrovsky Palace was remodelled, and its Gothic elements were even more obscured by neo-Russian details.

Petrovsky, like the Alekseyevskoye Palace ④, served as a resting place for the tsars and emperors travelling from St Petersburg to Moscow. The emperors usually stayed overnight at the Petrovsky Palace before making a formal entry

EXCURSION 3

The Petrovsky Palace features red bricks and white trim in a combination of Moorish, Gothic, and Old Russian styles.

into the old capital. The palace now houses the **Zhukovsky Aero-Engineering Academy**.

Rubstsev Pereulok
Metro: *Baumanskaya*

Rubtsevo

Only the Church of Pokrov (Intercession of the Virgin), 1619–26, remains of the former palace of Tsar Michael Romanov. The church has an interesting tiered gable construction which counterbalances its massive base.

PART II

MOSCOW OF THE TOWNSPEOPLE

INTRODUCTION

*T*he centre of Moscow is **Red Square**, the huge cobblestoned expanse separating the Kremlin from the old merchant quarter known as Kitai Gorod. The word 'red' comes from the Old Russian word *krasnaya* meaning beautiful.

For nearly five centuries, Red Square has been Russia's national forum. In the old days, merchants from afar would offer exotic wares alongside Russian traders who peddled their crafts, mead, furs, or honey. On festive days, the townspeople would meet in Red Square to watch ceremonies that started inside the adjacent Kremlin. Executions, the reading of royal edicts, and the proclamation of victories would also take place here.

Vending stalls, first built of wood and later of stone, existed in Red Square since the fourteenth century. Grand Prince Ivan Kalita, who understood the value of the central marketplace to Moscow, 'turned' the Kremlin toward Kitai Gorod, the city's earliest merchant suburb. In the eighteenth century all the wooden structures that cluttered Red Square were removed. For four centuries they presented a constant fire hazard and indeed caused the great fire of 1547 that ravaged most of Moscow.

When Ivan the Terrible built **St Basil's** in Red Square, the first royal church outside the Kremlin, he was breaking with tradition in an act as revolutionary as the design of the church. He intended the church to be a triumphal monument, not just for the royal family and the nobles, but for all Muscovites. He succeeded; St Basil the Blessed, or the Cathedral of Pokrov, as it is properly known, has been regarded as the leading architectural manifestation of the Russian spirit ever since it was completed in 1561.

Until the reign of Peter the Great, the Church of Jesus' Entry into Jerusalem of St Basil's provided the site of the annual celebration of Palm Sunday in Red Square, evoking the entry of Christ into Jerusalem. The white-robed patriarch of Moscow, preceded by chanting clergy and children, would emerge from the Saviour's Gates of the Kremlin, followed immediately by the tsar and his festively attired retinue. After a brief service in the Jerusalem Church, the tsar would move over to the *Lobnoe Mesto* elevation. From this vantage point he would watch the patriarch bless and distribute the pussy willows which are used instead of palm branches to celebrate Palm Sunday in Russia.

Between 1883 and 1893, Red Square assumed its pre-revolutionary appearance with the construction of the **Historical Museum** at the northern end and the Trade Mart (today's **GUM**, the Universal State Store) along the eastern side.

The square lost much of its commercial bustle in the Soviet period but continued to fulfill the same ceremonial functions. Today, perched on the balcony of the **Lenin Mausoleum**, Soviet leaders watch the civilian parade on 1 May (the traditional Marxist workers' day) and the military demonstration on 7 November. Long lines of people file daily into the mausoleum to see the embalmed body of Lenin.

Kitai Gorod, adjoining Red Square, was originally known as *Possad*, or merchant suburb, and was renamed following the construction of a brick wall between 1534–8. Kitai, literally China, has nothing to do with the name of

bronze memorial to Minin
Pozharsky in front of St
il's commemorates the Russian
stance to the Poles in 1612.

the wall. Rather it was the basket, *kita*, filled with earth and used in the construction of the wall, that may have led to its being called Kitai Gorod.

By the time the wall was completed, the only traders left in Kitai Gorod were the privileged wholesale *gosti* merchants. The other tradesmen were displaced by the noblemen and clergy whom Ivan III requested to vacate their wooden palaces in the Kremlin. Weary of fire hazards and congestion, the Grand Prince commanded all but a handful of boyars and churchmen to move out and offered them in exchange estates in the merchant suburb.

The presence of new palaces and monasteries did not however, alter the business character of Kitai Gorod. As before, it remained Russia's largest market place, famous for its textiles, furs, icons, jewellery and other wares ranging from the most exotic imports to the cheapest household goods.

Each line of goods was assigned its place in the rows of stalls known in Russian as the *riady*. Seventy-two rows of trading stalls lined Red Square and the three main streets of Kitai Gorod. The memory of the specialized trading stalls is still preserved in the names of Khrustalnyi (Crystal Row) and Rybnyi (Fishmongers' Row) located at the southern edge of Kitai Gorod.

When the Moscow merchants emerged as a powerful class in the 1860s, it was their turn to uproot the gentry. The ancient suburb became a jumble of storage houses, banks, and business concerns whose heartbeat was regulated by the **Stock Exchange** which the bankers founded in 1837 on Ilynka (Kuybysheva) Street.

Until 1918 this old quarter of Moscow gave the city a splash of colour and an atmosphere of solidity. Here banks and houses of business alternated with monasteries, churches, trading arcades, restaurants, and cafés. Famous restaurants, such as the **Slaviansky Bazar**, served the best pancakes in town, while the handsome houses and churches of the suburb, then as today, provided visual appeal and a link to Kitai Gorod's historic past.

No less significant in the history of Moscow was the aristocratic **White City**, so called for its white-washed walls which ran along the line of today's Boulevard Ring. Shaped in the form of a horseshoe, the settlement sprang up in the sixteenth century between the northern and eastern boundaries of the Kremlin and Kitai Gorod to accommodate the overflow from the congested merchant suburb. The proximity to the Kremlin made the White City particularly attractive to the nobles, who embellished it with crest-roofed palaces and splendid churches.

The most popular street in the White City was **Tverskaya**, the present-day **Gorky Street**. It started opposite the north-eastern corner of the Kremlin and ran north towards the city of Tver. In the sixteenth century, Tverskaya, an already well travelled trade road, also acquired an important role in royal pageantry. Even after Peter the Great shifted the capital to St Petersburg, all major state processions, including the formal entry of the new emperors, and military parades marched along this street.

At the end of the eighteenth century, Tverskaya became the setting for the gentry's pleasure as much as its business. The noblemen dined, gambled, and

discussed politics at the **English Club**, held balls and presented debutantes to the court at the **Nobles' Club**, and governed from the Tverskaya **Residence of the Governor-General**. Tverskaya's glitter reflected its mastery of the capital's cultural life, business, and government.

It was hardly surprising that the merchant barons who ran the business life of Moscow began to infiltrate the élite bastions of Tverskaya. The first attempt to unseat the gentry occurred in 1872 at the Duma (City Council) when Prince Cherkassky resigned, thus vacating the post of the Moscow mayor. The merchants' candidate was I. A. Liamin, a meek man whom the nobles ridiculed and even chastised for failing to appear in proper attire at the City Council meeting.

In the 1877 elections, the merchants' candidate was no longer a reticent Liamin, but the energetic textile merchant Sergei Tretyakov. Like his brother Pavel, Sergei was a famous art collector and co-founder of the Tretyakov Gallery of Art.

Gradually capitulating to what they called 'the dictatorship of the sales-counter', the nobles saw their houses pass into the hands of the newcomers, with even the exclusive clubs opening their doors to the industrialists.

In the 1930s Tverskaya underwent drastic alterations. Palaces, churches, convents and Moscow's famous Hunter's Row Market (Okhotnyi Riad) came down to make room for modern apartment houses, government buildings and hotels. The few landmarks which survived from pre-revolutionary days were moved backwards or encased into the new structures. Tverskaya was no more. In 1932 the enlarged avenue was renamed Gorky Street, after the writer Maxim Gorky.

The venerable institutions of the nobles became Soviet government buildings or museums. The English Club now houses the Museum of the Revolution of the USSR. The City Council, disbanded in 1917, was turned over to the Moscow City Council, or Mossoviet, which in 1936 occupied the former Residence of the Military Governors on Gorky Street. The Duma building itself was converted into the Lenin Museum, while the Nobles' Club is the present House of Trade Unions on Prospekt Marksa.

Like all ancient cities, Moscow needed modernization. But the General Plan of Reconstruction had as its goal to glorify Stalin at the expense of Moscow's treasured monuments. Churches, palaces, and chapels were eradicated to make room for modern houses, metro stations, or simply squares. The Kremlin and Red Square alone lost nine of its eighteen monuments. The most notable case of architectural barbarism was the demolition of the grandiose Saviour's Cathedral, which commemorated the Russian victory over Napoleon (see p. 337).

The General Reconstruction Plan radically altered the city, leaving only patches of its pre-revolutionary charm. Only with the coming to power of Mikhail Gorbachev was a formal ban placed on further annihilation of historical monuments previewed by Stalin's plan and pursued under his successors.

Excursion Plan 4
Red Square

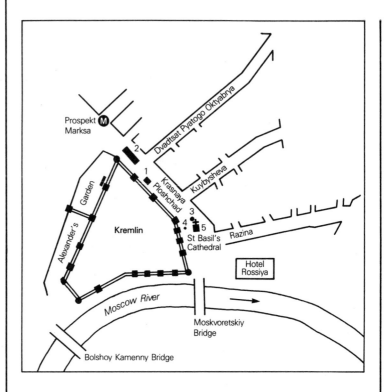

1. The Lenin Mausoleum
2. The Historical Museum
3. Lobnoe Mesto
4. The Memorial to Minin and Pozhansky
5. St Basil's

Excursion 4

RED SQUARE

A tour to Red Square that includes Lenin's Mausoleum — Historical Museum — Lobnoe Mesto Elevation — Memorial to Minin and Pozharsky — Cathedral of St Basil the Blessed.

① ## Lenin Mausoleum

The mausoleum housing Lenin's remains adjoins the eastern wall of the Kremlin. It was built by the well-known architect Shchusev in 1930 to replace an earlier wooden structure hastily erected in 1924. To avoid disrupting the architectural harmony of Red Square, Shchusev kept the building low and dressed the tomb in red granite and sombre shades of labrodite. He arranged the upper part as a tribune, the access to which is through a wide staircase on either side of the memorial. The glass sepulchre where Lenin's remains are displayed is kept in the underground vault of the mausoleum.

When Stalin died in 1953, his body was placed next to Lenin's in the Mausoleum. After Stalin was denounced in 1961, his body was removed and buried near the Kremlin wall behind the mausoleum among the graves of other revolutionary leaders and famous Communists.

② ## Historical Museum

Closest to the Lenin Mausoleum is the red brick building of the Historical Museum, located at the northern edge of Red Square. It was founded by Alexander III and executed by Vladimir Sherwood between 1878 and 1883 in pseudo-Russian style, inspired by Russian timber architecture then in vogue. An inventory of the museum's forty-seven halls makes the mind reel: four million exhibits and nearly as many documents trace the origin and history of the peoples of the Soviet Union from ancient times.

Halls 1–7 Archaeological finds trace the progress of the ancient tribes who inhabited the territory of what is now the USSR through the Stone, Bronze, and Metal Ages. Of particular note is a 5,000-year-old wooden boat discovered in the Ukraine at the end of the nineteenth century. Also note a suit of leather worn by a shaman, a religious head of a primitive tribe, dating back to the third century BC. In Hall 2 a painting by Vasnetsov in 1883 reconstructs scenes from the Stone Age. Hall 7 is devoted to the advent of Christianity in Russia.

Hall 8 Exhibits relate the development of the Kievan State from the ninth to the mid-eleventh centuries and include icons, marriage crowns, and replicas of mosaics from St Sophia's Cathedral in Kiev.

Hall 9 Exhibits cover the city of Novgorod and include models of Novgorod churches

Conceived in the joyful mood of victory, St Basil's Cathedral draws its inspiration from the wooden shapes of Russian timber architecture.

and icons from the fourteenth and fifteenth centuries. Note also the birch bark scrolls dating from the twelfth to the fifteenth centuries.

Halls 10, 11, and 12 | Exhibits relate the history of the ancient cities of Vladimir, Suzdal, and Rostov.

Hall 13 | Exhibits cover the Mongol period, ushered in by the invasion of Russia by the Tartar Khan Batu in 1237.

Hall 14 | Exhibits deal with the unification of the Russian state around Muscovy.

Halls 15, 16, and 17 | Exhibits examine the economic development of Russia and its internal and foreign policies in the sixteenth and seventeenth centuries. In Hall 15 is the first book to be published in Moscow in 1564, *Acts of Apostles*.

Halls 18, 19, and 20 | Exhibits highlight the reign of Peter the Great (1689–1725). In Hall 19 there is a replica of the room where Peter's half-sister, Sofia, was banished after she forced the coup in 1698, which nearly cost Peter his life. Included are displays relating to Peter the Great's military activities.

Hall 22 | Exhibits illustrate the economic development of Russia in the second half of the eighteenth century. Note displays of primitive farming tools in contrast to the fine apparel of wealthy nobility.

Hall 23 | Exhibits trace the reign of Catherine the Great (1762–96), during which the Peasant's Revolt led by Emilian Pugachev, a Cossack rebel, occurred. The cage in which he was captured and brought to Moscow for execution is on display. Note as well the portrait of Pugachev which was painted over the portrait of the empress.

Halls 24, 25, and 26 | Exhibits illustrate the internal and foreign policies of Catherine the Great. Note the Turkish armaments (war trophies) studded with coral, turquoise, and other semi-precious stones.

Hall 27 | Exhibits examine Russian cultural development in the eighteenth century. Note the intricately carved bone vases and chests of the period. Also of interest is a decanter divided into four parts to hold differently coloured wines.

Halls 28 and 29 | Exhibits deal with the Bolshevik Revolution in 1917.

Halls 30–47 | Temporary exhibits on contemporary subjects are held here.

EXCURSION 4

③ # Lobnoe Mesto Elevation

To the south in Red Square rises the Cathedral of St Basil and beneath it a rounded elevation known as the *Lobnoe Mesto*. Royal edicts and decrees were read from this elevation, and the tsar would present his heir-apparent here when the crown prince turned sixteen. The first historical mention of Lobnoe Mesto occurs in 1547, the year of the terrible fire, when Ivan the Terrible, builder of St Basil's, made a public confession of his misdeeds to the Muscovites.

④ # Memorial to Minin and Pozharsky

Also nestling in the shadow of St Basil's is a bronze memorial with statues of Minin and Pozharsky, commemorating the Russian resistance to the Poles in 1612. Prince Pozharsky organized the liberation movement that drove the Poles out of the Kremlin. The memorial cast by the Russian sculptor Ivan Martos in 1818 depicts episodes from the war of 1612 and was built with money received from public donations.

⑤ # Cathedral of Pokrov (St Basil the Blessed)

The story of St Basil's begins in May 1552 when Red Square was the site of a mass prayer meeting on the eve of the departure of the tsar and his armies to fight the Tartars. Mingling in the crowd was a barefoot holy man dressed in rags, well known to the crowd as Basil the Blessed for his humility and clairvoyancy. Even before Ivan unleashed his reign of terror, Basil was warning the tsar that his future crimes would condemn him to eternal damnation. On the eve of Ivan's departure for Kazan, Basil predicted that the tsar would murder his first-born son. Only the traditional immunity accorded to holy men saved him from Ivan the Terrible's wrath. St Basil died while Ivan was laying siege to Kazan, and his body was buried near the old Trinity Church on Red Square, the future site of the cathedral.

It took six months for the Russians to force their way into the Kazan fortress. Victory came on 1 October 1552, which, according to the Orthodox calendar, was the Feast of Pokrov, or Protection of the Blessed Virgin's Veil. Thankful for the help of the Virgin, the young monarch ordered a wooden church dedicated to the Pokrov to be built in Red Square. As more military successes followed, a series of wooden chapels took shape in Red Square, around the already existing Trinity Church, each commemorating the feast day on which Ivan had inflicted a new defeat on the Tartars. Finally, there were seven victories, and seven new churches in Red Square.

When the triumphant tsar returned to Moscow, he demanded that the Trinity Church and the wooden chapels be torn down to make the way for the Cathedral of Pokrov. The new cathedral was to surpass in size and splendour anything that the Russian rulers had built before, reminding future generations of Russia's victories and the tsar who had won them.

The tsar could not have suspected that the gaily coloured church would come to be associated in the popular mind not with his greatness but with his accuser, St Basil. Seventeen years after his death, St Basil was canonized and a chapel honouring the new saint was added to the north-eastern side of the Pokrov Cathedral. Since then the whole cathedral has come to be known by the name of the Church of St Basil the Blessed, although only one chapel was actually dedicated to him.

Architecture

St Basil's was conceived in the joyful mood of victory, a magnificent arch of triumph of its day. Its polychrome domes and vibrant colours amount to a Russian declaration of independence from the Byzantine past.

The two Russian masters summoned to build the cathedral, Postnik and Barma, drew on the wooden shapes of Russian timber architecture rather than on Constantinople for inspiration. The tent-roofed entries, the galleries, the porches with their picturesque stairways, the patterns of beads and logs, the many-faceted domes, and the beloved spade-shaped gables are all features

EXCURSION 4

79

of Russia's native timber churches. The architects skilfully translated the old wooden shapes into masonry, relying on foreign features only when national architecture was at a loss to supply a needed element. Thus, side by side with purely Russian features appear cornices handled in the Italian manner.

While popular legend holds that Ivan the Terrible put out the eyes of the architects to prevent them from building a rival to St Basil's, Postnik and Barma undertook the construction of the kremlin in Kazan after they had completed St Basil's.

Despite its complex exterior, the basic plan of the church is simple, resembling an eight-cornered star. Along the arms formed by the main axes are four octagonal churches with four smaller ones squeezed between the angles. The principal church rises above the centre of the cross in the shape of a tent-roofed pyramid. The subordination of the smaller churches to this central church resembles the design of Diakovo, near Kolomenskoye; but unlike Diakovo, the domes of St Basil's are onion shaped and vary widely in size and ornamentation. Some are twisted like oriental turbans, others are scaled like inverted pine cones, while still others are ribbed and faceted.

In contrast to its festive exterior, the interior of the cathedral is cavernous and sombre because of the enclosing of the open porches, which eliminated much of the light which once filtered into the church. Some of the smaller churches have recently been restored, displaying the graceful spiral patterns of the bricks in the ceiling.

Art

The sixteenth- and seventeenth-century icon screens in the chapels of the cathedral, with the exception of the iconostasis in the chapel honouring the *Entry of Jesus into Jerusalem*, are not the originals. As a result the visitor is not often aware that the separate churches which compose the cathedral are grouped according to canonical meaning. Going along the main axis, from east to west, for example, the three most important altars in terms of religious significance are carefully aligned: the *Trinity Church*, the *Church of Pokrov*, and the *Church of Jesus's Entry into Jerusalem*.

The central cathedral has become a state museum and contains an exhibit dealing with the cathedral's construction. Numerous engravings and miniatures allow the visitor to trace the evolution of the church from the sixteenth century to the present. A second exhibit, devoted to Ivan the Terrible's campaign against the Tartars, displays weapons and protective armour.

It is always difficult to explain the powerful effect of St Basil's. In winter, with the snow swirling like an enveloping mist, St Basil's and its clustered chapels seems to grow in size. In the summer, when the sun is reflected from its colourfully faceted surfaces, it looks something like the dazzling firebird of Russian folklore. During the holiday parades in Red Square it appears menacing and grotesque, and yet on a spring evening it can become gentle and friendly. Whatever lends to St Basil its ability to change with season and mood, it remains a purely Russian monument.

KITAI GOROD

Metro: *Prospekt Marksa*
or Ploshchad
Revolyutsii.

A tour that includes the Old Royal Mint — GUM Department Store — Street of 25 October — Kuybysheva Street — Razina Street — Church of St Anne — Church of the Holy Trinity 'in Nikitniki'.

Istoricheskiy Proyezd, 1
①

Old Royal Mint

The excursion begins with a visit to the Old Royal Mint, a cheerful red building tucked away in the courtyard of the tiny Historical Passage across from the Historical Museum.

The Old Royal Mint was built in 1697 by Peter the Great, as attested by the inscription above the gates. The contrast between the decor of the second floor, with its richly carved frames surrounding large windows, twisted columns, and tiled inserts, and the plain, windowless first floor was dictated by safety precautions. The cubicles built inside the thick wall on either side of the entry housed the mint guards who carefully checked each person entering and, particularly, leaving the building.

The right wing of the mint is shorter than the left because, during the eighteenth-century reconstruction, part of the old mint building was absorbed by the new wing.

In the 1770s, the mint was moved to St Petersburg and the empty building was taken over by the Moscow vice-governor for his administrative offices. The vice-governor, like the military governor, was traditionally a nobleman and a tsar's appointee. His task was to assist the governor in jointly running the city with the Moscow City Council.

This building was linked to the Historical Museum by the Resurrection Gates until the 1920s. Adjoining the gates stood the **Chapel of the Iberian Virgin**, the venerated gatekeeper of Moscow whose icon Tsar Alexis commissioned in Athos and for which the chapel was built. Both were demolished in the 1920s.

(25–Ogo Oktyabrya)

Street of 25 October

The street's original name, Nikolskaya, was derived from the fourteenth-century **Nikolsky Monastery** ④, turned over in the sixteenth century by Ivan the Terrible to the learned and needy Greek monks from Mount Athos. Only a disfigured twentieth-century bell tower now marks Nikolsky Monastery, which in 1724 became the burial vault of Kantemir princes from Moldavia.

Nikolskaya was also known as the 'Street of Enlightenment' because Moscow's earliest learning institutions and Russia's first printing press occupied the entire left side of the street. Moreover, Nikolskaya was the prime outlet of books and icons sold in the numerous stalls that lined the street. The right hand side of the street, by contrast, was occupied by large merchant arcades.

Excursion Plan 5
Kitai Gorod

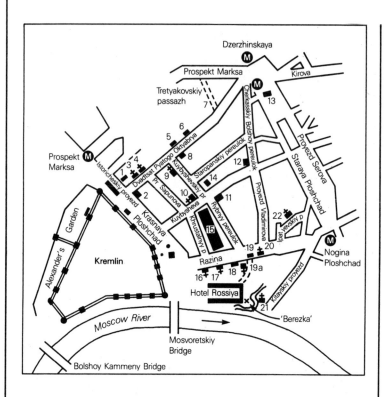

1. The Old Royal Mint (entrance from Istoricheskiy proyezd)
2. GUM (department store)
3. Saviour's Monastery
4. Nikolsky Monastery
5. The Old Printing House
6. The Slaviansky Bazar Restaurant
7. Tretyakovskiy Passage
8. Chizhov's Coach Exchange
9. Bogoiavlensky Monastery
10. Church of St Elias
11. Moscow Stock Exchange
12. Riabushinsky Bank
13. Moscow Merchants' Association Building
14. Trinity Sergius Hostel
15. The Old Merchant Arcade
16. St Barbara's Church
17. St Maxim's Church
18. Old English Embassy
19. House of the Boyars Romanov
19a. Znamensky Convent
20. St George's Church
21. St Anne's Church
22. Church of the Holy Trinity

GUM

(*Gosudarstvenny
niversalny Magazin*)
②

Until 1921, when Lenin nationalized it and renamed it 'GUM', this largest and most famous store in Moscow was known as the Upper Trading Arcades.

Designed by Aleksandr Pomerantsev betwen 1888 and 1893 the building was constructed of sandstone at the cost of six million roubles, not counting the price of the land. The three-storey-high building, occupying an area of some 24,500 square metres, replaced the old merchant arcades that existed on this site since the fifteenth century.

Three parallel glass-covered passages, each three storeys high, traverse the ground floor, with bridges linking the passages on the second and third floors. Each passage corresponds to what used to be the distance between the sixteenth-century trading rows. The offices located on the third floor once belonged to such Moscow merchants as the Tretyakovs, Alekseyevs, Riabushinskys, and a score of other wealthy textile traders anxious to keep an eye on the sale of their wares.

In pre-revolutionary days, GUM was famous for its textiles and furs. There was a wide assortment of fabrics, from coarse woollens to fine silks woven with gold and silver threads. No less impressive was the collection of furs ranging from expensive blue fox and sable pelts to cheap coats, derisively described by Muscovites as 'guardians of the house' because they were made from dog's fur.

Saviour's Monastery

(Zaikonospassky
Monastery)
③

Inside the courtyard of house No. 7 stands the Saviour's Church of the former Zaikonospassky Monastery. The name of the monastery is in itself proof that as early as the 1600s the icon trade was a flourishing industry on this street. The name means 'Saviour's Monastery Behind Icon-Trading Stalls'.

*our's Monastery 'Behind the
-Trading Stalls' attests to the
that the sale of icons was a
rishing business in the
nteenth century.*

The red and white church, built in 1661 and rebuilt between 1717 and 1720 by the architects Ivan Zarudny and Ivan Michurin, is tiered like the nearby Bogoiavlensky Cathedral, though the spread of its base is wider and the narrowing sections lighter and less burdened by white stone details. Western influence is also more pronounced in the treatment of the windows with key stones, the rounding of the arches, and the appearance of balustrades around the open platform at the upper storeys of the elongated church.

The Saviour's Church and its adjoining nineteenth-century buildings housed the **Slavic-Greek-**

EXCURSION 5

Latin Academy. Moscow's first higher education establishment, which functioned here between 1687 and 1814. It was Russia's largest secular school and staffed with Western-trained scholars from Kiev.

One of its graduates was Mikhail Lomonosov, a fisherman's son who later became the father of Russian science. Lomonosov was a Renaissance man, renowned as a scientist, educator, poet, orator, and historian. He modernized Russian poetry, creating new ground rules for the Russian literary language. In 1755, when Empress Elizabeth approved the founding of Moscow University, Lomonosov developed its curriculum.

(Pechatny Dvor)
⑤

Old Printing House

The spiked green building just beyond the Saviour's Monastery is still known as the Old Printing House, even though the original printing press founded by Ivan the Terrible in 1553 has long since gone. The nineteenth-century structure seen today was designed by the architects Mironovsky and Bakarev for the printing needs of the Holy Synod, the commission set up by Peter the Great to regulate Church affairs.

The real attraction of the Old Printing House is the Proofreaders' Building which stands inside the courtyard. The restored seventeenth-century mini-palace has a roof painted like a chessboard and a tent-roofed porch.

In designing the printing house, the architects made liberal use of Gothic motives, to which they added features of Russian seventeenth-century architecture. The mixture of styles produced an intriguing and highly decorative building in which the windows of the main facade and the two side wings are elongated like those of medieval churches. The many towers and turrets that rise from the building account for the spiky effect.

The building's decorations are so abundant that hardly a bare spot is left on the walls. Along with the carved flowers that embellish the pillars, the white insets above the doors and windows, and the bands on the walls, the architects managed to add two sundials and the figures of a unicorn and a lion above the portals.

The real attraction of the Old Printing House is the old proofreaders' building which can be seen only by those brave enough to push through the heavy black gates at No. 15 that lead to the inside court. Beyond the gates stands a restored seventeenth-

century mini-palace with a roof painted like a chessboard and a tented porch resting on pot-bellied columns. The windows have gaily coloured frames, and the walls are studded with bright ceramic tiles.

Inside the small, dark, and vaulted rooms, Ivan Fedorov, assisted by Petr Mstislavets, printed the *Acts of the Apostles*, Russia's first book. During the year it took Fedorov to produce the book, Ivan the Terrible paid a daily visit to the printing press. When it was finally finished on 1 March 1564, Ivan extended his hand to the kneeling printer and said: 'Today you have accomplished a great thing. Future generations will remember you for this.'

Acts of the Apostles did indeed become a major factor in bringing uniformity to Russian religious literature and in providing a base for the systematic development of learning in Russia. A **statue to Ivan Fedorov** was erected in 1909 just outside Kitai Gorod.

No. 17
⑥

Slaviansky Bazar Restaurant

The recently restored Slaviansky Bazar is one of Moscow's oldest and most colourful restaurants. It has recovered its former decor and some of its old gastronomic rating. When it opened in the 1870s, it was a popular meeting place for the intelligentsia. Here on 21 June 1897, during an 18-hour lunch, theatrical directors Stanislavsky and Nemirovich-Danchenko reached an accord on the formation of the Moscow Art Theatre. Million-rouble deals were negotiated by Moscow merchants inside the brightly painted rooms. The average order of pancakes, or *bliny*, ordered by these merchants was four dozen per person, served specially during the week preceding the pre-Easter period.

⑦

Tretyakovskiy Passage

The Tretyakovskiy Passage, which links the Street of 25 October to Prospekt Marksa below, was pierced through the Kitai Gorod wall to accommodate the textile merchant Sergei Tretyakov. Tretyakov, who lived on this street, wanted a quick access to the banks located on the other side of Prospekt Marksa. Permission was granted in 1871 after Tretakov agreed to pay for the piercing of the wall and for the construction of the arcaded passage with the red turreted gates above it.

(Chizhovskoe Podvorye)
⑧

Chizhov's Coach Exchange

Almost directly opposite the green Printing House is a sturdy building typical of nineteenth-century merchant design. This was the former coach exchange run by the Chizhov family, who made its fortune by hiring out horse-drawn carriages for public conveyance and carts for transporting goods to Moscow.

Since Russians hated to walk and Moscow streets were often muddy or snow-bound, there was a steady demand for taxis. According to the seasons, the coachmen drove carriages or sledges, usually pulled by one horse. In winter the Chizhovs hired out troikas with three fast horses to satisfy the Russian love of speed.

An unexpected bonus of visiting Chizhov's exchange is the seventeenth-century **Dormition (Uspenskaya) Church** adjoining Chizhov's former offices. Located inside the courtyard, the church is unusual since it combines the tiered construction of Moscow's Baroque style with classical pediments marking the transition to a thin drum and single cupola. Also noteworthy is the absence of apses which usually project from the eastern wall of Russian Churches.

(Ulitsa Kuybysheva)

Kuybysheva Street

Prior to 1935, Kuybysheva Street was known as Ilinka, named after the *Church of St Elias* (Ilia), tucked away in the jumble of the buildings which belonged to the Novgorod Exchange. At one time the main artery of Moscow's financial district, banks, money-changing places, and the Moscow Stock Exchange stood on or around this street. Its pride, however, was the Bogoiavlensky Monastery, Moscow's first educational institution and a magnificent architectural landmark.

Nos. 2–4
(9)

Bogoiavlensky Monastery

Bogiavlensky, or Epiphany, Monastery at Nos 2–4 was founded in the late 1290s by Prince Daniel, the energetic young prince who made Moscow his permanent residence. Daniel commissioned the building of Bogoiavlensky to reinforce the Kremlin and to protect the merchant settlement below the Kremlin fortress (defenceless until the Kitai Gorod wall was built in 1538). Located within walking distance from the Kremlin, Bogoiavlensky rose at the point where a well-travelled road, now Street of 25 October, emerged from the forest and turned toward the merchant suburb.

The fourteenth-century Metropolitan Alexis was one of the distinguished religious figures to emerge from Bogoiavlensky. This scholarly Churchman, who translated the New Testament from Greek into Church Slavonic, was also the man who preserved the unity of the Russian state during the infancy of Prince Dmitry Donskoy.

All that remains of the monastery is its Bogoiavlensky Cathedral, built between 1693–6. It is a superb example of the late Moscow Baroque style. The progressively narrowing sections extend from the arcaded cubic base and move toward an octagon and a single dome above. The finely profiled brick window frames on the second-storey level are inspired by Russia's wooden architecture. Those at the lower level feature columns and curvilinear pediments borrowed from classical architecture. No less splendid are the double stripes of patterned brick which create a rhythmical light and shadow effect and accentuate the massive volume of the church and its refectory.

The tall red church was once famous for its sculptures, now at Donskoy Monastery, that were commissioned as memorials by the Princes Golitsyn. The Golitsyns used the monastery's church as their family burial vault until 1771, when a cholera epidemic resulted in a ban on burials there and the family then switched their patronage to the Donskoy Monastery (see 'Moscow of the Clergy', Excursion 22).

*e Bogoiavlensky Cathedral is
that remains of the former
goiavlensky Monastery.*

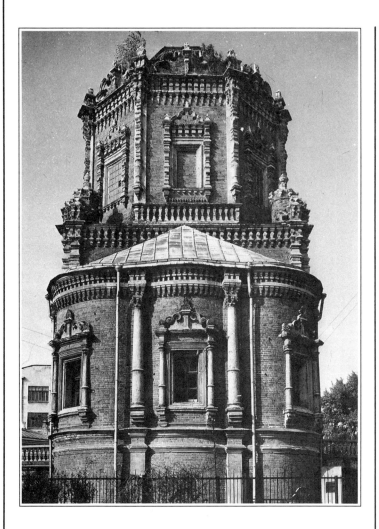

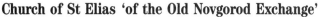

*Tserkov Ilii Proroka
'v Novgorodskom
Podvorye')
o. 3/8, opposite No. 4*
⑩

Church of St Elias 'of the Old Novgorod Exchange'

This pillarless, fifteenth-century church, reconstructed in the seventeenth and eighteenth centuries in a narrow passage between two warehouses, is recognizable by rounded *zakomar* arches and the eighteenth-century drum and single cupola. The Church of St Elias was built by rich Novgorod merchants next to the exchange on land the merchants received from Moscow grand princes when Novgorod was still independent. In 1497, Ivan III transferred five hundred ranking Novgorod families to Moscow; the exchange continued to operate and became the nucleus of the Novgorod community of merchants who settled around it.

EXCURSION 5

No. 6

⑪

Moscow Stock Exchange

The three-storeyed Stock Exchange (now the **Chamber of Trade of the USSR**), with its facade of enormous Ionic columns, was the work of architect Dmitry Bykov. Designed between 1873 and 1875 and reconstructed in the early twentieth century, it is an example of late Moscow classicism, better known for fine detail, as seen in the heavy wooden door with lions' heads, than the beauty of its architecture. The Stock Exchange was run by a committee selected by its five hundred members, who represented the most influential businessmen of Moscow.

Kuybysheva Ploshchad,
2

⑫

Riabushinsky Bank

The founder of this bank was Pavel Riabushinsky, an active Old Believer and dean of the Moscow business community, who did much to advance the cause of the constitutional government of Russia. He was frequently chosen as the spokesman for the merchant class; and whenever a delegation was sent to St Petersburg he was included, because the merchants believed that 'Riabushinsky will tell the truth to the tsar.'

The future of the merchants as the bulwark of Russia and the superiority of the merchants over the 'degenerate gentry' were Riabushinsky's favourite themes. His voicing such opinions as the president of the bank and the chairman of the Moscow Stock Exchange embarrassed his colleagues, many of whom were still beholden to the nobility. Riabushinsky not only ridiculed those who sought ennoblement but did everything in his power to destroy the myth of the gentry.

Moreover, unlike other leftist industrialists who financed the Bolshevik Revolution, Riabushinsky appealed to the Russian bourgeoisie to 'suffocate the Revolution with the bony hand of hunger'. As a true representative of his class Riabushinsky remained loyal to the crown until the end.

The bank, which Riabushinsky commissioned Fedor Shekhtel to design for him in 1904, is typical of the architect's mature work: rows of large windows dominate the pristinely pure, vertically oriented facade. The upward sweep of the building was somewhat disturbed when, in 1908, another architect added a sixth floor, wider than the five earlier ones. Despite reconstruction, the contrast between the severe facade and the sensuous glow of glazed tiles covering the bank's walls is as striking as ever.

Malyy Cherkasskiy
Pereulok, 2

⑬

Moscow Merchants' Association Building

The civically minded and philanthropical Riabushinsky was a member of the Moscow Merchants' Association, and probably he suggested Shekhtel, his favourite architect, for this project. Shekhtel designed the building (1909) in the modern style with stress on vertical alignment, big windows, and extensive use of glazed tiles for the facade.

Kuybysheva Ploshchad,
4
⑭

Trinity Sergius Hostel

It is interesting to contrast the Merchants' Association Building with the house built for the Trinity Sergius Monastery in 1875 by architect P. P. Skomoroshenko. Unlike the undecorated merchants building, the monastery's hostel was built in the then popular 'eclectic' style which relied heavily on Old Russian motifs: carved window frames, dentals, and pillars.

Kuybysheva, 4
⑮

Old Merchant Arcade

Though the arcade's formal address is usually given as Kuybysheva Street, it is best seen from Rybnyy Lane. The elegant white building with rhythmically distributed Corinthian columns was designed by St Petersburg's master architect, Giacomo Quarenghi, an Italian by birth. The building, completed in 1805, was acclaimed as an architectural *tour de force*.

It is worth going inside the building, now used for storage and offices, to admire the magnificent open arcade. Once lined with exclusive boutiques, it offered a spectacular view of the Kremlin. The Old Arcades (to distinguish it from the **New Arcades** built in 1839–42 directly opposite on Rybnyy Lane) occupies the whole block and curves towards the Kremlin as it reaches Razina Street.

(Ulitsa Razina)

Razina Street

Someone with a perverse sense of humour must have suggested renaming Varvarka Street, the citadel of Russian nobility and venerable merchants, Razina Street, which commemorates Stenka Razin, a Cossack rebel leader who was publicly executed in Red Square on 6 June 1671.

erkov Sv. Varvary)
No. 2
⑯

Church of St Barbara

The Church of St Barbara (Varvara), the salmon-coloured, cross-shaped building at the beginning of Razina Street, was designed by architect Radion Kazakov between 1796 and 1804 on the site of an earlier sixteenth-century church. Named after the church, Varvarka Street was first mentioned in the Russian chronicles in 1434, although Prince Dmitry Donskoy rode along it in 1380 on his way to the Battle of Kulikovo, where he defeated the Tartars. The street was then part of the old trade route to Vladimir and other points east.

(Tserkov Maksima
Blazhennogo)
No. 4
⑰

Church of St Maxim the Confessor

The church next to St Barbara's is dedicated to St Maxim, a Russian saint and one of the 'fools for Christ's sake' revered by the Muscovites. The fools for Christ's sake, like Maxim, were men and women who, in striving for humility, chose the ascetic struggle of acting half-witted and accepting ridicule to show their detachment from all material things. Many had a gift of prophecy. They spoke their mind, oblivious to the dangers their frankness could cause, and

pointed their accusing fingers even at the tsars. Maxim, who died in 1433, was particularly well known for his clairvoyancy.

In 1698 the Novgorod merchants who settled in this area donated money for the cube-shaped church crowned with five cupolas. When the church was finished, St Maxim's remains, encased in a silver shrine, were placed inside. Now stripped of all decorations, the empty church houses the **Society for Environmental Protection**.

Old English Embassy

(Angliiskoye Podvorie)
No. 6
(18)

This sixteenth-century white-washed house, with tiny windows, a peaked wooden roof, and a flight of steps leading to the second storey, originally belonged to a rich Russian merchant. In the mid-sixteenth century Ivan the Terrible presented it to the British traders who followed Sir Richard Chancellor, head of the English Trading delegation and later ambassador of Queen Elizabeth I.

The Old English Embassy originally belonged to a rich Russian merchant.

Sir Richard inadvertently arrived in Russia in 1553 when his three ships were caught in a storm and two foundered. Sir Richard survived and managed to reach the White Sea, thus demonstrating that the Baltic was not the only trade route to Europe.

Ivan the Terrible saw the hand of Providence in the arrival of the British traders; he had been seeking to establish relations with England in his effort to improve Russian technology and obtain an ally for his Livonian campaign. These motivations explain the great favours which the tsar later accorded Sir Richard and the six-hour-long feast which he offered the British captain in the Hall of Facets (see p. 36) at Christmas 1553.

Sir Richard's unexpected visit brought Russia in closer contact with

Elizabethan England. The agreement reached between Ivan the Terrible and Sir Richard stipulated that, in exchange for military supplies shipped to Russia through the mouth of the Northern Dvina, English traders were given the right to duty-free trade in Russia, free transit along the Volga route, and a firm footing in Moscow. Ivan's own feelings towards England were greatly coloured by his contacts with Sir Richard. At one point Ivan even considered marrying Queen Elizabeth, an honour she declined, though she graciously offered him asylum in England should he wish it.

The Old English Embassy was restored in the 1970s by architect Peter Baranovsky.

Hotel Rossiya

The huge modernistic hotel which dwarfs the lovely old buildings of Kitai Gorod was completed in 1967 under the supervision of the architect D. Chechulin. It houses one of Moscow's best stocked hard-currency *Beriozka* souvenir stores, the large Zariadie Cinema, and the Central Concert Hall and offers a beautiful view of the Kremlin.

The area it now occupies was formerly known as *zariadie*, or literally the place 'beyond the trading stalls'. Indeed, the old marketplace in Red Square stopped short of St Basil's. The slope descending from the cathedral once teemed with petty traders and artisans and had some of the oldest buildings in Moscow.

Below the overpass which leads to the second floor of the Hotel Rossiya is one of Moscow's most attractive architectural complexes: the adjacent buildings of the Znamensky Convent and the House of the Boyars Romanov, the birthplace of Tsar Michael Romanov, the founder of the Russian royal dynasty which ruled until 1917.

House of the Romanovs

(Dom Boyar Romanovykh) No. 10 ⑲

Among the earliest settlers on Razina Street were noblemen like Nikita Romanov, whose valiant deeds on the battlefield earned him this prized estate in Kitai Gorod. In 1547 Nikita's sister, Anastasia, married Ivan the Terrible and became one of Russia's most beloved tsarinas. Because of that marriage, Nikita's grandson Michael succeeded to the vacant throne in 1613 after Ivan the Terrible's sole surviving heir was murdered.

Over the years, the house fell into disrepair; only during the reign of Alexander II was the house 'rediscovered' and restored by painter Fedor Richter. All that remains of the original house is its white-stone basement.

Most striking about the Romanov house is its vertical plan, which contrasts with the horizontal alignment of other palaces that have survived in Moscow. Because of the slope of the ground, the house presents four storeys opening onto a courtyard. Within its four storeys, the Romanov house incorporates the basic features of a boyar's household. There is a high basement designed

EXCURSION 5

The House of the Romanovs.

as a wine cellar, a service floor, a living room containing a reception room, and the upper terem-turret, or women's quarters.

The exterior has been authentically copied. The visitor will recognize the similarity between the rusticated wall surface of the fifty-six-foot facade and the exterior of the Kremlin's Palace of the Facets. Small windows set into carved window frames, the filigree of the golden band beneath the eaves, the side entry with its stumplike columns, and the tall crested roof above all add to the quaint nature of the manor. A winged griffin — an inverted emblem of Livonia which the victorious Nikita Romanov adopted as the Romanov's coat-of-arms — is still affixed to the steeple of the turret.

After the house was reconstructed in the nineteenth century, it was turned into a museum to house various personal possessions of the Romanov family, including Michael Romanov's crib. Since then, the objects associated directly with the royal family have been removed and replaced by other furnishings typical of a nobleman's household of the seventeenth century. In the vestibule are painted chests, and in the cellar rooms are kitchen utensils and trunks for storing clothes, money, tableware, and other valuables. The upper floor is used for exhibits put on by the Historical Museum, which now administers the House of the Boyars Romanov.

Nikita Romanov was one of Moscow's legendary heroes, and a number of ballads sprang up about him because of his courage while battling Tartars at Kazan and for shielding his friends from the persecutions of Ivan the Terrible. The stories vary but the subject remains the same. Forewarned by his sister, Anastasia, Nikita gallops to the rescue of an innocent person, most frequently one of his royal nephews about to be executed by the order of Ivan the Terrible. Arriving at the crucial moment, Nikita strikes down Skuratov, the chief of Ivan's secret police and the villain of the ballad. Nikita then leads the intended victim away to safety while Skuratov plots revenge.

While legends inevitably obscure historical events, it is true that Nikita and Anastasia exerted a benevolent influence on the tsar. Anastasia's death in 1560 marks the beginning of Ivan's reign of terror.

After Anastasia's death, Nikita fell into disfavour and was banished to a distant province, while Ivan's police sacked the house. Four years before he died, Nikita was restored to power and was able to leave his oldest son, Fedor, a prosperous estate and a heritage of popular esteem.

This popular esteem, however, proved dangerous to Fedor, the father of the future tsar. In 1601 when Michael was barely three, Tsar Boris Godunov accused Fedor of plotting his death, using trumped-up charges to dispose of his popular Romanov competitors one by one. Michael and his sister were exiled to their country estates: Fedor was forcibly separated from his wife and made to take monastic vows and change his name to Filaret.

The family was briefly reunited after the death of Boris Godunov but not for long. Filaret became a hostage of the invading Poles, while his wife and children sought refuge near Kostroma. It was there in 1613 that the 16-year-old Michael heard that he had been elected to the Russian throne. The election nearly cost Michael his life. A Polish detachment was looking for him to prevent him from taking power but was led into the woods by Ivan Susanin, one of Russia's folklore leaders and the subject of Glinka's opera.

Znamensky Convent

With Michael safely on the throne, Filaret became once again patriarch of the Russian Orthodox Church. Not wishing to return to his family home, Filaret founded the Znamensky Nunnery on the adjoining plot.

The convent honours the *Znamenskaya Virgin*, or *Our Lady of the Sign*, the family icon of the Romanovs. It was cherished by the Romanovs because of their associations with Novgorod, where they spent many years as military governors. In 1169, when Novgorod was under attack, the beleaguered residents of the city credited their salvation to the intercession of this icon. Since that time Novgorod residents regarded the icon of the Virgin of the Sign as their personal protector. Because of the icon's protective powers, Michael's mother carried it with her to Kostroma and ascribed Michael's narrow escape from death to its miracle-making powers.

The five-cupola, two-tier church is the largest of the convent's buildings and dates from 1684. It was erected by Fedor Grigoriev and Grigory Ansimov and is considered one of Moscow's finest, late seventeenth-century structures. The belfry was added by Matvei Kazakov in 1789. The upper storey of the cathedral is now used for exhibits and concerts, often featuring Russian religious music.

EXCURSION 5

The former refectory of the nuns, a contemporary of the cathedral, adjoins the Romanov house. Its new wooden roof was modelled after the seventeenth-century original.

(*Tserkov Georgiia na Pskovskoy Gorke*)
No. 12

Church of St George

Near Nogina Square is the Church of St George with its vibrantly coloured red walls and gold-studded blue cupolas, built in 1658 by Moscow's relocated Pskov merchants. The blue neo-Gothic bell tower with the stylized spade-shaped arches was added in 1818.

(*Tserkov Zachatiia Sviatoi Anny, chto v Uglu*)
Moskvoretskaya Naberezhnaya and Kitayskiy Proyezd

Church of the Conception of St Anne that Stands 'in the corner'

From the top of the terrace of the Rossiya Hotel facing the Moscow River, you can catch a glimpse of this white church. As the name suggests, the Church of St Anne stood in the corner created by the Kitai Gorod wall making a sharp turn southwards as it reached the Moscow River. A fragment of this wall still survives east of the hotel.

Only the white-stone foundations of the original Church of St Anne, built at the end of the fifteenth century, survived the fire in 1547. Ivan the Terrible, who rebuilt the church, gave it the typical features of the merchant settlement church, of which there are still many in Pskov.

The church, in fact, displays many features of Pskov architecture. The builders made use of a variation of cloister vault which permitted the elimination of interior pillars. The walls are rounded off by a trilobal arch, with the middle section rising above those on either side. At the heel of the arches, a carved stone cornice traverses four facades. The narrow pilasters divide the walls into vertical sections. A single apse and the treatment of a sole drum, which rests upon the base of small spade-shaped gables, are all reminiscent of another church, the **Church of St Trifon** in Moscow, built by Pskovian architects and probably served as a model for St Anne's (see p. 213).

The Church of St Anne was often the refuge of Solomnia Saburova, the barren wife of Basil III. Like many Russian women, Solomnia believed that St Anne could make her fertile, and thus provide the tsar with an heir.

Two side chapels were added in the seventeenth century. The chapel on the northern side of the church was dedicated to St Catherine, the namesake of Tsar Alexis' daughter and one of the saints most revered by the Romanovs.

In the early sixteenth century, the Church of St Anne (named after the mother of the Virgin Mary) was the frequent refuge of Solomonia Saburova, the barren wife of Basil III. Solomonia shared the belief of Russian women that the intercession of St Anne, who like her was long without a child, would help her provide an heir to the Russian throne.

While Solomonia prayed and hoped, a fight raged inside the Kremlin. In 1525 Basil III, concerned over the problem of succession, announced his decision to divorce Solomonia. He had fallen in love with the Catholic, Polish-born Helen Glinska, whom he intended to make his second wife. The tsar's advisory Duma, along with the Moscow metropolitan, took a strong stand against the divorce. They opposed Basil on two grounds: Solomonia's beauty and piety made her popular with the Muscovites, and she was also the daughter of a prominent Moscow nobleman. Moreover, they were suspicious of the Catholic influences which they feared Helen Glinksa would introduce to Russia.

Returning to the Kremlin from the Church of St Anne, Solomonia was informed of the tsar's decision to divorce her and to exile her to a nunnery in Suzdal. Neither knew that Solomonia's prayers were answered after all. Several months later Solomonia gave birth to a son, Georgy. News of the child reached Moscow and an investigation was promptly launched. Solomonia, fearing for the life of her son, quietly arranged for his adoption and simultaneously staged a mock burial, using a child-sized doll in place of her son.

Church of the Holy Trinity in Nikitniki

(Tserkov Troitsy v Nikitnikakh)
Nikitnikov Pereulok, 3

The last noteworthy landmark of this excursion is the Church of the Holy Trinity, now the **Simon Ushakov Museum**. Concealed from the public view by the tall buildings of Kitai Gorod and the Central Communist Party Committee Headquarters, the best way to reach it is to turn left immediately after the Church of St George into **Ipatyevskiy Lane**, which soon veers to the right to climb a hill. From the crest one finally gets the first glimpse of the splendid five green-domed Church of the Holy Trinity.

The Trinity Church, rightfully described as the 'jewel of merchant architecture in Moscow', was built in 1634 for the pious and enterprising Grigory Nikitnikov, a wealthy merchant from Yaroslavl who was enlisted in 1620 by Tsar Michael Romanov into the financial administration of the state.

Gregarious and erudite, Nikitnikov ably carried out the numerous tasks assigned to him by tsars Michael and Alexis, for which he was generously rewarded.

As his place of residence, Nikitnikov decided on **Nikitnikov Lane** in Kitai Gorod, wanting to be near the Church of St Nikita the Martyr, the family saint. The church stood on the crest of the hill overlooking the Kremlin on one side and the Kitai Gorod wall on the other. Next to the church Nikitnikov built an impressive brick mansion, which he completed and occupied by 1625. When the wooden church burned down three years later, the pious merchant decided to construct a glorious new church in gratitude for his good fortunes and dedicated it to the Holy Trinity.

As was the case with many seventeenth-century churches, the Trinity Church was built on top of a brick storage basement. Square in plan with rounded

EXCURSION 5

95

The Holy Trinity Church 'in Nikitniki' has been described as the 'jewel of merchant architecture in Moscow'.

apses and a tent-roofed bell tower, the Trinity Church stood guard over the goods below. The interplay of carved white stone and red brick endowed the asymmetrically designed church with a fairy-tale quality much valued by the Muscovites. Though the Trinity Church proper is miniscule, it owes its monumental appearance to the side chapels, refectory, and closed gallery which adjoin it from the south and west.

The frescoes of the Trinity Church were begun a year after Nikitnikov died in 1651. One of the artists engaged was Simon Ushakov, a parishioner of Trinity, whose house still stands a block away, at the end of the Nikitnikov Lane.

With Vladimirov, Kondratiev, and Kazantsev, royal iconographers like himself, Ushakov strove to capture the spirit of Christianity and translate its message to the people. It is not the deep spiritual feeling that gives the frescoes of the Trinity Church their significance but the narrative depiction of the New Testament scenes. The artists incorporated into the painting a good deal of robust humour, boldness of colour and design, and especially vivid glimpses of the life and customs of seventeenth-century Russia. The style of dress, the boisterous raucous feasts, the wine drinking, and dancing all join together to give the feeling of a temporal rather than a purely spiritual interpretation of the New Testament lessons.

The themes of the frescoes above the carved portals on the western wall were chosen specially for a merchant audience: the central *Parable of the Ten Wise and Foolish Maidens* was meant to remind the merchants' wives of the value of virtue. The *Parable of the Rich Man* cautioned merchants to be hospitable and generous to the poor by depicting the suffering of the rich man in the harrowing fire of hell. On the other hand, the wealthy tradesmen must have taken comfort in contemplating God's forgiveness shown in the *Parable of the Prodigal Son* depicted to the right of the maidens.

A number of outstanding icons survive in the superbly gilded and carved iconostasis executed in 1640. The icon carrying the name of the Trinity Church is to the right of the central royal gates of the icon screen. The icon of the *Old Testament Trinity* depicting the three angels as they appeared to Abraham and Sarah was executed by Kazanets and Kondratiev. The icon of the *Annunciation of the Virgin*, with twelve border scenes depicting New Testament scenes, was painted by Ushakov specially for the Trinity iconostasis. It is to the left of the royal gates. This is one of Ushakov's first icons to show the influence of Western art on Russian iconography, most noticeably in the fleshiness of the faces. Equally remarkable is Ushakov's icon of *Our Lady of Vladimir* surrounded by the geneological tree of the Russian tsars. Metropolitan Peter and Prince Ivan Kalita are in front of the Kremlin's Uspensky Cathedral watering the tree, while Tsar Alexis Romanov and his family look on. The last important icon, painted by Vladimirov, in the bottom tier of the icon screen,

Trinity: icon of Our Lady of ... *a, which is said to have the ... to cure the sick.*

next to the Trinity, depicts the *Descent of the Holy Spirit* on the enthroned Virgin and the twelve attending apostles.

The oldest icon in the church is the sixteenth-century panel of *St Nikita*, which Grigory Nikitnikov rescued from the burning wooden church. Executed in vibrant red, green, and mellow blue with a full-length figure of Nikita, it is surrounded by fourteen episodes from his life.

To the right of the main altar a carved stone portal leads to the burial chapel of the Nikitnikovs. The bare-headed figures in the fresco on the

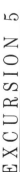

EXCURSION 5

wall to the right of the iconostasis are believed to be portraits of the Nikitnikov family.

Beautiful and grand as it was, the Trinity Church would have remained but another merchant's church if it were not for the outbreak of cholera in 1654. When the news of the plague reached Yaroslavl, a friend of the Nikitnikovs decided to take the icon of *Our Lady of Georgia* to Moscow, for it was said to have been endowed with the power to cure the sick.

Unfortunately for the Nikitnikovs, the icon arrived too late. The brothers were among the first victims of the plague. But thousands of other Muscovites who heard of the icon's arrival came to invoke its miracle-making powers and many were cured, so that deliverance of Moscow from the plague was attributed to the intercession of the Georgian Virgin. The Nikitnikov church became a national shrine, and some Muscovites still call it 'Our Lady of Georgia'.

Excursion 6

GORKY STREET

A tour of Gorky Street: The English Club (Central Museum of the Revolution of the USSR) — Credit Bank — Sytin's Printing House — Izvestia Building — Church of the Nativity of the Virgin — Pushkin Square — House of Rimsky-Korsakov — Gastronom No. 1 — Sovetskaya Square — Residence of the Military Governor-General — State Committee for Science and Technology — Church of the Resurrection — Savvinskoye Monastery building — Central Telegraph — Manor House of Boyar Fedor Troyekurov — Nobles's Club — Moscow City Hall (Central Lenin Museum).

(Angliisky Klub)
Gorkogo Ulitsa, 21
①

The English Club

This classical mansion was built by the architect Manelas in 1780 for Count Razumovsky and reconstructed in 1832 when it was acquired by the English Club, founded in 1772 by foreigners residing in Moscow. It has been the **Central Museum of the Revolution of the USSR** since 1924, with exhibits documenting the period since 1917.

This Moscow landmark was referred to many times in Russian classics. Leo Tolstoy recalled the banquet given for General Bagration in 1806 by its members, 'old venerable gentlemen with self-assured faces'; and Pushkin referred to the English Club in *Eugene Onegin* as the 'House with Lions at the Gate' (two frivolous-looking lions, their mouths half-open as if singing a naughty song, still guard the entry gates).

By 1830, most of its five hundred members belonged to the upper crust of Russian society. Nevertheless, some similarities to the British clubs remained:

e English Club is a Moscow
...dmark referred to many times
...Russian classics.

EXCURSION 6

Excursion 6
Gorky Street

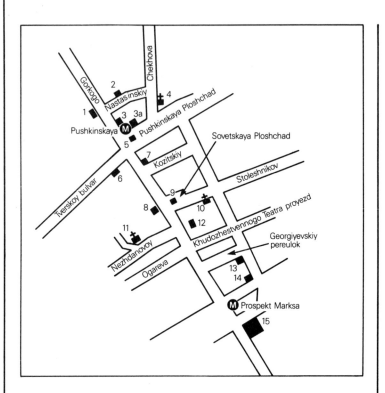

1. The English Club (Central Museum of the Revolution of the USSR)
2. Credit Bank
3. Sytin's Printing House (*Trud* Building)
3a. *Izvestia* Building
4. Church of the Nativity of the Virgin in Putinkakh
5. Pushkin's Statue
6. House of Rimsky-Korsakov
7. Gastronom No. 1
8. Governor-General's Residence (Mossoviet)
9. Sovetskaya Square, with statue of Yuriy Dolgoruky
10. Church of SS. Cosmas and Damian
11. Church of the Resurrection
12. Savvinskoye Monastery Building
13. Manor House of Fedor Troyekurov (State Planning Commission)
14. Nobles' Club (House of Trade Unions)
15. Moscow City Hall (Lenin Museum)

the 'Angliisky' Club was the Russian nobleman's castle, the one place in Moscow from which women and police were barred. The club evolved into Moscow's political and literary mecca, becoming a centre of enlightenment which brought together the best minds of nineteenth-century Russia. Members of the club included statesmen, publishers, military leaders, and scientists as well as Russia's men of letters — Pushkin, Chaadayev, and Tolstoy. It served as an arena for an open exchange of ideas and a catalyst for new concepts.

Though little remains of the original club building, a few features survive. The main staircase leads to the **vestibule**, whose portals rest on two gigantic women; here the 'blackboard of dishonour' was prominently displayed. Names of members who failed to pay their dues or to settle their gambling debts were marked in chalk and remained on the board until the accounts were settled or the members resigned.

The suite of rooms (6–9) now devoted to Lenin's role in the Revolution of 1917 was the club's sanctuary. The largest of these rooms was the **library**, a spacious hall where gray marble columns bear Corinthian capitols and whose ceilings are decorated with antique scenes done in *grisaille*. One of the two other rooms of the suite was known as *adskaya*, or 'infernal' room, where Leo Tolstoy once lost 1,000 roubles in a game of cards in a single night. The *umnaya*, or 'brainy' room, was the real core of the English Club and the room that made it famous, for it was here the Russian intellectual élite met to discuss and exchange ideas.

According to some, hall 11 — a red room with a ceiling covered with scenes of battles, naked goddesses, and Bacchus — was the club's dining room. Others claim that the members ate in room 22, an elegant hall with white marble walls. The presence of a balcony on pillared supports does suggest that this was the dining room, as it was customary for musicians to be placed in the choirs from where they entertained the dining guests during banquets. The favourite entertainers at the English Club were gypsies, for whom the ban against women was overlooked.

In the late nineteenth century, the aristocratic club reluctantly opened its doors to merchants, who improved the club's finances and livened up the card games but dimmed the old lustre. The last grand event at the English Club was a gala banquet given in 1913 in honour of Nicholas II on the occasion of the 300th anniversary of the Romanov dynasty.

(Ssudnaya Kassa)
②

Credit Bank

A quick detour into Nastasinskiy Lane leads to the Credit Bank, built between 1914 and 1916 by the architect V. N. Pokrovsky. This grey building halfway down the lane is an architectural flight of fantasy. Its wings, a replica of a seventeenth-century Russian palace, contrast sharply with the central section, where the faceted, multi-windowed treatment of the facade shows Gothic, Moorish, and Russian influences. No less striking is the contrast between the Western-looking spire on the bank's roof and its tent-roofed entry, recalling

EXCURSION 6

an old Russian chapel. The vaulted interior of the bank was inspired by Art Nouveau.

(*Trud* Building)
Gorkogo Ulitsa, 18

Sytin's Printing House

The publishing house of Ivan Sytin, unlike the Credit Bank, was designed as a single architectural unit and represents a fine example of Moscow's Art Nouveau. Its few decorative details, such as round windows, tiled insets, and curved wings, do not detract from the building's rectangular shape.

The purposefulness of the building reflects the character of its former owner, the foremost publisher in Russia. Barely fifteen when he went to work in a bookshop in 1866, Sytin realized the need for inexpensive books and purchased a small printing shop ten years later. By the turn of the twentieth century, Sytin owned his own newspaper, *Russkoye Slovo*, and headed Russia's largest publishing empire.

(Pushkinskaya Ploshchad)
③a

Izvestia Building

Not to be outdone by Sytin, the Bolshevik government set up the headquarters of its own newspaper in 1917 just around the corner on Pushkin Square. *Izvestia* remains the official organ of the Presidium of the USSR.

The central, and largest, building dates from 1926. Designed by G. Barkhin, it is considered an outstanding example of the Soviet architecture of its time. The stark rectangular construction is softened and enlivened only by concrete bands on the balconies and the row of round windows on the top floor.

(Tserkov Rozhdestva Bogoroditsy v Putinkakh)
Chekhova Ulitsa, 4
④

Church of the Nativity of the Virgin in Putinkakh

Nearby in Chekhov Street, this wonderful small church, built between 1649 and 1652, with spires recalling the turretted gates of old Russian timber fortifications, is famous for its multi-pyramid construction. It is one of the last of its kind, as Patriarch Nikon banned the construction of any more tent-type churches in the middle of the seventeenth century, on the grounds that they were patterned on secular architecture.

The main building of the Nativity Church, a broad rectangle crowned with three pyraminds on tall drums, lies on a north-south axis. Next to it is the chapel dedicated to the icon of *Our Lady of the Burning Bush*. A tall rectangular bell tower links the two buildings and provides the church with a focal point. The crosses of all the cupolas display a half-moon, a symbol of the Russian victory over the Muslim Tartars.

The most ornate part of the church is the one-storey refectory, which provides the main entry to the church. For this reason, its festive tent-roofed porch, the belt of patterned brick, the carved window frames, and the band of indented rectangles near street level are particularly elaborate.

Legend has it that the original Church of the Nativity of the Virgin was commissioned by a noblewoman who gave birth as her carriage drove past the spot and had the church built to celebrate the event. When the wooden Church of the Nativity burned down in 1648, the congregation petitioned Tsar Alexis Romanov for help. He agreed to spend three hundred roubles on the condition that the new stone church be dedicated to *Our Lady of the Burning Bush*, the icon which Russians venerate as a safeguard against fires.

The icon inspired by Moses' vision on Mount Sinai is easily recognizable. The figure of the Virgin is enclosed in an eight-cornered star consisting of two superimposed quadrangles; the green quadrangle symbolizes the bush and the red one, the flames which engulf the bush without burning it.

The Muscovites built two churches: the first dedicated, as they had promised Alexis, to *Our Lady of the Burning Bush*, and the other, like the original, honouring the *Virgin's Nativity*.

Pushkin Square

(Pushkinskaya Ploshchad) ⑤

At the intersection of Gorky Street and the Boulevard Ring, opposite the Nativity Church, where a square and the Rossiya cinema are now seen, stood the sixteenth-century White City walls and, beyond them, the **Strastnoy Convent** commemorating the Passions of the Lord, which gave the square its original name of Strastnaya. The convent dominated the crest of the hill, one of the seven hills of Moscow.

At the end of the eighteenth century, the walls were removed and the square was widened and incorporated into the Boulevard Ring. In the 1930s, the nunnery was dismantled to make room for the cinema, which the architect Sheverdiayev, Solopov, and Gadzhinskaya completed in 1961. The old mansions on the northern edge of the square gave way to the *Izvestia* newspaper complex. The square was renamed Pushkinskaya to honour the poet, whose statue had stood at the western side of the square since 1880 but was then moved to its present position near the Rossiya Theatre.

Sculptor A. M. Opekushin, who executed the statue of Aleksandr Pushkin (1799–1837) in 1880, depicted the poet in a brooding mood. The bronze likeness of Pushkin, standing with his head downcast and

...ue of Aleksandr Pushkin, ...pleted in 1880 by the sculptor ...M. Opekushin, depicts the poet ...rooding mood.

his right hand over his heart, conveys his resignation to a destiny beyond his control. When he died from a duelling wound at the age of thirty-eight, Russia lost its 'national poet-prophet of international renown', as Dostoevsky described the artist at the unveiling of the statue on one of the three days commemorating the hundredth anniversary of Pushkin's birth.

Both in spirit and execution, Pushkin's memorial differs from that of the poet Vladimr Mayakovsky (1893–1930), whose oversized statue is farther along Gorky Street on the Mayakovskogo Square.

House of Rimsky-Korsakov

Tverskoy Bulvar, 24–6
⑥

One of Pushkin's closest friends was Lt. General Rimsky-Korsakov, who earned the description of 'the king of the epicurian feasts' for his gourmet dinners. Rimsky-Korsakov lived in a house overlooking Tverskoy Boulevard, the widest, oldest, and handsomest of the nine tree-lined avenues that make up the semicircular Boulevard Ring. In 1796 the area in front of the house was cleared from the debris of the White City wall and planted with birches and, later, linden trees. Tverskoy became the model for other boulevards and the favourite promenading area for fashionable Muscovites.

The Rimsky-Korsakov mansion consists of two adjoining two-storey houses and was built in the eighteenth century and reconstructed in the nineteenth. The double mansion preserves its finely sculptured details, typical of late Moscow classicism and, less usual for that age, a row house effect.

The Rimsky-Korsakov whom Pushkin knew owed his career to the patronage of Catherine the Great, who promoted the dashing guardsman to the rank of lieutenant general. Catherine's friend and lady-in-waiting, Princess Dashkova, thought that he 'shone like the sun and spread sunshine around' because of his splendid clothes and his beguiling manners.

Rimsky-Korsakov brought on his own downfall, however, by spreading altogether too much sunshine on Countess Stroganova. When news of Rimsky-Korsakov's affair with the countess reached Catherine, the empress dismissed him from her service; and the nobleman gathered up his diamond-studded wardrobe to move back to Moscow, where he continued to entertain his friends with epicurean feasts. The house is now the **'Melodia' recording studio**.

Gastronom No. 1

(Eliseyevsky Store)
Gorkogo Ulitsa, 14
⑦

Returning to Gorky Street and continuing the descent towards the Kremlin, we come to the building of Gastronom No. 1. The grocery store has an imposing salmon-coloured facade enlivened by white garlands above the windows and a mezzanine with two whitestone sculptures.

As store interiors go, the opulence of Gastronom No. 1 compares with Paris's Fauchon or London's Fortnum and Mason's. The lights, the gilded bunches of grapes draping from marble columns, the stained glass displays, and the English clock on the wall complete the sumptuous decor of Moscow's largest

*...astronom No. 1 has a salmon-
...loured facade and an opulent
...terior. It originally belonged to
...rincess Zinaida Volkonskaya
...ntil she moved her literary salon
to Rome. The house was then
...urchased by a merchant who
...ade millions on the sale of
...mported foods and vintage wines.*

and most crowded grocery store. Moscovites still call the store 'Eliseyevsky' after the name of its former owner, a merchant from St Petersburg who made millions on the sale of imported foods and vintage wines.

Eliseyev paid a fortune for the palatial eighteenth-century mansion which the architect Matvei Kazakov created for Princess Zinaida Volkonskaya, famous for her literary salons. After acquiring the house in 1898, he hired the architect Baranovsky to remodel it and staged a gala opening for his new store in 1901.

As Eliseyev had overlooked the city ordinance prohibiting the sale of alcoholic beverages within forty-five feet of a church, the store was ordered shut. When it reopened, the wine counter was located in the farthest corner of the store — forty-six feet from the nearest church.

*(Sovetskaya
Ploshchad)*
⑨

Sovetskaya Square

Continuing the descent towards the Kremlin, we come upon Sovetskaya Square, previously known as Tverskaya or Skobelevskaya Square. The square has radically changed its appearance over the last two centuries. The aristocratic mansions of the Princes Dolgorukov, the descendants of Moscow's founder, Yuriy Dolgoruky, whose statue now stands in the centre of the square, have vanished, as has the turreted building which the Tverskaya police shared with the fire department. The mansion of the military governor-general, still existing at the western end of the square, is now Moscow's City Hall. The other survivor is the 1722 Baroque Church of **SS Cosmas and Damian** ⑩, which has occupied this site since the fourteenth century. Like many Moscow churches, it misses its bell tower and domes, as it has been turned into a printing shop.

**(Moscow City
Council or
Mossoviet)**
⑧

Governor-General's Residence

The original mansion was designed by architect Matvei Kazakov in 1782 for Count Zakhary Chernyshevsky, Moscow's first military governor-general. Catherine the Great appointed Chernyshevsky to his Moscow post for his victories in the Russo-Prussian war of 1760. After Chernyshevsky willed his residence to the city of Moscow, it served as the official residence of Moscow

EXCURSION 6

governors until 1917. In 1939, architect D. N. Chechulin moved the building fourteen metres back from the street and added two more storeys to the old building.

The Residence of Moscow's Military Governor-General until 1917. Before it is a statue of Yury Dolgoruky, founder of Moscow.

Several of Moscow's pre-revolutionary governors who lived here are remembered to this day through literature and the roles they played in Russian history. One such governor-general was the tall and dapper pink-cheeked Prince Dmitry Golitsyn, who governed from 1820 to 1844. During his term the city streets were paved and properly illuminated. Golitsyn also commissioned the system of water pipes which provide Moscow with excellent drinking water to this day.

No less popular was the jovial Vladimir Dolgorukov, a descendant of Yuriy Dolgoruky. Prince Dolgorukov was renowned for his elaborate charity balls, which brought together bejewelled nobles and long-robed merchants. The proceeds went to charities which Dolgorukov had organized and to which he contributed most of his fortune. Dolgorukov's openness and dedication to charity were once put to the test by a group of adventurers. Their leader, Speier, gained access to one of the governor's balls by parading as a landowner and secured Dolgorukov's permission to show his mansion to a rich English lord on the pretext of raising money. Soon after a grand tour of the house, a caravan of carriages loaded with the lord's possessions pulled up to the mansion. Finding the house still occupied, the lord unfurled a deed of sale and showed it to Dolgorukov. The deed had been prepared by Speier, who had sold the estate to the Englishman for one hundred thousand roubles and was never heard from again.

Nezhdanovov Street is linked to Gorky Street by a large gateway marked No. 11. The nineteenth-century pistachio-green building on the right is now occupied by the **State Committee for Science and Technology**. A few steps

further stands the Church of the Resurrection, whose golden dome dominates the tiny square.

(Tserkov Voskreseniya na Uspenskom Vrazhke)
Nezhdanovoy Ulitsa, 15
⑪

Church of the Resurrection

This is one of the few churches in central Moscow still open for worship. According to Moscow legends, the church stands on the spot where Tsar Michael Romanov welcomed his father, Patriarch Filaret, upon his return from captivity in Poland in 1619. To commemorate his father's return, Michael commissioned a church, which he dedicated to the prophet Elisha, on whose feast day the Romanov family was reunited. When the wooden Church of St Elisha burned to the ground in 1629, it was rebuilt in stone and renamed the Church of the Resurrection. The refectory and bell tower were added in the 1820s, and the latter was heightened in 1879.

The greatest treasure of the church are the icons, which were rescued from demolished churches in the neighbourhood and brought here for safekeeping. Noteworthy are: *Our Lady with the Dove*, a seventeenth-century icon of the Virgin with the Child hanging on the southern wall, immediately to the right of the entry; *Our Lady of the Passions*, an icon of Mary with Jesus which hangs directly across from *Our Lady with the Dove* is known as *Our Lady of the Passions (Strastnaya)* because the angels depicted on either side of the Virgin display symbols of the Crucifixion. It was brought here from the destroyed **Strastnoy Monastery** on Pushkin Square. The icon of *St Nikita the Warrior*, is to the left of the St Nicholas chapel; and the icon of *SS Cosmas and Damian*, the two healers from Asia Minor, hangs closer to the entry.

A seventeenth-century full-length icon of *Savva Storozhevsky*, founder of a monastery, hangs in the choirs of the right-hand side chapel; an icon of *St Elisha*, on the icon screen of this side chapel. The icon of *St Nicholas*, Bishop of Myra who died in 324, is displayed twice in the left-hand chapel honouring this popular saint, to the right of the royal gates and affixed to the choir.

Additional icons are displayed in the passage which links the refectory to the main church. *The Iberian Virgin*, a highly revered icon, hangs on the left side of the passage, nearest to the refectory. A distinguishing mark of the icon is the bleeding scar on Mary's right cheek. No less famous is the icon of *Our Lady of Kazan*, which hangs next to the Iberian Virgin. The icon is mounted into a frame of chased silver and surrounded by border scenes. Dated by some as late sixteenth century and by others as seventeenth, this is a copy of the original.

A rare and unusual icon of *St George* hangs opposite the Kazan Virgin. According to art critics the icon was painted in the seventeenth century, possibly by a Western painter, as Russians usually represent St George on a horse fighting the dragon or as a warrior with a sword.

The **crucifix** in front of the iconostasis was carved by a blind man in the seventeenth century, who recovered his sight upon completing his lifelong task.

On the left side wall of the church, there is another rare icon executed in

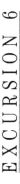

EXCURSION 6

enamel and chased silver. This is the icon of *St Spiridon, the Miraculous*, who took part in editing the Nicene Creed in AD 325. The icon also contains the saint's relics.

Savvinskoye Monastery Building

(Savvinskoye Podvorye)
Gorkogo Ulitsa, 6

The representational building of the former monastery of Savva Storozhevsky of Zvenigorod is an architectural treasure trove. To see it, one must go inside the narrow courtyard of the apartment building at No. 6 Gorky Street.

Intended to accommodate the monks from the Savva Storozhevsky Monastery during their stays in Moscow, the building was designed by architect I. S. Kuznetsov and completed in 1907. Borrowing from seventeenth-century Russian architecture, he decorated the fortress-like forms of the tall building with ceramic tiles, sculptured ornaments, and handsomely worked windows and doors.

The festive monastery fronted on Gorky Street until 1938, when it was moved back and other buildings razed to make room for the apartment houses.

Central Telegraph

(Tsentralny Telegraf)

The grey building at the corner of Gorky and Ogareva Streets, designed in 1927 by Ivan Rerberg, is a handy place from which to make an international telephone call. An English-speaking attendant is usually on hand.

Manor House of Boyar Fedor Troyekurov

Georgiyevskiy Pereulok, 4

Now the reception quarters for foreign visitors to the State Planning Commission, the red, crested manor house of nobleman Fedor Troyekurov is the only survivor of its kind in central Moscow. Its rectangular construction shows the influence of Western architectural styles, which Russian builders had begun to emulate when the house was erected in the 1690s.

Fedor Troyekurov's decision to commission a new residence was spurred by the building activity of his neighbours: Prince Vasily Golitsyn, the lover of the Regent Sofia, whose palace occupied the corner of today's Gorky street and Prospekt Marksa, and Prince Matvei Gagarin, who made a fortune as a governor in Siberia and whose house was rising next to Troyekurov's.

Troyekurov felt challenged. He, too, came from a noble Russian family and was Peter the Great's lord of the bedchamber. However, despite his birth and rank, Troyekurov lacked financial resources. Peter the Great solved Troyekurov's problem by appointing him to supervise the building of the **Sukhareva Tower**, destroyed in 1934. Providence itself thus provided Troyekurov with choice brick for his project.

Troyekurov came off best in both the building contest and his personal destiny. Just as he had completed his house, Golitsyn was banished to Siberia for his association with Sofia, and Gagarin was caught stealing on a grand scale in Siberia and had his head chopped off. Although Troyekurov's appropriation

of royal brick for his house did not go unnoticed, Peter the Great chose to limit his bedchamberlain's punishment to a whipping.

The Gargarin and Golitsyn houses were razed in the 1930s to make room for the **USSR State Planning Commission** on Prospekt Marksa.

Prospekt Marksa, 10
(14)

Nobles's Club

Like a venerable eighteenth-century aristocrat thrust into the mileu of avant gardists, the classical facade of the former Nobles's Club, now the **House of Trade Unions**, looks out of place in its current surroundings on Prospekt Marksa. The large green mansion with its white Corinthian porticos appears miniscule in comparison to the building of the State Planning Committee of the USSR to its left, and the Moskva Hotel across the street.

The former Nobles' Club has a white and gold ballroom with 28 artificial white marble columns and two sets of gold and crystal chandeliers.

The mansion originally belonged to Prince Vasily Dolgorukov-Krymsky, who received his epitaph *Krymsky*, or 'Crimean', for annexing Crimea to Russia in 1771. Dolgorukov suffered two setbacks in his career. As a young man he was demoted to a private after the ill-fated attempt of his relative Ivan Dolgoruky to arrange his sister's marriage to Emperor Peter II. His second disappointment came soon after the victory in Crimea, when his superiors denied him the rank of field marshal because they ascribed his victory to 'a stroke of luck' rather than merit.

Crestfallen, Dolgorukov retired to Moscow in 1781, where he became Moscow's commander in chief. Three years later, he sold his house to the Assembly of the Nobles, which was founded in 1783.

Dolgorukov's mansion was enlarged and reconstructed by master architect Matvei Kazakov over the next twenty years. After the fire of 1812, which demolished the facade, the club was rebuilt and then again between 1903 and 1908, when a third storey was added.

The only part of the building that retains the master's touch is the **Hall of the Columns**. The white and gold ballroom is Kazakov's finest interior and an outstanding example of early Moscow classicism. The **ballroom** is built entirely of wood and measures 1,000 square metres. Twenty-eight Corinthian columns dressed in white artifical marble span the regal dimensions of this hall that is lit by two sets of gold and crystal chandeliers.

During the two hundred years of the club's existence, the Hall of Columns witnessed many splendid assemblies. It was also here that Alexander II addressed

EXCURSION 6

109

Moscow nobility on the issue of serfdom on 30 March 1856, warning them that it was 'better to abolish serfdom from above than wait until it abolishes itself from below'. The emperor's speech was a prelude to the decline of the nobles, whose wealth depended on their lands and the number of their serfs.

The balls became less lavish as the nobility slowly abdicated its role as intellectual leaders, philanthropists, and liberal dreamers to the merchant barons who gained access to the Nobles's Club in the late nineteenth century. The end of the Nobles's Club came in 1919, when Lenin signed an edict transferring its ownership to the labour unions. After Lenin died in 1924, his body lay in state at the Hall of Columns and more than one million people came to pay their respects.

The House of Trade Unions is open to visitors on the days when concerts are held in the Hall of Columns.

Ploshchad Revolyutsii, 4

⑮

The Lenin Museum was formerly the Moscow City Hall and meeting place of the Duma.

Moscow City Hall (Lenin Museum)

The huge red-brick building in Revolution Square which now houses the Lenin Museum was formerly the home of the Moscow City Council, known as the *Duma*. The word *Duma* is a derivative of the Russian verb *dumat*, or 'to think', and was used to designate the tsar's Advisory Council of the Nobles. Architect D. Chichagov, who completed the City Hall in 1892, patterned it on seventeenth-century Russian palaces. Like the Terem Palace in the Kremlin, the building features barrel-shaped and crested roofs, complicated cornices, and a variety of window frames — some rounded, some triangular, and some arched.

The *Duma* was formed in 1870, when elections were held and Moscow's first mayor was elected. Although most of the councilmen were nobles, the merchants had gained the upper hand by the time the council had moved to its new quarters in 1892.

Converted to the Lenin Museum in 1936, more than 7,000 exhibits, including manuscripts, books, brochures, photos, portraits, and personal belongings of Lenin, are on display. Lectures and films on Lenin are available in Russian and foreign languages.

PART III

MOSCOW OF
THE NOBLES

INTRODUCTION

*T*he colourful saga of the Moscow nobles opened on a note of high drama. In the mid-twelfth century, Prince **Yuriy Dolgoruky**, the founder of Moscow, clashed violently with the boyar **Ivan Stepanovich Kuchka**, the area's richest landowner. Although the feud was sparked by Yuriy requesting the hand of Kuchka's beautiful daughter, **Ulita**, for his son **Andrei Bogoliubsky**, the real cause was the prince's encroachment on Kuchka's fertile lands. Kuchka was ultimately executed and his estates were confiscated, while comely Ulita was whisked off to Vladimir and married to Bogoliubsky.

Kuchka's story may be apocryphal, but not the nature of his dispute with Yuriy. For centuries to come the boyars' beautiful daughters would continue to entice the Russian rulers, and their fathers guard their privileged status, particularly the ranking noblemen or boyars (a word of uncertain origin, possibly a derivative of the Bulgarian *bolyarin*, meaning lord or seigneur). The boyars were courtiers, members of the tsar's advisory *Duma*, his military leaders, heads of ministries, and governors. In addition to their court duties, the boyars were also landowners. Their tenure of land was predicated on supplying the tsar in times of war with 'men, horses and weapons'.

The boyars prided themselves on their standing at the court and resented challenge to their hereditary lands and titles. The princes, on the other hand, in their effort to strengthen and unify Russia, were often forced to curb the nobility's selfish interests.

At the end of the fifteenth century, **Ivan III** and his son **Basil III**, having overcome the Tartars and consolidated Muscovy, asserted their rights as sovereigns by further reducing the privileges of the haughty boyars and their freelancing retinues that could move, at will, from one grand prince to another. They also infused new blood into the administrative and military apparatus of the state by creating a new serving class of gentry or *dvoriane*.

The lives of Moscow's upper nobility, like those of their contemporaries at the court of Louis XIV, centred around their sovereign. With **Tsar Alexis**, the model of a Christian and genuinely paternal ruler, the ideals of Muscovy seemed achieved. Still, for all the apparent harmony, chinks were beginning to appear in the nobles's secure existence. The lack of a reliable standing army and the need to resist Russia's enemies placed a particularly heavy burden of military support on the nobles. A stream of foreigners brought alien costumes and ideas which shocked the conservative Russian nobles. Moreover, Alexis began to pick his closest advisors from among commoners, some of whom went so far as to wear Western clothes and imitate foreign ways. Finally, no sooner did Alexis die than a revolution broke out in the *terem*, the secluded quarters of the royal women, when two strong personalities, **Sofia Miloslavskaya** (1657–1704), **Peter the Great**'s half-sister, and his mother **Natalia Naryshkina** crossed swords over the issue of regency.

With Peter the Great's triumph over Sofia and his transfer of the capital to St Petersburg in 1712, the Moscow of the nobles, as such, ceased to exist until the manifesto of 18 February 1762, by which **Peter III** freed the nobles from the obligation of the compulsory service to the state. The third half of

Reconstructed bust of Yuriy Dolgoruky.

the eighteenth century, until the Emancipation of Serfs by **Alexander II** in 1861, was the golden age of the Moscow aristocracy. Their legal status boosted by the Charter of the Nobility of 21 April 1785, and their privileges expanded, they returned to Moscow, eager to build, to indulge in cultural and pleasurable pursuits, and to apply their newly acquired Westernized ways to the old capital.

The land reforms and the change in the status of the serfs which occurred in the mid-nineteenth century, altered the life-style and impact of the nobles on Moscow. The rising class of the merchants and industrialists began to make their own mark on the city. Moscow University, which the nobles created and patronized, was producing a new class of intellectuals, the *raznochintsy*, who joined the ranks of the new Russian *intelligentsia*. Apart from those who had kept their fortunes intact, the bulk of the impoverished nobility had to forfeit their role as the sole leaders of Russian thought and cultural superiority.

Nonetheless, until the advent of the Bolshevik Revolution, the Russian gentry continued to produce outstanding military and state leaders. Ranging from the descendants of the old boyar families to the courtiers of Peter the Great and **Nicholas II**, the last Russian tsar, Russia always found 'Men of the Empire' who attempted to bring about needed reforms within the framework of the state.

Excursion 7

THE BEARDED ADVISORS OF THE TSARS AND THEIR BEAUTIFUL DAUGHTERS

The Manor House of Averky Kirillov — Church of St Antipy — The Palace of Prince Viazemsky and Prince Dologoruky — The House of the Lopukhins — House of the Princes Golitsyns — The House of the Pashkovs — The House of Prince Dmitry Ivanovich Shuisky — Shchusev Museum of Architecture — The Lenin Library — Church of Znamenie.

*e marriage of Ivan the Terrible
Anastasia Romanov.*

*I*n 1547 Ivan the Terrible announced his decision to marry. Couriers were immediately dispatched to every corner of the Russian realm, summoning the daughters of the nobles to the Kremlin. The young tsar would pick his wife from amidst the well-born maidens of his estate in a special ceremony of Old Muscovy. While the boyars of the *Duma* Council, looking dignified in their tall hats and fur-lined caftans, stroked their beards and deliberated with the tsar, each hoped that his daughter would be chosen and that he would become Ivan's father-in-law.

On a given day, the boyars's daughters were assembled in the Kremlin. Attired in their best *sarafan* dresses and high peaked jewel-encrusted *kokoshniki* headgear, the girls stood blushing while Ivan passed through their ranks. As the choice narrowed, the maidens and their chaperones were assigned special dormitories and remained in the palace until the tsar made his selection. Ivan dropped his embroidered handkerchief at the feet of the beautiful Anastasia Romanova, thus signalling his choice of wife. After the wedding, the bride's family were generously rewarded with grants of land and her brother Nikita promoted to the boyar's rank.

Anastasia's death in 1560, which marked the end of Ivan IV's benevolent period, had an adverse effect on the boyars's destinies and estates. Obsessed with the idea that the nobles had poisoned his wife, Ivan the Terrible fled the Kremlin and confiscated the boyars's estates in the White City. The sombre palace of the mania-ridden tsar became the headquarters of the dreaded *oprichniki* militiamen. Clad in black, carrying on their saddles a dog's head and a broom, the *oprichniki* were charged with ridding the tsar's realm of 'traitors'.

Those who survived Ivan the Terrible's persecution and reclaimed their houses did not keep them for long: many houses perished in the fire, many were repossessed by the crown, and many were abandoned. Nonetheless, a few old boyar manor houses still exist to this day, even if the bride-picking ceremony died with Peter the Great.

The Manor House of Averky Kirillov

*Bersenevskaya
Naberezhnaya, 20*
①

The seventeenth-century architectural ensemble of Averky Kirillov, located across the Moscow River from the Kremlin, is the best preserved landmark of the city's boyardom. Now the **Institute for Museum Sciences**, it borders

EXCURSION 7

115

Excursion Plan 7
The Bearded Advisors of
the Tsars and their
Beautiful Daughters

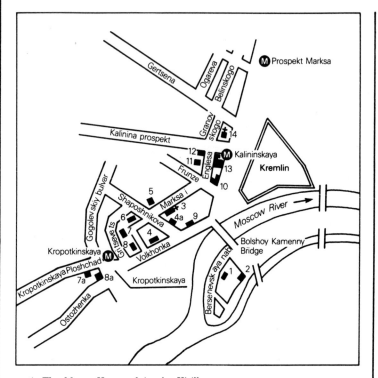

1. The Manor House of Averky Kirillov
2. Udarnik Theatre
3. Church of St Antipy
4/4a. Pushkin Museum of Fine Arts (former site of the Carriage House)
5. The House of Maliuta Skuratov
6. The Palace of Prince Viazemsky and Prince Dolgoruky (Marx and Engels Museum)
7/7a. Houses of the Lopukhins
8/8a. Houses of the Princes Golitsyn
9. Prince Volkonsky's house
10. The House of the Pashkovs (annex of the Lenin Library)
11. The House of Prince Shuisky
12. The Old Apothecary Office (Shchusev Museum of Architecture)
13. The Lenin Library (former site of the Streshnev estate)
14. The Church of the Sign (Znamenie)

on the narrow **Bersenevskaya Embankment**, named after boyar Ivan Bersenev-Beklemishev, first to live in the house. The palace and its church, which once stood in the Royal Gardens, are now dwarfed on the right by the massive **Udarnik Theatre** ② dating from the 1930s and a red-brick chocolate factory on the left.

Architecture

Begun in 1656 the manor house incorporates all the main features of Russian seventeenth-century residential architecture: the formal 'red' or 'beautiful' porch, the living quarters on the second floor, the elevated stone basement, and the house church of **St Nicholas**. The house is painted a rich shade of red and trimmed with white stone details. A vaulted attic was added to the second storey in the eighteenth century. The shape of the attic and the garlanded designs which decorate it suggest the authorship of Ivan Zarudnyi. Zarudnyi used similar motifs in the **Archangel Gabriel's Church** commissioned by Prince Menshikov (see Excursion 9).

manor house of Averky lov, 1656–7 (rebuilt 1703–11)

The Hall of the Cross

The vaulted chamber on the second floor of the house, known as the **Hall of the Cross** (*Krestovaya Palata*), served as the owner's reception room where, enthroned, he would entertain his guests. The inscription circling the chiselled crucifix on the keystone of the vault gives the year 1657 (7165) as the date of its completion, making it the only dated civic construction in Moscow.

The Church of St Nicholas (1656–7)

Originally the palace and the **Church of St Nicholas** were one architectural unit bound together by an arcade. The arcade is gone, but the two buildings are still interlinked by the use of various ornamental details inspired by timber architecture, such as the urn-like columns of the porches, festive main entries, brick work details, and elaborate window mouldings. What is missing in the house but can be seen in the church are the rows of *kokoshniki* or spade-shaped gables. The gables decorate the church's lower rectangle and its upper octagon which supports the five chiselled drums and cupolas.

The church's main or northern entry is also worthy of note. Its unique feature is the cornice with twin arches ending in a round pendant. The cornice repeats the contours of a barrel-shaped roof which must have also surmounted the original seventeenth-century manor house. The porch is set with majolica tiles. Amidst floral designs of the tiles are figures of double-headed eagles which suggest that Tsar Alexis Romanov participated in the building of the church.

The Cursed Palace

Despite its beauty, the garden palace had a sinister reputation, due to the fact that all of its owners died a violent death.

The first victim was Ivan Nikitich Bersenev-Beklemishev, the original owner of the palace in the Royal Gardens. He was a member of Ivan III's *Duma* and the tsar entrusted him with many diplomatic missions involving the Holy Roman Emperor and the Tartar Khan, Megli Girei. Since Ivan 'favoured opposition and honoured those who contradicted him', Bersenev was named the tsar's Garden Warden and rewarded for his frankness with a large plot of land along the Moscow River embankment, adjoining the Gardens of the Tsar.

Bersenev's candour served him less well under Ivan's son, Basil III. For Bersenev's opposition to the Smolensk campaign, the tsar had him decapitated in the Kremlin tower that still bears his name.

Averky Kirillov, the last owner of the estate was a son of a rich merchant. He, too, held the high position of Garden Warden and was also a member of the *Duma*. Since he was a commoner, and thus precluded from holding the title of boyar, he was given the important rank of a *Duma diak*, or Secretary-Scribe. Without him the *Duma* could not convene or a state document be validated. His successful career ended abruptly when he died during the musketeer rebellion of 1682 instigated by Regent Sofia (see Introduction to 'Moscow of the Tsars', p. 12).

Kirillov's and Bersenev's ownership of the old garden manor is confirmed by historical records. On the other hand, the presence there of Grigory Lukianovich, better known as 'Maliuta' or 'Babe' Skuratov, may be part of the Moscow lore which surrounds the palace and villainous deeds of Ivan the Terrible's powerful henchman.

According to the nineteenth-century author Alexei Tolstoy:

> The gaze of [Maliuta's] faded eyes was never direct, but struck with horror those who happened to meet his bleak look. Not a single human emotion ever stirred in this thick, deformed skull, overgrown with coarse hair which covered most of his forehead. He fled everyone, lived without friends, having reduced himself to the status of a royal bloodhound ready to pounce on whomever the Tsar would designate. So great was his thirst for blood that at night he stole back to the scene of the execution to cut up the bodies of his victims and toss them to the dogs. Allegedly a secret passage led from Skuratov's palace to the Tsar's bedchamber.

Skuratov's only love was for his beautiful daughters. He chose their husbands with great care. For his eldest daughter, Maria, Skuratov picked Boris Godunov, displaying acute political foresight. Boris, then a junior member of the *oprichnina* police force, ascended the Moscow throne and proclaimed Maria the Tsarina of all Russia in 1598.

The second daughter was too young for marriage when Maliuta went off to fight in Lithuania. He died while storming the Weissenstein fortress in 1573, thus missing the wedding of his younger daughter Ekaterina to Prince Dmitry Shuisky, whose brother Vasily became tsar in 1606.

Church of St Antipy 'By the Carriage House'

(Tserkov Antipiia 'Na Kolymazhnom Dvore')
Corner of Pereulok Marshala Shaposhnikova and 'litsa Marksa i Engelsa
③

On the opposite side of the Moscow River, directly across from Averky Kirillov's palace, stands the small white mid-sixteenth-century Church of **St Antipy**. It is now obscured by the nineteenth-century **Pushkin Museum of Fine Arts*** ④ ④ₐ, built on the former site of the *Kolymazhnyi Dvor*, or the Tsar's Carriage House. In addition to the royal horses and bejewelled saddles, the Carriage House also served as headquarters for the *oprichniki*, Ivan the Terrible's secret police.

Church of St Antipy.

* See Modern Moscow, p. 354.

The architecture of St Antipy reflects the deformed character of its builder, Maliuta. While most Moscow churches had either single or triple-altar apses, St Antipy has two asymmetrical apses, which make the church appear askew. Its other peculiarity is a row of unusual *kokoshniki* gables, resembling festoons — an uncommon feature for a sixteenth-century church.

Above the scalloped edges of the wall, two more rows of ogee-shaped gables mark the transition to a small, rounded drum with a cupola, while another drum, with a depressed dome and small cross, rises above the side chapel. The interior of the church has a groined pillarless vault. Two eighteenth-century additions adjoin the sixteenth-century church: a refectory with beautiful classical details and a cylindrical belltower. All three buildings have been taken over by the Pushkin Museum as exhibition halls.

The identity of the church's builder was long an object of speculation, but a tombstone bearing Skuratov's name was uncovered during recent renovations on what was once the cemetery. This confirmed that Maliuta not only commissioned the church but also lived nearby, supposedly in the building inside the courtyard of **Ulitsa Marksa i Engelsa 7 and 9** ⑤.

Skuratov's atrocities may have prompted the Muscovites to give the name of *Chertolie*, or 'devil's land', to the area surrounding the church. The sinister name may have also come from an unruly ('devilish') brook which ran down the present Kropotkinskaya and Volkhonka streets, frequently flooding them. In the seventeenth century the brook was bridled and the main street renamed Prechistenskaya or Prechistenka to honour the *prechistaya* or 'most pure' image of the *Virgin of Smolensk*. This much revered icon, still at **Novodevichiy Convent** (See 'Moscow of the Clergy', Excursion 23, p. 296), was the frequent object of royal pilgrimages.

(Marx and Engels Museum)
Ulitsa Marksa i Engelsa, 5
⑥

The Palace of Prince Viazemsky and Prince Dolgoruky

Open: 10:30 to 18:00 daily
Closed: Tuesdays, last Monday of the month.

The **Marx and Engels Museum** we visit next was once the palace of two noble Russian families: the Viazemskys and Dolgorukys or Dolgorukovs. The building stands on the foundations of a sixteenth-century house which once belonged to Prince Afanasy Ivanovich Viazemsky, Ivan the Terrible's favourite *oprichnik*. The prince's noble blood, his dashing looks, and his disregard for death endeared him to the tsar, but not the the the tsar's henchman, Maliuta Skuratov. Jealous of Viazemsky's good fortune, Skuratov masterminded his rival's demise. In 1560 he told the tsar that Viazemsky dabbled in witchcraft. This sealed Viazemsky's fate, even though Viazemsky had merely obtained potions in order to win a lady's favours. The tsar sentenced the prince to death, while Skuratov took pains to select the cruelest punishment.

The mansion's present decorations date from the mid-nineteenth century when a Prince Dolgoruky purchased it from a descendant of the executed Prince Viazemsky. The many pillars, friezes, vases, and balconies which adorn the main facade and the adjoining wings do little to offset the monotony of its overall appearance.

The Dolgorukys were latecomers to this area. Their original estates were in **Dolgoruky** (now **Belinskogo**) **Lane**. But they were banished from Moscow when they tried unsuccessfully to arrange their second royal marriage in 1730.

The lady in question was Ekaterina Dolgorukaya (1712–54), sister of Ivan Dolgoruky, the favourite of Emperor Peter II (r. 1727–30). Ivan was an ambitious and unscrupulous youth, but a master at organizing sumptuous parties and feasts. This talent won him the friendship and trust of the young emperor. On 30 November 1729 the triumphant Dolgoruky clan gathered in St Petersburg to witness Ekaterina's engagement to Peter II. Royal favours were showered on the in-laws, but the Dolgorukys enjoyed their new status for exactly 49 days. On 19 January 1730, the day Ekaterina was to be wed, Peter II died of smallpox. Ivan Dolgoruky hastily falsified Peter's will, making Ekaterina Dolgorukaya his successor. Four years later, this act sent Ivan to his execution in Siberia, where the rest of the disgraced Dolgorukys lived in exile. The survivors of the purge, the less prominent members of the family, later settled at **Volkhonka Street, No. 16**.

After the Revolution of 1917, the Dolgoruky estate was confiscated, and became the Marx and Engels Museum in 1962. It is difficult to imagine a less likely place to exhibit the documents and belongings of Marx and Engels than the former stronghold of the conservative Constitutional Democratic Party (*Cadets*), headed by the last two Dolgorukov owners of the house.

The House of the Lopukhins

(Soiuztrak-mashtekhnika)
Ulitsa Marksa i Engelsa, 3
⑦

The house of Evdokia Lopukhina, another royal bride who brought her family into the limelight, adjoined the Dolgoruky estate on the left. The two-storey house, at first glance, resembles a typical eighteenth-century Moscow nobleman's residence, with six columns rising from a finely rusticated basement, medallions on the walls, a frieze with griffins, and a coat of arms embellishing the pediment. Closer examination of the back of the house, however, reveals earlier foundations and seventeenth-century window mouldings. The restored hind facade confirms that the original building, though smaller, was most impressive — not surprisingly, given that it was the residence of the father-in-law of the tsar.

The pretty, appropriately plump, and easy-going Evdokia Lopukhina was twenty in 1689 when Natalia Naryshkina picked her as a bride for her seventeen-year-old son, the future Peter the Great. The Lopukhins were a conservative, devout family, and valuable allies against Peter's rival, the Regent Sofia. Moreover, Evdokia's father commanded the musketeer regiment which guarded the Kremlin.

After the wedding, Fedor Lopukhin, the father of the bride, was granted a governorship and a large tract of land in Moscow. He celebrated the royal kinship by building or refurbishing the house we now see.

Evdokia's inability to share Peter's ambitions, and her endless nagging, drove him away from home and into the arms of a German mistress. Evdokia was banished to a nunnery in Suzdal, and a year later, in 1698, her father was ordered out of Moscow. Evdokia's and Peter's first born son Alexis was accused of treason against his father and died under torture in 1718.

The Lopukhin estates survived only because Evdokia's niece married Mikhail Mikhailovich Golitsyn, a close friend and associate of Peter the Great. Golitsyn, Peter the Great's drummer at the age of twelve, went on to become a field-marshal and a senator. Some seventy years later, another beautiful Lopukhin woman rescued her family's fortunes and estates. Anna (1777–1805) caught the eye of Emperor Paul I at a Moscow ball on the occasion of his coronation in 1796.

Barely nineteen, the dark-eyed Anna became the most influential person at the imperial court in St Petersburg. The emperor saw her daily and had her accompany his retinue on trips. Nevertheless, Anna was apparently never Paul's mistress, only a close friend. While she had no taste for political intrigues, she often used her influence on Paul to shield an innocent person's life or career. She fell in love with Prince Pavel Gavrilovich Gagarin, whom Paul finally allowed her to marry in 1800. But Anna remained the emperor's trusted friend even after her marriage, until the day she died of consumption at the age of twenty-eight.

Anna's beautiful sister Ekaterina (1783–1830) almost followed in Anna's footsteps: at another coronation ball in Moscow, she turned the head of Emperor Alexander I. The watchful court quickly put a stop to that. The beguiling Ekaterina was married in haste to the millionnaire Demidov, descendant of a clever but common village smith. A distant relative sold the house to the state, and it was finally converted to a school.

Ulitsa Marksa i Engelsa,
Volkhonka, 14
⑧

House of the Princes Golitsyn

The Princes Golitsyn, next-door neighbours and relatives of the Lopukhins, were descendants of Lithuanian princes. From the middle of the sixteenth century, when the first Golitsyn arrived in Moscow, until 1917, at least one member of this prolific clan would occupy an important post in the service of the Russian tsars.

When the ownership of any imposing house in Moscow is uncertain, it usually belonged to the Golitsyns, as did the grand estate on Marksa i Engelsa Street. The family's initials are woven into the design embellishing the pillared entry. The gateway (1759) by the architects Ivan Zherebtsov and S. Chevakinsky is imposing, though cumbersome. By contrast, the small house to the right of the entry is a jewel of classical Russian architecture. Matvei Kazakov, who designed this service building, gave it an elegant pillared facade and a pediment worthy of a palace. Between 1759 and 1761, he also designed the main house set in the back of the courtyard. All that remains of Kazakov's work now is a touch of rustication here and a window casing there: the house's original proportions were distorted in 1928 when two more storeys were added, eliminating the old entablature.

Kazakov worked on the Golitsyn house twice: first in 1759, when the house was built, and again in 1762, when it was enlarged for the coronation of Catherine the Great. The empress, who normally resided in St Petersburg, took one look at the crumbling Kremlin palaces which had not been lived in since Peter the Great's time, and sought something more suitable. She chose the residences of Mikhail Mikhailovich Golitsyn and his neighbour Prince Dolgorukov, at No. 16, who had no alternative but to surrender their palaces.

On Catherine's instructions, Kazakov linked the Golitsyn and Dolgorukov palaces by several halls and passages, thus creating the central part of a huge new palace. The project took three and a half months and cost 70,000 roubles — a staggering sum, even for an empress. Catherine praised Kazakov, but complained in secret to her friend Baron Grimm that 'the house is a masterpiece of confusion'. The empress also complained about the stench: the tsar's old stables stood just outside her bedroom. After the coronation, the portions linking the Dolgorukov and Golitsyn residences were dismantled and the palaces returned to their owners.

The Golitsyn residence gained even greater celebrity when its then owner, Prince Sergei Mikhailovich (1774–1859), already famous as a philanthropist, unveiled his art collection there. He owned some 132 paintings, including works by Rubens, Leonardo da Vinci, and Corregio. The Hermitage Museum purchased the collection for 800,000 roubles in 1886. Golitsyn also collected marble, silver, and bronze art objects and was the first private collector to open his house to the general public. Two rooms of the former art gallery survive on the second floor of the house and have the original painted ceilings.

The spirited and gifted poetess Evdokia Ivanovna (*née* Izmailova), whom Emperor Paul had ordered to marry Sergei Golitsyn in 1799, was as much of an attraction as her husband's art. After a gypsy told Evdokia that she would die during the night, Princess Golitsyn developed a habit which earned her the sobriquet of 'Princess Nocturne'. She slept by day and wrote poetry all the night.

Golitsyn willed his house to charity. After the Revolution in 1917, the building, another Golitsyn-endowed hospital, was taken over by the **Academy of Sciences**.

In 1972, on the occasion of President Nixon's visit to the Soviet Union, the Moscow City Council decided to widen Kropotkinskaya Square. When the workers began the demolition work, they uncovered two seventeenth-century manor houses at the south-western corner of Kropotkinskaya Street: the nineteenth-century house which once belonged to the Lopukhins concealed a still earlier Lopukhin building ⑦ⓐ, and the nineteenth-century Golitsyn

e S.M. Golitsyn.

residence facing Kropotkinskaya Square contained the red-brick house of Mikhail Mikhailovich Golitsyn (senior) within its outer walls ⑧a.

After visiting Kropotkinskaya Square, we walk back towards the Kremlin along **Volkhonka**, one of the few streets in central Moscow to have kept its pre-revolutionary name. The name comes from the Princes Volkonsky, whom Leo Tolstoy immortalized as the Bolkonskys in *War and Peace* and who lived at **Volkhonka, No. 8** ⑨.

Across from the Volkhonsky estate stood the tsar's **Swan Court**, an office which handled royal swans and sold the feathers they produced. The Swan office bordered on **Lenivka**, or the 'Lazy Street', once Moscow's shortest and least travelled lane. Today it is quite busy, since it provides access to the Moscow River embankment.

Ulitsa Marksa i Engelsa, 14 ⑩

The House of the Pashkovs

The celebrated **Pashkov mansion** on the crest of the hill opposite the Kremlin's Borovitskaya Gates, is the eighteenth-century counterpart of Averky Kirillov's manor house (p. 115) and a masterpiece of Baroque architecture. The main building is flanked by service buildings, an estate church, and gardens.

Architecture

In the Pashkov mansion, the decorative stress is on the back facade overlooking Prospekt Marksa, the pre-revolutionary Mokhovaya.

Petr Egorovich Pashkov (1721–90), who commissioned the mansion on a former site of a royal palace, spared no means to impress the residents of the

The house of the Pashkovs (1784–6), rebuilt in the early nineteenth century by Osip Bove.

Kremlin with the splendour of his own home. He instructed the architects to raise the palace on a high basement in order to stress its importance and had the tall central part of the building treated with columns, sculptures, and topped off by a round belvedere. The side wings received Ionic columns and pediments. The airy white structure is believed to be the creation of Vasily Ivanovich Bazhenov (1738–99). The subsequent reconstructions were carried out by Osip Bove (1784–1834) in the early nineteenth century.

The main facade which fronts on Marx and Engels Street is less flamboyant. Seen through the entry gates decorated with columns and a lion's mask clutching two garlands, the palace appears small and compact as it curls around the front garden. Adding to the crowded effect are the auxiliary structures and the former manor church of **St Nicholas**.

The house figures prominently in the writings of Johannes Richter, a German advisor to the Russian textile industry. According to Richter, it was a 'magic castle' with 'remarkable gardens'.

The source of the Pashkovs's wealth was a well-concealed Moscow secret. Egor Ivanovich Pashkov, the father of the palace builder, was Peter the Great's orderly who amassed his fortune by compiling an incriminating dossier on Prince Matvei Petrovich Gagarin, Governor of Siberia. Though an effective administrator and immensely popular, Gagarin, according to Pashkov's dossier, was trafficking in grain and diamonds and imposing illegal levies on Chinese imports. On the strength of Pashkov's dossier, Gagarin was hanged in 1718, while the dutiful orderly was given a large share of the princely estate and several thousand serfs.

In addition to the estates, Pashkov took over Gagarin's licence to sell spirits, which brought his only son, Petr Egorovich, handsome revenues. The latter was appointed Governor to the seat vacated by Gagarin and later promoted to the rank of major general. When the last Pashkov died in 1839, Moscow University restored the mansion and presented it to Count Rumiantsev for his art collection and rare manuscripts in 1861. Vladimir Lenin, who had been a frequent visitor to the Rumiantsev Museum, nationalized it, and had the paintings divided between the Hermitage and the Pushkin Museum of Fine Arts. The book collection remained at the Pashkov House, today known as the **Lenin Library Annex**.

Ulitsa Marksa i Engelsa, 17

⑪

The House of Prince Dmitry Ivanovich Shuisky

At the turn of the seventeenth century, the Princes Shuisky owned a large estate on the present Marx and Engels Street, then alternatively known as **Shuisky** and **Blagoveshchensky Lanes**. Part of the estate, including the site of the Pashkov Mansion, belonged to Prince Vasily Ivanovich Shuisky. When Vasily became tsar and moved to the Kremlin in 1606, his brother Dmitry, whose house was further down the street, kept his share of the estate until he died in 1613.

EXCURSION 7

The house of Prince D. I. Shuisky
(twentieth-century reconstruction)

The manor house of Dmitry Shuisky has been recently restored and fitted with a crested roof, a porch, and small, square windows. Like many other sixteenth- and seventeenth-century dwellings (see Excursion 10, Yussupovs' Palace, p. 156) that have been rebuilt from scratch by Moscow restorers, however, the Shuisky residence has become an architectural museum piece. The only genuine parts are the solid brick walls that have sunk below street level. The rest represents a well-documented, but artificial, recreation of the past.

The estate's original owner was the popular Prince Ivan Shuisky, whose military leaership won him, as it had his predecessors, the title of boyar. Ivan the Terrible appointed Shuisky as one of the four regents to his son, Prince Fedor. Had Shuisky aspired to become tsar, he may have well been elected to the throne after Fedor's death, but he chose to become a monk, and leave his estates to his sons.

Shuisky's sons, Vasily and Dmitry, did not resemble their father. Though they had ample chance to prove themselves in battle, they chose political conspiracy instead. Boris Godunov, who sought the crown for himself, had good reasons to fear the two brothers. On his instigation, Vasily and Dmitry were banished, and their elderly father Ivan strangled inside his monastery.

The resourceful Dmitry, however, repaired his fortunes by marrying Ekaterina Skuratova (the daughter of Ivan's henchman, Maliuta), Boris's sister-in-law. This earned him a boyar's title in 1591 and helped his brother Vasily's return to Moscow. No sooner were the Shuiskys reunited that they began to plot anew against Godunov, and later his successor, until Vasily had himself successfully proclaimed tsar in 1606.

With the Shuiskys in power, things went from bad to worse. Moscow was threatened by rebellions, and would have fallen but for Mikhail Skopin-Shuisky (1586–1610), Dmitry's and Vasily's nephew. Mikhail's reward, however, was

Mikhail Skopin-Shuisky (d. 1630).

a cup of poisoned wine: Tsar Vasily Shuisky was childless, and Dmitry, who aspired to become his successor, had valid motives to murder the popular Skopin-Shuisky.

For once, Dmitry miscalculated. The death of Skopin-Shuisky put the entire burden of military command on Dmitry's back, and the Russian troops were defeated. Tsar Vasily had to step down from the throne, and both he and Dmitry died as prisoners of the Poles, who occupied the Kremlin until 1612.

The poison in Skopin-Shuisky's wine may have well come from the **Old Apothecary Office** located inside the courtyard of today's **Shchusev Museum**, only a few steps away from Dmitry Shuisky's residence.

Prospekt Kalinina, 5

Shchusev Museum of Architecture (The Old Apothecary Office)

Open: 10–6. Closed: Tuesday

This part of the **Shchusev Museum** is devoted entirely to the Soviet period of architecture. Of note are plans by the early twentieth-century architects such as Tatlin and Vesniny brothers. The division dealing with the pre-revolutionary architecture is located at the **Donskoy Monastery** (see 'Moscow of the Clergy', Excursion 22, p. 289).

The restored seventeenth-century fragment, cleaved inside the neo-Classical mansion which houses the museum, is the tsar's **Old Apothecary Office**. A ranking boyar personally appointed by the tsar oversaw the preparation of the medicinal potions and emergency measures during the epidemics. The preparations were rigidly controlled since they were destined for the tsar and his entourage. The next in line for the medicines were orphans and widows.

When Peter the Great moved the medicinal herb gardens which grew alongside the Kremlin wall to a new location and commissioned a new apothecary building, Stefan Talyzin purchased the vacated lot. Talyzin's neo-classical mansion, finished in 1773, incorporating the Old Apothecary Office, may have served Tolstoy as the model for the house of Prince Bolkonsky in *War and Peace*, although it is more likely to have been based on the house at No. 9 Kalinina Prospekt.

(Vozdvizhenka)

Kalinina Prospekt

We next reach **Kalinina Avenue**, so named in 1946 after Mikhail Kalinin,

EXCURSION 7

who had just died, and some twenty years after the **Krestovozdvizhensky Monastery** was torn down and **Vozdvizhenka**, named after it, ceased to exist.

Vozdvizhenka, like **Gertsena Street** further west, was once a trade route to Novgorod and subsequently the seat of the Moscow aristocracy.

The Lenin Library

Prospekt Kalinina, 3
⑬

The grey, monolithic mass of the **Lenin Library** occupies the entire block between **Kalinina Prospekt** and **Frunze Street.** It was built in 1941 according to the design of V. Shchuko and V. Gel'Freikh. It is one of the world's largest libraries with 30 million titles in 247 languages. The bulk of its precious manuscript kept in the Pashkovs' former house (see p. 124) came from the famous Rumiantsev (see p. 133) collection.

The library stands on the land which once belonged to the Streshnevs. The marriage of Evdokia Streshneva to Tsar Michael Romanov in 1626 was a true Cinderella story. The girl came to the Kremlin palace as an attendant to a rich relative, only to be chosen by the tsar for his wife over all of the other maidens of the realm. The Streshnevs received the estate bordering on that of the Romanovs, whose **Church of Znamenie** we will visit next.

Znamenie Church
(Church of Our Lady of the Sign)

*(Tserkov Znamenia
'na Starom
Sheremetievskom
Dvore')
Ulitsa Granovskogo, 14*
⑭

The **Church of Znamenie** was built by Ivan Romanov, who, like the Streshnevs, profited from a royal marriage. Ivan's father was the legendary Nikita Romanov, whose sister Anastasia married Ivan the Terrible in 1547. For Anastasia's wedding Nikita received in addition to the boyar's title, some 8,000 acres of land. The Znamenie Church rose on the land donated by the tsar, within walking distance from the Kremlin.

By a curious twist of history the sixteenth-century Romanov Church of Znamenie displays features of the seventeenth-century Naryshkin Baroque and the finishing touches of the eighteenth-century Classicism. This is how it happened.

Ivan Romanov, who had commissioned the church, died childless. His estate passed into the hands of the Naryshkins, relatives of Peter the Great's mother Natalia. The Naryshkins, anxious to stress their ties to the royal house, rebuilt the old Romanov church in the 1690s, but kept its dedication to Znamenie, the favourite icon of the Romanovs. When the Counts Sheremetievs (see p. 201) acquired the Znamenie Church in the eighteenth century, they did not change the name nor touch its exterior appearance. They only altered the interior to suit their Westernized tastes. The Romanov church, built in the Naryshkin Baroque, thus became part of the Sheremetievs' estate. In time, the Sheremetievs became Russia's richest aristocrats and the builders of famous

amenie Church (Church of Our dy of the Sign, 1690–1704): tail.

palaces, including the one adjoining Znamenie Church, now the Kremlin Hospital.

Architecture

Znamenie Church is a city cousin of the Naryshkin out-of-town churches* with their sweeping wingspan of terraces stretching into the countryside. Its terraces are neatly tucked under to conform to the restricted surroundings. But, like other Naryshkin churches, that of Znamenie displays the vertical flight of superimposed octagons which create an impression of a circular building as the narrowing octagons sweep upwards. The church also shares the wealth of white stone ornaments applied to red brick walls that typifies the Naryshkin Baroque. Unfortunately, the crested and rounded pediments which outline the windows and individual tiers with lacy grace suffer from the crowded effect produced by placing the three cupolas above the altar projections, like soldiers in a row. The church seems free of its confines only in the upward reach of its central dome.

The classical interior of the Znamenie Church is the contribution of the Sheremetievs, whose lives spanned the transition from Old Muscovy to Imperial Russia. This is best seen in the tall iconostasis, which, were it not for the familiar arrangement of icons in the eighteenth-century altar screen, would make one believe one was in a Catholic church. Tucked away in **Granovsky Lane** and barely visible from **Prospekt Marksa**, the Znamenie Church is unique for it spans three lives, three generations, and three different outlooks.

*See the Pokrov Church in Fili, Minskaya and Oleko Dundicha streets, and the Church of the Saviour in Ubory village.

EXCURSION 7

Excursion Plan 8
Nobility at the
Crossroads

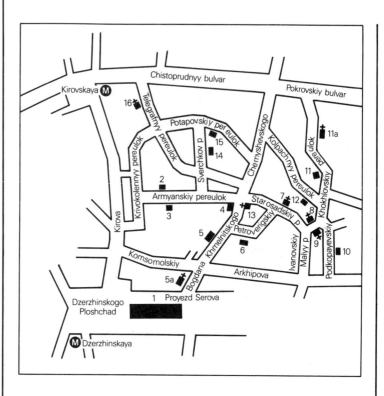

1. The Polytechnical Museum
2. The Manor Houses of Ivan Miloslavsky and Artamon Matveyev
3. House of the Lazarevs
4. Palace of Field-Marshal Rumiantsev
5. Old Ukranian Embassy
5a. Church of St Nicholas 'v Blinnikakh'
6. House of P.K. Botkin
7. Lutheran Church of SS. Peter and Paul
8. St Vladimir's Church 'in the Old Gardens'
9. Ivanovsky (St John's) Convent
10. House of Boyar Shuisky
11. House of Emilian Ukraintsev
11a. Trinity Church
12. House of Ivan Mazepa
13. Church of SS. Cosmas and Damian
14. House of Ivan Sverchkov
15. House of the Princes Golitsyn
16. Church of the Archangel Gabriel (Menshikov Tower)

NOBILITY AT THE CROSSROADS

Armyanskiy Lane — The Manor Houses of Ivan Miloslavsky and Artamon Matveyev — The House of the Lazarevs — The Palace of Field-Marshal Petr Alexsandrovich Rumiantsev — Bogdana Khmelnitskogo Street — The Church of St Nicholas — The House of Petr Kononovich Botkin — The Church of SS. Peter and Paul — The Church of St Vladimir — Ivanovsky Convent — The House of Boyar Shuisky — The House of Emilian Ukraintsev — The Trinity Church — The Manor House of Ivan Mazepa — The House of Ivan Sverchkov — Menshikov Tower and the Church of the Archangel Gabriel.

bove The Regent Sofia, Peter the reat's half-sister and rival for e throne.

elow Natalia Naryshkina, Peter e Great's mother.

Armyanskiy Pereulok, 3 and 9

②

*T*he reign of the paternal *batiushka* Tsar Alexis (*r.* 1645–76) was perhaps as epoch-making for the Russian courtiers as that of his tempestuous son, Peter the Great. The difference between the father and the son lay in their methods of modernization. Alexis welcomed and fostered Western ideas, but introduced them gradually without disrupting the deeply rooted traditions of Muscovy. Nonetheless, the influx of 28,000 foreigners, mostly Protestants, made itself felt. The Russian nobles did not so much object to the professional, industrial, and military contributions of the newcomers as to the impact they were making on the court. What upset the old-fashioned boyars most were the Westernized ways of their tsar's closest advisers.

The dilemma between adherence to native roots and the espousal of the Western ways was even more intensified after Alexis's death, when the conservative supporters of Regent Sofia clashed with the Western-minded adherents of Natalia Naryshkina, Alexis's second wife and mother of Peter the Great. The nobles were caught in the middle of the Great Feud, which in the end was won by Peter the Great and his westernized 'fledglings'. Peter's victory, however, did not resolve the dilemma: for years to come the Russian nobility continued to be torn between their heritage and their loyalty to the reform-minded tsar.

Nowhere in Moscow was the battle between the conservative old guard and the Westernized courtiers of Tsar Alexis fought with greater vehemence than in the quiet, twisting **Armyanskiy Lane**, off **Bogdana Khmelnitskogo Street** in eastern Moscow.

The opening salvo of the feud between the Miloslavskys, relatives of Sofia, and the Naryshkins occurred in the mid seventeenth century with Artamon Matveyev purchasing a house in Armyanskiy Lane, *next door* to Ivan Miloslavsky, the tsar's brother-in-law.

The Manor Houses of Ivan Miloslavsky and Artamon Matveyev

Aside from the memory of their strife, all that remains of the Miloslavsky and

Matveyev estates is a small white structure at No. 3, possibly a service building of the Miloslavskys'.

The well-born, influential Miloslavsky took an intense dislike to his neighbour Matveyev, a commoner by birth whose fascination with Western culture was gaining him favour with Tsar Alexis. Ivan watched Matveyev become the commander of a musketeer regiment, then head of the Secret (Police) Department, and finally the Minister of Foreign Affairs.

Miloslavsky's abhorrence increased when Matveyev, in defiance of Russian traditions, married Mary Hamilton, the daughter of a Scottish royalist from the 'German Suburb'. The wench wore Western clothes and mingled with guests rather than keeping to the *terem*. Furthermore, she encouraged Matveyev's interest in chemistry and had theatrical performances staged at their home.

This was bad enough, but when Alexis's first wife Tsarina Maria Miloslavskaya died the tsar avoided his father-in-law's company in preference to Matveyev. It was at Matveyev's home that Alexis met his second wife, the lively black-eyed Natalia Naryshkina, whom Mary Hamilton had raised in the Western manner. The tsar married Natalia in 1671. On 30 May 1672, she gave birth to a healthy son, the future Peter the Great. Matveyev's furture was assured; the disapproving Miloslavsky was sent as governor to distant Astrakhan.

But the victory proved short-lived. In 1682, Matveyev perished during an anti-Naryshkin coup instigated by Sofia. As soon as she became Regent, she had her uncle Ivan recalled from Astrakhan. Ivan died peacefully in his bed and was buried in the cemetery of **St Nicholas Church** which stood at the end of the Lane. His body came to rest next to the tomb of the tortured Matveyev. And still the Westernizers triumphed. In 1689 Peter reclaimed the throne from Sofia and immediately ordered the body of Ivan Miloslavsky to be dug up, loaded on a cart drawn by pigs, and dumped outside of Moscow.

A century later the Lane was taken over by relatives of Lazar Lazarian or Lazarev, who arrived from Persia along with other Armenian families and the street was henceforth known as the **Armenian Lane**.

Armyanskiy Pereulok, 2
③

The House of the Lazarevs

Lazarev selected a tract of land opposite the Miloslavsky estate on which he erected his house and, in 1781, the **Armenian Church of the Resurrection**, demolished by Stalin in 1930.

Catherine the Great elevated Lazarev to noble rank in recognition of his commercial successes and philanthropy, which entitled the Armenian merchant to buy land and build several factories for manufacture of fine silks and brocades. The extent of his wealth may be confirmed by the fact that Lazarev owned the famous Orlov Diamond which Count Orlov bought from him as a present for Catherine the Great. The diamond is now on display at the Kremlin Diamond Fund Exhibit.

After Lazarev's death in 1782 his sons inherited a vast fortune. Ivan, the

The house of the Lazarevs: formerly the Lazarev Institute of Oriental Languages, now the Armenian Embassy.

elder of the two Lazarev brothers, commissioned the large pillared house built between 1815 and 1823 by Lazarev's serfs I. Podiachev and T. Prostakov. The mansion is set back into the garden, with two wings curving towards the street. Its fine workmanship extends to the wrought-iron fence and the entry gates. The **obelisk** in front of the house commemorates the Lazarev brothers who donated their house to an Armenian School, which became the **Lazarev Institute of Oriental Languages** in 1848. For many years, the Lazarev Institute was a training place for Russian diplomats.

When the Soviet Armenian Republic sought new quarters, they chose the Lazarev mansion as the **Armenian Embassy**, thus providing a modern reason for Armenian Lane to retain its historic name.

The red-brick building at the corner of **Armyanskiy** and **Malyy Komsomolsky** lanes was the former site of the famous sixteenth-century Church of St Nicholas 'of the Pillars', the burial place of Ivan Miloslavsky, his antagonist Artamon Matveyev, and Matveyev's grandson, Field-Marshal Petr Ruminatsev. When the church was levelled in the 1930s, a chest of gold was allegedly discovered in the passage linking St Nicholas' Church to Matveyev's house.

Ulitsa Bogdana Khmelnitskogo, 17

④

The Palace of Field-Marshal Petr Aleksandrovich Rumiantsev

Armyanskiy Lane ends at the broad **Bogdana Khmelnitskogo Street** near the pale-green palace which Petr Rumiantsev purchased from Mikhail Khlebnikov, his aide-de-camp. The well-heeled colonel, who came from a family of wealthy Kolomna merchants, commissioned the fashionable architect Matvei Kazakov to build him a house in 1780. Count Rumiantsev hired artists to

EXCURSION 8

The palace of Field-Marshal Rumiantsev (1725–96), a brilliant strategist whose victories during the Seven Year War and in Turkey earned him the title of Count (1744) and then Field-Marshal (1770).

decorate the reception rooms with battle scenes of his victories in the Russo-Turkish war of 1768–74. The palace was later rebuilt, losing its wings and gardens but preserving the fine sculptures and the white ornamentation on the facade.

When Catherine the Great visited Moscow after the signing of the Kuchuk-Kainardzhi Treaty with Turkey, Rumiantsev modestly declined the honour of riding through the Triumphal Gates built for the occasion in **Tverskaya (Gorky) Street**, apparently preferring to savour his victories in the privacy of his own home.

Rumiantsev's son, Nikolai Petrovich (1754–1826), Minister of Foreign Affairs under Alexander I, was the palace's next owner. In 1814 he retired from the service and moved to his Moscow home to devote himself fully to rare books and paintings. His fabulous collection was later bequeathed to the **Rumiantsev Museum**, which Nikolai Petrovich helped to endow and which Lenin unceremoniously divided between various libraries and museums.

Moscow's nineteenth-century 'grandmother' — chronicler Yankova (see page 185) — lamented that:

> The magnificent palace of the Rumiantsev with its battle frescoes was bought by some merchants . . . who, of course, removed them . . . [They] did away with the park and finally the last owners used it as an apartment house and kept a store. Only the fine sculptures of the facade and the delicate stone ornamentation on [the remaining] wing bespeak the old glory.

The Church of SS. Cosmas and Damian

(Tserkov Kosmy i Damiana)
Ulitsa Bogdana Khmelnitskogo, 14/2
⑬

This unusual church was built on Lt.-Colonel Khlebnikov's initiative. In 1792 Field-Marshal Rumiantsev's aide raised 14,525 roubles, a regal sum for the time, though not for the sought-after architect Matvei Kazakov.

From its very inception the church, commemorating SS. Cosmas and Damian, the two healers of Asia Minor, was praised for its innovative design and clever juxtaposition of cylindrical and cubic volumes. The body of the church is made up of four cylinders, of which the largest and the tallest dominates the curved projections of the apse and the two side chapels. The refectory and the bell-tower, adjoining the church from the west, are cube-shaped. To stress the architectural perfection of his building, Kazakov deliberately omitted all decorative trimmings. This dark green church is among Kazakov's best works.

Bogdana Khmelnitskogo Ulitsa

The street on which Rumiantsev decided to purchase his palace and Khlebnikov build his church owes its original name, **Marosseika**, to the *malorossy*. The *malorossy*, or Ukrainians, settled here in the seventeenth century while seeking refuge from the religious persecution of the Catholic Poles, who then ruled the Ukraine. But when in 1667 Tsar Alexis reclaimed Kiev and the eastern Ukraine, the *malorossy* established their Embassy on **Marosseika**, now **Bogdana Khmelnitskogo Street**, No. 9.

Nikita Khrushchev, a Ukrainian by birth and later First Secretary of the Communist Party, celebrated the 300th anniversary of the reunification of Russia with Ukraine by rededicating the street to Bogdan Khmelnitsky, the first Ukrainian *Hetman* or Governor of the Ukraine.

The anti-Catholic *malorossy* took exception to the foreigners who 'invaded' their street. As soon as they settled in, the irate residents petitioned Alexis to expel the 'Germans', as all foreigners were called, from their neighbourhood. The 'Germans', mostly Protestants, were accused of inflating the property prices and of building their own houses of worship, thus diminishing the revenues of local churches. At first Alexis dismissed the petitions, but in 1652 he reluctantly moved all foreigners to the 'German Suburb' (see p. 143) on the left bank of the Yauza River.

(Tserkov Nikoly 'v Blinnikakh') ogdana Khmelnitskogo Ulitsa, 5
(5a)

The Church of St Nicholas 'of the Pancakes'

The many guilds who enjoyed a brisk trade in this Ukrainian settlement added to the bustle of the area. The richest of all was the pancake-makers' guild. With profits from their pancakes (*bliny*) they financed their splendid **Church of St Nicholas 'of the Pancakes'**. In 1920 the red Baroque church of the pancake-makers had its crosses and cupola torn down to the distress of all Muscovites.

Another peculiarity of this commercial street was the presence of many palatial establishments, such as the Rumiantsev mansion. The reason was strictly that of political expediency: Bogdana Khmelnitskogo Street led to the summer residences of the tsars. The more resourceful noblemen, such as the Sheremetievs,* Golitsyns (see p. 122) and Dolgorukys erected their own houses along the royal route in the hope that the tsars would pay them a visit on their way to or from their country residences.

etroverigskiy Pereulok, 4
(6)

The House of Petr Kononovich Botkin

For those who enjoy Russian literary history, a quick glance at the early nineteenth-century mansion of Petr Botkin (1781–1853) may be rewarding.

*The restored palace of Sheremetievs, blood relatives of the Romanov tsars, is located inside the courtyard of house No. 11.

EXCURSION 8

The house stands a few yards from where **Petroverigskiy Lane** veers towards **Starosadskiy Lane**, which links it to **Bogdana Khmelnitskogo Street**.

The classical mansion of the wealthy tea merchant and art collector Botkin was a famous nineteenth-century literary salon. Almost every important Russian writer, critic, and poet attended the soirées given by Botkin and his sons.

The **Botkin Hospital** in Moscow bears the name of Botkin's son Sergei (1832–89), a famous physician, who is sometimes confused with Evgeniy Botkin, Nicholas II's court physician. The latter was shot by the Bolsheviks in Ekaterinburg on 16 July 1918 with the imperial family.

Corner of Petroverigskiy and Starosadskiy Pereulok

⑦

The Church of SS. Peter and Paul

The U-shaped **Petroverigskiy Lane** ends directly opposite the former eighteenth-century Lutheran **Church of SS. Peter and Paul**. Built in the neo-Gothic style, it was one of the several non-Russian churches in this area.*

(Tserkov Valdimira v 'Starykh Sadekh')
Starosadskiy Pereulok, 9

⑧

The Church of St Vladimir 'in the Old Gardens'

The name of the church and the **Starosadskiy** or **Old Garden** lane on which it stands recall that the royal orchards once grew along the sloping hill running down to **Solyanka Street** (see p. 220). The church was built between 1514 and 1516 for Tsar Basil III by the Italian architect Alevisio (Novy) then working in the Kremlin. Basil took a keen interest in the church and the rare fruits grown in his royal gardens. The present building was altered in 1689, but remains a landmark of sixteenth century Russian architecture: square, pillarless, with a single dome and a low bell-tower.

Ivanovsky Malyy Pereulok and Zabelina Ulitsa

⑨

Ivanovsky (St John's) Convent

The nunnery was founded by Helen Glinska, second wife of Tsar Basil III, to commemorate the birth of her son, the future Ivan the Terrible. The elated tsarina dedicated the main church to St John the Baptist, patron saint of the new-born child Ivan or John, hence the name *Ivanovsky*.

This convent, like all monastic institutions at that time, was circled with strong walls capable of repelling enemy attacks. When built in the mid-sixteenth century, the nunnery stood inside the royal gardens, which were gone by the time architect M. Bykovsky had rebuilt the main church in the 1870s.

Ivanovsky gained notoriety as the place of confinement for noble women: Maria Shuiskaya, the wife of Tsar Basil IV, was the first lady of noble birth to be so committed after her husband Vasily (Basil) Shuisky was overthrown.

---

*The Jewish Synagogue, The Church of Eastern Orthodoxy, The Roman Catholic Church of St Louis, and the Baptist Church. See 'Moscow of the Clergy', p. 328.

The true identity of the second victim, the ill-fated Princess Tarakanova, was kept secret for thirty-two years. Known to the nuns only as Sister Dosifeya (see Excursion 24, p. 308), the prisoner was the daughter of Empress Elizabeth and Count Razumovsky. The royal origins of Tarakanova were denied during her lifetime. When she died in 1810 she was buried at the **Novospassky Monastery**, the traditional burial grounds of the Romanov family, though even in death her true identity was not disclosed.

But for the ordinary Muscovite, the prime attraction of the Ivanovsky Convent was the notorious murderess Daria Saltykova, a demented noblewoman who served a life sentence for having murdered 138 serfs, mostly young women whom she beat to death for trivial housekeeping mistakes.

...wers of the Ivanovsky (St John ...e Baptist) Convent.

After the great fire that followed Napoleon's occupation of 1812 the convent became a home for widows. The twin towers of the former nunnery and the **St Elizabeth Church** they frame date from the late nineteenth century. The convent is now in ruins, having been used as a prison for victims of Stalin's secret police. It still remains closed to the public.

Podkopayevskiy Pereulok, 5
(10)

The Manor House of Boyar Vasily Shuisky

Leaving Ivanovsky Convent on our right, we turn the corner and descend a few steps into **Podkopayevskiy Lane**. The restored red-brick manor house on the left is believed to be the former summer residence of Tsar Vasily Shuisky (r. 1606–10), a master of court intrigue whose second wife Maria ended her life as a prisoner in the convent. In the course of reconstruction, the seventeenth-century building lost its window mouldings, the festive porch which led to the second floor, and the women's quarters, the *Terem*.

From the crest of the hill occupied by Shuisky's house, one sees the bell-tower and the dome of **St Nicholas 'v Podkopayakh'**, Podkopayevskiy Lane No. 13. The name *podkopai* is a derivative of the verb *kopat*, 'to dig', which suggests that the church adjoined an old quarry. It occupied the site from 1493, although the present building dates from 1750. The church was used by the Patriarchs of Alexandria during their visits to Moscow.

The summer residence of Boyar Vasily Shuisky, whose successful intrigues won him the Russian throne in 1606. His second wife, Maria, ended her days as a nun in the nearby Ivanovsky Convent.

Khokhlovskiy Pereulok, 7

The House of Emilian Ukraintsev

A famous Ukrainian diplomat lived in this house, built around 1655. Although the seventeenth-century exterior is concealed beneath a nineteenth-century facade, three large pillared chambers dating from the original construction are still preserved within.

Emilian Ukraintsev (1641–1708) picked the lane because of its association with his native Ukraine: his neighbours were the *khokhly*, or Ukrainian Cossacks, so named for the long mesh of hair (*khokhol*) which they kept on their otherwise shaven heads. An accomplished diplomat, Ukraintsev protected his personal interest with the same zeal as the three rulers he served. Having started his career under Tsar Alexis Romanov in 1665, he became the head of the Foreign Affairs Department. He was also Alexis's envoy to Sweden, Denmark, and Holland.

Instead of taking sides in the power struggle between Sofia (1682–89) and Peter the Great, Ukraintsev tactfully ceded his post to Prince Vasily Golitsyn, Sofia's influential advisor. This proved most prudent: he reclaimed his job immediately after Peter banished Sofia to the Novodevichy nunnery. Working for Peter, who was given to violent outbursts, had its drawbacks, however. When Ukraintsev failed to deliver a message to the Austrians during the campaign against the Turks in 1696, in which the tsar urged them to rush reinforcements to him, the siege of the Azov fortress was delayed by four months. Confronted by the enraged Peter, Ukraintsev confessed that he had disobeyed orders for fear that the message would be intercepted by the Turks.

To avoid any more similar encounters. Ukraintsev had himself assigned to the court of the Turkish Sultan, where he painstakingly negotiated the Thirty-Year Peace, signed on 3 July 1700. For his success at the Sublime Porte, Peter appointed Ukraintsev supervisor of the royal provision stores. For once

Ukraintsev could not resist. He dipped into the state funds, for which he was knouted and fined. After having to pay for 7,400 cloaks and hats for the Preobrazhensky and Semenovsky regiments out of his own pocket, the impoverished diplomat had to seek a new post in Hungary, where he died in 1708.

(Tserkov Troitsy)
Khokhlovskiy Pereulok
⑪a

The Trinity Church

On the right hand side of **Khokhlovskiy Lane**, hidden by the bend of this steeply rising street, stands the **Trinity Church**, dated 1696. It was built by the prominent nobleman Lopukhin as a memorial to his daughter.

Considering that this period was the height of the Moscow Baroque style, the Trinity Church displays unusual restraint in its decorative statement. Both the square-shaped base and the superimposed octagons that lead to the dome are free of the usual profuse profiling: the main decoration consists of cherubs on tiles by the noted ceramist Stepan Polubes. The bell-tower also dates from the seventeenth century.

For those who want to save themselves steps, a narrow passage which starts below the church cuts through to **Kolpachnyy Pereulok** and emerges in the lane just above No. 10, the house of Ivan Mazepa.

Kolpachnyy Pereulok,
10
⑫

The Manor House of Ivan Mazepa

This austere two-storey manor has a colourful past. It was built by Ivan Mazepa (1644–1709), the conniving *Hetman* or leader of the Ukrainian Cossacks, who is remembered as a dashing cavalier and a ladies' man. Ivan's adventures began at the court of Jan Kazimir, the Polish King. He made rapid strides as a page, even though he was a Russian Orthodox Christian in Catholic Poland, but his career was interrupted when an outraged husband found Ivan in his wife's bed. Mazepa was tarred and feathered, tied to a wild horse, and cast out of town.

...e manor house of Ivan Mazepa.

Mazepa moved to the Polish part of the Ukraine and soon became the spokesman for the Cossacks living along the shores of the Dniepr River. When Ukrainians loyal to the tsar captured him and sent him to Moscow, Mazepa was questioned by Artamon Matveyev, then head of the Secret (Police) Department. Impressing the erudite Matveyev with his quick mind and gift for languages, Ivan became the *Hetman* of the Ukrainian Cossacks, by the appointment of Tsar Alexis, at the age of 45.

Again, complications arose. The contest between Peter the Great and his half-sister Sofia came to a head soon after Alexis died, requiring a quick decision in Mazepa's part. He opted for Sofia, but news that Peter had triumphed reached him when he was *en route* from the Ukraine to Moscow, allowing him to indulge in dramatic demonstrations of loyalty to Peter. The tsar rewarded Ivan with favours and wealth, even taking his side in the Ukrainian's amorous escapade with a 19-year-old general's daughter.

Ivan Mazepa, Hetman of the Ukraine (d. 1709).

The dark-eyed Matrena Kochubey, smitten with the dashing (if ageing) *Hetman*, sought refuge in his house. Her father, the general, appealed to Peter the Great, claiming that Mazepa was guilty of treason. Peter decided in Mazepa's favour and had Matrena's father punished for spreading lies.

Peter erred in his judgement, however. In 1708, when Charles XII invaded Russia, Mazepa, loyal to the cause of independent Ukraine, joined forces with the Swedish king at the very moment when Charles's lucky star was about to forsake him.

From **Kolpachnyy Lane** one can cut through to **Starosadskiy Lane** by crossing the courtyard of the dilapidated **Golitsyn palace** at **No. 6 Kolpachnyy Lane** which once offered the tsars hospitality.

Behind the palace, a flight of stairs leads to another courtyard which opens on **Starosadskiy Lane** just below the already familiar Church of SS. Cosmas and Damian.

Turning right at the church, we come back to **Bogdana Khmelnitskogo** Street and then turn left into **Sverchkov Pereulok**.

Inside the courtyard of Sverchkov Pereulok, 8

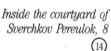

The House of Ivan Sverchkov

The narrow **Sverchkov Lane** bears the name of Ivan Sverchkov, an enterprising merchant whom Peter the Great charged with raising money for building the royal fleet. Sverchkov raised enough money to satisfy the tsar and to commission the **Uspensky Church** (1696–9), which was often likened to **St Basil's** (1696–9) because of its many domes and polychrome appearance. Like most churches in this neighbourhood it was pulled down in 1930.

The recently restored house of the merchant Sverchkov stands in the back of the courtyard, behind contemporary buildings which block it from the street. The manor house is a fine example of a seventeenth-century house, complete with whimsical window mouldings, designs of patterned brick, a crested roof, and all the other attributes of Russian timber architecture. Inside, there are

several vaulted halls and a basement dating from the sixteenth century, indicating a still earlier origin.

At the junction of **Sverchkov** and **Potapovskiy Lanes**, note a small **Empire house** with a pillared facade on your right ⑮. It once belonged to the Princes Golitsyn. We turn left instead and walk down **Potapovskiy Lane**, which leads us to **Telegrafnyy Lane** and the famous **Menshikov Tower**.

(Tserkov Arkhangela Gavriila/ Menshikova Bashnia) ⑯

Church of the Archangel Gabriel (Menshikov Tower)

The Church of the Archangel Gabriel reflects a midpoint between old and new Russia. The tower-like building is the final expression of old Muscovy, with its colourful baroque, and, at the same time, the first monument to be based on clearly classical architecture. Ivan Zarudnyi used Russian tent-type architecture but, rather than superimpose one tier on another, he separated them by curvilinear roofs. The edges are stressed by sculpture decorations, such as the vases above the first octagon, or the ornamental details which outline the curvature of the roof.

Church of the Archangel Gabriel. It was Menshikov's intention to have his church rise above the Kremlin's Bell-Tower of Ivan the Great.

Despite its immense height — originally, it measured 83 metres — the church appears surprisingly graceful and light, as Zarudnyi grouped the heavy ornamental elements (including the enormous *valutas*, which he applied to the western and eastern facades and the colossal porches projecting from the tower) at its lower levels. Particularly handsome is the western facade, where giant scrolls frame the entry's portico and underline the delicate columns supporting it. To lighten the burden of the lower mass, the architect elongated the fluted colums of the porticos, extended the embrasures of the octagons, and marked each vertical detail with a corresponding projection of the cornice.

In decorating the church, Zarudnyi also demonstrated his talent as a sculptor. He treated stone and brick with artistic delicacy and sense, using the pink of the walls to bring out the white of his carved details. The flower

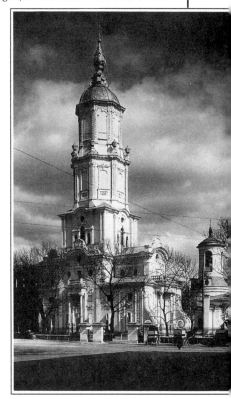

garlands and cartouches enliven the brick with fluidity and movement. The fragments of the interior decorations, such as the elaborate stucco reliefs and the altar sculpture, contribute to the decorative entity of this remarkable church.

Adjoining the Church of the Archangel Gabriel is the **Church of Fedor Stratilat** (*Theodore Stratilatus*), dating from 1806. Both churches are open for worship, administered by the Patriarchate of Antioch. The towering church is also a milestone in the history of the Russian nobility. Its builder, Aleksandr Menshikov (1673–1729), was a vendor of meat pies who became a Prince of the Russian empire. This unprecedented promotion proved that for Peter the Great nobility was a 'quality of the character and of the mind'.

The lifelong friendship between Peter and Menshikov began at the house of Francis Lefort (see p. 145), the tsar's Swiss-born friend and drinking companion. Peter took an immediate liking to Menshikov and enrolled him in the Preobrazhensky Regiment, in which Menshikov doubled as the tsar's orderly and aide-de-camp. Peter valued Menshikov's courage in battle, his quick mind, and his infectious gaiety; Menshikov never spared himself in advancing the cause of westernizing Russia and thought of himself as Peter's creation — 'a fledgling of Peter's nest'. This did not prevent Menshikov, however, from feathering his own nest: during his years of service, he amassed tens of millions of roubles.

The son of a stable boy, Aleksandr Menshikov (1673–1729) thought of himself as Peter the Great's creation and a 'fledgling' of Peter's nest. For his loyal service to the emperor, Menshikov was made a prince in 1707.

By 1699, Menshikov was sufficiently rich to buy a large property near the present **Kirov Gates** and to commission the Church of St Gabriel, which he wished to rise above the Bell-tower of Ivan the Great in the Kremlin. Zarudnyi complied with Menshikov's request, adding yet another tent to the tall body of the church and affixing to it a tall spire with a copper statue of an angel. The building was completed in 1707 and exceeded its Kremlin rival by 1.7 metres.

Fifteen years later, the Church of the Archangel Gabriel was struck by lightning. As Muscovites watched the flames envelop the copper angel and attack the upper reaches of the tower, no one moved to extinguish the blaze. They saw it as the sign of God's displeasure with the arrogant favourite ('the overbearing Goliath') of the tsar. Although these predictions seemed unfounded at first — after Peter's death in 1725, Menshikov gained even more power as advisor to his widow, Catherine I — his days were numbered. No sooner did Catherine die than the generalissimo, prince, and member of the Supreme Privy Council was accused of treason and exiled to Siberia, where he died in 1729. The copper angel and the upper tier of the Menshikov Tower were never rebuilt: a twisted cupola now graces the top of the church. The Church of Archangel Gabriel was never again to rival the Bell-tower of Ivan the Great.

Excursion 9

THE FLEDGLINGS OF PETER'S NEST

Lefortovo: The 'German Suburb' — Menshikov Palace — The House of Anna Mons — The Palace of Count Bestuzhev-Riumin — Palace of Fedor Golovin (Yekaterinskiy Palace) — Church of SS. Peter and Paul — The Military Hospital.

***P*eter the Great** called his closest associates the 'fledglings of his nest'. Their common bond was 'nobility of soul', rather than rank or birth. As the historian Sergei Platonov put it, 'the principle of individual merit triumphed over aristocratic lineage.' To serve Peter's state, a young man needed knowledge and skills which, at that time, could be acquired only abroad, or in the new Russian educational institutions patterned on those of the West. Every year, talented young men were despatched to Europe to study subjects ranging from shipbuilding to architecture, so that Western education became a mark of high rank, much as the high hats and beards of Muscovy had once been. While some fledglings were members of the Russian aristocracy, others were sons of stable boys or falconers. There were also the parvenus of the 'German suburb', a settlement of foreigners adjoining Preobrazhenskoye, the royal estate where Peter had spent much of his adolescence.

'Lefortovo', the German suburb

The 'German Suburb', which drew the 18-year-old Peter, was established in 1652. His father, **Tsar Alexis Romanov**, had granted foreigners land on the banks of the Yauza River in north-eastern Moscow. During Peter's youth, this was an international colony of some 30,000 Western Europeans known as *nemtsy*, or mutes — a word later used to mean Germans. Actually, the settlement included very few Germans: most of the residents were Dutch, English, and Scots fleeing from the persecutions of Oliver Cromwell. They came to Russia to join the army, or as professional men: doctors, pharmacists, merchants, or schoolmasters.

The self-contained Western European town extended from the present **Baumanskaya Street** down to the left shore of the **Yauza River**. The quadrangle was bordered by **Radio Street** (formerly **Voznesenskaya**) and **Krasnokazarmennaya Street** in the south and **Soldatskaya** and **Gospitalnaya Streets** in the north. The wide, straight avenues were lined with stately houses boasting columns and cornices, European-type gardens, and reflecting pools. The sizes of the houses and their gardens were determined by the rank of the occupant and the value of his service to the crown.

The residents of 'German Town' wore foreign-made clothing and ordered their books and magazines from the West. They entertained themselves with concerts, balls, and picnics, drank alcohol, smoked tobacco, and generally kept themselves amused to the abhorrence and criticism of the Patriarch Joachim (1674–90).

Two men from the German suburb played a decisive role in the life of the orphaned Peter the Great, who after his father's death was left to his own

EXCURSION 9

Excursion Plan 9
The Fledglings of
Peter's Nest

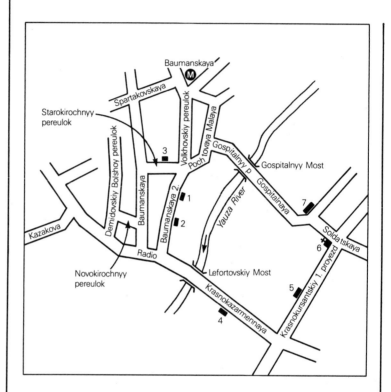

1. Lefortovo or Menshikov Palace
2. Palace of Count Bestuzhev-Riumin
3. House of Anna Mons
4. Krasnokazarmennye Military Barracks
5. Palace of Fedor Golovin/Yekaterinskiy Palace
6. Church of SS. Peter and Paul
7. Military Hospital

devices. One was **Karsten Brandt**, a Dutch carpenter who taught Peter the
principles of shipbuilding. The Scottish-born **Patrick Gordon**, a soldier of
fortune who attained a general's rank in the Russian army, was the second.
Gordon helped Peter train his 'mock regiments' drafted from the royal entourage.
Sofia, who saw no harm in Peter's hobbies, obligingly provided weapons and
ammunition. Little did she know that in the final contest for power, the
professionally-trained 'toy' soldiers would topple her from power in 1689.

The power struggle with **Sofia** crystallized Peter's decision to remove the
seat of government from the Kremlin, full of hateful memories of her plots.

Out of respect for the Patriarch, Peter postponed his decision until the prelate died. He then moved his headquarters to the German Suburb, where he met **Francis Lefort**, the future mentor of his 'fledglings'. The German Suburb was renamed **Lefortovo** after him.

Baumanskaya (2.)
Ulitsa, 1
①

Lefortovo or Menshikov Palace

The palace which Peter the Great commissioned for Francis Lefort was executed by the architect D. V. Aksamitov between 1697 and 1699. The original palace was asymmetrical, with wings projecting from the central building, each part topped by an individual tent-type roof. The Italian architect Domenico Fontana expanded the palace in 1708. He spruced it up with wide stone pilasters and Corinthian capitals and surrounded it with rectangular buildings, creating a massive entry in the middle. The third reconstruction took place in the nineteenth century and made the palace look like military barracks. It now houses the historical archives of the **Soviet Ministry of Defence** and is closed to visitors.

While Francis Lefort (1656–99) was nominally the owner of the palace, he

efortovo or Menshikov Palace
Historical Archives of the Soviet
Ministry of Defence).

EXCURSION 9

145

Above *The fun-living Swiss-born Francis Lefort (1655–90) introduced Peter the Great to the joys of wine, women, and song. In 1697 he helped Peter lead 'The Great Embassy' to the European capitals.*

Peter the Great in his youth.

*Baumanskaya 2.
Ulitsa, 5*
②

managed it as an open house for the members of the 'Jolly Company', a motley crew of Peter's closest Russian and foreign associates. Peter paid for all of the expenses of running the 'club', and took it over for himself whenever an occasion called for pomp.

The handsome, easy-going, Swiss-born Lefort did not mind this arrangement. Until he met Peter, Lefort had a chequered career as a mercenary soldier with loyalty to no one flag or leader. From 1690 on, however, the two men were inseparable. Thanks to Lefort, Peter was accepted by the colony of foreigners and became a welcome guest at balls, baptisms, and weddings; the 34-year-old Lefort also introduced Peter the Great to the pleasures of wine, women, and song and became the heart of the 'Jolly Company'.

Peter appointed Lefort to head his diplomatic Great Embassy, which numbered some 250 men. Its purpose was to visit the West and hire technical specialists. The Embassy set off from Russia in the spring of 1697. A year later the tsar and Lefort were forced to interrupt their mission and return to Moscow to deal with Sofia, who in their absence had incited the musketeers to yet another riot.

Peter made Lefort the admiral of the Russian navy, a responsibility for which he had little training, and then his chief ambassador, a rôle in which Lefort excelled. He died, however, before Peter the Great fulfilled his dreams of building St Petersburg: Lefort's prodigious capacity for alcohol deserted him at the age of 43. Peter sped back to Lefortovo to personally arrange for his friend's funeral, and to attend to Lefort's family, who were left virtually penniless. In this, Lefort was an exception. The majority of Peter's 'fledgloings', particularly the low-born Alexandr Menshikov, whom Peter met through Lefort and who later inherited Lefort's palace, amassed large personal fortunes at the tsar's expense.

The Palace of Count Aleksei Petrovich Bestuzhev-Riumin

Next to Lefort's palace stands a large building which belonged to several distinguished Russian statesmen, including the 'iron chancellor', Count Aleksei Petrovich Bestuzhev-Riumin. It is now the **Bauman Technical Institute**, named after Nikolai Ernestovich Bauman (1873–1905), active member of the Bolshevik revolutionary movement, killed in 1905.

The central part of the building facing the street dates from 1749. The palace was totally reconstructed by Giacomo Quarenghi between 1788 and 1789. The splendid semi-rotunda of the garden facade dates from this period. Damaged by the fire of 1812, the palace was rebuilt for the last time between 1827 and 1830 in the monumental and severe style of late Classicism. Loggias with two columns surmounted by arches divide the walls and are the main decoration of the building's gigantic facade. The centre is enlivened by a sculpture designed by Ivan Vitali.

e Palace of Count Bestuzhev-umin (Bauman Technical titute), 1788–9, 1827–30. The om chancellor' influenced the eign policy of four Russian ers.

Count Aleksei Petrovich Bestuzhev-Riumin (1693–1766) was a worthy graduate of Peter the Great's 'Men of the Empire' school. Educated and trained abroad, he understood the complicated political intrigues of the European courts better than any of his contemporaries. Count, field marshal, and statesman, he served Peter the Great, Anna, Elizabeth, and even Catherine, earning himself the rank of chancellor and the reputation of being the moulder of Russian foreign policy under Elizabeth. Catherine the Great, finding a worthy ally in Bestuzhev-Riumin during those ambiguous years when she was Elizabeth's daughter-in-law, described him as 'tricky, suspicious, inflexible in his opinions, determined, despotic, avenging, and petty'.

Bestuzhev-Riumin was greedy as well. One of the richest men of eighteenth-century Russia, he always wanted more: he accepted bribes from the English king, took money from Maria Theresa of Austria, and demanded loans from Louis XV, only refusing a bribe from Prussia's Friedrich II. Accepting money from Prussia ran contrary to the chancellor's 'system', based on Russia's close alliance with England and a hatred for all things Prussian. The Seven Years War, however, altered political alliances, and found France and England on the side of Friedrich II. Bestuzhev-Riumin's carefully devised 'system' crumbled, precipitating his downfall in 1758 and nearly causing his death. Elizabeth never forgave her chancellor for the disastrous retreat after the Russian victory over the Prussians at Gross Jaegerndorf, which cost Russia 30,000 men and 30 million roubles.

After Bestuzhev-Riumin died, his palace was given to another astute chancellor and favourite of Catherine, **Aleksandr Andreyevich Bezborodko** (1747–99) who ceded it to Paul I. The emperor satisfied his passion for military matters by converting it into a barracks.

EXCURSION 9

*Starokirochnny
Pereulok, 6*
③

The House of Anna Mons

It was at one of Lefort's parties that Peter the Great met Anna Mons, daughter of a Westphalian wine merchant for whom he was to build an elegant yellow mansion with pillared facade and the dignified pediment of the early classical style.

Described as an 'exceedingly beautiful blonde, with flashing eyes and a bold, easy laughter', Anna was exactly what Peter wanted as a mistress. He showered her with jewellery, country homes, and estates, and even promised Anna that he would marry her when he divorced his tiresome wife. The liaison lasted twelve years. Peter did divorce Evdokia and banished her to a nunnery, but he never married Anna: in 1703, he met a simple girl of Lithuanian extraction named Catherine, whom he wed in 1712 and crowned Empress in 1725. Catherine was a real 'trooper's wife' whose earthy sense of humour, loyalty, and ability to soothe Peter's nervous seizures made her as invaluable as the late Lefort.

Anna, in retaliation, announced her intention to marry the Prussian envoy Keyserling. Peter's immediate reaction was to reclaim the estates and the diamond-studded portrait of himself which he gave to his mistress, but he later relented, allowing Anna both to marry and to keep his gifts.

The excursion to Lefortovo continues on the other side of the **Yauza River** which is reached by taking the **Lefortovskiy Bridge**. On the right-hand side is a long block of military barracks* ④ built in the eighteenth century and rebuilt several times since.

Turning left from **Krasnokazarmennaya Street** into **Krasnokursanst-skiy 1. Proyezd,** one comes to a huge red palace which stands on the former estate of Fedor Alekseyevich Golovin.

*Krasnokursanstskiy 1.
Proyezd, 3/5*
⑤

Palace of Fedor Golovin/Yekaterinskiy (Catherine the Great's) Palace

Fedor Alekseyevich Golovin (1650–1706) was the descendant of a noble Greek family which settled in Moscow at the end of the fourteenth century. Always close to the royal court, Fedor was assigned to Peter the Great and though he was twenty years older than the young prince, he participated in Peter's mock battles and the revelries of the 'Jolly Company'. Later assuming command of Peter's real troops, Golovin's extraordinary talent lay in diplomacy. He received his training during the Great Embassy where he acted as Lefort's deputy, and graduated to become Peter's first professional ambassador. In 1699, at the age of 53, he was General-Admiral, and also the first man to receive both the coveted Order of St Andrew and the rank of Prime Minister.

*The original red colour of the barracks gave the street its name Krasnokazarmennaya (Red Barrack Street). From 1866 it housed the Alekseyev Military School. In 1912–18, it was a centre of the Cadet Corps who resisted the Bolsheviks.

One of the lessons Peter the Great learned during the Great Embassy is that medals cost less money than grants of land. In 1698 he introduced the Order of St Andrew, honouring Apostle Andrew, the Patron of Russia, who is believed to have visited and blessed the site of the future Kiev, Russia's first capital. This white and black enamel cross worn on a bright blue ribbon was Russia's highest and most coveted Order.

Architecture

The palace which Golovin built on the Yauza River opposite Lefort's palace has not survived, nor has the palace which Peter the Great erected in its place when Golovin died in 1706. The

enormous red palace one sees today dates from the reign of Catherine the Great. It was begun in 1774 by Giacomo Quarenghi but was finished only at the end of the eighteenth century by Domenico Gilliardi. The palace is famous for its huge Corinthian colonnade consisting of sixteen grey columns. Despite their beautiful proportions, the columns make the palace appear morose, which may be why Catherine the Great chose not to live here. The building stood empty until her son, Paul I, came to the throne. Wishing to eradicate all memories of his despised mother, Paul turned her palace into military barracks. Since 1866, it has been a military school, first housing the Cadet Corps and, later, the students of the Soviet Mobile Units (Tank) Academy.

The garden, which runs down from the palace to the Yauza River, once renowned for its artificial lakes with cascades and whimsical bridges, dates from 1724.

Further down, at the corner of **Krasnokursantskiy** and **Soldatskaya Streets**, stands a tiny white church with five blue domes, which we visit next.

Palace of Fedor Golovin/ herine the Great (Yekaterinskiy ice), begun in 1774 by omo Quarenghi. Now an lemy for the Soviet army's units.

The Church of SS. Peter and Paul

(Tserkov Petra i Pavla v Soldatskoi Slobode)
Corner of Krasnokursantskiy Proyezd and Soldatskaya Ulitsa
(6)

This cheerful church, built in 1711 for the soldiers of Lefort's regiment and dedicated to Peter the Great's patron saints, retained the rectangular plan of the seventeenth century. It consists of a cube-shaped church, a small refectory, and a tent-shaped bell-tower. The interior decorations include a superb eighteenth-century red and gold iconostasis and a number of outstanding icons, dating from the same period. The finesse of their colour and composition suggests the hand of a royal iconographer.

The icon of *Apostles Peter and Paul* occupies the bottom tier of the iconostasis. Next to it is the image of the *Saviour* known as 'Veronica's Veil', which shows only the face of Christ. On the opposite side of the royal gates,

EXCURSION 9

149

we find the historical icon of *Our Lady of Smolensk* (see 'Moscow of the Clergy', Excursion 23, p. 296), and a large icon depicting the *Resurrection*. *Christ rising to Heaven* is shown in the top part of the composition, while his *Descent to Hell* is depicted below.

The *Pochaevskaya Virgin* icon, a type rarely found in Moscow, hangs on the left wall of the church near the iconostasis. The original of this icon, showing Mary and Jesus in Western-looking crowns, was presented by the Countess Anna Gojska in 1599 to the newly founded Pochaevsko-Uspensky Monastery in the south-western Ukraine, one of the few monasteries still to have a theological seminary. This icon is also venerated in Poland.

The full-length figures of *SS. Basil, Gregory, and John Chrysostom*, the three luminaries of the Orthodox Church, are on the icon nearest to the *Pochaevskaya Virgin*.

The chapel occupying the left (northern) side of the refectory honours St Sergius, in whose monastery (see 'Moscow of the Clergy', Excursion 21, p. 280) Peter found safety when he fled from Sofia in 1689. The icon of the saint as he kneels in front of the Virgin, on the pillar nearest the chapel, depicts his vision of her assuring the safety of his monastery, shortly before his death in 1391.

The oldest icon is that of *St Nicholas*. It is on the right side of the church, near the chapel dedicated to *St John Chrysostom** encased in a golden cover which conceals all but the face and hands of the saint. It was rescued from a church which had served as a memorial chapel for soldiers but which perished in the 1930s. The many crosses affixed to the icon may have been donated by the families of the deceased.

Among other icons rescued from neighbouring churches is a composition known as the *Indestructible Wall*, a variation of the *'Znamenie'* icon prophesying the birth of Christ. In both, the Virgin is shown without Jesus. The icon hangs on the southern wall of the refectory.

Turning left immediately after the Church of SS. Peter and Paul, we come to a large building, which occupies the entire block adjoining **Gospitalnaya Square**.

(*'Voennaya Gofshpital'*) *Gospitalnaya Ploshchad, 1/3* ⑦

The Military Hospital

The first hospital that Peter the Great commissioned and the square on which it stands retain the rectangular plan of the German suburb. Designed by architect Ivan Vasilievich Egotov (1756–1814), a student of Matvei Kazakov, the building's composition is similar to that of the **Pashkov House**, the white Baroque mansion opposite the Kremlin (p. 124). Like his teacher, Egotov lived to build facades with shallow loggias, Cornithian columns, and pediments. The inscription inside the pediment reads 'Voennaya Gofshpital', the original name for 'Military Hospital'.

*Possibly the patron saint of Peter's half-brother and co-ruler Ivan (John).

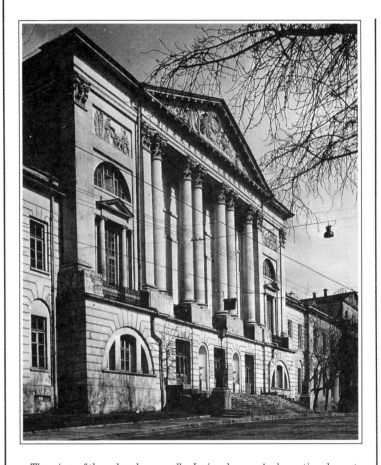

*...he Military Hospital, 1798–1802.
...e military hospital built by
...ter the Great contained Russia's
...st medical school and retained
...e rectangular plan of the
...iginal 'German suburb'.*

The wings of the palace have smaller Ionic columns. As decorative elements (pilasters, semi-rounded Italian windows, G. Zamaraev's bas-reliefs) are concentrated on the central part of the building, the hospital resembles a palace, with its location on the crest of the hill from which **Gospitalnaya Street** steeply descends to the Yauza River accentuating the effect.

Here ends our excursion to the stomping grounds of Peter the Great where, in 1703, he made the decision to move the capital of Russia from Moscow to St Petersburg.

EXCURSION 9

Excursion Plan 10
Elizabeth's Favourites

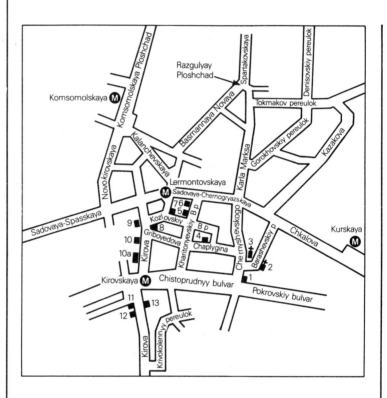

1. House of Razumovsky/Palace of Count Apraksin
2. Church of the Presentation 'in Barashakh'
3. Church of the Resurrection 'in Barashakh'
4. Old Lithuanian Embassy
5. The Manor House at 13/17 B. Kozlovskiy Lane
6. Manor House of the Princes Yussupov
7. Corner house at B. Kozlovskiy Lane
8. House of Baryshnikov and Begichev
9. House of Prince Lobanov-Rostovsky
10. Le Corbusier Building (Central Statistical Management of the USSR)
10a. House of Kozma Soldatenkov
11. The Yushkov Palace
12. The 'Tea House' of Perlov
13. Post Office

ELIZABETH'S FAVOURITES

The House of Razumovsky and the Palace of Count Apraksin — The Church of the Resurrection 'in Barashakh' — The Church of the Presentation — The Manor House of the Princes Yussupov — The House of Prince Lobanov-Rostovsky — The House of Baryshnikov and Begichev — Central Statistical Management of the Soviet Union — The House of Kozma Soldatenkov — The Yushkov Palace — The 'Tea House' of Perlov.

zabeth I (r. 1741–61).

*O*n the night of 25 November 1741, **Elizabeth**, the 32-year-old daughter of **Peter the Great**, led the crack *Preobrazhensky* regiment into the Winter Palace and overthrew **Anna**, Regent to her infant son Ivan VI. The nobility welcomed Elizabeth with open arms and hearts. After a succession of ruling mediocrities and German favourites, the nobles wanted a return to the glorious days of Peter the Great.

Elizabeth, responding to the nobles' yearning for internal stability, put an end to the German domination of the state, and saw to it that power was exercised by Russian-born representatives of the Senate. Although Elizabeth despised paper work, she had a keen political sense and surrounded herself with intelligent advisors.

Internally, Elizabeth's reign marked an upsurge of Russian nationalism and the bettering of everyday life: the draft requirement was reduced, and State banks were set up, enabling the gentry and the merchants to take out loans at six per cent interest, the lowest in Europe. The 1762 decree freeing the nobles from obligatory service to the State, signed by Elizabeth's nephew **Peter III** less than two months after her death in 1761, was essentially Elizabeth's doing.

Unlike her father, Elizabeth loved Moscow and encouraged the nobles to reinstate it as a centre of learning. **Prince Dmitry Ukhtomsky** (1719-74), Moscow's first city planner, founded the Moscow School of Architecture in 1749. Six years later, **Ivan Shuvalov**, Elizabeth's erudite favourite, and the eighteenth-century genius **Mikhail Lomonosov** (1711-65), created the Moscow University. The rivalry between Moscow and St Petersburg nobility took on an intellectual and scientific aspect.

The return of the affluent aristocracy to Moscow manifested itself in new and vigorous building activity, which had been brought to a stop by Peter's ban on stone construction outside St Petersburg.

The few landmarks left by Elizabeth's favourites are in the area east of **Pokrovskiy Boulevard**, near Metro stop **Kirovskaya**.

*itsa Chernyshevskogo,
(corner of Pokrovskiy
Bulvar)*
①

The House of Razumovsky/The Palace of Count Apraksin

While art experts disdain the claim of this green mini-palace to the authorship of Bartolomeo Rastrelli, the Baroque architect and builder of St Petersburg's

Above Count Aleksei Razumovsky (1709–71), the morganatic husband of Empress Elizabeth who shunned honours and to his dying day remained 'a humble servant and a devoted admirer' of the empress.

Right *The Razumovsky/Apraksin Palace (1766–8).*

Winter Palace, and historians acidly deny that Elizabeth commissioned the palace for Count Aleksei Grigoriyevich Razumovsky, whom she wed in a morganatic marriage in November 1742, it could have been built by Rastrelli's student. Enough historic proof does exist to support the romantic notion of this being Elizabeth's quondam love nest.

Architecture

Built between 1766 and 1768, the palace owes its curious appellation as 'the chest of drawers' to the effect created by its many projections. The curved surfaces outlined with columns and sculptured Baroque frivolities do remind one of a French or an Italian commode. The house should be seen from the garden, rather than from **Chernyshevskogo Street**. The central part of the garden facade is three storeys high and rises over the side wings, marked by twin and single columns bearing a large entablature. The corner sections, made to resemble towers, have columned porticoes and broken pediments. The decorative value of the Baroque window frames is stressed by keystones, cartouches, and other such ornaments. The pleasing turquoise of the walls, outlined with white details, accentuates the resemblance of this mansion to the Winter Palace in St Petersburg.

The beautiful voice of Count Aleksei Grigoriyevich Razumovsky (1709–71), the alleged owner of the green palace, led to his first encounter with Elizabeth and his subsequent fame. When Elizabeth heard him sing at the court chapel in 1731, she insisted on meeting him. The prettiest princess of the eighteenth century and the broad-shouldered cossack, who had sung in a country choir before coming to St Petersburg, were never to part: they married, and Elizabeth made Razumovsky a field-marshal, and later a count. With the title came gifts of land in the Ukraine and vast estates in Moscow.

Deeply religious and generous to a fault, Razumovsky stayed clear of palace intrigues. He preferred to patronize Russian and Ukrainian arts and to champion the cause of his native Ukraine. To please Razumovsky, Elizabeth journeyed with him to Kiev in 1744 and later appointed his brother Cyril to be *Hetman* of the Ukraine.

No sooner did Elizabeth die than Catherine the Great dispatched her Chancellor Vorontsev to Moscow, instructing him to verify Razumovsky's wedding documents, under the pretext of wishing to reward him with the official title of 'His Imperial Highness and Royal Consort'. Razumovsky drew the papers from the secret drawer of his desk, and tossed them into the fireplace. Watching the fire consume the papers. Razumovsky reportedly said: 'papers and honours mean nothing to me. I was always a humble servant and a devoted admirer of her highness Elizabeth.'

While Razumovsky's *beau geste* may have saved the family from Catherine's persecution as possible rivals for the crown, Catherine still ordered Elizaveta Tarakanova (see pp. 137, 308), the only child of Razumovsky and Empress Elizabeth, to be jailed at the Ivanovsky Convent, where she remained for thirty-two years.

The Church of the Resurrection 'in Barashakh'

(Tserkov Voskreseniya 'v Barashakh') Corner of *Chernyshevskogo Ulitsa* and *Barashevskiy Pereulok* ③

The **Resurrection Church** at the back of the Razumovsky Palace provides historical support to Elizabeth's morganatic marriage to Razumovsky, which supposedly took place here on 12 November 1742. A crown once decorated the dome of the church in commemoration of this occasion.

Built in 1734, the Resurrection Church is a typical creation of the post-petrine era. Hardly a distinguished work, it is even less attractive after the Soviet destruction of its domes and crosses. The designation *in barashakh* recalls the existence of the ancient *baryshniki* guild which once lived here, pitching tents and preparing bivouac accommodations for the tsars.

The Church of the Presentation 'in Barashakh'

Tserkov Vvedeniya 'v Barashakh') *Barashevskiy Pereulok* ②

This single-domed church, dated 1701 and rebuilt in later years, is one of the few Elizabethan landmarks in Moscow. Perched in the bend of **Barashevskiy Lane**, it is noteworthy as an example of the Moscow Baroque, receiving a Western interpretation, and has a bell-tower showing old Russian forms mixed with Dutch influences.

Turning left at the Presentation Church we follow **Lyalin Lane** which cuts across **Chernyshevskogo Street** to become **Chaplygina Street**. Though the street honours Sergei Alekseyevich Chaplygin (1869–1942), a leading Soviet scientist in the area of aero- and hydromechanics, this narrow lane has hardly been touched by time. There are no remarkable buildings (save possibly the **Old Lithuanian Embassy** at No. 3 ④), but this quaint street provides a convenient link to **Bolshoy Kharitonyevskiy Lane**, which owes its literary fame to poet Aleksandr Pushkin and its artistic renown to the splendid manor house of the Princes Yussupov.

Kharitonievskiy Pereulok
21
⑥

The Manor House of the Princes Yussupov

Most foreigners associate the name Yussupov with Prince Felix Yussupov, the Russian aristocrat who assassinated Rasputin in 1916. Felix Yussupov was also the last owner of the manor house in Bolshoy Kharitonyevskiy Lane, once a hunting lodge of Ivan the Terrible. From Ivan the Terrible the lodge passed into the possession of the prominent Volkov* family and was later given to the Yussupovs, descendants of the Tartar Khans who sought refuge at the Kremlin.

The Yussupov manor house, now the **Institute of the Academy of Agricultural Sciences**, is Moscow's foremost seventeenth-century residence, and possibly the best preserved. The whimsically shaped house was gradually enlarged throughout the years, but never lost its original seventeenth-century character, lacking in other Moscow houses of this period.

The three separate units that make up the palace vary in height, as do the turreted roofs, once decorated with chequerboard motifs. The vivid green facades are further emphasized by white columns, carved window frames, and portals. The palace's turrets and projections give the building its original appearance and create the asymmetrical look prized in old Russia.

The Yussupov manor house (now the Institute of the Academy of Agricultural Sciences): detail of rear facade. It is one of the few preserved seventeenth-century residences in Moscow.

The covered staircase in the back of the house leads directly to the second floor, where it opens on to the unique **Chinese Vestibule**: Dragons glare down from the seventeenth-century vaulted ceiling of what used to be the 'Red Porch', where the host traditionally met his honoured guests with offerings of bread and salt.

The grandest hall in the Yussopov mansion is its **Krestovaya Palata** or **Hall of the Cross**, where guests

*Aleksei Volkov was the ranking secretary at Alexis Romanov's advisory *Duma*.

were received or festive functions held. The hall is fourteen metres high, ending in a chamber vault. The swelling cupola is painted with the signs of the zodiac executed in silver against a dark red background. Below, there is a series of fabled animals, birds and other fairytale creatures painted in gold on a blue background. Bronze portraits of Russian tsars line the shelf along the walls. The frescoes were restored in 1893 by N. V. Sultanov, who reproduced the original seventeenth- and eighteenth-century designs.

The private church of **St Vladimir**, where the Yussupovs worshipped, no longer exists, although the **Portrait Gallery** of the owners is intact.

Passing along brightly coloured corridors, one finds another interesting room on the ground floor of the palace's western wing. The frescoes decorating the four faces of the chamber vault recall the palace's early history. One depicts Ivan the Terrible in a falconer's dress, another has the festively attired tsar surrounded by his nobles and flanked by the white-robed *rynda* bodyguards.

Regrettably, this — Moscow's only genuine seventeenth-century building with intact interior — is closed to visitors.

The Yussupovs are descended from Yusuf Murza (d. 1556) who sought refuge at the court of Ivan the Terrible. At the turn of the twentieth century, the family's fortune was valued between 350 and 500 million dollars. One of the main contributors was Grigory Dmitrievich Yussupov (1676–1730), a close associate of Peter the Great who became President of the Kamer-Kollegia (an office established to manage State revenues), and, finally, the rector of the cadet corps. The man who turned the old manor house into a luxurious palace, furnishing it with marble, mahogany, velvet, and silk, was Nikolai Borisovich Yussupov (1750–1831), the grandson of Grigory Dmitrievich and the 'nobleman' of Aleksandr Pushkin's verse.

...ai Borisovich Yussupov ...–1831). At the turn of the ...ieth century the Yussupov ...e was estimated at between ...nd 500 million dollars.

Pushkin's family occupied the garden cottage of Yussupov's second palace, which stood across from the seventeeth-century manor. In 'I Remember the School of my Youth', Pushkin recalls:

> I loved to listen to the hum of lucid waters and murmuring leaves
> To watch the statuary in the shadow of the trees
> And capture, on their faces, the trace of frozen thoughts.

The other landmarks of Bolshoy Kharitonyevskiy Lane proved as perishable as Pushkin's nobleman. The house of the poet's ailing aunt, described in *Eugene Onegin* ('At last the carriage comes to rest, before the house's gates, in Kharietonievo — inside the lane'), has disappeared, along with the **Church of St Kharitony**, which gave the lane its name. Fortunately, the seventeenth-century house* at **13/17 Bolshoy Kozlovskiy Lane** ⑤ has been restored.

There is an unusual corner house ⑦ in **Kozlovsky Lane**, although it is quicker to take **Griboyedova Street**, which leads off Bolshoy Kharitonyevskiy Lane and ends a few hundred metres later at **Kirova Street**, where we turn left and retrace our steps to the Boulevard Ring.

---

*Possibly the house of Peter Shafirov, an enterprising 'fledgling' of Peter the Great's 'nest'.

EXCURSION 10

Kirova Street

A Soviet writer described **Kirova Street** as being 'a kilometre and a half long and five hundred years old'. The street was first mentioned in 1472, when it became the home of Pskov and Novgorod merchants resettled by the grand princes to Moscow. By the seventeenth-century, however, the butchers or 'Miyasniki' took it over, and gave it its pre-revolutionary name 'Miyasnitskaya'.

Aleksandr Menshikov (see p. 142), Peter the Great's *Herzenkind* and orderly, was the first nobleman to build his palace in this stench-filled neighbourhood. Wanting the visibility occasioned by Peter the Great's use of the street to Preobrazhenskoye and Lefortovo, others followed suit. Before long, the energetic Menshikov had the butchers resettled. A pond, which still exists on Chistoprudnyy Boulevard, was drained and cleaned of slaughter wastes, changing its name from *pogannyi* (filthy) to *chistyi* (clean) in the process.

As we emerge onto Kirova Street, we see the house built for Prince Aleksandr Lobanov-Rostovsky in 1790.

Ulitsa Kirova, 43
(9)

The House of Prince Aleksandr Ivanovich Lobanov-Rostovsky

This two-storey villa is a far cry from the sumptuous palaces of Elizabeth's 'favourites' or Catherine's 'eagles'. Built in 1790 by Francesco Comparesi, it illustrates this architect's individualistic interpretation of Classical orders.

The Corinthian capitals of the columns are endowed with unusual proportions and executed with a touching naïveté. A tall arch resting on double columns marks the centre of the house. Set into a semi-circular arch is a window of similar design.

The house of Prince Lobanov-Rostovsky (1790). Descendants of Kievan Prince Riurik, the Lobanovs were entitled to full honours when visiting Rostov.

The hyphenated part of Prince Lobanov's name comes from the city of Rostov in north-east Russia, which the Lobanov-Rostovskys, the direct descendants of Prince Rurik, sold to Ivan III in 1475. The Lobanovs stipulated that their male descendants be entitled to full honours when they visited Rostov. The last of their line to benefit from this agreement was Prince Aleksandr Ivanovich (1752–1839), the builder of the house, whose subsequent career as a senator and a major-general was less impressive: he was removed from his post as the Marshal of Moscow district nobility by Paul I, who accused the prince of faulty military draft procedures.

Despite his difficulties with Emperor Paul, Aleksandr Ivanovich had a distinguished military record, as did all Lobanov-Rostovskys. Art collecting was their vocation, even in exile: one of the finest collections of Russian Theatre costumes and stage designs is now in the United States owned by a Lobanov-Rostovsky.

Ulitsa Kirova, 42
⑧

The House of Baryshnikov and Begichev

Directly across from the Lobanov-Rostovsky house is another eighteenth-century residence which belonged to several people including Ivan Ivanovich Baryshnikov, a major in the artillery and Colonel Begichev, a close friend of the poet/diplomat/dramatist Aleksandr Sergeyevich Griboedov (1795–1829). Having been cleared in the Decembrist revolt, Griboedov headed a diplomatic mission to Teheran to enforce the peace treaty with Persia (1828), and was the victim of a mob attack on the Russian legation. Shah Nadir presented Nicholas I with a huge diamond in atonement, which is now displayed in the Kremlin's Diamond Fund.

Baryshnikov/Begichev house
7–1802).

This charming yellow house is typical of the noblemen's residences built on Kirova Street at the turn of the eighteenth-century. Designed by the prolific Matvei Kazakov and erected between 1797 and 1802, the house incorporated foundations of a seventeenth-century building.

A superb iron grille, extending from the central gates, links together the side wings and separates the main facade and the formal garden from the street. A well-designed portico attests to Kazakov's mastery.

The reception rooms preserve their original frescoed and sculptured ceilings, gilded woodwork, and columns faced with artificial marble.

This hospitable house of Vladimir Petrovich Begichev (1828–91), Director of the Bolshoy Theatre, was famous for its literary evenings. Pushkin's close friends, poets Kuchelbecker and Davydov came here almost daily while

Griboyedov, Begichev's protégé, was working on the manuscript of *Gore Ot Uma*. The play made a brilliant debut at the Malyi Theatre in November 1831. The 'Hairy' Davydov (see p. 183), whom Leo Tolstoy portrayed as 'Vaska' Denisov in *War and Peace*, argued with the fun-loving Begichev and cracked jokes, while the composer Verstovsky, accompanied by Griboedov, sang his 'Black Stole', a popular song which Verstovsky had just composed.

Another landmark of Kirova Street is Le Corbusier's 'Living Machine' (1933), which now houses the **Soviet Union's Statistical Management Centre**.

(Tsentralnoe
Staticheskoye
Upravlenie USSR)
Ulitsa Kirova, 39

Central Statistical Management of the Soviet Union

Stalin asked Le Corbusier (Charles Edouard Jeanneret, 1887–1965), who was then on one of his visits to the Soviet Union, to propose a reconstruction project for Moscow. Le Corbusier suggested that everything except the Kremlin be razed, and that a new, functional city be built along four huge avenues, which were to start at the Kremlin and run north, south, east, and west. The project struck even Stalin as too avant-garde, though he had done his own share of 'reconstruction' from 1929 to 1936. Le Corbusier's sole contribution to functional living in Moscow was thus the glass and Armenian-tufo structure we see today.

Because he lacked the technical know-how, Corbusier could not fully realize his design for the eight-storey house. He failed to neutralize the double glass walls, between which warm air was to circulate in winter and cool air on hot summer days. None the less, the house is recognized as a major contribution to modern architecture, even if it is a less than perfect 'living machine'.

Ulitsa Kirova, 37

The House of Kozma Terentiyevich Soldatenkov

Dwarfed between Le Corbusier's Statistical Centre and the large corner building of the **Ministry of Trade of the RSFSR**, is the house of Kozma Terentiyevich Soldatenkov, one of Moscow's beloved merchant princes.

Soldatenkov's house resembles Begichev's villa at No. 42, but has lost much of its original decor to nineteenth-century reconstructions. The late neo-Classical columns and pediment are mediocre; hardly anything survives of Osip Bove's original design.

Kozma Terentiyevich Soldatenkov (1818–91) made millions of roubles on the sale of textiles and on his banking transactions, which he conducted from the offices at the Old Gostinnyi Dvor (see 'Moscow of the Townspeople', Excursion 5).

He devoted his spare time to publishing works of young or unknown writers; the windows of his study aglow long after midnight as he planned with them 'some useful, but unprofitable volumes'.

On many occasions Soldatenkov's hunch was correct. He brought out the early editions of writers and historians who became world famous: Turgenev, Ogarev, Kliuchevsky, Granovsky, Zabelin (the historian of Moscow), and others.

Soldatenkov displayed equal zeal in helping young painters, their works indiscriminately displayed along with old masters in the merchant's art gallery. The bulk of Soldatenkov's collection is now at the Tretyakov Gallery of Art, which became the recipient of the Rumiantsev Art Collection (see p. 125), after being nationalized by Lenin. Along with the Rumiantsev Museum, Soldatenkov endowed several schools and Moscow's leading **Botkin Hospital** (Botkinskiy Pereulok 2. 5. Also see p. 136).

Soldatenkov was brought up as an Old Believer and even had a private chapel in his home; this did not, however, prevent him from keeping a French mistress or a smoking den with low oriental divans.

Generous as an art patron, Soldatenkov was frugal with himself and his guests. When someone suggested asparagus for lunch, Soldatenkov snapped back, 'asparagus bites, my friend, five roubles per pound!' He also hated fads. When a fashionable hostess offered Soldatenkov a menu from which to select his meal, he balked: 'If you invite me, spare me, darling, the agony of decision making'.

Kirova Ulitsa, 21
⑪

The Yushkov Palace

The grand style of architecture which once characterized Kirova Street is probably best represented by the **Palace of Yushkov**, who, unlike Soldatenkov spent more money on parties than charity. The house occupies the corner position on Kirova Street, on the opposite side of the wide boulevard.

In the 1780s, after numerous unsuccessful attempts to produce palaces for Catherine the Great, the crestfallen architect Vasily Bazhenov was pleased to accept a commission from General Ivan Ivanovich Yushkov,* a wealthy aristocrat and freemason. The imposing mansion, finished in 1793, is a monumental example of Moscow's classicism. The best-preserved part of the building is its rounded Ionic colonnade which serves as the focal point of two side wings, of which one faces Kirova Street and the other the boulevards.

The wings, particularly those of the garden facade, bear the scars of frequent and careless reconstructions. Still, the surviving corner colonnade, set on a rusticated pedestal above the two lower floors, evokes the former splendour of the palace. Moscow records preserve an account of a three-day ball which Yushkov's son gave in this palace. Its festivities interrupted the commerce of the street, as the crowds listened to music, watched fireworks, and stared at Yushkov's guests.

From 1844 until fairly recently, Yushkov's palace was **Moscow's Academy of Art and Sculpture**. The first artists to paint and exhibit here were the

---

*This Yushkov could have been either a descendant of the Tartar Prince Zeusha, or else came from a rich, crafty merchant 'Yushka', known as the 'Tail Grabber', whose house was turned over to the old English Embassy still on Ulitsa Razina (see 'Moscow of the Townspeople', Excursion 5, p. 90).

EXCURSION 10

'Wanderers', who had broken away from the more conservative school in St Petersburg. The first classes were organized by General Mikhail Orlov (see p. 180).

The **Post Office** ⑬ opposite Yushkov's palace dates from 1912. It replaced an earlier eighteenth-century building, which had stood on the land confiscated from Aleksandr Menshikov (see p. 142) whose **Church of the Archangel Gabriel** still stands behind the post office. The church can be reached by walking down **Telegrafniy Lane** and **Chistoprudnyy Boulevard**.

Ulitsa Kirova 19 ⑫

The 'Tea House' of Perlov

The last thing that one would expect to find on Kirova Street is a neo-Chinese creation, but the building which the architect Roman Ivanovich Klein created between 1890 and 1895 for the tea merchant S. V. Perlov is just that. The flat facade of the three-storey house, designed as a residence and tea shop, has pagoda-type roofs, canopies, lamps, and other pseudo-Chinese details affixed to an otherwise Classical building.

In 1894, Moscow was preparing for the coronation of Nicholas II. Among the invited guests was Lee Hung Chang, the Regent of the young Chinese Emperor. Two Russian tea firms, one belonging to S. V. Perlov, the builder of the tea shop, and the other to V. Perlov & Son, invited Lee Hung Chang to stay with them. The Perlovs' invitation was accepted, though the letter of acceptance failed to specify which of the Perlovs. S. V. Perlov, confident that the regent had picked him, hastened to add Chinese touches to his nearly finished residence, only to be disappointed when Lee Hung Chang chose to stay with the other Perlov on what is now **43a Prospekt Mira**.

The Tea house of Perlov (1890–5). In 1895 Perlov affixed Chinese details to his house's classical facade, but Lee Hung Chang snubbed the tea merchant and chose to stay with a relative of Perlov's.

Another amusing Moscow tale involves Perlov's neighbours on Kirova Street. The childless Kuskovnikov couple lived at No. 17 (now destroyed). Fearing robbery or murder, they slept during the day and spent the nights riding along the streets of Moscow, carrying all of their valuables with them.

Kirova Street evokes many more stories and legends, but most of its houses have either disappeared or been reconstructed beyond recognition by businessmen who spilled beyond the walls of crowded **Kitai Gorod** at the end of the nineteenth century and set up their offices, storage houses, and banks here, in the gentry's former palaces.

CATHERINE'S EAGLES

The Church of St Nikita the Martyr — The House of Count Demidov — the Church of the Resurrection — The Palace of the Razumovskys — The House of Ivan Muravyev Apostol — The House of Vasily Pushkin — The Mansion of Count Musin-Pushkin — Cathedral of the Epiphany — The House of Demidov — The House of the Perovskys — Church of SS. Peter and Paul — The Houses of the Princes Kurakin — Komsomolskaya Square.

*C*atherine the Great ruled the empire with the help of her 'eagles', the aloof and educated nobles whom she enriched through enormous grants of land and serfs. A cultivated woman who corresponded with the leading intellectuals of her time, Catherine also encouraged the nobles to travel, fostered their love for French culture, and patronized the arts. Her 'eagles' became an affluent, privileged class and contributors to Russia's cultural golden age.

The liberal views which Catherine had presented in 1766 to the 565-man Legislative Commission to modernize and codify Russian laws were stunted by the revolutionary developments in France and the United States: Catherine dealt harshly with **Aleksandr Radishchev** (1749–1802) and **Nikolai Novikov** (1744–1818), noblemen who spoke out against serfdom. Although the empress remained intellectually opposed to slavery and harsh punishments, she, like the other sovereigns of her time, felt compelled to fall back on regimentation.

More and more nobles made Moscow their home during Catherine's reign. Having fulfilled their State obligations in St Petersburg as military leaders or government officials, they could abandon themselves to a life of leisure. Moscow's lavish dinners became legendary, as did the intellectual debates of the **English Club** (see 'Moscow of the Townspeople', Excursion 6, p. 99) and the performances of the serf theatres.

The informal way of life which had characterized Elizabeth's favourites was replaced by Catherine's orderliness and refinement. Russian architects, sensitive to the change, adopted a Classicism more attuned to Catherine's tastes in place of Elizabeth's Baroque.

A number of classical mansions and churches built by Catherine's 'eagles', grace the **New** and **Old** (now **Karl Marx**) **Basmannaya Streets** which form the side of an equilateral triangle whose summit is **Razgulyay Square** and whose broad base is formed by the **Sadovoye Ring**.

The Basmannaya Streets received their name from the local bakers' guilds which supplied the crown with the *basman* breads. As the royal court grew and the 'old' basman guild was unable to supply enough breads, a 'new' basman guild was founded in the 1640s on what is still the New Basmannaya Street (Basmannaya Novaya).

The tsars passed by the bakers' guilds each time they went from the Kremlin to **Rubtsevo**, **Izmaylovo**, or **Preobrazhenskoye**, their out-of-town estates on the eastern outskirts of Moscow. The route followed either **Kirova** (see

...therine the Great II 1762–96).

Excursion Plan 11
Catherine's Eagles

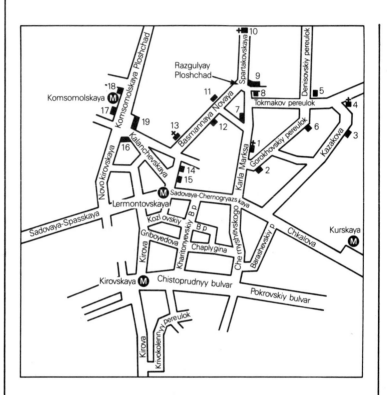

1. Church of St Nikita the Martyr
2. Mansion of Count Demidov
3. Palace of the Razumovskys
4. Church of the Resurrection
5. House No. 21
6. Equadorian Embassy
7. House of Ivan Muravyev-Apostol
8. House of Vasily Pushkin
9. Mansion of Count Musin-Pushkin (Decembrists' Museum)
10. Cathedral of the Epiphany (Yelokhovsky)
11. The Perovsky House
12. The House of Demidov (Sixth City Hospital)
13. Church of SS. Peter and Paul
14/15. Houses of the Princes Kurakin
16. Leningradskaya Hotel
17. Leningradskaya Station
18. Yaroslavl Station
19. Kazansky Station

p. 158) or **Bodgana Khmelnitskogo** (see p. 135) Streets and then switched to the appropriate Basmannaya.

The late resurgence of both Basmannaya Streets as a fashionable residential area accounts for the mostly Classical style of the churches and houses. The **Church of St Nikita** is an excellent example.

(Tserkov Nikity Muchenika)
Ulitsa Karla Marksa, 16
①

The Church of St Nikita the Martyr

This large church is one of the first attempts to introduce Western Baroque to Moscow. Even so, Prince Dmitry Ukhtomsky, who designed the church in 1751, found it difficult totally to forsake the Russian building traditions on which he was raised. This accounts for the contrast between the heavy old-fashioned silhouette of the building, and its Western-looking dome and bell-tower which are closer to eighteenth-century German and Italian prototypes.

he Church of St Nikita the
Martyr (1751), designed by D.
khtomsky, a master builder with
penchant for the Baroque.
khtomsky's students included
zzhenov, Starov, and Kazakov.

Gorokhovskiy
Pereulok, 4
②

The presence of a church honouring St Nikita prompted Nikita Akinfiyevich Demidov to buy the former estate of Prince Kurakin, which was located behind the church.

The Mansion of Nikita Akinfiyevich Demidov

Matvei Kazakov built this mansion in the late 1780s. Since land was plentiful, he extended the wings on either side of the main house, thus creating a huge facade turned towards the street to impress passers-by on **Old Basmannaya** with the owner's wealth and taste. The main portico on six Corinthian columns stresses the central part of the house. The mansion was even more majestic when a wide-arched entry below the columns provided access to the estate.

The **'golden salons'** and **ballrooms**, aligned on a straight axis, are well preserved, and, unlike the Baroque palaces of St Petersburg, do not seem opulent. The delicate carving and the moderate gilding enliven, rather than overpower, the decorations of the rooms. Not coincidentally, there is a similarity between the golden rooms of Demidov's palace and Catherine's palace in Tsarskoye Selo, as both architects — Matvei Kazakov and Charles Cameron — drew their inspiration from the frescoes of the Pompeii palaces, which were then all the rage.

The owner of five metallurgical plants in the Ural mountains, Nikita Demidov (1724–89) owed his fabulous wealth to his grandfather, whose financial

EXCURSION 11

The mansion of Count Nikita Demidov (Moscow Geodetic, Aero-photographic, and Cartographic Engineering Institute).

beginnings are unique, indeed. According to several different accounts, while Peter the Great was visiting an iron foundry in Tula, he asked to have his German pistol repaired and summoned Demidov's forebear, the city smith. As Peter raved about West European workmanship, Demidov acidly remarked that he could make a better pistol. The tsar took up the smith's challenge, telling him that he would shower him with gold if he succeeded — or have his head chopped off if he failed. Demidov was given two weeks.

When Peter was presented with three excellent pistols in a fortnight, he rewarded the smith and made him the manager of the plant. The enterprising Demidov expanded his empire, as did his son Akinfy. Akinfy left all of his foundries to Nikita, his youngest son, considering him the most business-oriented.

The older brothers brought a suit before Empress Elizabeth who decided in favour of the plaintiffs. She redistributed the iron works between the three brothers keeping a large share of the property as payment for royal justice.

Count Nikita Demidov (1724–89). Demidov's wealth and taste matched his generosity. He was one of the main contributors to the construction of Moscow University.

Nevertheless, Nikita justified his father's expectations, expanding his share of the inheritance while his brothers lost most of theirs through bad management. Well educated and widely travelled, he was an honorary member of the St Petersburg Academy of Arts and contributed 5,500 sheets of iron, and money, for the construction of Moscow University.

The mansion is now the **Moscow Geodetic, Aerophotographic and Cartographic Engineering Institute**.

(Tserkov Voskresenya 'Na Gorokhovom Pole')
Corner of Kazakova Ulitsa and Tokmakov Pereulok
④

The Church of the Resurrection

The Resurrection Church in the 'Pea Fields', was built between 1790 and 1793, by Matvei Kazakov, whom the street honours. In the eighteenth century the vegetable and pea fields amidst which stood the Resurrection Church were purchased by two nobles: the field to the right of the church was bought by Cyrill Razumovsky for his out-of-town residence, while to the left rose the Musin-Pushkin Palace.

One or both of Catherine's favourites participated in the reconstruction of the Resurrection Church, notable for its size, and fine proportions. The massive rotunda, crowned by a cupola, rests on a white stone colonnade. From the west, the building was extended by the addition of a refectory and a bell-tower with a tall spire. Set on the crest of a hill above the Chechera River (now in an underground pipe) the Resurrection Church provided a focal point for three intersecting streets.

Ulitsa Kazakova, 18
③

The Razumovsky Palace

This sprawling mansion, now the **Institute of Physical Culture**, is one of the best-preserved nests of Catherine's 'eagles'. Originally considered the work of Matvei Kazakov, Soviet art specialists now date its construction to 1800 or 1803, and attribute it to Nikolai Aleksandrovich Lvov (1751–1804), an architect who contributed greatly to the evolution of the classical style in Russia.

Architecture

When first built, the estate consisted of the main house with short rounded wings and separate side buildings which Lvov placed close to the street. In 1842, Afanasy Grigoriyev, a famous architect of the so-called Moscow 'Empire' style, was asked to rebuild the mansion. He linked the buildings together and curved them around a *cour d'honneur*.

The focal point of the palace is its elaborately sculptured, arched entrance set between porticos with double Ionic columns. Ionic columns also support the entablature which starts at the base of the arch and extends on either side of it. A wide staircase providing access to the reception rooms on the second floor follows from there as well.

The ground floor of the palace and the wide wings are brick, while timber reception and living quarters above, stuccoed to resemble stone, reflect the Russian belief that wooden dwellings are healthier and warmer than those made of stone.

Aleksei Kirillovich Razumovsky (1748–1822) inherited the estate from his father Kirill (Cyril), who had received it from his brother Aleksei Grigoriyevich

EXCURSION 11

167

The Razumovsky Palace (Institute of Physical Culture), built between 1800 and 1803 and now attributed to Nikolai L'vov.

(see p. 154), the morganatic husband of Empress Elizabeth. Aleksei Kirillovich, who claimed to be Elizabeth's nephew, spent one million roubles on the palace, ordering logs of entire oak trees and furnishing it with imported mirrors, paintings, and Goebelins. The window sills of the ballroom were lined with lapis lazuli.

In 1778, Razumovsky petitioned Catherine the Great to release him from government service in order that he might 'fulfil his obligations towards embellishing his ancestral home'. The Empress, who was tired of Razumovsky's bragging and suspected him of being a freemason besides, agreed to his retirement. Razumovsky began to devote himself to botany, personally supervising the planting of his magnificent park, and kept his doors closed to Moscow society.

Alexander I (r. 1801–25) and his liberal politics drew Razumovsky out of his retreat. He became Rector of Moscow University in 1807 and Minister of Education between 1810 and 1816. No longer advocating the virtues of West European culture, Razumovsky declared over-exposure to Western influences as harmful to young Russians, and insisted that Russian history, language, and catechism be introduced into Russian schools.

The Razumovsky estate extends to the **Tokmakov Lane**, where we turn left at the Resurrection Church and follow the lane back to **Karl Marx Street**.

Ulitsa Karl Marksa, 23
⑦

The House of Ivan Matveyevich Muravyev-Apostol

The comfortable yellow house, wooden beneath its stuccoed finish, is a well-

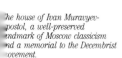

preserved landmark of late eighteenth-/early nineteenth-century Moscow Classicism. Its only ornaments are the six-column portico and bas-reliefs executed in white. The elegant living room, still decorated with frescoes and pillars, was a well-known literary salon.

*The house of Ivan Muravyev-
Apostol, a well-preserved
landmark of Moscow classicism
and a memorial to the Decembrist
movement.*

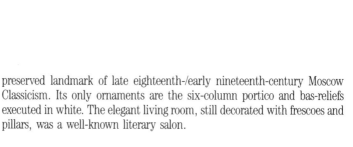

The owner of the house, Ivan Matveyevich Muravyev-Apostol (1762–1810), was a senator, special counsellor, ambassador, and Minister of Education. He also had three sons who participated in the Decembrist (see p. 178) plot to keep Nicholas I from ascending the throne. The idealistic streak which they inherited from their father prompted their disenchantment with Alexander I's latter-year policies and, then, their rebellion.

Lt.-Colonel Sergei Muravyev-Apostol was one of the five key organizers of the Decembrist conspiracy who were hanged on 13 July 1826. Ipolit was wounded and, seeing the rebellion crushed, committed suicide. Matvei, the only one to survive his father, was banished to Siberia. (The house is now a museum dedicated to Decembrists.)

Ulitsa Karla Marksa, 36
⑧

The House of Vasily Lvovich Pushkin

The memorial plaque near the entry of this dark, wooden house announces that it belonged to the uncle of Aleksandr Pushkin a venerable gentleman immortalized in several of his nephew's poems. On 8 September 1826, Pushkin burst in here to tell his uncle that Nicholas I, with whom he had just met for two hours, had pardoned him for his subversive activities. The cautious old gentleman reserved his greetings and, wanting to be assured that his exiled nephew was not in breach of justice, dropped a sentimental tear on his Bukhara

EXCURSION 11

robe only when Pushkin's friends thronged in to congratulate him.

News of Pushkin's pardon travelled quickly through Moscow; he became the toast of the town overnight. The same evening, ten houses away, Emperor Nicholas I recounted his meeting with the poet to the French ambassador, saying that 'Today I spoke with the smartest man in Russia'.

Not far from Pushkin's house is the mansion of Aleksei Ivanovich Musin-Pushkin, also a writer, but not a relative of the poet.

Spartakovskaya Ulitsa, 2
(9)

The Mansion of Count Aleksei Ivanovich Musin-Pushkin

The **house of Musin-Pushkin**, now the **International Building Institute of Moscow**, stands on a small square formed by the junction of **New Basmannaya** and **Karl Marx** streets. It is called '**Razgulyay**', or 'the live-it-up' place because Moscow's first bars opened here, even before Peter the Great lifted the ban on the sale of alcoholic beverages, and attracted, needless to say, throngs of Muscovites.

The noise bothered Count Musin-Pushkin, who had built his palatial establishment on this now rowdy spot. He often complained that he could not enjoy the singing of the nightingales in his park until the last drunk had left. His house still stands, though both bars and nightingales are long gone and only the noise of traffic now fills the street. The rounded colonnade of the original mansion designed by Kazakov in 1780 survived the fire of 1812, while all the rest perished, along with a collection of priceless manuscripts.

Musin-Pushkin (1744–1817) was a typical representative of the well-educated, refined, and wealthy noblemen whom history remembers as Catherine's 'eagles'.

The mansion of Count Musin-Pushkin (International Building Institute of Moscow). Count Musin-Pushkin (1744–1817) was an outstanding historian, archaeologist, and collector.

He was an archaeologist, historian, and president of the Russian Academy of Arts in St Petersburg from 1794 to 1799. Thanks to his father, who headed the Monastery Office which administered church property, Musin-Pushkin had access to valuable manuscripts kept in the monasteries. As a young man, Musin-Pushkin began the systematic collection and publication of manuscripts, including the historic *Tale of Igor's Host* (*Slovo o Polku Igoreve*). Fortunately, he published the Igor tale before 1812, when the fire ravaging his house destoyed the original manuscript.

Musin-Pushkin's collection and his own works were turned over to the

Russian Historical Society, providing the historian Nikolai Mikhailovich Karamzin (1766–1826) with materials for his history of Russia, as well as historical documentation for Pushkin's novels.

Continuing on Karl Marx Street, past **Razguliay Square**, we come to the large **Cathedral of the Epiphany**, now the seat of the Moscow Patriarchate.

Cathedral of the Epiphany (Yelokhovsky Cathedral)

(Bogoiavlensky Sobor 'v Yelokhove')
Baumanskaya Ploshchad 15
⑩

Cathedral of the Epiphany 1837–45), also known as Yelokhovsky' because it once stood in Yelokhovo village. Since the eviction of the clergy from the Kremlin cathedrals, Epiphany is the officiating church of the Patriarch.

This church, built by the architect Evgraf Dmitrievich Tiurin between 1835 and 1845, attests to the decline of Moscow Classicism. It is huge and cube-shaped, with five Western-style domes, the largest of which is at the centre. The bell-tower's first tier, which dates from the end of the eighteenth century, is all that has survived of the original church.

After Patriarch Tikhon was evicted from the **Uspensky Cathedral** in the Kremlin in 1918, the seat of the Russian Orthodox Church moved several times until, in 1943, it came to rest here, at the **Epiphany Cathedral**. The church was chosen more for its size than its artistic merit.

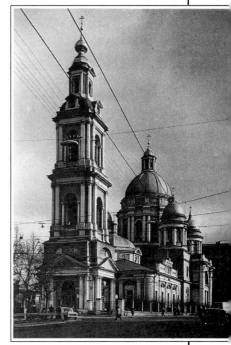

The only relic that the Russian clergy was allowed to remove from the Kremlin was the remains of Metropolitan Alexis, Moscow's fourteenth -century saint. Until Stalin's order of 1930, leading to the destruction of the Kremlin's **Chudov Monastery**, the shrine with the remains of Alexis was kept there. It is now preserved in the Epiphany Cathedral in front of the iconostasis, to the right of the royal doors.

Now that the Uspensky Cathedral (p. 19) is a museum, the Epiphany Cathedral serves as the burial place of Russian patriarchs.

The **tomb of Patriarch Sergius**, who succeeded Patriarch Tikhon as the head of the Russian Church in 1925, is also at the Epiphany Cathedral and is located in the northern side chapel honouring St Nicholas. Since Sergius's appointment came to the height of the anti-religious campaign, the metropolitan was not allowed to assume the patriarch's title until 12 September 1943, when

Stalin decided actively to seek the support of the Church against the Nazis. Sergius died a year later and was succeeded by the Patriarch Alexis (1944–70).

The Iconostasis and Icons

The iconostasis of the Epiphany Cathedral, whose opulence borders on Roccoco, rests on four sets of double columns carved with a motif of interwining grapes. The order of the tiers is no longer clearly defined, but the iconostasis, as a whole, is skilfully inscribed into the huge interior space of the church.

The icons are mostly nineteenth century. The icon on the extreme left of the bottom tier is a collective representation of all iconographic types of the Virgin. Near the main altar is the revered image of the *Joy to all Sufferers*, an icon of the Virgin thought to be endowed with miracle working powers. Also noteworthy are icons of the *Annunciation of the Virgin*, in the right side chapel, and a famous icon of *St Nicholas* on the opposite side of the refectory where lie the remains of Patriarch Sergius.

The patriarch frequently officiates at this cathedral. The most festive service is the midnight Easter celebration, which starts at 11.45 p.m. and lasts until the early hours of the morning. The candlelit service is enhanced by the choir, whose members include soloists from the Bolshoy Theatre.

Having visited the cathedral, we will retrace our steps to **Razgulyay Square** and take the right fork leading towards the **Sadovoye Ring**. The grey building of **City Hospital 6**, which we see next, once belonged to the rich Demidov clan.

(Sixth City Hospital)
Basmannaya Novaya, 26

The House of Demidov

Even the most devoted student of Matvei Kazakov would fail to discern the master's touch on this bleak hospital, built in 1790. The facade still preserves delicate ornaments, slender pilasters, and the partially destroyed church in the back.

Some guidebooks claims that the bleak hospital was once a palatial establishment of Prokofy Demidov, the wealthy owner of **Neskuchnoye**.* When Catherine the Great needed four million roubles for her Turkish wars she turned for help to Prokofy, the 'cheeky, wise guy', as she called him. Demidov refused the loan to Catherine because she had the authority to whip him, but gave it to Fedor Orlov, one of the five Orlov brothers who brought Catherine to the throne. Overriding Orlov's objections, Catherine agreed to Demidov's conditions: the loan would be repaid on time, failing which Demidov could whip the royal favourite.

Despite the amusing tale, the facts point to Prokofy's nephew Nikolai (*b.* 1773) as the true owner of the house. An heir to his father's foundries, precious metals mines and some 11,000 serfs, Nikolai developed spending habits which outraged Catherine the Great. After she imposed control over her 'eagle's'

---

*Now the **Presidium of the Academy of Sciences**. Built in 1756, the palace boasted a marvellous park with pavilions; since Soviet days — **Gorky Park**.

expenditures, Nikolai promptly retired from her majesty's service.

He travelled to Europe to study mining techniques, which he was later to apply in Russia. Nikolai enhanced his fortune in 1827 by marrying a Stroganoff heiress, and presented Nicholas I with a platinum bullion weighing ten pounds. As an ambassador in Florence, Demidov endowed a museum; the grateful Florentines erected a statue of their Russian *patrone* which still stands in the Piazza Demidov.

The Perovsky House

Basmannaya
Novaya, 27
⑪

The ancestral house of Sofia Perovskaya, a noblewoman who devoted most of her life to planning Emperor Alexander II's assassination, is directly opposite Demidov's estate.

This wooden house, executed in the Empire style and dated 1819, belonged to Countess Perovskaya, mistress of Count A. K. Razumovsky. On 1 March 1881, their descendant, Sofia Perovskaya, masterminded the assassination of Tsar Alexander II.

Built of wood in 1819, stuccoed and embellished with sculptural ornaments, the house is more of a historical curio than an architectural landmark. It was built originally for the mistress of Count Aleksei Kirillovich Razumovsky who bore him several children (known as Counts Perovsky).

Sofia, the daughter of Count Lev Perovsky, who was later appointed governor-general of St Petersburg, was born in this house. Rejecting the luxury and the social whirl of St Petersburg, she became a revolutionary, moving from peaceful propaganda to terrorism. Ironically, the tsar whose assassination she masterminded on 1 March 1881, was the emancipator of the serfs. On the day of his death, Alexander II had planned to sign the document which would have granted Russia constitutional monarchy.

The assassination attempt on 1 March almost failed, as had two previous efforts to kill the tsar, for he changed his route at the last moment. Sofia,

EXCURSION 11

173

however, foresaw this possibility. When the moment came, she signalled Ignaty Grinevitsky, one of her four associates, to throw the bomb which mortally wounded Alexander II. Sofia could have fled, but she decided to share the fate of her lover, Andrei Zheliabov, the leader of the 'People's Will' terrorist party who was arrested the day before. Both were executed on 3 April 1881.

The Church of SS. Peter and Paul

(Tserkov Petra i Pavla)
Basmannaya Novaya, 11
⑬

Peter the Great commissioned this church honouring his patron saints. Its architecture reflects his experimentation with the West: although the placement of an octagonal tower on a square base goes back to traditional seventeenth-century architecture, Peter also used Classical pilasters (betraying a lack of familiarity with their placement and distribution), semi-circular pediments, and a cone-shaped spire crowning the church. The influence probably came from Holland, where Peter had seen similar spires.

The church was finished in 1744 by Karl Blank, who added the large bell-tower. Its heavy proportions and details overwhelm the rest of the eighteenth-century church. Also of note is the fine eighteenth-century iron grille, taken from another church.

The last two interesting houses on **New Basmannaya Street** belonged to the Princes Kurakin, who displeased Catherine by befriending her son, Paul I.

The Houses of the Princes Kurakin

Basmannaya Novaya, 4 and 6
(14/15)

Shortly before he died in 1727, Prince Boris Ivanovich Kurakin, related through marriage to Peter the Great,* vowed to build an almshouse for destitute soldiers. His son, Aleksandr Borisovich (1697–1749), carried out his father's last wish. He donated part of his estate for the building of an almshouse and the Church of St Nicholas, which perished in the 1930s. The Kurakin Almshouse, finished in 1742, became the first of many such charitable institutions built by the Russian aristocracy in Moscow.

Next to the Almshouse, Kurakin commissioned a three-storey palace for himself at **No. 6 Basmannaya Novaya**. The first storey has now sunk below the street. The architectural details of the upper floors appear simplified and naive. Only Kurakin's coat-of-arms and haut-reliefs decorating the pediment and the sections above the second-storey windows attest to its former glory.

Two Kurakins were worthy of the title 'Diamond Prince': both were wealthy, both were named Aleksandr Borisovich, and both served as ambassadors in France.

The 'Diamond Prince' was probably the builder of the palace, for he was a passionate lover of the sparkling stones, which embellished his fingers, shoes,

*He married the sister of Peter's first wife, Evdokva.

and waistcoats. He studied abroad, served as the Lord of the Equerry, and was sent as a diplomat to France by Peter II. His grandson Aleksandr (1752–1818) had fewer chances to flash his diamonds, because he spent years in exile at his country estate, a punishment Catherine the Great imposed on him for befriending her son, Paul I.

After being brought back to St Petersburg by Alexander I, Prince Kurakin wrote a treatise on the liberation of serfs, and was a staunch supporter of Alexander's early reforms. As an ambassador in France, the younger Kurakin had the foresight to warn the emperor of Napoleon's plans to attack Russia.

For those who still have energy and appreciate good early-twentieth-century architecture, we suggest a visit to the **Komsomolskaya Square**, known as the Square of the Three Railway Stations.

The tall building rising near the junction of the **Sadovoye Ring** with **Kalanchevskaya Street** is another of Stalin's twenty-eight-storeyed wedding cakes, the **Leningradskaya Hotel** ⑯. We follow Kalanchevskaya Street to **Komsomolskaya Square**. The right side of the square is dominated by the red brick **Kazansky Station** ⑲, which the architect Aleksei Viktorovich Shchusev began in 1913 and finished in 1926. Shchusev relied extensively on old Russian building styles, including the original Kazan fortress, modelling the main turretted entry to the railway station on one of its towers.

The Kazansky railway station, completed in 1926.

Yaroslavl station, designed by Fedor Shekhtel and completed in 1904.

Compare the Kazansky Station with that of **Yaroslavl** ⑱, completed in 1904. There, the architect Fedor Ossipovich Shekhtel, created a modernistic building which he endowed with fairy-like details.

The third station (**Leningradskaya**) ⑰ from which the trains leave for Leningrad is built in a nondescript, neo-Classical style, hardly reflective of its magnificent namesake on the Neva River, for which Peter the Great and his successors abandoned old Moscow.

PLOTTERS AND PARTYGOERS

The House of Vsevolod Vsevolozhsky — The House of Mikhail Orlov — The Krushchov-Seleznev House (Pushkin Literary Museum) — The House of Lopukhin (Leo Tolstoy Museum) — The House of Denis Davydov — The House of Dashkov, Arkharov, and Naryshkin — The Prechistenskaya Fire Depot — The House of Aleksei Yermolov — The Okhotnikov Palace — The Palace of Andrei Dolgorukov — The House of Aleksei Tuchkov.

> The splendid mansions stand aglow
> In shadow play across the shutters
> Flit profile heads of demoiselles
> And fashionably well-groomed swells.
> *Eugene Onegin*
> Aleksandr Pushkin

*T*he golden age of the Russian nobility ended abruptly with Napoleon's invasion in the summer of 1812, which produced an immediate and sobering effect on the haughty and self-centred élite. For the first time since the troubled days of 1612, the noblemen were forced to think of themselves as part of the Russian people. While the fires set by the retreating Muscovites raged for six days and six nights, the nobles recognized how much the old capital had meant to them.

The Great Patriotic War of 1812, as it came to be called, was won by **Alexander I**, the handsome, liberal monarch whose ascent to the throne in 1801, with the promise of reform, had been greeted with jubiliation. The officers of his victorious army which entered Paris in 1814 shared Alexander's views. Their sojourn abroad and consequent exposure to the ideals of the European Enlightenment made them aware of their obligations, not only to the State, but also to the Russian people, particularly the serfs, whose toil had given them wealth, leisure, and education.

The officers had every reason to believe that their emperor, the Liberator of Europe and the author of the Holy Alliance, would free the serfs and grant Russia the promised reforms. The war and radical changes within Russia, however, altered Alexander's assessments: he granted constitutional institutions to Poland and Finland, but not to Russia.

The Spark that Kindled the Flame*

Outraged, the officers took matters into their own hands. On the surface, life in Moscow went on as usual: well-groomed guardsmen danced with bright-eyed debutantes at the Nobles's Club while elders scrutinized prospective marriage partners for their offspring. Behind the facades, however, secret societies and clubs were springing up in St Petersburg and Moscow. Initially

*Pushkin's dedication to the Decembrists: 'From the spark, the flame will come'.

EXCURSION 12

Excursion Plan 12
Plotters and
Partygoers

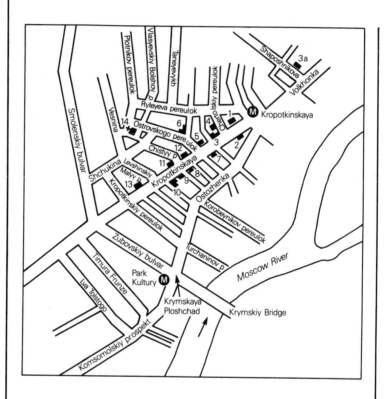

1. House of Mikhail Orlov
2. House of Vsevolod Vsevolozhsky
3. Khrushchov-Seleznev House (Pushkin Literary Museum)
3a. Pushkin Fine Arts Museum (Western Art)
4. House of the Boyars Saltykov
5. House of Dashkov, Arkharov, and Naryshkin (House of Scientists)
6. Mindovsky Villa (Austrian Embassy)
7. House of Lopukhin (Leo Tolstoy Museum)
8. House of Denis Davydov
9. House of Andrei Dolgorukov
10. Tuchkov Palace (Academy of Art of the USSR)
11. House of Aleksei Yermolov (UPDK)
12. Prechistenskaya Fire Depot
13. House of Pavel Okhotnikov
14. Church of the Dormition (Uspenya)

social in character, they became politically oriented by 1818. The most prominent of these, formed along the lines of the German Tugenbund and influenced by the teachings of Scottish freemasons, was the Union of Welfare.

Its members wanted to spread enlightenment, to improve the lot of the serfs, and to limit autocracy. The union split over the future of the emperor in 1821, when one member's offer to assassinate Alexander I was voted down. Alexander's unexpected death in 1825 and the succeeding interregnum brought on the hastily hatched coup of 14 December 1825, which earned its organizers, a handful of élite guards officers, the name of **Decembrists**. **Nicholas I** (1825–55), whom the Decembrists had tried to keep from the throne and from putting an end to their liberal dreams, quashed the revolt. Of the 121 Decembrists brought to trial, thirty-six were sentenced to death. Thanks to Nicholas's personal intercession, however, only five were executed.

The Decembrist coup in St Petersburg failed because it was poorly organized and lacked leadership. But the liberal searchings of the nobility were not a Decembrist monopoly and did not cease after their demise. The example set by the Decembrist inspired many activists, publicists, and writers, including **Aleksandr Gertsen** (Herzen), **Aleksandr Pushkin**, and **Count Leo Tolstoy**, for decades to come.

The Flame that Changed Moscow

The war of 1812 affected the external lives of the Russian nobility at least as much as it did their inner lives. Architecturally, the fire which ran uncontrolled through Moscow, finally contributing to Napoleon's departure, did much to improve the appearance of the city. Destroying some eighty per cent of the buildings, it cleared the way for systematic reconstruction. Under the supervision of the architect **Osip Bove** (1784–1834), the Moscow Building Commission drew up plans to modernize the metropolis.

In conformity with Moscow building tradition, the commission decided on the semi-circular distribution of squares around the Kremlin and the orientation of the main buildings on each square towards the royal citadel. Moreover, private builders were instructed to harmonize both the style and the positioning of their homes accordingly. The recommended style was the Russian Empire, admirably displayed by the mansions on **Kropotkinskaya Street**, named after **Prince Peter Kropotkin** (1842–1921), writer and theorist of 'scientific anarchism'. Such one- or two-storey houses have a portico supported by columns, geometrical decorations, and seven to nine windows; they front directly on to the street, rather than standing at the back of a courtyard.

Kropotkinskaya, previously called **Prechistenka**, came into its own at the end of the eighteenth-century. Its residents were the courtiers of **Catherine the Great** and their heirs, the warriors of 1812 and the plotters of the 1820s. Balls and social reforms, gambling and secret societies, flourished side by side in the beautiful mansions, colouring a way of life described in Pushkin's and Tolstoy's masterpieces.

EXCURSION 12

Kropotkinskaya, 7
②

The House of Vsevolod Andreyevich Vsevolozhsky

Truly representative of its time is this substantial mansion of Vsevolod Vsevolozhsky on **Kropotkinskaya**. Severe, with seventeen windows on all three floors, it bears witness to its nineteenth-century Classical origin. Twelve semi-columns of complicated profile combining Corinthian and Ionic features serve as a link between the second and third storey. The two lower floors are rusticated. Today, the house looks more like an office than a private home because of the reconstructions undertaken in the late nineteenth century when it was acquired by the Moscow Military District. The plaque on the wall commemorates a battle between young White cadets and Red revolutionaries in 1917.

The Vsevolozhkys had entered the service of the Moscow Grand Prince Basil I in 1389. By the end of the seventeenth century, they were immensely rich, owning metallurgical plants, sheep farms, textile mills, fisheries, and lands stretching from Perm to the Caucasus. Vsevolod Andreyevich Vsevolozhsky was the happy heir to these fortunes. Moscow's darling, he gave parties with abandon, and held private dramatic and musical soirées. His son Nikita became the master of ceremonies at the court of Alexander I, ending his career as a senior state counsellor.

Nikita Vsevolozhsky was the archetypal golden youth flitting between Moscow and St Petersburg. Active and ebullient, Nikita participated in *Arzamas** parties but, eventually disappointed by their superficiality, founded the Green Lamp † Club. Pushkin, who had met the 'restless' Nikita during their days at the Foreign Affairs department, recalled these meetings in his 'Adieu, The Son of Happy Feasts'.

Kropotkinskaya, 10
①

Count Mikhail Fedorovich Orlov (1788–1842).

The House of Mikhail Fedorovich Orlov

Count Mikhail Fedorovich Orlov (1788–1842) purchased his house on Kropotkinskaya fourteen years after the Decembrist uprising. Two storeys high and fronting directly on the street, it is smaller than Vsevolozhsky's, but also displays two sets of pilasters with Corinthian capitals. The small balcony over the entry has a lace-like grate. Above, a cornice of patterned brick makes a transition to the roof, and, together with the mouldings of the upper storey, completes the decorative statement of the house. Its present appearance dates from 1886, when the house was acquired by rich merchants.

Before his retirement in Moscow, Orlov was part of Petersburg's *beau monde*. A liberal dreamer and an excellent orator, Orlov was the descendant of one of the five Orlov brothers who helped Catherine the Great stage her palace coup in 1762. Decorated for bravery in 1812, Orlov was congratulated by

*A St Petersburg literary circle named after a town famous for its geese: each *Arzamas* meeting ended with a lavish goose dinner.
†The colour green symbolized hope and enlightenment.

Alexander I for his handling of the treaty negotiations governing the capitulation of Paris in 1814. When he wrote to the emperor about liberating the serfs and received no reply, however, he despatched another, more sharply worded, missive, and was transferred to Kishinev. During his years there as commanding general of the 16th Infantry Regiment, Orlov abolished corporal punishment and taught his soldiers to read and write.

house of Mikhail Orlov. Its *ent appearance dates from* *5.*

Although he was never directly involved in the Decembrist uprising, his offer to march the 16th regiment against the government led to his arrest in 1822. When Nicholas I came to the throne, he pardoned Orlov, but restricted him to Moscow.

Gertsen,* who knew Orlov during these years, observed that he 'resembles a lion in a cage with nothing to do, with no place to move to . . . condemned to live between *Arbat* and *Basmannaya*, having been denied even the right to let his tongue run free'. After buying the house on the future Kropotkinskaya, Orlov devoted himself to art. He started a drawing class which became the **School of Painting and Sculpture**, with its own house on **Kirova Street, 21** after his death in 1842.

Chertolskiy Pereulok, on your right as you pass Orlov's house, comes from the word devil and recalls a devilish brook which once flowed down **Prechistenka**. Also note the restored seventeenth-century residence ④ of the Boyars Saltykov.

Kropotkinskaya, 12
③

The Khrushchov-Seleznev House

The most charming Empire house in Moscow, further up Kropotkinskaya, forms

*Aleksandr Ivanovich Gertsen (1812–70), writer, journalist, philosopher. In 1827, at the age of 15, he took an oath to struggle against autocracy in memory of the Decembrists. Gertsen's house-museum is nearby. **Sivtsev Vrazhek, 27.***

a corner with **Khrushchevskiy Lane**. Known alternatively as the residence of the Khrushchovs and the Seleznevs, it is now a museum housing the manuscripts and paintings of the poet Aleksandr Pushkin. (This Pushkin Literary Museum is not to be confused with the Pushkin Fine Arts Museum: see p. 354). Many of the papers and the portraits relate to the residents of Kropotkinskaya Street. The house itself, furnished and decorated in the fashion of its heyday, gives an insight into the lifestyle of the plotters and the partygoers.

The house is raised on a high rusticated basement with columned facades facing the main street and the lane. The sculptured reliefs, the masks and the locks above the windows are executed with the felicitous grace that earned its builder, Afanasy Grigoryev, fame. Originally built by the retired Captain Aleksandr Petrovich Khrushchov, it was redone by Afanasy Grigoryev in 1814 to repair war damages.

The Krushchov-Seleznev house (A. S. Pushkin Literary Museum). Rebuilt by Afansy Grigoryev in 1814.

A Decembrist in spirit, Pushkin was never implicated, partly because his friends, Rayevsky and Orlov, had managed to keep him at arm's length from the plot, and partly because his tempestuous outbursts against Alexander I had resulted in his exile to the provinces. Nevertheless, he stayed in close touch with the conspirators and dedicated many of his most beautiful poems to them or their wives.

Many lanes in this neighbourhood are named after the former house owners, hence the **Krushchevskiy,*** **Vsevolozhskiy**, and **Lopukhinskiy Lanes**. To the right of the **Pushkin Museum** is the former **Mertvyi Pereulok**, or the **Lane of the Dead** (**Ostrovskogo Lane** since 1937) named after the victims of the plague which ravaged Moscow in 1771. They were buried at the cemetery adjoining the **Church of the Dormition (Uspenie) On The Gravesites (Na Mogiltsakh)** (14), built on the order of Catherine the Great in 1779. Although heavily damaged, it survives, as does the once famous **Zachatievsky Convent**, founded in 1584 as a refuge for the aristocratic spinsters and widows of Prechistenka. Because of the filling station in front of the gutted nunnery, diplomats call the surviving gate church 'Our Lady of Gasoline'. The church is located at the intersection of the **2nd** and **3rd Zachatievsky Lanes**, one block south of **Ostozhenka** (formerly **Metrostrayevskaya**) **Street**. The lack of churches on Kropotkinskaya is not to be interpreted as reflecting the nobility's atheism; the pre-revolutionary Prechistenka had four churches, many house chapels, and the Saviour's Cathedral.

As you pass **Ostrovskogo Pereulok**, note the charming yellow corner

*The lane known originally at Khrushchovsky after A. P. Khrushchov, was renamed to honour Nikita Sergeyevich Khrushchev who lived nearby. There are rumours that the appellation will soon be readjusted.

mansion, an eloquent example of Moscow Empire. It is now the **Austrian Embassy** (6).

(Leo Tolstoy Museum)
Kropotkinskaya, 11
(7)

The Lopukhin House

The house opposite Pushkin's Museum is devoted to the works, photographs, portraits and personal papers of Leo Tolstoy, another Russian literary giant. The small yellow house, built by an unremarkable Lopukhin, is a fine example of the Moscow Empire style. The stucco finish conceals the original wooden building material. The six elegant Ionic columns supporting the portico are also imitation stone. The bas-relief and sculpturing above the window and house itself bears the signature of Grigoriyev, the architect who built the house for the Khrushchovs. The well-preserved interior of the villa, completed in 1822, features grisailled ceilings.

Lopukhin house (Leo Tolstoy Museum).

Though Tolstoy's children attended a school on Kropotkinskaya, he preferred to reside in less-aristocratic districts. During his time in Moscow he chose a quiet wooden house near the Decembrists' headquarters at **Shefsky Dom** (Komsomolskiy Prospekt, 13). That house, with Tolstoy's personal possessions, has also been made into a museum.

The exhibits housed at the **Tolstoy Museum** on Kropotkinskaya provide valuable insights into life of the 1820s. One room, the former ballroom of the house, is devoted entirely to Tolstoy's epic novel *War and Peace*. There are numerous lithographs pertaining to this period, including one depicting the burning of the Kremlin by Napoleon's soldiers. The detailed rendering of the Battle of Borodino, the decisive encounter between the French and the Russian army in 1812, shows the extent to which Tolstoy studied the Napoleonic campaigns. A portrait of Prince Sergei Volkonsky (the Bolkonsky of *War and Peace*), a relative of the writer's mother, is also displayed. Other inspirations for *War and Peace* include Denis Davydov (Vaska Denisov), who lived at **Kropotkinskaya, 17**, and Nastasia Dmitrovna Ofrosimova (Akhrosimova, the dragon lady-referee of proper behaviour), who lived on the nearby **Starokonyushennyy Pereulok**. Begun as a book about the Decembrists, *War and Peace* gradually evolved into an epic about the Napoleonic invasion.

A portrait on the wall to the left of the entry provides a direct link between Tolstoy and Pushkin. Tolstoy saw Maria Gartung, the oldest daughter of the poet, only once, but her classical features changed and inspired Tolstoy's visual concept of Anna Karenina.

Kropotkinskaya, 17
(8)

The House of Denis Davydov

Denis Davydov (1784–1839), the Vaska of *War and Peace*, had a brief and

EXCURSION 12

183

worrisome stay on Kropotkinskaya. The plaque on the door dwells on the memory of the tempestuous poet-partisan Davydov, who bought the house on impulse. An ebullient, much-decorated officer who organized raids into Napoleon's flank, Davydov was captured well in Tolstoy's novel: it is easy to imagine the 'dark, hairy Vaska' purchasing the house on Prechistenka with the same spontaneity as he proposed to Natasha Rostova. Denis soon realized that his funds were insufficient to maintain the princely mansion, and promptly put it up for sale — in poem form — to the Moscow Building Commission. His advertisement ran:

> Help me peddle to the state
> A fancy estate,
> A grand palace,
> My Prechistenka house.
>
> Too restricting for a partisan,
> friend and companion of the hurricane, —
> I, the Cossack and fighting man,
> love houses without windows and halls,
> without doors and brick walls,
> a house for endless outings
> and happy landings.

The house where Denis lived, despite his light-hearted lament is a worthy monument to Prechistenka society. The main building, recessed into the depth of the garden, features two sets of columns on either side of the entry with a balustrade above; the central part is extended by a mezzanine with a rounded window. The left wing no longer exists. The remaining right wing bears the coat of arms of a previous owner, possibly Mrs Arsenyieva who ran a women's high-school here in 1917. The building is now the administrative centre for one of the Moscow city districts.

(The House of Scientists)
Kropotkinskaya, 16
⑤

The Dashkov, Arkharov, and Naryshkin House

The present house reflects the tastes and reconstructions of its many owners. The main facade is partly concealed by a tall fence surmounted by vases and two puzzled lions. The walls are divided by means of vertical flat pilasters with bas-reliefs on the capitals. The pilasters accentuate the rhythmical distribution of the sixteen windows (including two false ones) of the main facade. Above the three central windows there is a triangular pediment, with a lovely sculptured frieze embellishing the cornice. The semi-columns above the windows end in Doric capitals. The side facing **Ostrovskogo Lane** depicts three graces and a chariot executed in bas-relief.

Andrei Yakovlevich Dashkov, the original owner of the house, sold it in 1793 to General **Ivan Petrovich Arkharov**, the redoubtable chief of police under

he house of Denis Davydov, the /aska' of War and Peace.

Catherine the Great. Arkharov was the terror of Moscow, as were his specially trained and personally financed troops, known as *Arkharovtsy*. To this day, *Arkharovets* has a derogatory meaning — a recollection of the undisciplined troops who looted helpless Muscovites during the cholera outbreak of 1771.

In 1829 the house was acquired by **Ivan Aleksandrovich Naryshkin**. According to *babushka* Yankova, Prechistenka's grandmother-chronicler, Ivan Aleksandrovich was 'small, fragile, cute, very polite, and a great hand-kisser. He kept his hair short to conceal his balding . . . and had a strong penchant for diamond rings'.

Naryshkin married Ekaterina Aleksandrovna, *née* Stroganoff, a great friend of *babushka*, who remembered her as a 'large woman of imposing appearance, unsociable and very proud of the family link to Prince Sergei Mikhailovich Golitsyn, owner of the palace on Volkhonka Street, 14.

Naryshkin's younger son Aleksei married Elizaveta Alekseyevna Khrushchova, daughter of his neighbour from Prechistenka, 12. The other son died in a duel with the disreputable Count Fedor Ivanovich Tolstoy, a distant cousin of the writer Leo Tolstoy. Since duels were forbidden, Tolstoy took a hasty trip to the United States, which earned him the nickname 'the American'. After his return to Moscow he devoted himself to his favourite pursuits: women and gambling. In her chronicle, Yankova noted both his dark good looks and his reputation for not settling his gambling debts.

Kropotkinskaya, 22

⑫

The Prechistenskaya Fire Depot

In about 1835, when Yankova moved to Prechistenka, the property at No. 20 had just been split in two. The government got half the plot, turning it into a fire depot that became known for an ingenious method of replenishing its stables: anyone caught speeding on Prechistenka forfeited his horse.

Kropotkinskaya, 20
(11)

The House of Aleksei Petrovich Yermolov

The house which stood at No. 20 before the estate was divided belonged to Pushkin's idol, General Aleksei Petrovich Yermolov (1777–1861). The flamboyant, eclectic extravaganza is now the headquarters of the UPDKa, a Soviet organization set up to provide support services to the foreign diplomatic and business community in Moscow. Its façade is barely visible under sculptured eagles, scrolls, coat of arms, shells and every other conceivable ornament known to the nineteenth-century architects.

The house of Aleksei Yermolov (UPDKa Headquarters).

In ancient Greece, Yermolov would have been the hero of a tragedy. In 1835 a friend wrote that he was enormously tall, 'with a head of a lion and a body of Hercules. His small grey eyes peered from beneath a mane of coarse grey hair. His whole being exuded the lore of undeserved suffering and repressed sadness.' At balls, he wore nothing but black and the cross of St George pinned on him by General Suvorov for leading the storming of Prague in 1794.

Yermolov started his career under Catherine the Great, who despatched him on a diplomatic mission to Persia, but died before she could give him a high government rank. Emperor Paul I, who disliked Yermolov's biting remarks, banished him from Moscow. Unperturbed, he began to study Latin.

Recalled from exile, the twenty-five-year-old Yermolov was said to have exclaimed 'I need a war!' Four years later, his wish was granted: he was sent to fight against the French. Rapidly promoted to general in the war of 1812 for his legendary, savage, bravery, Yermolov was put in charge of the northern Caucaus, which was teeming with Muslim rebels. At the zenith of his career, however, Yermolov's outspoken criticism of the court reached Nicholas I, who relieved Yermolov of command when the Decembrists designated the young

General A. P. Yermolov (1777–1861) Pushkin's idol.

general as one of four candidates to head the temporary Russian government. In 1827 Yermolov returned to Moscow where he purchased the house on Prechistenka. His wife was the aunt of the poet-partisan Denis Davydov, who lived at Kropotkinskaya, 17.

Subsequent occupants of Prechistenka, 20 were no less colourful. The prosperous **Vladimir Dmitrievich Konshin**, a State commercial counsellor, partner in the Tretyakov Textile Factory, and a generous contributor to charity was next.

Then came the **Firsanovs**. Along with the house, Vera Ivanova Firsanova inherited millions from her miser-father, a timber merchant, although when he died no one could find the key to his money box. Despite her good business sense, Vera Ivanova married the no-good Gonetsky. One of their joint ventures was the building of the **Sandunovsky Sauna-Palace** in 1890. But the marriage soon broke up over his passion for horses, wild parties and gambling. Firsanova moved out and her husband, deprived of his wife's income, sold the house in 1899 to **Nikolai Petrovich Smirnoff**, the vodka king.

Eleven years later, **Aleksei Konstantinovich Ushakov**, State counsellor and owner of chemical plants, acquired the Smirnoff mansion. He, too, had a stormy marriage. His wife refused to understand his attraction for the Bolshoy's Ballerina Balasheva. Mrs Ushakova moved to the present house at Kropotkinskaya, which she purchased for 108,000 roubles, while Balasheva joined Ushakov at his house next door. Ushakov spruced up the conjugal bedroom with gilded columns, bronze eagles, and the finest of silks, and emigrated to Europe with his prima ballerina in 1918.

The American dancer **Isadora Duncan**, who came to Moscow in 1921, found the bedroom intact, and decided to share it with her husband, the blue-eyed Russian poet **Sergei Esenin** (1895–1925), adding another tempestuous short marriage to No. 20's history. Isadora believed that her dancing style, devoid of the trappings of classical ballet, would move the Russian people who had thrown off the bonds of the old regime, but her barefoot prancing in free-flowing tunic failed to entrance the working classes. She taught ballet to the children of the Russian proletariat for three years and then left the country. Yesenin traced 'Isadora, I love you', with his wife's lipstick on the dust of their gilded bedroom mirror, and committed suicide a year later. This time he wrote the poem in his own blood:

> My poems are no longer needed,
> And I, too, by your leave, am no longer needed.

Kropotkinskaya, 32
⑬

Okhotnikov Palace

The palace belonged to Pavel Yakovlevich Okhotnikov, a dashing officer in His Majesty's Guard. The romance of his brother Aleksei Okhotnikov with one of the princesses of the royal house eventually drew the attention of the vigilant court, and Aleksei Okhotnikov was stabbed during a theatre performance in St Petersburg in the autumn of 1806. Bleeding heavily, he wrote a hasty note to the princess, who sped to rejoin her dying lover. Okhotnikov kissed her, asked for a lock of her hair, and asked that it be buried with him. Their child, a daughter, died soon after birth. Pavel Okhotnikov resigned from the Guard Regiment and came to settle in Moscow.

The house remained in possession of the Okhotnikov family until 1879. It was sold to the State for 100,000 roubles and became the famous **Polivanov Gymnasium** where Leo Tolstoy sent his children to school. The building, which is remarkably well preserved, is now a musical school. It consists of a main house with two wings and extensive service buildings behind. The facade is tastefully ornamental with its late eighteenth-century Classical attributes: columns, masks, balconies resting on ornamental supports, and the family's coat of arms. The coach houses behind the main building are gracefully curved and arcaded.

The last two houses on the street, often mistaken for one large building, are the adjoining palaces of the Princes Andrei Nikolayevich Dolgorukov (No. 19) and Aleksei Alekseyevich Tuchkov (No. 21). Both are painted in a light shade of burnt sienna. Close scrutiny of the architectural detail reveals where one palace ends and the other begins.

Kropotkinskaya, 19
⑨

The Palace of Andrei Nikolayevich Dolgorukov

Dolgorukov's palace, designed by Matvei Kazakov in 1790, is one of the architect's finest works. After being disfigured by the fire of 1812, it was rebuilt in 1837. A tall portico with Ionic columns highlights the centre, while the Corinthian columns of the second storey loggia appear delicate in contrast. The bas-relief work is ascribed to the sculptor Vitali.

The palace of Andrei Dolgorukov, designed by Matvei Kazakov in 1790. The palace was damaged in the fire of 1812 and rebuilt in 1837.

Andrei Nikolayevich Dolgorukov (1797–1843) was the namesake of Moscow's jolly governor (see 'Moscow of the Townspeople', Excursion 6, p. 105), whilst his son is the 'cautious Ilya' in Pushkin's *Eugene Onegin*. He and 'restless Nikita' Vsevolozhsky of No. 7 were both members of the Welfare Union, but broke from the Decembrists before 1825. While his friends whiled away the days of their exile in Siberia, Ilya (1797–1843) went on to make a brilliant career in St Petersburg.

In 1836, the house was turned into a school. The building now belongs to the **Moscow Military District**.

Kropotkinskaya, 21
⑩

The Palace of Aleksei Alekseyevich Tuchkov

The large and sombre structure which adjoins Dolgorukov's palace was famous for its gambling parties and its art collections. The first collection to be housed here belonged to Aleksei Alekseyevich Tuchkov (1766–1853), the original builder of the palace. Tuchkov was one of the five sons of a famous military engineer who served Catherine the Great. All five brothers participated in the war of 1812. One was wounded at Smolensk, two died in the Battle of Borodino. Tuchkov, who had become a major-general, retired to Moscow and was asked to head the Moscow nobility, a task that he performed with zest.

Tuchkov's true interests, however, were art, architecture, and gambling. His gallery contained a number of European masters, for which he paid a fortune. He also collected houses, which he would level to their foundations and rebuild to his own specifications. With gambling, however, his luck was worse. Losing first his collection, then the palace, and finally his Prechistenka residence, he moved to his country estate, nearly destitute, in 1817.

Count Sergei Pavlovich Potemkin acquired the house from Tuchkov in 1817. A relative of the lover of Catherine the Great, the General was born with a silver spoon in his mouth: he was made an officer of the Guard Regiment on the day of his birth.

He married Elizaveta Petrovna Trubetskaya, sister of the Decembrist Sergei Grigorievich Trubetskoi. Countess Potemkina was a close friend of Pushkin's and stood in for the poet's mother at his wedding with Natalia Goncharova on 18 February 1831. Pushkin, a frequent guest at the house of the warm-hearted Potemkins, dedicated a poem to Sergei Pavlovich:

> When in the twilight [*potemki*]* to Potemkin
> I walk along Prechistenskaya Street
> I hope that the future generations
> Will mention me along with Bulgarin.†

How much work was done by Potemkin and how much by his successors is not known. In 1870, the house belonged to **Dmitry Solomonovich Martynov**,

*In Russian, *potemki* is a play of words with Potemkin.
†Bulgarin was a conceited literary contemporary of Pushkin.

whose brother mortally wounded the Russian poet Mikhail Lermontov in a duel.

Dmitry Martynov was no luckier at cards than Tuchkov. He lost 60,000 roubles to the merchant **Konshin** (Kropotkinskaya, 16). Lacking cash, the loser rented his own house to the winner for twelve years at 5,000 roubles a year.

Ivan Avraamovich Morozov, Moscow's art patron and merchant baron, was the last man to own this unlucky gamblers' house. He lived here until 1917.

A descendant of Moscow's textile kings, Morozov was famous in the West for his superb collection of French Impressionists, featuring Cezanne, Monet, Gaugin, and Renoir. An artist himself, he studied drawing and painting in Moscow and at the Zurich Polytechnikum, returning from Europe in 1892 to attend to the family business and to start collecting art in earnest. Morozov proceeded cautiously, relying on the advice of specialists and personally visiting studios (he visited Matisse in 1908). He also acquired some Russian painters — Korovin, Golovin, Serov, and Vrubel; the two latter lived on Kropotkinskaya, 38 and 4, respectively.

Morozov's closest friend was a fellow merchant and art collector, Shchukin (see 'Moscow of the Art Patrons', Excursion 19, p. 263), with whom he compared notes and occasionally disagreed. The museums were closed to the public, but easily accessible to young artists. Two great modern Russian painters, Mikhail Larionov and Natalia Goncharova, were frequent visitors to these galleries.

By the decree of 8 December 1918, signed personally by Lenin, the gallery was nationalized and opened to the public. Assured that his priceless collection would remain intact, Morozov left Russia.

He had an affair with a nightclub singer, Evdokia, whom he married after the birth of their daughter, but he could never overcome society's refusal to accept his wife. Morozov died abroad in 1921.

His museum was liquidated in 1948; the collection was divided between the Pushkin Fine Arts Museum and the Hermitage. The house proper is now the art gallery of the **USSR Academy of Art**. The first-storey vault, intended for Morozov's valuables, now safeguards the handwritten manuscripts of **Leo Tolstoy**.

The Last of the Decembrists

The heavily guarded **Serbsky Central Scientific Research Institute of Forensic Psychiatry** on Kropotkinskiy Pereulok, 23, opposite the **Art Academy of the USSR**, is a building dreaded by Soviet dissidents. Those who openly challenged the Soviet regime were sent here for 'psychiatric evaluation' and were inevitably pronounced schizophrenics and locked up in insane asylums. Ironically, Professor Vladimir Petrovich Serbsky (1858–1917), after whom the Institute is named, caused the closure of the Psychiatric Congress in 1911 by speaking out against autocracy, though he personally suffered no punishment.

Excursion 13

INTELLECTUALS AND THE INTELLIGENTSIA

Ostozhenka Street — The Mansion of A. I. Derozhinskaya (Australian Embassy) — The House of Varvara Turgeneva — The House of Vsevolozhky and Kireyevsky — The Palace of General Eropkin — The Katkov Gymnasium — Food Depot — The Leo Tolstoy House-Museum.

*W*esterners are apt to call all Russian intellectuals, *intelligentsia*. Yet this term, and the concept of intellectuals bound by socio-political ideas rather than by class origin, dates from the mid-nineteenth century. It roughly corresponds to the appearance in London of **Alexandr Gertsen**'s* revolutionary *Kolokol (The Bell)* magazine. Until then Russian intellectuals were mainly scions of the nobility. They were the heirs of the Decembrists (see p. 179), a handful of Westernized and political secularized liberal dreamers who attempted to bring about political reforms. Their failure, in 1825, produced a generation of 'fathers' aptly described by **Ivan Turgenev** in his *Fathers and Sons*. Grouped in circles around the Moscow University, the intellectuals of the 1830s and the 1840s fought a passionate war of ideas, but abstained from overt political action. Their intellectual searches, influenced by the German Romantic philosophers and the French Socialists, culminated in the historic debate between the 'Westernizers' and the 'Slavophiles' on Russia's place in the world and on the country's ultimate destiny.

The **Westernizers** saw their ideal in the reforms of Peter the Great. They felt that Russia's backwardness should be honestly admitted and that the tsar's methods of imposing Western European models on Russia should continue. The Westernizers differed from one another only on which political structure to adopt, with suggestions ranging from constitutional monarchy to a parliamentary republic.

The **Slavophiles**, by contrast, argued that Peter the Great had departed too far from Russian national traditions. Unlike the Westernizers, they did not rely on borrowed metaphysics. The Slavophile philosophy was based on Russian national identity, the experience of the Russian Orthodox Church, on its ideology and to a certain extent on the Transcendental Idealism of the German philospher **Friedrich Schelling** (1775–1854). What is often forgotten is the fact that Slavophiles were not opponents of Western culture. They considered Russia to be a part of Europe and proposed returning not to some 'peasant Mother Russia', as their critics accused them, but to the Christian roots common both to Russia and Western Europe.

Both schools of thought, however, were equally liberal. Though differing in their views of Russia's past and future, the Westerners and the Slavophiles vied vigorously for the abolition of serfdom. They often worked hand-in-hand to promote local self-government, and judicial, educational, and other progressive reforms which were carried out during Alexander II's reign.

*Gertsen (Hertzen) was an illegitimate son of a nobleman.

Excursion Plan 13
Intellectuals and the
Intelligentsia

1. Mansion of A.I. Derozhinskaya (Australian Embassy)
2. Zaïrean Embassy
3. House of Varvara Turgeneva
4. House of Vsevolshky and Kireyevsky
5. House of Kudriatseva
6. Palace of General Eropkin (Maurice Torez Institute of Foreign Languages)
7. Food Depot
8. The Katkov Gymnasium (Institute for Foreign Relations)
9. Church of St Nicholas
10. Weavers' Guild Workshops (17th century)
11. Leo Tolstoy House-Museum
12. Khamovnicheskie Barracks

The Kremlin: view from the Moscow River. Compare the Renaissance features of the Archangel Michael's Cathedral on the right with the Pskov-influenced Annunciation Cathedral on the left. The neo-Russian style of the adjoining 19th-century Great Kremlin Palace was inspired by 17th-century timber architecture. **Excursion 1**. (Evi Musser)

Above *Izmaylovo: Pokrov Cathedral. The five-domed Cathedral (1671-2) was modelled on the Kremlin's Uspensky, the matrix for all the major cathedrals built within monasteries or royal estates.* **Excursion 3**. (Evi Musser)

Right *Rising above a sharp bend of the Moscow River, the Ascension Church (1532) of the royal estate at Kolomenskoye is a fine example of 'tent-type' churches, patterned on wooden defence towers which one can also see at Kolomenskoye.* **Excursion 3**. (Evi Musser)

Right *House of the Romanovs. In the mid 1850s, while restoring the palace of the Boyars Romanov, Fedor Richter preserved features typical of 16th-century manor houses: the tall basement, the festive 'red porch', and the women's turret or teremok.* **Excursion 5**. (Evi Musser)

Below *The manor house of Averky Kirillov, with its Church of St Nicholas, is one of Moscow's few remaining 17th-century town estates.* **Excursion 7**. (Evi Musser)

Above *The Church of St Antipy 'by the Carriage House'. The builder was allegedly 'Maliuta' Skuratov, Ivan the Terrible's formidable henchman.* **Excursion 7**. (Evi Musser)

Right *Znamenie Church is the city cousin of the circular multi-tiered churches built by the Naryshkins in what is known as the 'Naryshkin Baroque'.* **Excursion 7**. (Evi Musser)

*...ove Once a hunting lodge of ...n the Terrible, the 17th-century ...ace of the Yussupov princes ...plays to advantage the formal ...d porch' where guests were met ...h bread and salt, symbols of ...pitality. It is the best preserved ...mple of a boyar's residence in ...scow and was patterned on ...er prototypes. **Excursion 10**. ...Musser)*

...t Ostankino. The quiet ...nce of the Ostankino palace ...the exuberance of the 17th- ...ury Trinity Church recall ...t Sheremtiev's two great ...ions: his wife Praskovia, a ...er serf, and his theatre. ...rsion 14. (Evi Musser)

Above *The Old Believers' Cemetery (Rogozhskoye Kladbishche): Gate-Tower and Church of St Nicholas.* **Excursion 16**.

Right *Novodevichiy. The Transfiguration Gate-Tower Church (1687-9) exhibits features of the 'Moscow Baroque' in which western features blend with Russian ornamentation.* **Excursion 23**.

ove The Church of St Nicholas 'Khamovnikakh' (1679–82), ...ecting the artistic skills of the ...vers who built it, is an ...mple of Moscow's 'ornamental ...e'. Above the entry to the church ...gs a copy of the miracle-...king icon Helper of All Sinners. **...ursion 25.** (Evi Musser)

...t Trinity: central angel, by ...ei Rublev, 1422–7. The icon ...nspired by the story from ...sis of God appearing in the ...of three angels to Abraham ...arah and was commissioned ...e Trinity Church of Trinity ...us Monastery. (Tretyakov ...ry of Art)

Above *The Church Militant, 1550, commissioned by Ivan the Terrible to celebrate the Russian victory in Kazan. The youthful tsar is shown riding behind the winged archangel Michael. The icon was moved from the Kremlin's Uspensky Cathedral to the Tretyakov Gallery of Art.*

Right *'Of Thee We Sing', Dyonisius, early 16th century. Behind the Virgin stand Archangels Michael and Gabriel. Their halos are outlined against the background of an enormous five-domed church with zakomar arches and green cupolas typical of Moscow churches. (Tretyakov Gallery of Art)*

After the emancipation of serfs in 1861 these ideologically-oriented, predominantly upper-class intellectuals divided themselves into two opposing socio-political camps: *Narodniki* or Populists, and the liberal to conservative *Pochveniki*, who advocated closer ties between the social élite and *pochva*, the grass-roots.

Fedor Dostoevsky (1821–81) reflected in his works the *Pochveniki* view of Russia's special historical role. As the first person to perceive Russia's eventual redemption and renaissance, Dostoevsky anticipated the many horrors and upheavals his country would undergo by abandoning the Christian faith for a godless materialism. In *The Possessed* he vividly depicted the sinister images of Russia's revolutionaries of the 1860s and 1870s.

The Revolutionary Sons

These impatient 'sons' of the mid-eighteenth-century armchair revolutionary 'fathers' demanded radical action. Their ranks were now swollen by the influx of *raznochintsy* — intelligentsia. Having benefited from their education at Moscow and other universities, the sons of merchants, clergymen, and eventually of workers and peasants clamoured for their own place in the shaping of Russia's future. Noblemen and commoners found themselves writing for the same magazines, even belonging to the various factions of the same *Narodniki* movement. This loosely-knit movement embraced a variety of often antagonistic political groups, ranging from democrats and utopian socialists to radical revolutionaries, anarchists, terrorists, and, from 1879, Marxists.* Interestingly, it was the gentry intelligentsia that formulated most of the philosophy of revolution, while action was advocated mainly by the *raznochintsy*. In time, as the various elements amalgamated, there emerged a new type of 'professional revolutionary' as exemplified by **Lenin**, **Trotsky** and **Stalin**.

In talking about Moscow, one is apt to forget that the court and the centre of political and intellectual activity was none the less in St Petersburg. It was in the northern capital on the Neva River, that the best minds and talents of the Russian nobility were placed at the service of the crown. The frivolities and idiosyncrasies one encounters among the aristocracy in Moscow is explained by this very fact. While their counterparts in St Petersburg served their country as State and military leaders, the Moscow gentry engaged in pursuits of their choice.

Ostozhenka Street

The conflicts, aspirations, and gradual impoverishment of the intellectual

---

*By the end of the century the *Narodniki* movement disintegrated and gave birth to two major revolutionary parties: the violently anti-Marxist Social Revolutionary Party and the smaller Marxist Russian Social-Democratic Workers Party. In 1903 the latter broke up into the *Bolsheviks*, led by V. Lenin, and the *Mensheviks*, headed by L. Martov and G. Plekhanov. The Constitutional Democratic Party emerged in 1905 primarily from the *Pochveniki* and other liberal groupings that strove to establish in Russia a constitutional monarchy. The Octobrists party rallied the supporters of autocracy. Such was the political constellation on the eve of the February 1917 Revolution.

Russian nobility are admirably portrayed by the buildings of **Ostozhenka* Street**, whose image as the poor cousin of Kropotkinskaya is as striking as ever: aristocratic palaces on Kropotkinskaya still overshadow the modest Empire houses of Ostozhenka. The first house we see is named after Prince **Petr Alekseyevich Kropotkin**† (1842–1921), the theorist of scientific anarchism.

(The Australian Embassy)
Kroptokinskiy Pereulok, 13

The Mansion of A. I. Derozhinskaya

The present **Australian Embassy** is another masterpiece of the Art Nouveau architect Fedor Shekhtel, who designed it in 1901 for a mysterious woman, known only by her initials and last name. She may have been a mistress of the textile baron Sergei Ivanovich Zimin (1875–1942), the owner of a private opera house in Moscow, who also paid this mansion's bills. Unlike Shekhtel's earlier buildings, it is starkly geometrical, with a tiled façade, enormous windows, and a tower-like projection above the centre: the stress is on the relationship of masses, and not on decorations.

As in his other houses, however, Shekhtel's genius manifests itself in the interior of the Derozhinskaya mansion. Simultaneously functional and aesthetic, it was meant to make people forget life's trivia. The central hall is the pivotal point of the mansion: twice as high as the other reception rooms, it recalls a huge Gothic chapel. Nothing inside the hall or in the adjoining rooms detracts from their airiness. The panelling is light, the lamps resemble clusters of pearls strung on slender threads, and the custom-built furniture blends into the walls. Every detail is functional, and every functional feature is a work of art.

Ostozhenka Ulitsa, 37
③

The House of Varvara Petrovna Turgeneva

Kropotnkinskiy Lane ends at Ostozhenka, where at No. 37 lived the mother of Ivan Sergeyevich Turgenev. This powder-blue wooden house, featuring a pediment and white columns, closely, resembles the crisp eighteenth-century colonial houses in the United States.

The house of Varvara Petrovna Turgeneva, where Turgenev wrote Mumu *in which he portrayed his despotic mother.*

Varvara Petrovna, the mother of the well-known Russian writer Ivan Sergeyevich Turgenev (1818–83), moved from her country estate to settle here in the early 1840s. When Turgenev visited Moscow, he usually stayed in this house, although he hardly shared the views of his despotic mother. Turgenev portrayed her in his short story 'Mumu', which he wrote here and which also took place in this

*The name comes from *ostog*, or grazing lands, which existed in medieval times.
†Kropotkin's birthplace is now the **Spanish Embassy**, Kropotkinskiy Pereulok, 26.

house. In his *Notes of a Hunter*, on which he worked here between 1850 and 1851, the writer masterfully depicted the lives of ordinary peasants. A typical Westernizer, more by nature than philosophical or political conviction, Turgenev felt restless at home and homesick while abroad, spending half his life in France.

Turgenev played an important role in raising Russian prestige abroad. His works were widely translated and became popular in Western Europe, as many of his heroes resembled universal types akin to Lear, Werther, Romeo, and so on, in a Russian setting. Turgenev opened a window to Europe for other Russian writers, particularly Tolstoy and Dostoevsky.

Ostozhenka Ulitsa, 49
④

The House of Vsevolozhsky and Kireyevsky

Timber boards lie beneath the yellow stucco of this one-storey house. It is a typical representative of the Empire style which the impoverished Russian gentry commissioned for themselves in Moscow after the fire of 1812. Six Doric columns support a well-proportioned portico, which ennobles the facade without burdening it. Conversely, the house next door (**No. 47**) looks pompous, decorated with, in the words of the academician Igor Grabar, 'Empire slap-ons' and Ionic columns too heavy for its modest proportions ⑤.

A poor relative of the Prince Vsevolod Andreyevich Vsevolozhsky (Kropotkinskaya 7, see p. 180) occupied this house between 1899 and 1908. Unable to match Vsevolod's grand style, the owner of the house on Ostozhenka signalled his noble birth by decorating the portico of the mezzanine with the family's coat of arms.

Vsevolozhsky bought the house from Alexsandr Bakunin, who, unlike his revolutionary-minded brother Mikhail (1814–76), preferred botany. Here, too, lived Ivan Vassilivich Kireyevsky (1806–58), Russia's foremost Slavophile. He seemed undisturbed by the fact that five houses down resided Ivan Turgenev, his Westernizing antagonist.

Kireyevsky was born in Moscow but spent his childhood at the family's estate in Tula where his personal tutor was the famous Romantic poet Vasily Zhukovsky.

As a child, Kireyevsky was exceptionally gifted. He could defeat adult partners in chess at the age of seven, and had read most of Russian and French literature, as well as speaking fluent German, by the age of twelve. Unfortunately, his acute sensitivity proved a hindrance: after Nicholas I banned an article Kireyevsky wrote, considering it seditious, Kireyevsky published nothing more for eleven years.

Kireyevsky's works, which form the base of the Slavophile ideology, were devoted to the philosophy of total knowledge. Believing that man would attain truth only if it was sought simultaneously with the mind, the senses, and with life itself, he opposed the rationalism underlying the ideology of the Westernizers who, following in the footsteps of French and German rationalists, proclaimed the supremacy of the intellect, often ignoring man's intuitions and

EXCURSION 13

195

the wisdom he gained from life. Kireyevsky, who stressed the need for all of these sources, rejected rationalism precepts as untenable.

Ostozhenka Ulitsa, 38

(6)

Above *Petr Dmitrievich Yeropkin (1724–1805).*

Right *The Yeropkin Palace (1771), now the Maurice Torez Institute of Foreign Languages.*

The Yeropkin Palace

This grand palace (1771), with ten Corinthian columns spanning the second and third storeys, arcaded ground floor and rusticated facade, belongs to a different era from the neighbouring houses. Now the **Maurice Torez Institute of Foreign Languages**, it was built to the tastes of General Petr Dmitrievich Yeropkin (1724–1805), a hero of the Seven Year War and the most admired 'eagle' (see p. 163) of Catherine the Great.

Yeropkin demonstrated his courage when, at the height of the cholera epidemics in 1771, he took over the command of Moscow, which had been deserted by both the Governor General and the Chief of Police. Yeropkin calmed the people, undertook emergency action to arrest the spread of the disease, and ordered new cemeteries to be built outside Moscow's city limits for plague victims.

Catherine the Great decorated Yeropkin with the coveted Order of St Andrew, appointed him Governor-General of Moscow, and presented him with several thousand crown serfs, as well as gifts of money. Yeropkin accepted the governorship and the medal, but declined everything else: he even stayed in his own house instead of moving into the Governor's mansion (see 'Moscow of the Townspeople', Excursion 6, p. 105) and gave the representation allowance to charity.

After Yeropkin died in 1805, the mansion was turned into a commercial

school. A memorial plaque affixed to the wall of the building recalls two people whose lives were associated with the school: the religious philosopher Vladimir Solovyiev (1853–1900), a major contributor to Russian idealism and Symbolism who was born here, and Ivan Aleksandrovich Goncharov (1812–91), who attended the school.

Goncharov, master of the realistic prose of the 1840s and 1860s reversed rôles with the nobleman-dramatist Ostrovsky. Where Ostrovsky had once poked fun at the merchants, it was now the turn of the merchant's son Goncharov to portray in his 'Oblomov' the inefficiency of mid-nineteenth-century gentry.

Another important training ground of Russian intellectuals was the **Katkov Lyceum**, directly opposite Yeropkin's grand palace.

Ostozhenka Ulitsa, 53

The Katkov Lyceum

The green lyceum has somehow managed to preserve its palatial identity despite having been rebuilt, dewinged and crowded by the new overpass for traffic. The white stone statuary now surveys the bustle on the **Krymskiy Bridge** from its third-storey niches, rather than the park they once faced. As before, flat white pilasters with Corinthian capitals accentuate the palace's vertical movement. The building's last reconstruction was carried out by the architect A. E. Weber in 1875.

The palace was commissioned for the Grand Prince Michael, the uncle of Alexander II, and his wife, the German-born Princess Elena, who, like Catherine the Great, became more Russian than the Russians and won their hearts. The grand princess was a scholar, a fervent champion of serf emancipation, and a patron of the arts. When Anton Rubinstein came to St Petersburg, she helped him to organize the first class of the conservatory — in her palace.

Aleksei Alekseyevich Tuchkov (see p. 189), who made a hobby of collecting paintings and palaces, acquired the mansion after the grand prince. He redecorated it to his own taste, only to lose it immediately afterwards in a game of cards. The palace became a secondary school in 1868, honouring the memory of Prince Nicholas, the oldest son of Tsar Alexander II. Mikhail Nikiforovich Katkov (1818–87), an ex-professor of philosophy, editor of the influential *Moskovskiye Vedomosti* and publisher of the *Russkii Vestnik*, periodicals which provided a literary arena for the Slavophiles and the Westernizers, became its rector.

The **Institute of the Red Professors,** the ideological training ground of the revolutionaries, established itself at the Katkov Gymnasium in 1917. Graduates of the institute were automatically accepted into the Central Committee of the Communist Party or offered responsible positions in the State apparatus.

Mikhail Nikolayevich Pokrovsky (1868–1932), the Soviet historian and Deputy Commissar for Education, was the institute's first rector. His original vehement attack on the Russian tsars was revised under Stalin who rehabilitated Ivan the Terrible and Peter the Great. Joseph Stalin was a frequent visitor himself

EXCURSION 13

at the Institute, eager to meet with the students and to discuss a variety of subjects, ranging from collectivization to foreign policy.

Among the institute's graduates were Mikhail Suslov (1902–1982), the hard-line member of the Politbureau; the chess champion Alekhin; and Avtrokhanov, the author of a controversial book about Stalin's death.

After the Second World War, the institute, having fulfilled its task, ceded the building to the élite **Institute of International Relations** which trains Soviet diplomats and other specialists in foreign affairs.

Food Depot

(Proviantskie Sklady)
Krymskaya Ploshchad, 2
②

This white building across from the Institute of International Relations can hardly match the history of the green palace, but it is unique in its own way.

Hardly ever were utilitarian storage buildings designed with more grace than the three white-stuccoed food depots facing **Krymskaya Square**. Vasily Petrovich Stasov (1769–1848) was responsible for the architectural drawings, which were realized by the architect F. M. Shestakov between 1829 and 1831. The depots resembled early Renaissance palaces, the monotony of their rectangular shapes overcome by slight narrowing at the top. Decoration consists of fine geometrical friezes, medallions, and semi-circular second-storey windows. Magnificient wrought-iron gates and sculptures, which link the three buildings, accentuate the simplicity of the overall composition.

On the other side of the overpass which spans Krymskaya Square stands the beautiful **Church of St Nicholas 'of the Weavers'** (see 'Moscow of the Clergy', Excursion 25, p. 320) ⑨ which had among its worshippers members of Leo Tolstoy's family.

The House Museum of Leo Tolstoy

Ulitsa Lva Tolstogo, 21
⑪

Open: 10:00 to 15:00 daily.
Closed: Mondays.

Turning right immediately after the Church of St Nicholas, which is open for worship, we find ourselves on **Leo Tolstoy Street**, formerly known as **Khamovnicheskiy Lane**. Attesting to the presence of the *khamovniki* or weavers is the still-preserved white block-house where the guildsmen spun and embroidered their wares. The **Weaver's Guild House** ⑩ is of simple rectangular construction with small frameless windows and a steep shingled roof.

A few more steps and we reach the unprepossessing dark brown log house which once gave out on to trees, berry bushes, and a wall surrounding the old brewery. Between 1885 and 1901 this was the residence of Leo Tolstoy and his family.

The eighteen-room house, now a State-run museum, preserves the atmosphere of thoughtful reflection and of quiet family life occasionally interrupted by violent scenes of truly Tolstoyan proportions.

The long dining room table is still set for eleven persons, Tolstoy's immediate family. The writer's wife Sofia, sat at the head of the table: Countess Tolstoy was in charge of household activities, payments, and even her husband's manuscripts, which she used to copy. To her left was the youngest son, Vania, and next to him Tolstoy.

The study of Lev Nikolayevich is the main attraction of the museum. Besides the desk, which he bought in 1881 and where he worked on *Death of Ivan Illich*, *The Power of Darkness*, the *Living Corpse*, *Khadzhi-Murat* and *Resurrection*, are mementoes of his other activities. The cobbler's instruments recall Tolstoy's skill in making shoes. A visitor might also be astounded by a bicycle which was given to Tolstoy when he was 67 by the Society of Bicycle Lovers. Bicycling became the writer's favourite sport until he died. Always active and robust, Tolstoy used to get up with the morning whistle of the nearby factory. He then either chopped wood or saddled his horse and took a barrel to fetch water from the Moscow River.

One thing Tolstoy disliked intensely in his later years was any kind of formality. He left entertainment to his wife and children, although occasionally he would listen to Anton Rubenstein, Nikolai Rimsky-Korsakov, Sergei Rachmaninov, and other musicians, who were invited to his wife's tea-parties. These large gatherings took place in the main reception room on the second floor overlooking the overgrown garden which was so dear to the writer's heart. Two objects in this austerely furnished room are of note: the bearskin beneath the piano and a black table cloth. The bear was shot by Tolstoy in 1885. The black table cloth, on which some of the famous guests at the Tolstoy house signed their names in white chalk, was later embroidered by Tatiana Lvovna, Tolstoy's daughter.*

On 8 May 1901, Tolstoy returned to his family estate at Yasnaia Poliana, and stayed away from Moscow until 1909. The last letter he wrote from his Moscow home was the reply to the Holy Synod's announcement that they no longer considered him a member of the Russian Orthodox Church.

The Prophet of Non-Violence

Tolstoy was born in 1828, three years after the abortive Decembrist coup,† on the family estate at Yasnaia Poliana. Feeling honour-bound to share his wealth and knowledge with the masses, he emerged with his own brand of religious populism, even though he felt uneasy about the populist movement leadership. By the late 1870s, he had parted with the radical intelligentsia altogether; for, although his political teaching was essentially anarchist, Tolstoy

---

*Another of Tolstoy's daughters, Alexandra founded the Tolstoy Foundation, a major charitable organization for Russian newcomers from the Soviet Union and senior citizens of Russian descent.

†Prince Sergei Grigproevich Volkonsky (1788–1865), a relative of Tolstoy's mother, was one of the Decembrist leaders, who inspired Tolstoy to write a book on Decembrists. The book evolved into *War and Peace*, but Volkonsky served as the model for Prince Bolkonsky (see p. 183).

opposed forcible revolution. Even as he condemned the State as an instrument of oppression and censured the Church for sanctioning the State, Tolstoy believed that the liberation of humanity would come through the knowledge of truth and through moral regeneration.

The seventh, and successful attempt on the life of Tsar Alexander II confirmed Tolstoy's belief in non-violence, and coincided with a decline in Russian literature. With the deaths of Dostoyevsky in 1881, of Turgenev in 1883, and with his own abandonment of fiction in favour of moralistic writing, the great inspirers of the younger generation vanished. Tolstoy's rationalized version of Christianity, stripped of mystical dogma and ritual, found few followers.

By the end of the century, however, new writers with new ideas began restoring their country's literature. Bleakness and futility became the principal themes of the intelligentsia writers, such as **Anton Chekhov** (1860–1904). The hardships of the proletariat provided another young writer, **Maxim Gorky** (1868–1936), with subjects soon to become the rallying cry of political revolution. **Georgy Plekhanov** (1856–1918), himself a member of the privileged gentry, founded the first Russian Marxist organization in 1883.

The Revolution closed the chapter of the Russian nobles; many of them were driven into exile where writers like **Kuprin, Bunin** and **Nabokov**, to name a few, continued to serve as a link with the few intellectuals who either weathered the post-revolutionary period or miraculously survived Stalin's purges.

Excursion 14

THE OUT-OF-TOWN ESTATES OF THE NOBLES

Kuskovo Palace Museum — Ostankino Palace Museum of Serf Art — Arkhangelskoye Estate Museum — The Curch of Pokrov in Medvedkovo.

Ul. Yunosti 2
Metro: *Ryazanskiy Prospekt*

I. Kuskovo Palace Museum

Open 10:00 to 18:00, May-September.
10:00 to 15:00, October to April.
Closed: Monday, Tuesday.

Monuments

1. The Main House (1769-75) — Blank, Mironov.
2. The Dutch House (1749-51) — Argunov.
3. Hermitage (1765-7) — Blank, Kologvrivov.
4. Italian House (1755).
5. Orangery (1761-2) — Blank, Argunov.
6. Grotto (1756-71) — Argunov.
7. Kitchen Service Quarters.
8. Church (1737-39).
9. Gardens.

*F*rom the sixteenth century, Kuskovo was the patrimonial estate of the boyars **Sheremetiev**, descendants of **Andrei Kobyla**, the founder of many Russian noble families, including the **Romanovs**. The Sheremetievs distinguished themselves as military leaders and diplomats: in one of his celebrated letters to Ivan the Terrible, Prince Andrei Kurbsky, described Ivan Sheremetiev as 'a mighty wise man, foresighted, and from his youngest age skilful in chivalrous undertakings'. Another Sheremetiev, Petr (*d.* 1690), the military governor of Novgorod, had a chance to display his grace by helping a Swedish ambassador whose carriage could not clear the city gates. Sheremetiev first offered his own carriage, and then, when the envoy declined, dismantled the gates.

His son, Boris Petrovich Sheremetiev (1652-1719), hero of the Poltava victory over Carl XII of Sweden, received Kuskovo as an honour from Peter the Great.

The turning point in Kuskovo's history, and the highlight of that social season in St Petersburg, was the marriage of Count **Petr Borisovich Sheremetiev** (1713–1788) to **Varvara Cherkassakava** in 1743. The Cherkasskys were the descendents of the Carabidian Prince Temeriuk and were related to Tsar Michael Romanov. As a dowry, the bride brought Sheremetiev over 60,000 serfs and several estates, including Ostankino, that had been in the family since the sixteenth century. Together, the newlyweds owned about three million acres of land and 200,000 serfs. Among the 1,200 villages on their lands there were some famous textile and cabinet-making industries.

The Sheremetievs commissioned the best architects available to work at

Kuskovo Palace: main entrance.

Kuskovo and trained their own serfs in construction and design. The park, apty described as 'The Moscow Versailles', and the main buildings were started in the 1760s under the supervision of landscape architects Andrei Vogt and Yury Kologrivov (1697-1754), who had spent many years in Italy. Also participating in the project were Fedor Argunov (1732-1768), a former serf and an outstanding architect, and the renowned Karl Blank (1728-1793).

The grandiose palace designed by Karl Blank has not survived. A two-storey house now stands on its site, overlooking an artificial lake. It is an excellent example of the early Russian Classical style and displays the skill of Fedor

Kuskovo: the ballroom.

Argunov in handling wood to advantage. The façade of the building, with a double flight of stairs and a portico supported by double columns, was completed in 1775.

The rooms were decorated with paintings, tapestries, sculptures, and portraits of the owners which were executed by Argunov. The most beautiful room is the **White Hall**, a marvel of mirrors, crystal, and gilding set in white surroundings. In the **Crimson Drawing Room**, a big stove covered with coloured tiles manufactured by Moscow ceramists provides a contrast to the typically Western furnishings.

The garden buildings have kept their original appearance and carry one's imagination to different parts of the world. **The Dutch House** (1749-51), for example, is painted to resemble brick; its interior is faced with glazed Delfic tiles. **The Italian House** (1755) is a replica of an Italian country villa. **The Hermitage**, designed by Karl Blank, captures the spirit of French court life and offers a secluded place for intimate parties. The most famous of all the buildings, the **Orangery** (1761-2), has a two-story hall in the centre and two greenhouses with tropical plants on either side.

The Grotto

The Grotto was designed to give the impression of a water palace rising out of the sea. The wavy outline of the pedestal staircase, the tiered construction of the pillars, and the shape of the dome, all recall Venetian palaces. The warm-toned right-hand cavern is inlaid with Mediterranean shells and exotic underwater plants. The northern cavern, by contrast, is bluish in tone and its materials are of Russian origin.

...uskovo: the Grotto (1760).

The Orangery and the Open-Air Theatre

The orangery and the **Open-Air-Theatre** were the favourite gathering places of the Moscow nobility. Every Sunday and, in later years, every Thursday, the *beau monde* met at Kuskovo to enjoy the concerts and theatrical performances staged by the 250-member Sheremetiev troupe of actor serfs, all trained on the premises of the estate.

The Kuskovo Nightingale

Nikolai Sheremetiev (1751-1809), the son of Peter and Varvara, met his future wife **Praskovia** in Kuskovo, an encounter which gave rise to the Russian

EXCURSION 14

Kuskovo: the Orangery and statue of Scamander.

folk song 'One Evening as I was Driving the Cows from the Pasture'. The song describes how the lord of the manor (*barin*) noticed a peasant girl during one of his evening walks and, struck by her beauty, asked her where she was from — 'Kuskovo', she demurely replied. As it happened, Praskovia Zhemchugova-Kovaleva, the most famous actress in eighteenth-century Russia, had as much to do with household chores as did women of noble birth. From the age of ten, she was a member of Sheremetiev's theatrical company, and her education, conducted by foreign tutors, surpassed that of many of her noble contemporaries. Her voice and beauty won over Emperor Alexander I as well as Nikolai Sheremetiev, whom she married in 1801. To shield his wife from the snobbery of court society, Sheremetiev retired with her to Ostankino (see below), where they spent the happy but brief remainder of their married life: the young countess died during childbirth in February 1803. Kuskovo remains a memorial to her talent and beauty.

Pervaya Ostankinskaya Ulitsa 5
Metro: *VDNKh*

II. Ostankino Palace Museum of Serf Art

Open: 11:00 to 17:00, May to September
10:00 to 14:00, October to April
Closed: Tuesdays and Wednesdays

Monuments

1. Palace and Theatre (1792-8) — Argunov, Mironov, Dikushin, under the supervision of Quarenghi, Camporesi, Nazarov, and Blank.

2. Trinity Church (1683) — Pavel Potekhin. Bell-tower (1877-8) — Shultanov.
3. The Egyptial Pavilion, built as a concert hall, was converted into a banqueting house in the nineteenth century.
4. The Italian Pavilion used as the palace's sculpture gallery.
5. The Park (1793-5).

The museum is renowned for its collection of seventeenth- and eighteenth-century paintings, engravings, carvings, crystal, and porcelain.

Developed and embellished over four centuries, Ostankino now consists of a seventeenth-century church, a late-eighteenth-century palace and theatre, and a magnificent park with groves and ponds. For **Count Nikolai Petrovich Sheremetiev** (1751–1809), Ostankino, like the Taj Mahal, was a labour of love which reflected his two great passions: his wife, **Praskovia Zhemchugova-Kovaleva**, and his theatre. Sheremetiev studied at the University of Leyden and then lived many years in Paris, which he adored and where he befriended the philosopher Denis Diderot and learned to play the violoncello with considerable skill.

Sheremetiev treated his staff of serf-actors with affection and respect; his star singers and dancers all had names like Ruby and Pearl (the latter was his epithet for Praskovia his wife). Each actor and dancer developed his or her talent under the tutelage of Western teachers, as did Sheremetiev's architects and craftsmen. When Praskovia died in childbirth, the count abandoned Ostankino and its theatre. He contributed vast sums of money to the Strannopriimnyi Dvor, an almshouse he build between 1794 and 1804. The almshouse's hospital, now the **Sklifosovskiy Institute**, became a memorial to Praskovia. The Count endowed it with an annual income of 50,000 roubles and left an equal amount for the continued support of widows and orphans.

The Palace

The first plans for Ostankino Palace, which was to serve as a summer residence and theatre, were submitted by Quarenghi in 1794. When they fell short of Sheremetiev's expectations, he turned the project over to his own architect, Fedor Argunov. Under Argunov's direction, the palace grew into a building which combined the dignity of an urban residence with the ease of a country villa. It consists of three parts bound together by one-storey galleries which underline the formal portico of the central building, rounded off by a large cupola. The less-elaborate garden facade gives a majestic appearance by virtue of a loggia-portico supported by ten columns, encompassing the entire second storey. The elegant baulstrades of the porticos, as well as the niches with statues and bas-reliefs executed by F. Gordeev and G. Zamaraev, add to the refinement of the palace. One of the best examples of Russian Classical style, the palace is made of wood; its moulded stucco exterior is made to resemble stone.

Even as it contributes to the impression of a well-integrated architectural ensemble, each part of the group of buildings can also stand by itself. The same is true of the interior, where each hall is a separate work of art. Of particular

EXCURSION 14

interest is the elaborate use of carved wood, which is omnipresent. The characteristically Russian excellence of workmanship in wood also extends to the imaginatively designed parquet floors.

The bright colour-scheme of the halls introduces another feature of Russian art in this Western-style mansion. The ceilings are brightly painted, while vividly-coloured silks cover the walls. Each hall is arranged to display to advantage the art treasures Nikolai Sheremetiev collected. They range from antique statues to paintings of Dughet, Le Nain, Campidoglio, Ciniani, Palamedes, and others.

The Halls

Ostankino: the portrait gallery. For Count Nikolai Petrovich Sheremetiev (1751-1809) Ostankino reflected his two great passions: his wife and his theatre.

The **Blue Hall**, the main room of the northern suite, may have been intended as the guest bedroom for Catherine the Great. The Mahogany parquet floor has a large birchwood rosette. The oval Wedgwood medallions on the loggia wall portray Peter the Great and Catherine II. The most valuable works of art in the Blue Hall are the statues of three Egyptian slaves, exact copies of the Italian originals which Sheremetiev purchased in 1796. Chiselled in grey marble, the statues stand at the Blue Hall's doors.

The **Crimson Drawing Room** is dominated by the portrait of Emperor Paul I (the elaborate frame had been prepared for the portrait of Paul's mother, Catherine the Great, but political expediency and her sudden death made Sheremetiev change his plans).

The **Theatre Room**, constructed in a semi-circular form in 1793, is the most famous room of the palace: the auditorium acquired a semi-elliptical form after the reconstructions of 1796–7, when the balcony was removed and the annex was rebuilt into a picture gallery. In the stalls, the floor was covered with emerald cloth, which harmonized with the light-green upholstery in the rear rows and the apple-green colour of the walls.

When the auditorium was being rebuilt, F. Priakhin, a serf, designed an ingenious device which raised the floor of the auditorium to stage level, thus letting it serve as a ballroom at will. It was there that the serf-actress wife of Nikolai Sheremetiev, Praskovia Zhemchugova, made her last appearance in 1797. A portrait of her in a white dress hangs in the theatre's wings.

The Trinity Church

This ornamental seventeenth-century church differs in appearance and spirit from the quiet elegance of the Sheremetiev Palace. Like its builder, **Mikhail Cherkassky**, it belonged to the venerable boyardom of pre-Petrine Russia. (Cherkassky's loyalty to the reforming tsar was so great that he was the only man in Peter's court that was allowed to keep his beard.)

The church which Cherkassky commissioned incorporates the Moscow Baroque style in its exterior and a Western-influenced interior. The intricate massing of volumes contributes to the complex silhouette of the church, although the building consists simply of a central cube, flanked by smaller chapels on the north and south. All three churches are raised on a high substructure and linked by a terrace. Access to the terrace is by a covered staircase with rampart arches and a tent-type roof. The tapering silhouette of the belfry accentuates the picturesque shifting of the volumes and counterbalances the bulbous cupola. The building's festive appearance is further stressed by ceramic tile inlays, white stone carvings, spade-shaped gables, and archivaults lustily displayed against the red brick walls.

The carved iconostasis matches the opulent decorative statement of the rest of the Trinity Church, although its icons demonstrate the decline of Russian iconography as it begins to borrow from the West.

It is interesting to compare the Trinity Church with the **Church of the Archangel Michael**, executed by the same architect (Pavel Potekhin) for boyar Odoyevsky at the nearby **Arkhangelskoye estate** (see below) in 1667.

III. Arkhangelskoye Estate Museum

Open: 11:00 to 17:00, Wednesday to Friday (summer).
10:00 to 18:00, Saturday, Sunday (summer).
11:00 to 16:00, Wednesday to Sunday (winter).
Closed: Monday, Tuesday (all year).
Last Friday of each month (winter).

Arkhangelskoye is 21 kilometres (16 miles) from Moscow. It can be reached by bus 541 from *Metro Station Sokolniki*, by car, or with an Intourist-arranged tour. If you are driving, take *Rublevskoye Shosse*. Turn right at the *Militia Booth* towards *Ilinskoe* and take the right fork after you pass *Russkaya Izba Restaurant*. This quaint wooden cottage serves excellent food, but you must book ahead. There is an open-air restaurant at Arkhangelskoye, though the food is not as good.

Monuments

1. The Palace (1780–1831) — Chevalier de la Huerne, Yevgraf Tiurin.
2. The Theatre (1817) — Yevgraf Tiurin, Osip Bove, Stepan Melnikov.
3. The Church of the Archangel Michael (1667) — Pavel Potekhin.
4. Pavilion with statue of Catherine the Great depicted as the Goddess of Justice (1819) — Yevgraf Tiurin.

EXCURSION 14

5. Park with pavilions and statuary, including statue of poet Aleksandr Pushkin.

This ancient estate of **Boyar Odoyeysky** and later of Prince **Dmitry Mikhailovich Golitsyn*** gained its fame in 1810, the year **Prince Nikolai Borisovich Yussupov** (see p. 157) purchased it from the Golitsyns and made it the base of his collection of fine furnishings and art.

Yussupov (1750–1831) was a welcome guest at the court of Louis XVI and Marie Antoinette. He also knew the Holy Roman Emperor Joseph II and visited Friedrich the Great. He was so handsome that Catherine the Great commissioned a painting in which she had herself depicted as Venus and Yussupov as Apollo. His striking slightly Tartar looks inspired more than 300 conquests, the last of which occurred with an 18-year-old in 1831, when he was 81! Proud of his prowess, Yussupov commissioned portraits of all his mistresses, which he displayed in this country estate.

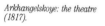

Arkhangelskoye: the theatre (1817).

Yussupov's sister was also a famous beauty. She married Herzog Peter Biron, Empress Anne's despised German favourite. When his wife died, Biron offered her silver and blue bedroom suite to Yussupov. Among the other mementoes and treasures Yussopov collected while serving as ambassador to various West European capitals and as director of the Hermitage museum are the furniture which once belonged to Marie Antoinette, a chandelier from Madame Pompadour's bedroom, and art exceeding that of many European museums in its quality. With all his wealth and position, Yussupov remained accessible and kind: Arkhangelskoye was always open to the public.

*Another great art collector and philanthropist. Golitsyn's collection of paintings was displayed at the **Golitsyn Hospital**, which still stands on Leninskiy Prospekt 8.

The Palace

One enters the palace through a handsome wrought-iron gate made by Stepan Melnikov to resemble a triumphal arch (1817). The building, situated inside a formal yard, is the work of French architect Chevalier de la Huerne. It consists of a **main building** with a belvedere and a four-column portico from which extends a Tuscan order colonnade, thus forming an honour guard on either side. The **portico** of the front facade is counter-balanced by a semi-circular projection turned towards the garden. The **garden facade** overlooks two terraces surmounted by statues and, beyond them, the magnificent **French park.** Impressed by Arkhangelskoye's dignity, poet Aleksandr Pushkin wrote that 'all that is beautiful must also be stately [*velichavo*]'. His statue is displayed in the park.

ight Arkhangelskoye: the court cade.

r right Arkhangelskoye: the rden facade. The beauty of khangelskoye inspired the poet eksandr Pushkin, whose statue ces the park.

Before visiting the palace, we turn left and follow a path across the park to the estate church.

The Church of Archangel Michael

The oldest and architecturally most interesting monument of Arkhangelskoye is its Church of Archangel Michael. Those familiar with the flamboyant **Trinity Church at Ostankino** will find it hard to believe that its architect, Pavel Potekhin, is the same one who completed St Michael's for Nikita Odoevsky (*d.* 1689) some twenty years earlier.

The church is small and compact. It consists of a main cube with tiered rows of *kokoshniki* gables leading to a scaled solitary dome and two smaller annexes, each with a similarly scaled onion-shaped cupola. The interior was gutted during the Revolution and is now used as an exhibition area.

Polyarnaya Ulitsa

Metro: *Sviblovovo and bus 23*

IV. The Church of Pokrov in Medvedkovo

Prince Dmitry Pozharsky (1578–1642) erected this church to commemorate his victory over the Poles in 1612. Its dedication to the Intercession of the

EXCURSION 14

Virgin (*Pokrov*) affirms the association of that feast with the triumph of Orthodoxy over its foes, a connection that first became established in Russia after the victory of Ivan the Terrible over the Tartars in Kazan. Much as Ivan had done in building the **Cathedral of Pokrov** (the Cathedral of St Basil) in Red Square, Pozharsky was expressing his gratitude to the Mother of God for delivering the Russians from their enemies.

The tapering mass of the Medvedkovo Church appears austere in comparison with its Red Square prototype because it was built to the modest Pozharsky's tastes. Architecturally, however, the Church of Pokrov in Medvedkovo is a masterpiece of Russian tent-type church style and a feat in its own terms.

The church stands on a high basement, from where an octagon placed over a lower cubic mass provides the transition to the tapering tent. The uniform

Church of Pokrov in Medvedkovo (1640). Prince Dmitry Pozharsky (1578–1642) erected this church to commemorate the victory over the Poles in 1612. Its dedication to Pokrov (or Intercession of the Virgin) recalls the association of that feast with the triumph of Orthodoxy over its foes. (Photograph: Evi Musser.)

Church of Pokrov: detail.

domes placed at each corner of the cube at Medvedkovo are a far cry from their extravagant models in Red Square, though their positioning is similar, emphasizing the cross shape of the church as do the towers of St Basil's.

The decorations of Pozharsky's church consist of ogee-shaped *kokoshniki* gables which provide a decorative setting for the four corner domes and stress the stepped silhouette of the tent-like pyramid. Also noteworthy is the jutting of the trisectional altar apse of the lower **Znamenie** church beyond the apse of the upper church of Pokrov. This peculiarity, while adding grace to the silhouette of the church, was dictated by a liturgical requirement prohibiting one altar being built directly over another. The dedication to the Icon of the Sign (*Znamenie*) comes from two sources: the icon belonged to the new ruling dynasty, the Romanovs, and the main victory over the Poles occurred on the feast day of the icon — 27 November.

PART IV

MOSCOW OF THE ART PATRONS

INTRODUCTION

*T*he art and art patronage of Moscow differ greatly from that of the earlier Russian cities. Unlike Kiev, Novgorod, Pskov, Rostov, or Suzdal, where art flourished since their very inception, Moscow came into being during the years of Tartar domination. This explains why the primary task of Moscow's early rulers was to protect, rather than embellish, the city. By the time the Tartar threat was overcome, Moscow had become a centralized state in which the role of art was to reflect the ambitions of its tsars: to visually document the emergence of Moscow as the Third Rome and its claim to the Kievan and Vladimir inheritance (see 'Moscow of the Tsars', Excursion 1, p. 11).

Little wonder, therefore, that the first art patrons in Moscow were the tsars and the upper clergymen, who strove to embed their aspirations into the stone and icons of the Kremlin. Only from the sixteenth century onwards, as the other strata of the Moscow population begin to share in the prosperity of Moscow, do the boyars, tsars' noble advisors, the rich *gosti* merchants (see 'Moscow of the Townspeople', p. 72) and even the artisan guilds, also begin to make their mark as the city's art patrons.

In Moscow, as in Europe, the early works of art that were commissioned were predominantly religious in nature. The churches and their interior decorations became in themselves a status symbol. It would be erroneous to think, however, that other forms of art did not flourish in Moscow. Had Moscow been built of stone like Florence or Venice, the city would have abounded in fanciful palaces with crested roofs, brightly painted window frames, grand porches, and equally opulent interiors. But stone was expensive. Moreover, because of their cold winters Muscovites preferred wooden dwellings, none of which survived to our days. One can, however, reconstruct the onion-domed, crest-roofed panorama of early Moscow thanks to the seventeenth-century boyar palaces and churches in which the timber motives were repeated in stone.

The high-ranking boyars and relatives of the tsar, such as **Prince Trifon Patrikeyev**, were the first to emulate royalty and the upper clergy. His fifteenth-century **Church of St Trifon*** escaped destruction in Stalin's days as miraculously as did Prince Trifon, who nearly forfeited his life for letting go of the tsar's favourite falcon. Though small because of the shortage of building material, St Trifon's Church is an example of the nobility's fine taste, which we also find in the icons, silver, and other articles of art commissioned at that time.

Russian merchants were another colourful group which from the seventeenth century, joined the aristocracy as Moscow's enthusiastic art patrons and philanthropists. Producing many of the nation's explorers and trade representatives abroad, their heavily laden vessels sailed for distant lands, where neither tsar nor boyar ever travelled. Operas were inspired by their adventures and legends grew around merchant families like **Nikitnikovs** (see 'Moscow

...rifon's Church (fifteenth ...ry). This first parish church ... of stone in Moscow, recalls ...egend of Prince Trifon and ...ost falcon of the tsar.

*Prince Trifon had a vision in which his patron saint Triphon told him where to find the lost bird. The church was built on the very spot where the prince recovered the falcon. When in the 1930s Stalin ordered the church destroyed, the workers uncovered on its facade an intact fresco of St Trifon and the church was spared.

Fresco of St Trifon (sixteenth century), now in the Tretyakov Art Gallery.

of the Townspeople', Excursion 5, p. 95) or **Stroganovs**, who acted as tsars' bankers, built beautiful churches, or in case of the Stroganovs, established the famous **School of Stroganov Icon Painting**.

Even the artisan guilds could hold their own when it came to church building. Numbering some 48,000 in the seventeenth century, they were grouped according to their skills and served the Tsar's court. After fulfilling their royal quota, some of the guilds had enough money to engage in church construction. Several of the guild churches still stand and are considered masterpieces of Russian architecture (see 'Moscow of the Clergy', Excursion 25, pp. 319–23.

Peter the Great's transfer of the capital to St Petersburg deprived Moscow of its art patrons, as the Russian nobility, merchants, and artisans followed their young tsar to the banks of the Neva. The heavy taxes he levied for the construction of St Petersburg and his military needs, depleted the funds of the merchants and artisans who stayed in Moscow. The depopulated city, which by then had become an international marketplace and the thriving centre of Russian manufacture, had gone into decline. Even those who could still afford to build, were no longer allowed to do so. All available stone went to St Petersburg.

Nearly a century passed, before Moscow started to recover from the blow it suffered in the early 1700s. Little by little the nobles, finally freed from compulsory service to the State, began to drift back and resume their cultural pursuits with renewed vigour. The historian P. P. Svinin in an article published

214

in the *Otechestvennye Zpaiski* declared in 1820 that: 'Only England can compete with Moscow in the number and the quality of fine paintings' — collected by the Russian aristocracy at their houses or out-of-town estates. It suffices to recall such world-famous collections as those of the Princes **Golitsyn**, **Yussupov**, **Shermetiev** and **Rumiantsev**, now divided between various art galleries of Moscow and Leningrad, to appreciate the scope and taste of Moscow's nobility.

The **serf theatres** which the nobles organized on their estates served as the training grounds for a generation of Russian dancers, singers, actors, painters, and architects. Many of the serf actors were either sent by their masters to study abroad or received training of the best European masters.

While Moscow's art patrons dined and danced in their luxurious mansions, they also saw to it that the lot of the poor was improved. Large-scale educational and philanthropical institutions, such as the **Foundling House**, built with the contributions of the nobility, made their appearance. For every theatre the nobles opened or collection they amassed, they would also endow a hospital or an educational institution. The nobles maintained their role as trend setters and art patrons until rapid industrialization in the mid-nineteenth century created a new class of benefactors. These were the former serfs and petty traders who had invaded Moscow after the war of 1812 and who by the 1850s had driven the *gosti* merchants out of business. Eighty per cent of the *gosti* wholesale enterprises and 200 factories passed into the hands of the out-of-town traders and peasants, turned large-scale manufacturers.

By the turn of the twentieth century, the emerging industrialist élite began to exert a preponderant influence on the country's economic and cultural life. Its influence increased at the expense of the nobility, whose wealth dwindled after the emanicipation of the serfs. But even when the industrialists gained access to the aristocracy's exclusive institutions (see 'Moscow of the Townspeople', p. 72), they chose to remain a tightly knit group. While a few joined the titled ranks, most of them shunned ennoblement, taking pride in their own merchant origins. This did not stop them, however, from trying to outbuild and outshine the gentry.

If *la grande noblesse* gave parties, so did the merchant barons. If the seigneurs had house theatres, the merchants sponsored, financed, and patronized the Russian opera, ballet, and theatres. If the aristocracy collected old books and art, the merchants also expended millions of roubles in purchasing the finest canvases and art works of Russian and Western masters. For every hospital or orphanage that the nobles founded, the industrialists endowed one or more of their own charitable institutions. These merchant barons infused enormous creativity into the competition, giving the old capital glamour and excitement in a civic outburst of pleasure and creativity.

The names of **Riabushinsky**, **Morozov**, **Shchukin**, **Demidov**, and **Tretyakov** who made enormous contributions to the culture and welfare of Moscow can take their eightful places alongside the Golitsyns, Rumiantsevs, and Sheremetievs who dominated the city during the eighteenth and early

INTRODUCTION

nineteenth centuries. **Pavel Pavlovich Tretyakov** and his brother **Sergei**, a one-time mayor of Moscow and textile baron like Pavel, turned their residences into a gallery of Russian paintings. When, in 1837, the collection outgrew their houses, they commissioned architect-painter Viktor Vasnetsov to build the large red gallery displaying Russian folk motives and a large spade-shaped gable above the main entry. Inside the gable is the figure of St George fighting the dragon, the pre-revolutionary emblem of Moscow. The **Tretyakov Gallery** houses the finest collection of icons and spans 1,000 years of Russian art.

FROM RAGS TO RICHES

Nogina Square — Church of All Saints — Solyanka Street — Church of the Nativity of the Virgin — Khitrovo Market — Church of SS. Peter and Paul — Court of Wards — Foundling Hospital — The Ustinskiy Proyezd — Church of the Holy Trinity of the Silversmiths — Palace of Ivan Batashev — Church of St Nikita on the Sewing Hill — The House of Aleksandr Bezborodko — The House of Klapovskaya — Taganka Theatre.

'*F*rom Rags to Riches' is a journey into the lives of artisans, merchants and noblemen who settled in the eastern sector of Moscow. The artisans lived much like their kinsmen in **Zamoskvorechie** (see 'Moscow of the Clergy', Excursion 25, p. 309), whose *slobody* or guilds were located south of the Kremlin. The difference between the two artisan suburbs lay in the nature of their occupation. The **Trans-Yauza District**, bordering on the Yauza River, was the heart of Moscow's metal-working and ceramic industries, which used open fires. In the sixteenth-century the tsars relegated these guilds to the eastern shore of the Yauza River in the hope that the river would prevent fires spreading to central Moscow.

While other guilds existed in the eastern merchant suburb, none were as popular as the potters and blacksmiths.

The beautifully coloured glazed faience tiles produced by the ceramists or *Gonchary* were used for the palaces and churches commissioned by tsars and wealthy clergymen. Iron-work was highly valued by all stratas of Moscow society: bolts and locks secured the homes of rich and poor alike. Fine blacksmith work was also required for the crosses, chandeliers, and other articles of forged iron still found in Moscow churches, museums, and houses.

Between the artisan settlements stood the out-of-town estates of the nobles and the houses of the merchants, many of whom were Old Believers who rose from rags to riches in less than a century.

The old eastern suburb of Moscow, well preserved and photogenic, can be walked in two hours. The excursion starts at **Nogina Square**.

Nogina Square

(*Varvarskaya Ploshchad*)

Until 1934, St Barbara's (*Varvarskiye*) Gates linked the walled merchant suburb of Kitai Gorod to what used to be called **St Barbara**'s (*Varvarskaya*) and is now Nogina Square. **St Barbara's Gates** marked a tragic episode which occurred during the outbreak of cholera in 1771. Desperate for healing and immunity, Muscovites flocked to kiss the miracle-working icon of *Our Lady of Bogoliubovo*, which hung on the city gates. When Archbishop Amvrosy, fearful that the crowds would spread the epidemic, ordered the icon removed, the angry crowd pursued Amvrosy to the Donskoy Monastery (see 'Moscow of the Clergy', Excursion 22, Donskoy Monastery, p. 289) and murdered him. St Barbara's Gates, along with the sixteenth-century brick wall, were

Excursion Plan 15
From Rags to Riches

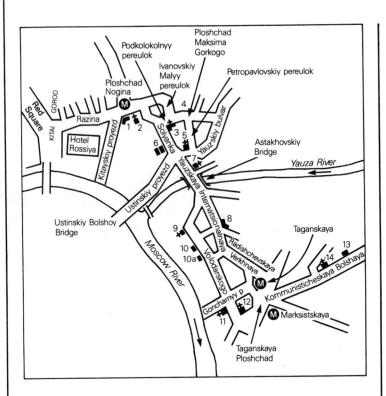

1. Delovoi Dvor (Business Centre)
2. Church of All Saints
3. Church of the Nativity of the Virgin
4. Khitrovo Market (Gorkogo Square)
5. Church of SS. Peter and Paul 'on Kulizhkakh'
6. Court of Wards (Soviet Academy of Medical Science) and the
   Foundling Hospital (Dzerzhinsky Artillery Academy)
7. Church of the Holy Trinity of the Silversmiths
8. Palace of Ivan Batashev (23rd City Hospital)
9. Church of St Nikita
10. House of Aleksandr Bezborodko
10a. House of Klapovskaya
11. Church of the Dormition of the Virgin 'in Goncharakh'
12. Church of St Nicholas 'na Bolvanke'
13. House of the Alekseyevs
14. Church of St Martin of the Confessor

demolished in 1930, and the square was widened to accommodate the flow of traffic.

St Barbara's Square was renamed after Victor Pavlovich Nogin (1878–1924), a veteran Bolshevik and member of the Central Committee of the Communist Party. Following the Revolution in 1917, Nogin headed the Supreme Soviet of People's Economy (VSNKh). The Soviet took over the **Business Centre** (*Delovoi Dvor*) ①, a large grey structure designed in 1913 by the architect I. S. Kuznetsov, at the southwest corner of the Nogina Square.

Other large buildings in the immediate vicinity of Nogina Square used to be luxury hotels for visiting businessmen. One was the **Boyar Hostel** (**Boyarsky Dvor**) built in 1901 by Fedor Shekhtel, the leading contemporary architect; it is now the **Central Party Committee Headquarters**.

(Tserkov Vsekh Sviatykh 'Na Kulizhkakh')
Ploshchad Nogina
②

Church of All Saints

The fourteenth-century **Church of All Saints** is the foremost landmark of Nogina Square. While some maintain that '*Kulizhki*' refers to the swampy ground beneath the church, a historically more plausible explanation is that '*Kulizhki*' is a derivative of '*Kulikovo*', the name of the battlefield near the River Don where the Moscow Prince Dmitry Donskoy challenged and defeated the vastly superior Tartar force in 1380. Some 80,000 Russian soldiers, two thirds of Dmitry's host, perished at Kulikovo and were buried at the field itself. Only the bodies of Dmitry's retinue were brought to Moscow. A church was built at each of the burial sites, with the Church of All Saints 'in Kulizhki' being the most famous.

The link between '*Kulizhki*' and the Kulikovo Battle was confirmed during construction work on the Moscow metro. While digging under All Saints' Church, workers discovered white stone tombs dating from the fourteenth

:h of All Saints, 'na
hkakh', viewed from the
Built in wood in the
enth century, it was rebuilt
ne in the fifteenth, enlarged
seventeenth, and restored in
'60s and 1970s.

219

century. The tombs and the bones of the Kulikovo heroes were unceremoniously dumped, but the historical church was spared.

Architecture

Between the 1960s and the 1970s, the All Saints' Church was restored to its fifteenth-century appearance; the red-brick building recovered its rectangular shape, the semi-circular apse at the eastern end and the tri-sectional octagonal tower at the western end. The original restraint of decorative statement was observed: only the green onion dome and a band of gold below relieve the monochrome effect of red brick.

The arches at the base of the drum and those crowning the walls have the curvilinear design of the *zakomars*, which predate the spade-shaped *kokoshniki* gables. A horizontal strip of ribbed brick provides a common link between the church and its bell-tower, which has, over the centuries, acquired a slant similar to that of the Tower of Pisa.

All Saints' Church marked the beginning of the old trade route to Vladimir, Kolomna, and other points to the East. The route followed **Solyanka Street**, cut through the artisan settlements on both sides of the Yauza River, and then continued after skirting the **Novospassky**, **Krutitsky**, and **Spaso-Andronikov Monasteries** (see 'Moscow of the Clergy', p. 301) guarding Moscow's south-eastern periphery. Dmitry Donskoy marched along this route to the Kulikovo Battle and the Russian princes used it to make their obeisances to the Tartar Khans of the Golden Horde, who confirmed their titles of 'grand prince'.

Solyanka Street

Solyanka, or **'Salt' Street**, derives its name from the seventeenth-century 'Salt Court' of the tsar, the site of the present nineteenth-century apartment house at **Solyanka, 1**. Salt was processed and sold there until 1733, when it stopped being the crown's monopoly. The petroleum tycoon Lianozov bought the house opposite the **Salt Court No. 2**, planning to replace it with a high-rise. The Bolshevik Revolution prompted his departure, however, and the old house survived.

Church of the Nativity of the Virgin

(Tserkov Rozhdestva Bogoroditsy 'Na Strelke')
Corner of Solyanka and Podkolokolnyy Pereulok
③

The **Nativity Church** was built in the 1760s by Karl Blank, one of Catherine the Great's favourite architects. Despite missing crosses and domes, the cylindrical bell-tower and the triangular refectory retain their classical silhouette and enhance the whole perspective of the street. The large yellow building further down Solyanka is another Karl Blank creation, the **Court of Wards**, which we will see on our return walk.

Leaving Solyanka on our right, we climb the steep **Podkolokolnyy Lane** to **Gorky Square**, once the site of the infamous **Khitrovo Market**, which Maxim Gorky (1868–1936) described in his *Lower Depths*.

Ploshchad Maksima
Gorkogo
④

Khitrovo Market

Gorky Square owes its original name to Major General Nikolai Khitrovo, a nobleman who bought Countess Shcherbatova's estate at **No. 38** with the idea of opening a market there. He died without building the market and his children sold the house to a merchant who converted it into slum dwellings. Before long, other mansions around the square also became boarding houses and bars, sporting names like The Exile, The Prison, and The Steam Roller. Eventually Khitrovo Market degenerated into a hangout for thieves, marauders, prostitutes, and other elements of Moscow society who preferred to shun the police. Up to 10,000 people slept in the dark, crowded houses which bordered the square.

An unwritten truce existed between the residents of the nearby fashionable **Pokrovsky Boulevard** and the Khitrovo thieves. So long as the houses of the rich were not burglarized, the trespasses of Khitrovo were tolerated: any breach resulted in an immediate police alert.

The market was cleaned up, reconstructed, and renamed Gorky Square in the 1930s to commemorate its connections with the writer's *Lower Depths*, which opened at the Moscow Art Theatre in 1902.

The **Petropavlovskiy Lane**, which leads from Gorky Square to **Yauzskiy Boulevard**, is named after the grand, Baroque **Church of SS. Peter and Paul** halfway down the lane.

(Tserkov Petra i
Pavla 'Na
Kulizhkakh')
Petropavlovskiy
Pereulok, 4
⑤

The Church of SS. Peter and Paul

The Church of SS. Peter and Paul was built in 1700, the year marking the transition between the late Moscow Baroque and early Classicism. The Baroque influences evidence themselves in the positioning of the octagonal volume on the cubic base and the bold display of white stone details against a red-brick surface. By the same token, with the exception of the curvilinear window pediments, the white stone work is opulent enough to be truly characteristic of Baroque.

The cornice, on the other hand, consists of a single row of zigzags, and the double columns at the corner of the building are slim and free of carving. The large western dome which tops the walls also introduces a note of Classicism, even if the octagonal drum with its faceted cupola above, are still remnants of the seventeenth-century Baroque style. The **bell-tower** adjoining the western portal of the Church of SS. Peter and Paul dates from 1771, the year of the Moscow cholera epidemic, while the rounded **refectory** was added in 1791. The eighteenth-century additions and projections contributed to the ship-shaped form of the church.

EXCURSION 15

Church of SS. Peter and Paul. Built in 1700, the bell-tower was added in 1771.

The Icons

The main altar of the church is dedicated to the icon of *Our Lady of the Sign (Znamenie)*, which hangs to the left of the Royal Gates. The Virgin, a medallion of Christ Emmanuel on her breast, is shown with both hands upraised. As the name 'Sign' (*Znamenie*) suggests, the icon prophesies the birth of Christ. The seventeenth-century panel is a copy of the famous icon from Novgorod to which the city's residents ascribed their rescue from the attack of Suzdal's Prince Andrei Bogoliubsky in 1169.

The *Icon of the Virgin Bogoliubskaya*, displayed in a special case, *kiot*, to the left of the main iconostasis is even more famous. It was this icon that surmounted St Barbara's Gates and caused the tragic cholera riot in 1771. The *Bogoliubskaya* is one of the few representations of the

Virgin Mary without the Child, for this is how She appeared in a vision to Prince Andrei Bogoliubsky.*

The icon of *SS. Peter and Paul* who are usually depicted together in the Russian Orthodox Church and in whose honour the church is named, hangs in the northern (left) chapel, to the right of the Saviour. The southern chapel is dedicated to the icon of *Our Lady of Kazan*, a present of Princess Shcherbatova, whose estate adjoined the church. When she died, her beautiful palace became a slum dwelling on Khitrovo Market.

After the Church of SS. Peter and Paul, the Petropavlovskiy Lane begins to descend. It leads to **Yauzskiy Boulevard**, which narrows as it progresses southward towards the Moscow River.

From the junction of the Yauzskiy Boulevard and Solyanka Street, we turn right on Solyanka to see the **Academy of Medical Sciences**, formerly the **Court of Wards**.

(Opekunsky Sovet)
Solyanka, 14
⑥
(Soviet Academy of Medical Science)

Court of Wards

The palatial Court of Wards was built between 1823 and 1826 by architects Domenico Gilliardi, and his favourite student Afanasy Grigorievich Grigoriev.

*The vision appeared to the prince, while he was moving the capital away from Kiev in 1159. Half-way between Kiev and Vladimir at Bogoliubovo, he saw the Virgin standing full length with a scroll in her hand, hence the name *Bogoliubskaya*.

The building is regarded as the finest example of Moscow Empire, the Classical building style which evolved during the reign of Emperor Alexander I (1801–25). Originally the main building stood apart from the two wings, but all three were joined, and the dome was moved closer towards the street in 1846. Only the large portico with eight Ionic columns resting on an arched base remains unchanged.

...urt of Wards (Presidium of the ...viet Academy of Medical ...iences), built between 1823 and ...26 by Domenico Gilliardi and ...s student Afansy Grigoriev.

The Court of Wards was a privately financed charitable organization, which raised money to help orphans, old people, and invalids. It derived its main income from the sale of playing cards and money lending. After the emancipation of the serfs in 1861, many impoverished noblemen mortgaged their houses to the Court of Wards, and Nikolai Gogol's Pavel Chichikov came here to try to pawn his 'Dead Souls'.

...ospitatelnyi Dom)
Solyanka, 12
(6)

Foundling Hospital

Further down, overlooking the Moscow River, we can see the former **Foundling Hospital**, now the **Felix Dzerzhinsky Artillery Academy**. Some 2,500 illegitimate children and foundlings were housed, fed, and educated here with the funds provided by the Court of Wards.

The colossal rectangular block of the Foundling Hospital was built on the initiative of the educator and philanthropist Ivan Ivanovich Betsky with private donations: 100,000 roubles from Empress Catherine the Great, 50,000 roubles from her son Paul I, and the rest from Prokofy Demidov (see 'Moscow of the Nobles', Excursion 11, p. 172), owner of the metallurgical plants, whose ancestor was a Tula smith. Architect Karl Blank, whom Catherine the Great summoned

EXCURSION 15

in 1764 to build the hospital, used the white stone from the recently dismantled White City wall to create this severe classical building surmounted by a single dome. Sculptures of *Charity* and *Education* executed by the sculptor Ivan Petrovich Vitali between 1830 and 1835 surmount the gates of the Court of Wards and the Foundling Hospital. Girls received special attention: some went to trade school, others could enroll in the hospital's School for Ballet, the first such school in Russia, which later furnished ballerinas for the **Bolshoy Theatre** (see p. 358).

The Ustinskiy Proyezd

After the detour to the Court of Wards, we return to **Ustinskiy Proyezd** at the junction of **Solyanka** and **Yauzskaya Streets**. From here, a marvellous view opens on the old artisan suburb dominated by the tall, blue silversmiths' **Church of the Holy Trinity** ⑦ and the red **Church of SS. Peter and Paul**.

The 176-metre-high apartment house on the opposite side of the square nearer to the Moscow River is one of Stalin's seven 'Wedding Cakes' built in 1952 by the architect Chechulin.

The house on the corner with a six-column portico, **Yauzskaya Street No. 1,** was allegedly built by Gilliardi between 1820 and 1824 for the Moscow University professor Smirnov, who found that being a business consultant was financially more rewarding than academia.

(Tserkov Troitsy v 'Serebryanikakh')
Serebryanicheskiy Pereulok
⑦

The Church of the Holy Trinity of the Silversmiths

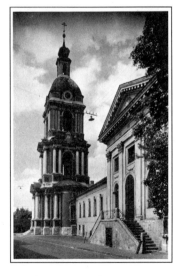

The blue and white Church of the Trinity, dated 1781, is ascribed to Karl Blank. The **bell-tower** owes its dynamic silhouette to a clever use of architectural orders: Doric columns at the base, narrower Corinthian columns on the second tier, and delicate pilasters on the third.

The church proper was built a century later. It is half hidden by the bell-tower which overshadows the Trinity Church located on the low-lying **Serebryanicheskiy Lane** rather than on the elevated Yauzskaya Street. A flight of stairs connects the belfry to the Trinity Church below, from where one can admire the architectural unity of this handsome

Church of the Holy Trinity of the Silversmiths (1781), ascribed to Karl Blank.

ensemble consisting of the belfry, the one-domed church, a free-standing refectory and a curvilinear entry gate. Trinity's original patrons were the tsars' silvermasters, whose guild minted coins and an array of art objects including icon frames.

The Trans-Yauza District

Guilds whose trade presented a fire hazard were located on the other side of the Yauza River, which one crosses at the **Astakhovskiy** (formerly **Yauzskiy**) **Bridge**. In 1812, a stormy exchange took place here between General Kutuzov, who commanded the Russian army during the Napoleonic War, and Moscow's governor Count Rostopchin. The scene was described by Leo Tolstoy in *War and Peace*.

The **Internatsionalnaya** (until 1922 called **Taganskaya Street**) was the main artery of the former Taganskaya guild of ironsmiths.

The architectural focus of the Internatsionalnaya is the House of Batashev, beautifully landscaped into the hilly terrain once cut in half by a deep ravine.

The Batashev Palace

Internatsionalnaya Ulitsa, 1 (formerly Yauzskaya) ⑧

The palatial establishment which now houses the **23rd City Hospital** was built by Ivan Radionovich Batashev, whom Catherine the Great ennobled for his humane and efficient running of seven foundries in the Ural Mountains. The grand colonnade of the palace's street facade was designed by the serf architect M. Miselnikov according to the plans of Radion Kazakov, or perhaps even the royal architect Vasily Bazhenov. The building was erected between 1798 and 1802 in the neo-Classical style of the time and was reconstructed after the fire of 1812.

A forged grille, similar to grilles designed by Giacomo Quarenghi for St Petersburg palaces, separtes the house from the street. The stone posts of the central gateway are flanked by four-columned porticos which serve as pedestals for two lions cast at one of the Batashev foundries. A two-storey gallery which runs perpendicular to the main house and adjoins it from behind, divides the estate into two parts. By turning right and walking around the building, one sees the service facade. The interior was spared by the fire of 1812 and hence preserves features of an earlier and purer Classical style.

By turning left and passing between the main house and the former estate church, one reaches the garden facade with its once famous rose garden that grew along the hill sloping down to the **Yauza**.

The focal point of the garden facade is an arched opening with a loggia. The keystone of the loggia's arch resembles a lion's mask, finely executed and reminiscent of a similar mask at the gates of the **Pashkov House** (see 'Moscow of the Nobles', Excursion 7, p. 124). The symbolism of the two bas-relief panels on either side of the arch is obscure, but suggests feverish building activity.

The Batashev empire did indeed grow rapidly. The dynasty founder was a blacksmith whose fine work caught the eye of Peter the Great. When Batashev

EXCURSION 15

The Batashev Palace (23rd City Hospital), built between 1798 and 1802 and reconstructed after the fire of 1812.

died, he left his sons Andrei and Ivan several foundries and a sizeable fortune. Andrei, the older of the two, took over the management of the plants and added a few new ones, but he behaved cruelly and recklessly. Anyone who stood in his way risked his life; a neighbour who refused to cede his wife to Andrei, for example, was shoved into a foundry oven during his tour of the plant. His 12,000 labourers fared no better. When Catherine the Great ordered an investigation of Batashev's abuses, the commission was greeted by a servant bearing a bowl of fruit. Tucked inside the fruit was an envelope with money and a note, which read: 'Enjoy the fruit and the money, but get out while you are still alive'. The investigators cleared Batashev.

Working conditions improved with Andrei's death. Ivan, who took over the seven family foundries, compensated the families of the workers and restored order. Catherine the Great ennobled Ivan and rewarded him with an order of St Vladimir.

From Batashev's house, one sees three neighbourhood churches: The **Trinity of the Silversmiths**, the large, round **St Simeon of the Pillar**, and the graceful white **St Nikita** of the 'Sewing' guild.

(Tserkov Nikity Na 'Ushivoi Gorke')
Ulitsa Volodarskogo, 4
⑨

The Church of St Nikita 'on the Sewing Hill'

The **Church of St Nikita**, overlooking the Moscow River, consists of four separate buildings grouped into an asymmetrical composition: the sixteenth-century Church of St Nikita, two **side chapels** and an eighteenth century **bell-tower** with a tent-type roof. The buildings are situated atop a steep hill that was once settled by the sewing guild, patrons of St Nikita's Church. Eventually, the name *Ushivaya*, meaning 'sewing', degenerated into *Vshivaya* meaning '*lousy*', or overrun by lice. The Soviet government searching for a more dignified name dedicated the street to Moisei Markovich Volodarsky-Goldstein, 1891–1918, member of the Presidium of the St Petersburg Soviet.

A foundation stone recovered in the wall of St Nikita's Church states that the church was founded in 1595 by Savva Yemilianov, a prosperous member of the sewing guild. The exterior appearance of the church and some of its details such as the three semi-rounded *zakomar* arches which top the walls, the finely profiled division of the facades, and the design of the cornices seem to validate this date.

Church of St Nikita on the Sewing Hill, founded in 1595.

Other evidence, however, suggests that despite Yemilianov's pretensions, St Nikita's Church had already been in existence for nearly a century. The earlier origins are substantiated by Moscow chronicles which state that the Church of St Nikita was built on the spot where two rays of sun struck the ground on 11 March 1476, and again that in 1543, a bolt of lightning damaged the wall of the church and the iconostasis. Since there is no mention of the church burning down, it was presumably already built of stone.

Evidence has been uncovered to substantiate this version: during 1958 restorations, the architects found a massive pillar made with the same type of brick that the Italian architect Alevisio used in the early sixteenth century in the basement. They also

discovered pilasters without capitals in the apse of the church. All this proves that Yemilianov did not build St Nikita's Church from scratch, but rather repaired it after it was hit by lightning.

Note the difference between the western and northern portals. The **western portal** which leads to the wide terrace has noticeably enlarged details, while the **northern portals** are finely chiselled in white stone. The contrast comes from practical considerations: the western portals were meant to be admired from the Moscow River embankment, while the others were intended for close-up contemplation.

Ulitsa Volodarskogo, 12
⑩

The House of Aleksandr Andreyevich Bezborodko

The Classical mansion designed by the architect Matvei Kazakov in the eighteenth century was rebuilt beyond recognition in the 1930s when a third

EXCURSION 15

Bezborodko — possibly Count Bezukhov's house in War and Peace.

storey was added. Only the grand concept of the estate which once commanded a panoramic view of the Moscow River survived. The house is interesting because of its historic and literary associations.

The original owner of the house was Aleksandr Andreyevich Bezborodko (1747–99) an accomplished Russian diplomat under Catherine the Great and her son Emperor Paul I. From 1783 onwards, Bezborodko virtually ran Russian foreign policy, becoming chancellor in 1797 and being granted the title of prince shortly before he died in 1799, at the age of 53.

Bezborodko started life as a son of an impoverished nobleman. But his diplomatic triumph earned Bezborodko a 220,000 roubles a year income which he owed to Catherine the Great's grants of money, lands, and serfs. These grants were a reward for Bezborodko's successful negotiations of the Peace of Jassy in 1792 and the Convention of 23 January 1793, which provided for the second partition of Poland.

Bezborodko's only weakness was women. The Italian singer Davia who caught his fancy received a monthly income of 8,000 gold roubles. When Bezborodko presented Davia with 40,000 roubles in one lump sum, Empress Catherine ordered her to leave St Petersburg on 24-hours notice. As a parting present to his mistress, Bezborodko gave her diamonds valued at 500,000 roubles. He died nearly destitute.

The house is also known as the **house of Tutolmin**, who participated in General Suvorov's epic march across the Alps. Possibly Leo Tolstoy had Tutolmin's residence in mind when he described the House of Count Bezukhov in *War and Peace*, and it may have been Count Bezukhov's father who inspired Leo Tolstoy's portrayal of Pierre in that book.

Ulitsa Volodarskogo, 16
⑩ₐ

The House of Klapovskaya

The immediate neighbour of Bezborodko was the noblewoman Klapovskaya. Her well-preserved late-Classical house, built on the arcaded basement of an earlier seventeenth-century building, features six Doric columns which carry an entablature of such decorative exuberance as to stand out even among the opulent neo-Classical buildings of early nineteenth-century. A decorative frieze similar to the band which adorns the house, also embellishes the entry gates which consist of pylon-type posts.

Since 1930, the house of Klapovskaya has been the headquarters of **Moscow Scientific Atheism**. Ironically, there is said to be a high rate of conversion to Christianity among the attendees of the anti-religious seminars. For many this was their first formal exposure to religion and its appeal occasionally proved stronger than the planned counter arguments put forward by the lecturers.

House No. 7, opposite Klapovskaya mansion, has a wooden top floor extending from a stone basement, and features carved window frames and bands under the eaves and dormer windows. These timber decorations inspired the white stone window frames that one sees on Moscow Baroque churches.

Volodarskogo Street runs down from the 'Sewing Hill' and rises again as it reaches **Taganskaya Square**. From the crest of the hill one sees two beautiful churches, the blue domed **Church of the Dormition of the Virgin in Goncharakh** ⑪ and, at the other end of the street, the elongated **Church of St Nicholas 'na Bolvanke'** ⑫ (see also Excursion 25, p. 323). Both are surrounded by quaint two-storey houses once settled by the members of the two rival guilds.

The houses nearest the Dormition Church formerly belonged to the prosperous *gonchary* whose pottery and glazed, ingeniously coloured tiles were in great demand at the royal court and elsewhere in Moscow. The houses closer to St Nicholas Church were those of the *Bolvanka* guild who earned their living by supplying wooden forms to hatters. When the ceramists claimed that theirs was the most beautiful church on this side of the Yauza River, the builders of St Nicholas responded with, 'these peasants rake in shovelfuls of gold'. They would not concede, however, that their church, grand as it was, paled in comparison with the jewel-like Church of the Dormition of the Virgin.

Chkalova Ulitsa, 76

Taganka Theatre

On the opposite side of **Chkalova Street** from St Nicholas's church is the new building of the **Taganka Theatre**, Moscow's experimental avant-garde theatre. Foreign plays, works of contemporary Soviet playwrights, Trifonov's *House on the Embankment*, and modernized versions of such classics as Chekhov's *Three Sisters* are played there. The brick block design of the theatre building is as controversial as the manner in which the plays are staged. Taganka was the home of the rebellious idol of the Muscovites: the actor–poet **Vladimir Vysotsky** (1938–80).

EXCURSION 15

Taganskaya Square

The nearby Taganskaya Square owes its name to an ancient guild of ironsmiths who produced metal tripods, known in Russian as *tagany*. The tripods served as supports for pots in which soldiers cooked their food during field marches. Taganskaya was one of the guilds settled by the tsars on the eastern shore of the Yauza River to protect the wooden houses of Muscovites from the smithies whose smelting contributed not only to Moscow's art works but also to the frequent fires which ravaged the city.

The present Taganskaya Square evolved in the early nineteenth-century when the Earthen City fortifications were removed and the square was rebuilt as a large circular marketplace serving the needs of local residents.

The guild character of the Taganskaya area changed radically when Peter the Great moved the Russian capital to St Petersburg. The artisans' land passed into the hands of petty merchants, mostly Old Believers, who were attracted to this area by its proximity to the **Old Believer's Cemetery** (see p. 232) at the nearby **Rogozhskiy Val**.

By the end of the nineteenth century, most of the houses on the streets radiating from the Taganskaya Square belonged to Old Believers, such as, for example, the Alekseyevs, who lived ⑬ on the **Bolshaya Kommunisticheskaya**, formerly **Alekseyevskaya Street**. Alekseyev's forebear was the stable boy of Prince Shermetiev. Starting as a salesman in the silver row on Red Square, he ended up as an owner of cotton and woollen mills, sheep herds, gold-thread and electric-cable factories. The Alekseyevs used their wealth to improve the lot of those less fortunate than themselves. The family also gave the city two of its most popular mayors and the great **Konstantin (Alekseyev) Stanislavsky**, the theatrical innovator and co-founder of the Moscow Art Theatre.

Opposite top *Patriarch Nikon, who became patriarch in 1652, and was deposed by the Church Council in 1667. His attempts to correct old religious texts led to the Great Schism. Nikon's downfall was a result of his interfering with the state affairs of Tsar Alexis Romanov.*

Opposite bottom *The departure of Boyarina Morozova by Vasily Surikov (1887). Morozova was one of the leading non-conformist Old Believers. The painting depicts the boyarina being forcibly removed from Moscow. She holds up two fingers, which the Old Believers used to make the sign of the cross, unlike the Nikontites who crossed themselves with three fingers.*

THE SACRED TREASURES OF THE OLD BELIEVERS

The Old Believers' Cemetery — The Cemetery Churches: Church of Pokrov — Church of the Nativity of Christ — Church of St Nicholas

*T*he successors to the Moscow guild merchants and their art patronage were the traders of the Old Believers' denomination. They belonged to the conservative segment of the Russian Orthodox population who rejected the reforms imposed by **Patriarch Nikon** in the mid seventeenth century. The very thought of destroying their old sacred books and printed liturgies and replacing them with corrected ones, conforming to the modern Greek texts, made them rebel. In 1653, those who considered themselves the recipients of 'unsullied Orthodoxy' broke away from the main body of the Church, the Nikonites, who accepted Nikon's reforms.

Many Old Believers fled to the northern forests to prepare for their end. They firmly believed that Nikon was the Antichrist sent by the Lord to punish them for their sins. Their apocalyptical misgivings were reinforced by the second appearance of the Antichrist in the person of **Peter the Great**, who ordered Christians to shave their beards. The only way to be spared this was for the Old Believers to pay 'beard tax'. In fact, most Old Believers still wear beards, a distinction on which they insisted even during Stalin's time.

Years of persecution strengthened the Old Believers' attachment to their faith and brought them into closely knit groups. This explains why the Moscow merchant community continued to keep to themselves even after **Catherine the Great** granted them freedom of worship in 1771 and allotted them land in north-eastern Moscow. Their preference was to cling together, building their houses near their new centre at **Rogozhskiy Val**, where they erected churches,

worshipped their marvellous icons and buried their dead. Some of the richest merchants emerged from these patriarchal collectives. Some traded in grain, others combined trade with manufacture. The great merchant dynasties like the **Riabushinskys** (see pp. 88, 247), the **Morozovs** (see p. 249), and the **Soldatenkovs** (see p. 160), the great art patrons of Moscow, belonged to the latter group.

By the turn of the twentieth century, the Old Believers' merchant settlement at Rogozhskoye had assets estimated at 20–25 million roubles. Although their old-fashioned ways were ridiculed by the nobility and provided fertile material for satire, the Moscow merchants were pious, hard-working people, as solid and sturdy as the heavily shuttered houses in which they lived behind locked gates. Dawn found them at their trading stalls in **Kitai Gorod**, where they remained till nightfall.

(Rogozhskoye Kladbishche)
Ulitsa Voytovicha, 29
Metro: *Taganskaya*
(plus bus or taxi)

The Old Believers' Cemetery

The Cemetery Churches

With Catherine's permission, the Old Believers began large-scale construction. The first church to be finished was the **Church of Pokrov**, fittingly dedicated to the *Protection of the Virgin's Veil*.

Next to this yellow, single-domed building, a typical representative of Moscow Classicism, rose the more ornate and mildly Baroque **Church of the Nativity of Christ**. Soon yet another building was finished — the diminutive **Church of St Nicholas**. The ornamental **Gate-Tower of St Nicholas** (which leads to the Old Believers' burial grounds*) gives the Old Believers' Cemetery its fairy-like aspect of Old Muscovy. In later years, this church was taken over by the *Yedinovertsy* or 'co-religionists', who recognized the hierarchy and dogma of the Nikonite Church, while still observing the old rituals.

The building zeal of the Old Believers was interrupted in 1827 by Nicholas I, who retracted the freedom of worship. The churches remained closed until Nicholas II, the last Russian tsar, published his manifesto of religious tolerance in 1905. The grateful Old Believers, then numbering some 17 million, celebrated the unsealing of the altars by building the mammoth white **Bell-Tower**, somewhat reminiscent of the Kremlin's Bell Tower of Ivan the Great. Other buildings sprang up in rapid succession. The cemetery evolved into an architectural complex with bishop's residence, almshouses, and hotel for visiting Old Believers.

The Icons

One of Moscow's (and Russia's) finest collections of pre-seventeenth-century icons is to be found in the still-functioning **Pokrov Cathedral**.

*Many of Moscow's great merchant dynasties, including that of the Morozovs have erected their family mausoleums at the Rogozhsky Cemetery; along with Riabushinskys, Morozovs and Soldatenkovs they are buried at the Rogozhskiy Cemetery.

As traditionalists, the Old Believers preserved and venerated only those icons that pre-dated the Great Schism, rejecting the Westernized religious paintings which began to appear in mid seventeenth century. Furthermore, the Old Believers were among the first to appreciate icons as works of art. Thus, the icons which the wealthy merchants collected and bequeathed to the cemetery represented the very best of what was produced by the various Russian schools of icon-painting.

The representation of Christ, known as the *Saviour of the Burning Eye*, is the oldest icon in the Pokrov Cathedral. In this fourteenth-century panel one sees some distinctly Greek characteristics. They are expressed in the sombre tonality of the face, the abrupt lines of drawing and the haughty demeanour so typical of the Byzantine style. This priceless icon is kept in a glass kiot near the southern entry.

Equally noteworthy are the six enormous icons partially hidden by the altar screen. They are waist representations of *St John the Baptist, Archangel Gabriel, Apostle Paul, the Virgin, Archangel Michael*, and *Apostle Peter*. The icons are attributed to the school of Andrei Rublev. They once formed the deisis row of a fifteenth-century church. The seventh icon, believed painted by Rublev himself, is located in the icon screen. The *Saviour's* image stands out by its graceful lines, harmonizing with the serene and gentle expression of his face.

Another famous icon is the fourteenth-century image of *Our Lady of Bogoliubovo*, displayed on the right-hand wall. The Virgin is represented standing with a scroll in her hand. At her feet, tsars and other mortals are kneeling. Attesting to the Vladimir-Suzdal origin of the panel are the elegant proportions of the saints and its colour scheme tinged with blue and silver.

ht The Entry of Christ into ısalem, *Pokrov Church. Late rteenth/early fifteenth century, ıgorod School.*

right The Miracle in Cannae, *rov Church. Late fourteenth/ ıy fifteenth century, Tver school ᴣonography.*

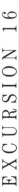

Icon of the Saviour, *Pokrov Church. Fifteenth century. Probably painted by Rublev.*

Across from the Virgin is the icon of *St Paraskeva*, patron saint of the merchants. merchants.

The fire-red cloak of Paraskeva and the bold composition of the icon bespeak the individualist Novgorod style of painting.

The church elder and the deacon, the only persons authorized to show the church to tourists, take great pride in attracting the visitors' attention to other famous icons: these are the *Entry of Christ into Jerusalem* and the *Miracle in Cannae*.

The community numbers two million people. Officially recognized by the Soviet government, the Old Believers are allowed to worship in their cemetery churches. They exist, however, under the same difficulties as the remainder of the Russian Orthodox population.

THE ARISTOCRATIC ART LOVERS OF BOLSHAYA NIKITSKAYA

The Orlov Palace — The House of the Boyars Kolychev — The Palace of Princess Vorontsova-Dashkova (Moscow Conservatory) — The Palace of Prince Menshikov — The House of Yakov Brius — The Church of the Little Ascension — The Streshnev House — Mayakovsky Theatre — The House of Major-General Pozdniakov — The Stanislavsky House Museum — The Church of the Great Ascension — The Church of St Theodore Studitus.

*E*ven the boldest of the merchant princes demurred from settling on **Bolshaya Nikitskaya**, though, in fact, this aristocratic avenue started its existence as the Novgorodskaya trade route. The transformation took place in the sixteenth century when **Nikita Romanov** (see 'Moscow of the Townspeople', Excursion 5, p. 91), the brother-in-law of Ivan the Terrible, founded there the **Nikitsky Convent** and renamed the commercial thoroughfare Bolshaya Nikitskaya. By the time **Natalia Naryshkina**, the mother of Peter the Great, decided to build her own palace on Bolshaya Nikitskaya, it was already a stronghold of the aristocracy and famous for its grand estates and churches.

Because of the street's proximity to the Kremlin hardly anything of this period survives; the destiny of the residents was governed by the whims of their rulers who took a heavy toll of the area. The old estates abandoned during Peter the Great's rule had fallen into disrepair and were replaced by Western-styled houses. Most of the buildings we see today on **Gertsena Street** reflect the tastes of the affluent, Westernized aristocracy who repossessed their ancestoral estates after being freed from the service to the crown in 1762.

The life of the nobility centred around the **Moscow University** founded by Empress Elizabeth in 1755. Directed and patronized by the Moscow aristocracy, the university served as the cradle for Russian intellectuals whose literary and philosophical circles met in the brightly lit mansions on Bolshaya Nikitskaya.

The Moscow University still stands, but the **Nikitsky Convent**, the *raison d'être* of Bolshaya Nikitskaya, together with four other churches disappeared on Stalin's orders in 1930. It was in the same year the street became **Gertsena Street**, after Alexandr Gertsen, the nineteenth-century writer and philosopher, and a frequent visitor of Bolshaya Nikitskaya salons.

Ulitsa Gertsena, 5

①

The Orlov Palace

The mansion at Gertsena 5 belonged to Count Vladimir Orlov, the youngest of the five Orlov brothers who brought Catherine the Great to the throne in 1762. The three-storey-high palace bears the signature of Matvei Kazakov, father of Moscow's eighteenth-century Classical architecture. Just as its counterpart did in America, Kazakov's style conveyed an intimate quality lacking in the palatial establishments of St Petersburg. The pillared mansion, softened with light pastels and delicate Baroque ornaments, symbolized Moscow's new

Excursion Plan 17
The Aristocratic Art
Lovers of Bolshaya
Nikitskaya

1. The Orlov Palace
2. House of the Boyars Kolychev
3. Palace of Prince Menshikov
4. Palace of Princess Vorontsova-Dashkova (Moscow Conservatory)
5. House of Yakov Brius
6. The Streshnev House
7. Mayakovsky Theatre
8. Church of the Little Ascension
9. House of Pozdniakov
10. Stanilavsky House Museum
11. Church of the Great Ascension
12. Church of St Theodore Studitus

tastes. Its wings form one block with the main building which is set off by four Corinthian semi-columns and a portico.

Vladimir's brother, Alexei Orlov, the hero of the naval victory at Chesame over the Turks in 1770, owned the famous swift-legged Orlov thoroughbreds which he raced at his **Neskuchnoye estate**, now the **Presidium of the Academy of Sciences** on Leninsky Prospekt. Orlov's thoroughbreds are still prized and are an important export item for the Soviet Union.

Ulitsa Gertsena, 11
②

The House of the Boyars Kolychev

Nearly three centuries before Count Orlov raced his stallions on the grounds of the Neskuchnoye Palace, the venerable Kolychev boyars already owned the neighbouring estate. In 1566, Ivan the Terrible confiscated the land after executing Metropolitan Philip, an illustrious member of the Kolychev clan. But in the eighteenth century, after making a comeback as diplomats and politicans, the Kolychevs reclaimed their estates and commissioned two adjoining houses from Matvei Kazakov.

The building at **No. 9** is disfigured beyond recognition. The second house, at **No. 11**, was altered in the nineteenth century, but retains the original part with the characteristic Corinthian pilasters on a tall socle base. From 1886 until 1918, this was the home of the **Synodal School**, which prepared singers and directors for church choirs. **The Moscow Conservatory of Music** (next door) acquired the building for its voice department in 1923; after the reconstructions (1988), the building recovered its seventeenth-century acoustic system and interior.

(Tchaikovsky Conservatory of Music)
Ulitsa Gertsena, 13
④

The Palace of Ekaterina Romanovna Vorontsova-Dashkova

Kazakov also designed the building which now houses the Musical Conservatory, originally the residence of Princess Ekaterina Romanovna Vorontsova-Dashkova (1744–1810), the founding mother of the Russian Academy in St Petersburg and the prototype of the energetic art patroness of Moscow's **Arbat**. The semi-rotunda projecting from the central facade and the right wing (1770s) survive from Vorontsova-Dashkova's days, while the left wing and the curving extensions were added in the 1780s.

Vorontsova-Dashkova was an exceptional woman: like her famous uncle Chancellor Mikhail Vorontsov, she combined a fine political sense with a keen intellect. Her interest in politics found practical application when she befriended the sixteen-year-old German princess, the future Catherine the Great, who married Emperor Peter III in 1755 and overthrew him seven years later. While the Orlov brothers rallied the support of the guard regiments, Vorontsova-Dashkova sought to win the St Petersburg courtiers to Catherine's side. On 28 June 1762 dressed in a guard's uniform, the young woman rode on horseback beside the future empress at the head of the regiments which brought down Peter III.

Widowed after six years of marriage to Prince Mikhail Dashkov, the princess spent many years abroad where she befriended Voltaire and Diderot. Her association with some of Europe's great literary figures heightened Vorontsova-Dashkova's interest in classics and her own native language.

In 1783, upon Vorontsova-Dashkova's return to St Petersburg, Catherine the Great appointed her to head the Academy of Sciences, a post which she held with distinction until 1796. She encouraged learning by providing scholarships to needy students, sponsoring free lectures and starting several publications, among them *Lovers of Russia*. This magazine, which featured poems by Gavrila Derzhavin and other literary figures who had assimilated the experiences of European literature, created the formal linguistic base for Russian literature. She also found time to oversee translations of classics into Russian, work on Russia's first dictionary, direct plays, and to write her own plays and poems. Her memoirs provide a fascinating account of Catherine's the Great's court.

After the death of Princess Vorontsova-Dashkova, the estate was placed in the custody of her relative, General Vorontsov, and purchased for the **Moscow Conservatory of Music** in 1859.

The Conservatory owes its existence to Nikolai Grigorievich Rubinstein (1835–81), the youngest son of a Moscow pencil manufacturer. He followed in the footsteps of his famous brother, the composer Anton Rubinstein, who had founded the St Petersburg Conservatory four years earlier and, like Nikolai, was an accomplished pianist and conductor. But unlike Anton, who was backed by the imperial family, Nikolai had to raise the funds to open the Moscow Conservatory. Fortunately, in addition to his organizational and fund-raising talents, Nikolai also had a knack for surrounding himself with talented people. One of the first teachers he hired for the conservatory, after whom it is now named, was Petr Ilich Tchaikovsky (1840–93).

Besides Tchaikovsky, Taneyev, Ippolitov-Ivanov, Glier, and Neuhaus all taught at one time at the Moscow Conservatory. Their most famous students included Rakhmaninov, Skriabin, Goldenweiser, and Oistrakh.

Every four years, aspiring violinists, pianists, and celloists from all over the world convene at the **Great Hall** of the Moscow Conservatory to compete in the International Tchaikovsky Competition. The American pianist Van Cliburn won the first prize for piano in 1958, the year the competition was initiated.

The **Small Hall** is reserved for chamber music and organ recitals.

Ulitsa Gertsena, 12
③

The Menshikov Palace

One must cross the street and retrace a few steps to see this marvellous palace erected in 1775 by Matvei Kazakov for Prince Sergei Aleksandrovich Menshikov

The Menshikov Palace (1775).

(1746–1815) who inherited his grandfather's taste (see 'Moscow of the Nobles', Excursion 8, p. 142), though fortunately not his arrogance. Since the access to the palace is blocked by a polyclinic, the only approach to the building is from **Ogareva Street.**[*]

At first glance, the palace has all the hallmarks of the Moscow Empire Style, but closer scrutiny reveals earlier origins. The palace was built in three stages. The first and the most interesting period of construction is preserved only in the rear facade, where one sees the unspoiled forms of early Classicism.

The fragment of the curving passage which once linked the main house to its side wings is dated 1778–82, and represents the second stage of construction. Only the left part survives. After the fire of 1812, the palace was rebuilt for the third time. Then, the six-column Corinthian portico on the arched socle appeared on the facade turned towards **Gertsena Street**, the rustications became more pronounced, and the sculpture ornaments got the typical Empire look.

Ulitsa Gertsena, 14
⑤

The House of General Field Marshal Yakov Brius

Directly opposite the conservatory is the house of Yakov Brius (1670–1735), general field marshal under Peter the Great. The resourceful Yakov, who had been trained abroad, was keenly interested in mathematics and the natural sciences. Peter appointed him to supervise book printing in 1706 and, later, to head the astrological observatory in the upper storey of the **Sukhareva Tower.**[†] Muscovites suspicious of Yakov's experiments dubbed them 'witchcraft', and his Society of Neptunes as 'devil worshippers'.

Brius's intellectual endeavours did not keep him from the drinking bouts of Peter's 'Jolly Companions', nor from the military campaigns of the tsar. His performance in the battle of Narva during the war with Poland, and especially his successful command of the artillery at the Battle of Poltava, earned him a field marshal's rank and the order of St Andrew. Among the important diplomatic missions entrusted to Yakov was the Nystadt Peace Treaty negotiations with Sweden in 1721.

[*]Until 1920, Ogareva Street was known as 'Gazetnyi' or Newspaper Lane to commemorate Moscow *Vedomosti*, a newspaper which was published here by the Moscow University Press.

[†]Located on Kolkhoznaya Square until destroyed in 1934.

Four years later, grieving over Peter's death, Yakov asked permission to retire to Moscow, where he commissioned the present house.

Originally one storey, Yakov's residence was enlarged in the 1770s by his namesake and grand-nephew, General Yakov Brius. This distinguished general and favourite of Catherine the Great was unpopular with the Muscovites, even after he was made their Governor-General, for his constant degrading of the city, and, to everyone's relief, was removed from that post in 1789. General Brius never finished the house: except for the projecting wings, which he embellished by adding Ionic pilasters, it remained unadorned.

Despite the general's unpopularity, the lane running along the house bore his name. Now it is **Nezhdanovoy Street**, renamed for a Bolshoy Theatre soloist who lived here.

Ulitsa Gertsena, 18a
⑧

The Church of the Little Ascension

This small, deformed church, which had occupied the corner of Gertsena and **Stankevicha** Streets since 1584, was reconstructed by General Zakhary Chernyshev in 1739. The general was the first man to occupy the post of (military) Governor-General of Moscow and to bequeath his residence to the governors that followed him. The Bolshevik Revolution cost the church its crosses and iconostasis, the military governors their jobs and their mansion (see 'Moscow of the Townspeople', Excursion 6, p. 105), and the street its name. The former **Chernyshevsky Lane** now bears the name of the philosopher-poet Nikolai Vladimirovich Stankevich (1813–40), founder of a famous literary circle in Arbat.

Ulitsa Gertsena, 19
⑥

The Streshnev House

From the middle of the eighteenth-century until 1919, house No. 19, diagonally across from the **Ascension Church,** belonged to the Streshnev family, whose fortunes soared when the widowed Tsar Michael picked Evdokia Streshneva as his second wife in 1624.

The house is unique, for it expresses Russia's conflict between devotion to native sources and fascination with the Western styles. Its street facade is a Classical Western eighteenth-

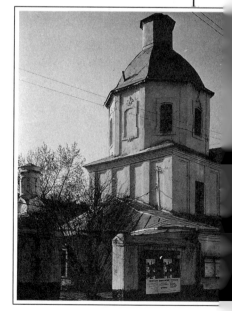

Church of the Little Ascension, reconstructed in 1739.

240

century building, coarsened through nineteenth-century reconstructions. Once beyond the massive arched entry, however, you are in old Russia: there is not a single Western feature in the red brick palace, which forms a quadrangle around the interior court. Stout pillars, not ordered columns, support double arches with pendatives; brick dentals, not friezes, traverse the walls.

Mayakovsky Theatre

Ulitsa Gertsena, 18/19
⑦

The Theatre which Streshneva commissioned next door to her palace, designed by the architect Fedor Shekhtel in 1866, is boldly neo-Russian, though the stylized barrel-shaped roofs and gables give it a touch of Art Nouveau. Streshneva's theatre had no permanent troupe, renting itself out to various entrepreneurs. In the 1920s, the theatre enjoyed a brief, but brilliant, stint as the **Theatre of Revolutionary Satire** under Vsevolod Emilievich Meyerhold (1874–1940). This former student of Stanislavsky, having abandoned his Symbolist searchings, was experimenting with Constructivist ideas in his own playhouse. In 1928, he staged Vladimir Mayakovsky's *Bath House*, and his *Bed Bug* in 1929. When Meyerhold was arrested ten years later, one of the accusations was that he had staged Mayakovsky's works — whom, ironically, the theatre now honours. Meyerhold died in prison, and his ideas of bringing everyday life into the theatre, the 'theatre-in-the-round' being one of the more ingenious manifestations, died with him.

House No. 23, beyond on **Kalashnyi* Lane**, preserves the memory of many notable figures, among them Nikolai Platonovich Ogarev (1813–77). While a student at Moscow University, the poet convened his famous literary and philosophical circle at his family's home. Ogarev's closest friend and fellow student was the revolutionary writer and publisher Aleksandr Ivanovich Gertsen (Hertzen, 1812–70), after whom the street is named.

The house on the opposite side of the street belonged to two great theatre lovers: General Pozdniakov and Prince Yussupov.

The House of Major-General Pozdniakov

Ulitsa Gertsena, 26
⑨

Built for a Count Orlov in the late eighteenth century and reconstructed in the late nineteenth, the house seems small and unprepossessing: its only luxurious room was the hall on the second floor, to which Major-General Pozdniakov added choirs and a gallery with a theatre stage when he purchased the house from Orlov shortly before Napoleon invaded Russia. While the general battled with the French, Napoleon used this house to stage French plays. The house miraculously escaped the fire of 1812, but the furniture and even the stage screen were gone when the French left. Undaunted, Pozdniakov rebuilt

*Until the seventeenth century, the royal bakers who provided the palace with *kalachi*, white bread loaves, lived here.

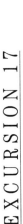

EXCURSION 17

his troupe with the help of Sandunovskys* famous actors from St Petersburg's Imperial Theatre.

Pozdniakov, whose company enjoyed considerable success in Moscow, willed the sizeable proceeds from these performances to the invalids of the Napoleonic wars and the widows of the Russian soldiers who had died in them. The theatre patron himself had a heart attack on the eve of a performance in honour of the new Persian ambassador.

When the ambassador arrived at the appointed hour, he was greeted by his host's comedian. Solemn for once, the actor bowed to the ambassador and announced: 'his lordship wishes to apologize for the inconvenience, but, for reasons beyond his control, the show has had to be cancelled'. The house and the troupe were purchased by Prince Nikolai Yussupov, a noted theatre lover who also owned a serf theatre at his summer estate in **Arkhangelskoye** near Moscow (see Excursion 14, p. 207).

Ulitsa Stanislavskogo, 7
(10)

The Stanislavsky House Museum

Open: 14:00 to 19:00, Wednesday, Friday
13:00 to 18:00, Thursday, Saturday, Sunday
Closed: Monday, Tuesday

It seems in keeping with the traditions of the old Arbat that the name of Konstantin Sergeyevich (Alekseyev) Stanislavsky (1863–1938), a merchant turned theatre patron, be given to the lane we cross next. Only a few houses down the lane, one finds the **Stanislavsky House Museum**, a well-preserved Empire mansion where this famous actor, director, and theatre innovator lived from 1920 to 1938.

Stanislavsky made a major contribution to the Russian theatre when he founded the *Moscow Art Theatre* (MKHAT) in 1897. This theatre put an end to the artificiality and conventional styles of the State-run theatres which had dominated Russia until then. Discouraged by the academic approach and the mediocrity of the teachers at the Moscow School for Theatre, the 23-year-old textile merchant Alekseyev left the school to help organize the **Moscow Society of Art and Literature** (1888), intended to provide a new school for young Russian actors and opera singers. The first performance of the society set the history of the **Moscow Art Theatre** in motion.

The theatre took form during an eighteen-hour lunch in Kitai Gorod between Stanislavsky and his future partner, Vladimir Sergeyevich Nemirovich-Danchenko. During their marathon session, the two men decided on the reforms that would place MKHAT into the foreground of the artistic world: the star system was to be replaced by team-work of a high degree of perfection, the

---

*Sila Sandunovsky fled to Moscow to protect his beautiful actress wife from the amorous advances of the St Petersburg dandies.

author's concept was to be observed, and his characters to be truthfully portrayed. *Tsar Fedor*, a tragedy by Count Alexei Tolstoy (1817-75), was chosen for the première.

Stanislavsky's goal of portraying truth and art realism met its challenge in the works of Anton Chekhov. Although his *Seagull* had had a disastrous opening at the St Petersburg Alexandrine Theatre, Stanislavsky's staging made it a success in Moscow. Chekhov later presented Stanislavsky with an engraved booklet whose inscription read: 'You gave life to my *Chaika* [Seagull]. Thank you.' *Chaika* became MKHAT's emblem, its symbol of success. Maxim Gorky's *The Lower Depths* and Leo Tolstoy's *The Power of Darkness* followed this success.

Papers, photographs, manuscripts, and mementoes of the Stanislavsky and Nemirovich-Danchenko collaboration on MKHAT are divided between the Stanislavsky House Museum and the MKHAT Museum. It is, however, the mansion which preserves the memory of Stanislavsky's last years: his bedroom, his study, and the ballroom which he converted into a theatre with a stage, used for rehearsals of the **Opera Dramatic Group**, which Stanislavsky founded in his later years.

(Tserkov Bolshogo Vozneseniya)
Ulitsa Gertsena, 36
⑪

The Church of the Great Ascension

At the intersection with **Suvorovskiy Boulevard**, Gertsena Street veers off to the left, allowing the **Church of the Great Ascension** to dominate the **Nikitskiye Vorota Square**. The name of the square retains the memory of the city gates which were taken down in 1784, along with the White City fortifications, and replaced by boulevards.

The Church of the Great Ascension was begun in the eighteenth century,

...urch of the Great Ascension,
...un in the 18th century and
...npleted in 1840 by Shestakov. It
...s here that Pushkin married
...alia Goncharova in February
...1.

Aleksandr Pushkin (1799–1837), poet, writer, and father of Russian literature.

but finished only in 1840 by Fedor Shestakov along the plans drawn up by Afanasy Grigoriev, a successor to Matvei Kazakov. The church, executed in the style of late Classicism, owes its severe monumentality to the huge expanses of bare walls and its laconic geometric forms: the rectangle of the church, its large frameless windows, the semi-spherical apse extending from the eastern wall, and two Ionic porticos. The large western dome is shifted towards the east, giving the building a ship-like appearance.

The Ascension Church has a special meaning for Muscovites. Aleksandr Pushkin, Russia's literary idol, married Natalia Goncharova, Moscow's most beautiful débutante, here on 18 February 1831. Although the church was not yet finished, the bride's parents insisted that the wedding take place here in their parish. Several omens during the ceremony presaged tragedy: a crucifix fell to the ground, a gust of wind blew out the candles — and six years later, Pushkin, lured into a duel to defend his wife's honour, was dead. Because of its association with Pushkin, his admirers did their best to keep the church open. But despite the fierce resistance of the Muscovites and even the intervention of foreign diplomats, the church was closed and its altar screen carted away to another church.

(Tserkov Fedora Studita)
Suvorovskiy Bulvar, 25
⑫

The Church of St Theodore Studitus

Directly across from the Church of the Great Ascension and barely visible from the street is the tiny church where Generalissimo Aleksandr Vasilievich Suvorov was baptized in 1730. Built in 1626 by Patriarch Filaret, the father of Tsar Michael Romanov, it now houses the **Institute of Fats**. Efforts are underway to turn the church into a Suvorov museum. Suvorov is a legendary figure to this day, both because of his military genius and his popularity with the Russian soldiers.

Paul I fired Suvorov for his anti-Prussian sentiments, but recalled him from his Moscow retirement to head the Russian army during the Italian campaign in 1799. Suvorov stunned the world by leading his army across the snow-capped Alps, a feat which won him the title of 'the Italian Prince'.

Excursion 18

THE MERCHANT BARONS

*A*s the industrialists moved into the territory that had been the private preserve of the nobles, they advanced on all of Moscow's fronts, almost literally leaving no stone unturned. Their infiltration was so profound and so rapid that Boris Pasternak, the Moscow-born author of *Dr Zhivago*, could write that:

> In the 90s, Moscow still preserved its old appearance of a picturesque, provincial town with her famous 'forty times forty churches . . .' At the beginning of the new century, everything was transformed, as if by magic. Moscow was seized by the business fever of great capital cities. Brick giants, which seemed to grow imperceptibly, suddenly shot up to the very sky. Moscow, too, grew in stature and overtook St Petersburg: it inaugurated new Russian art, the art of a great city, a young, modern art.

Two sorts of new rich were rising. The more conservative tried to emulate the nobles, acquiring their mansions and estates. The other, younger generation of merchant barons, such as the Shchukins, the Morozovs, and the Riabushinskys, went a step further. Declining the ennoblement to which many were entitled, they held on to their class origins proudly. In his New Year's address, **Pavel Pavlovich Riabushinsky** spoke for all of the liberal industrialists when he said,

> Our New Year's toast is addressed to the bourgeoisie — the third class of contemporary Russia. It is directed to the rising power which, because of its spiritual and material riches, has overtaken the degenerating gentry and the ruling bureaucracy. We, the carriers of this high, historic mission, welcome creative egoism, striving towards self-perfection and the well-being of each of us. The sound, constructive egoism of the State and of the individuals who constitute the State is the foundation for a new and powerful Russia.

When the merchant barons commissioned their houses, they gave the architects free rein in inspiring new styles: determined to assert their status as innovators and art patrons, they poured their millions into creating a life-style uniquely their own. Their enthusiastic support of the national and the individualistic made Moscow the natural focus of their self-expression and the birthplace of specifically Russian art, for St Petersburg was still under the sway of foreign influences. The efforts of the merchant barons helped move Moscow into the cultural mainstream. **Nikolai Riabushinsky's** magazine popularized Western

Excursion Plan 18
The Merchant Barons

1. House of Nikolai Riabushinsky (Maxim Gorky Museum)
2. The Mansion of Savva Morozov
3. House of the Tarasovs
4. The Palace of Prince Ouroussov
5. The Palace of the Scherbatovs (Filatov's Children's Hospital)
6. The House of Basilevsky
7. The House of Count Bobrinsky
8. The House of 'Natasha Rostova' (USSR Union of Writers)
9. The House of Prince Gagarin (Maxim Gorky Literary Museum)
10. The House of Prince Volkonsky (USA and Canada Institute)

art in Moscow and Russian art abroad; **Ivan Morozov** and **Sergei Shchukin** acquired the finest collection of Impressionist paintings in the world. On the eve of the Bolshevik Revolution, Moscow's opera house, ballet, music, art, and literature could rank with the best.

The **Suvorov Boulevard**, immediately behind the **Church of St Theodore Studitus** (see Excursion 17, ⑦), marks the border line between the realm of the old aristocracy and the baronial estates of the industrialists. The contrast is clearly visible even today as one starts to explore the northern segment of **Gertsena Street** and the quiet lanes that branch off behind the Church of the Ascension. **Kachalova Street**, the little sister of Gertsena Street, is a good case in point.

Kachalova Street

Once called 'Little Nikitskaya', in deference to the splendid 'Great' Nikitskaya, or Gertsena Street, the present Kachalova Street has had its share of beautiful people and houses. In the eighteenth-century **villa of the Count Bobrinsky** ⑦, set back into the garden of **No. 12**, for example, sculptures of *Paris* and *Helen of Troy* frame the entrance of the Classical mansion, the lone survivor amidst the nineteenth-century merchant mansions still dominating the rest of the street.

The first Count Bobrinsky was allegedly the son of Catherine the Great and Grigory Orlov. Bobrinsky's extravagance during his travels in Europe incurred imperial wrath and a ban on coming to St Petersburg. By the time Bobrinsky revised his ways, Catherine died, and Paul I gave Bobrinsky permission to return, even placing Orlov's palace in St Petersburg at his disposal.

(Maxim Gorky Museum)
Ulitsa Kachalova 6/2
①

The House of Nikolai Pavlovich Riabushinsky

Open: 8:00 to 10:00 Wednesday, Thursday, Friday
8:00 to 20:00 Saturday, Sunday
Closed: Monday, Tuesday

The pale yellow villa belonged to the banker Nikolai Pavlovich Riabushinsky, publisher of the sumptuous *Golden Fleece* magazine and a representative of the younger merchant élite that settled near Arbat. Unlike his conservative older brother Pavel Pavlovich, chairman of the Moscow Stock Exchange, and pillar of the Old Believers' community, Nikolai placed his artistic pursuits above business endeavours and pursued art for art's sake. Art patronage was his consuming passion; bordering on obsession.

Not in the least concerned with the staggering cost of the publication, Riabushinsky had launched the first issue of the *Golden Fleece* magazine in

The house of Nikolai Riabushinsky (Maxim Gorky Museum), commissioned in 1900 from the architect Fedor Shekhtel.

1906. In its editorial he declared: 'We intend to propagate Russian art beyond the country of its birth, to represent it in Europe, in a whole and integrated fashion in the very process of its development'.

The *Golden Fleece* followed the pattern of the St Petersburg based *World of Art* magazine which ceased to exist in 1904. Like the *World of Art*, the *Golden Fleece* was at once a society, a publication, and an organizer of exhibits. Taking up the banner of 'Art for Art's Sake', it

championed the cultural and avant-garde movements in Russia and in the West, and sought to turn Russian talent into a contributor to the mainstream of Western culture. The magazine also intended to familiarize Russia with Western art by exhibiting works from the West in Moscow and St Petersburg.

The *Golden Fleece* brought the French Post-Impressionist and the Fauve exhibits to Moscow, and it was Riabushinsky who encouraged the Primitivist trend in Mikhail Larionov and Natalia Goncharova, the two artists who created a bridge between the Mamontov group and the Russian school of abstract art. Despite its brief existence (1906–9), the magazine did much to make Moscow an art centre in its own right and to create a middle-class buying audience.

The *Golden Fleece* and other extravagant undertakings strained the resources of even the fabulously wealthy Riabushinsky. He lost his fortune before the advent of Communism, a staggering loss when we consider that the Riabushinsky Brothers' Bank had a turnover of 1,423 million roubles in 1911.

Architecture

The house which Riabushinsky commissioned in 1900 reflects both his infatuation with Art Noveau as well as the many-sided talent of its builder, Fedor Shekhtel (1859–1926). This Saratov-born, Moscow-trained architect whom all the Riabushinskys patronized worked in a variety of styles ranging from neo-Russian eclecticism to style moderne. The mansion of Nikolai Riabushinsky represents a mid-point in Shekhtel's creative process. In designing the house, Shekhtel combines angular forms with the fluid design of the wrought-iron grating of the balconies and the windows. He contrasts massive volumes, such as those of the entries or the balconies on omega-shaped supports, with mosaic friezes: bands of delicately designed orchids whose golden shimmer brings out the lustre of ceramic tiles covering the facade.

The house itself is not unusual for its day, in terms of basic form (rectangular with the large overhang) and layout.

Detail and the subtle changes distinguish it from the Art Nouveau houses

Staircase in the Riabushinsky house.

designed by Frank Lloyd Wright, Joseph Maria Olbrich, and Scotland's Charles Rennie Mackintosh. Like his contemporaries, particularly the Secessionists, Shekhtel was searching for the revival of life-beautifying concepts of visual culture in an attempt to break away from academic constructions.

Shekhtel's experience as a freelance theatre designer influenced his dramatization of interiors. The inside of Riabushinsky's house, for example, recalls an underwater kingdom: the railing of the circular staircase resembles a medusa rising out of the sea. The fine furniture and woodwork for which Shekhtel was famous are preserved mainly because writer Maxim Gorky lived here after the Revolution. Gorky's personal belongings and books are displayed in the house which in 1965 became the **Gorky Museum** despite Gorky's dislike of both the house and its original owner.

(The Reception House of the Ministry of Foreign Affairs)
Ulitsa Alekseya Tolstogo, 17
②

The Mansion of Savva Timofeyevich Morozov

No less dramatic was the saga of Savva Timofeyevich Morozov, whose baronial castle on **Ulitsa Alekseya Tolstogo** is another important work by Shekhtel.

The Morozovs were a family of Old Believers who came to Moscow shortly after Napoleon's invasion and managed to retain the leadership of the cultural, social and financial life of Moscow until 1917. Their scope of activities was immense: they published the influential newspaper *Moscow News* (*Vedomosti*), organized the **Moscow Philosophical Society**, financed the **Moscow Art Theatre** (MKHAT) and founded several hospitals. Leading shareholders in the **Moscow Merchant Bank**, the Morozovs owned four major textile factories equipped by Ludwig Knopp with the latest British equipment.

Architecture

The residence which Shekhtel designed for Morozov between 1893 and 1898 differs so greatly from Riabushinsky's that it is hard to believe that it was the work of the same architect. Built for one of the richest and greatest romantic extraverts of his time, the mansion seems to have no limits save for its architect's imagination. It is a huge pile, half house, half stage set for a medieval Passion play. The asymmetrically grouped forms are reminiscent of English Perpendicular Gothic, dressed in a wealth of medieval trappings which one usually associates with ecclesiastical rather than secular architecture: flying

EXCURSION 18

buttresses, oriels, oversized gargoyles and tall lanceted church windows. The details executed in a contrasting brown have no structural function, but are there to emphasize the conceptional grandeur and the dynastical aspirations of Morozovs, 'the kings of them all'.

The mansion of Savva Morozov (Reception House of the Ministry of Foreign Affairs), designed by Shekhtel between 1893 and 1898. Morozov, patron of the Moscow Art Theatre, killed himself in 1905.

The interior shows Shekhtel's expressive handling of natural materials and his penchant for the theatrical. The most dramatic part of the house is its **entry hall**: a huge vaulted space encased in dark carved wood, where figures of knights line the walls and black wolf-like creatures guard access to the staircase. To the right of the hallway is a **white and gold ballroom**, decorated in the Empire style. Next to it is the former **library**, a large, dark, vaulted room with fine stained-glass windows. The vitrages depicting medieval knights are the work of painter Mikhail Vrubel, protégé of the mechant art patron Savva Mamantov (see p. 266). The moody Impressionistic visions suit the neo-Gothic decor.

The **dining-room** situated on the opposite side of the hall is also large and sombre. It is furnished with the heavy oak furniture so popular with the Russian merchants. The mansion is now used as reception quarters for the Ministry of Foreign Affairs.

Savva Morozov (1862–1905), who commissioned the mansion, was a grandson of a serf who by 1820 managed to buy his freedom with the proceeds from a wool factory he had acquired and converted to cotton. When he died, he left a flourishing business to Timofei, Savva's father, Russia's counterpart of Andrew Carnegie: ruthless in business, Timofei spared no money on improving engineering standards of the now numerous mills, and sponsoring technical scholarships for his workmen.

When Savva inherited the mills, he continued to expand the business, though his concern was directed towards improving the working conditions of his employees and organizing charities. His wife was a daughter of a textile operator from one of his mills.

After a period of feverish business activity and art collecting, Savva gave himself wholeheartedly to the Moscow Art Theatre (MKHAT). He financed a new building, bought out all of its shares, invested large sums of money in the productions, and even helped lay electric cables. He threw himself into the Revolution with the same abandon. Vladimir Neimirovich-Danchenko, co-founder of the Moscow Art Theatre watched Morozov's dilemma with concern:

> Human nature cannot withstand two opposing and equally powerful passions. A merchant has no right to be carried away. He must remain

faithful to his own element: the element of self-control and common sense. A betrayal leads inevitably to tragic conflicts and Savva Timofeyevich was a man of unbridled passions . . . Not a passion for women . . . but a passion for his role as a merchant . . . passion for Stanislavsky . . . passion for Maxim Gorky . . . passion for the Revolution.

The tension inside Savva Morozov finally snapped when the General Strike broke out in 1905: he fired a bullet into his head at Nice.

The House of the Tarasovs

*Ulitsa Alekseya
Tolstogo, 30*
③

The palazzo which the textile wholesaler Gavril Gavrilovich Tarasov commissioned from the architect Ivan Zholtovsky (see Introduction to 'Modern Moscow', p. 333) at the turn of the twentieth century is less flamboyant than Morozov's Gothic castle, but it, too, stands out from other buildings. It was inspired by the Palazzo Thiene designed by Andrea Palladio in Vincenza. The grey, square building does, indeed, recall a High Renaissance palace by its use of orders and other ancient Roman details expressed with considerable power, severity, and restraint.

The Tarasovs' first commercial undertaking was a cotton factory in Siberia. In 1899, the brothers founded the Tarasov Manufacturing Company with a capital of four million roubles. Their success impressed the art collector Peter Shchukin, who recalled:

> At first the Tarasov brothers lived modestly. They wore old coats, travelled in 3rd class coaches and ate dried biscuits which they brought along to save money on club cars. By the time I saw them again, they had struck it rich and were sporting sable coats with beaver collars.

Unlike other textile merchants who moved to Moscow, the Tarasovs owned no warehouses or offices in Moscow, but ran all of their purchasing operations out of the Renaissance palazzo.

While his two elder brothers attended to business, Nikolai Tarasov devoted his energies to the Moscow Art Theatre (MKHAT). First a shareholder, then a member of the board of directors, he bailed out MKHAT by lending it 30,000 roubles while the company was stranded during a German tour. His mild-mannered ways were deceiving, for Nikolai had a gift for satire and the grotesque. He soon became the motivating force and gagwriter for the first theatre cabaret, known as 'The Bat'. Each performance consisted of ten to fifteen comic numbers accompanied by songs.

The Palace of Prince Ouroussov

*Ulitsa Alekseya
Tolstogo, 40*
④

Tarasov's immediate neighbours were the Princes Ouroussov, also theatre lovers, but belonging to the generation of blue-blooded aristocracy who preceded the merchants on this street.

EXCURSION 18

251

Architecturally, the former Ouroussov mansion offers no attraction. Years of neglect and the subdivision of the palace into communal apartments has cost the building its former grand appearance. After the reconstructions are complete, the building may recover some of its Classical decor, but it will never again see its original setting or splendid gardens. When it was built, in the eighteenth century, the palace faced the **Sadovoye (Garden) Ring** from which it was separated by a beautiful park.

The Ouroussovs are credited with founding Moscow's first professional theatre, the forerunner of the famous **Bolshoy**. In the 1770s Prince P. V. Ouroussov, Moscow's district attorney and owner of a private serf-theatre, petitioned Catherine the Great for a ten-year concession on a public theatre in Moscow. He offered to finance all performances during these ten years, to contribute 3,100 roubles annually to the **Court of Wards** (see p. 222) (where Moscow's first ballerinas were trained) and to build a theatre 'suitable for holding operas and pleasing to the eye' with his own means. Permission granted, Ouroussov engaged the English-born M. E. Maddox to help him realize the project.

Ouroussov's serf-actors and graduates of the Moscow drama department comprised the first company which performed in private theatres until the Bolshoy Petrovsky Theatre was built in 1780. The expenses, aggravated by constant fires, exceeded Ouroussov's estimates and nearly sent Maddox to a debtor's prison. In 1805, the theatre burned to the ground. The company had to keep changing its quarters until 1825, when the Bolshoy Petrovsky Theatre was rebuilt, under the aegis of the Imperial Theatre Administration. It has been known as the Bolshoy Theatre ever since, being the second largest in Europe, after Milan.

It was not the theatrical achievements of the family, however, that drew the poet Alexandr Pushkin to the hospitable household, but one of the Ouroussov daughters, Sofia — a dazzling creature who set many hearts ablaze. Pushkin translated Voltaire's verses for her and was challenged to a duel on her behalf. Fortunately, the duel never took place: a level-headed friend settled the differences between Sofia's admirers at an early morning champagne breakfast.

Vorovskogo Street

(Ulitsa Vorovskogo, formerly Povarskaya)

By turning left onto **Vspolnyi Pereulok** at the Ouroussov House, we reach the quiet, narrow **Vorovskogo Street**, which derived its original name **Povarskaya** from Ivan the Terrible's cooks or *povary*, whose settlements were located here in the sixteenth century. The neighbouring lanes still preserve the association with the guilds that catered to royal needs: the **Stolovyi** (table), **Skaternyi** (tablecloth), and **Khlebnyi** (bread) **Lanes.** In 1923 the old Povarskaya Street was given the name Vorovskogo, after Vatsliav Vorovsky, the Moscow Bolshevik killed by the Whites.

Turning right on Vorovskogo Street towards **Vosstaniya Square,** one passes the former residences of millionaires, now foreign embassies, until one comes upon an ex-nobleman's residence at No. 50.

Ulitsa Vorovskogo, 50
⑧

The House of 'Natasha Rostova'

Since 1932, this huge, estate-like residence of the Princes Dolgorukov and, later, the Counts Sollogub, has been the home of the **Union of Soviet Writers**. Built in 1802, the house owes its fame to the belief that it once belonged to the Rostovs, and thus provided the setting for the coming-out party of Natasha Rostova, Leo Tolstoy's heroine in *War and Peace*.

The country-like aspect of the house is stressed by the informal, even loose, arrangements of numerous side wings and structures around the garden. The garden with the seated statue of writer **Leo Tolstoy**, erected by G. Novokreshchenova in 1958, appears to be the focal point of the architectural ensemble. The main house and the arcaded wings show Palladio's influence despite anaemic Corinthian capitals and the absence of a formal entry. The coat of arms inside the pediment are those of the Counts Sollogub, the last owners of the house before the Revolution.

house of Natasha Rostova'
R Union of Writers), the
ed setting for Natasha's
ng-out party in War and
e.

(Maxim Gorky
Literature
Museum and the
Institute of World
Literature)
litsa Vorovskogo, 25a
⑨

The House of Sergei Sergeyevich Gagarin

Open: 8:00 to 20:00 Tuesday, Friday
10:00 to 17:00, Wednesday, Thursday, Sunday
Closed: Monday

The salmon-coloured mansion was finished in 1829 as the residence of Prince Sergei Sergeyevich Gagarin (1795–1852), privy councillor, Director of the Royal Horse Farms, and, later, Director of the Imperial Theatres. Designed by the prominent architect Domenico Gilliardi, the building differs from most Empire

EXCURSION 18

houses: instead of a collonade, Gilliardi designed three powerful arches covered with drawings which frame the deep recesses of the central projection. Simple in form, monumental in design, the house shows a new sensitivity to the needs of a nineteenth-century nobleman looking for a well-planned building. Note the unusual detail of the facade: above the interwoven laurel wreaths with symbols of art, appears a solitary six-cornered star. This may have been a reminder of Gagarin's affiliation with the lodge of the freemasons.

The house of Prince Sergei Gargarin (Maxim Gorky Literature Museum/Institute of World Literature), completed in 1829 to a design by Domenico Gilliardi.

Gilliardi applied the same fresh and inventive approach to the interior. He borrowed the idea of toplighting from the Roman Pantheon and made the ceiling above the entry swell into a dome with a large central skylight. The Doric columns framing the landing are severely Classical in style, as are the cornices bordered with Greek motives, the statuary lounging in the semi-circular niches, and the repetitive use of lyre designs.

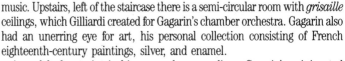

The frequent evocation of musical symbols reflects Gagarin's love for music. Upstairs, left of the staircase there is a semi-circular room with *grisaille* ceilings, which Gilliardi created for Gagarin's chamber orchestra. Gagarin also had an unerring eye for art, his personal collection consisting of French eighteenth-century paintings, silver, and enamel.

A model of restraint in his personal surroundings, Gagarin's opinionated views caused problems in his official life: shortly after being appointed Director of the Imperial Theatres, he clashed head on with Charles Didelot, the proud and choleric French choreographer. Didelot resigned in a fit of temper, but returned to mould the Russian ballet company into the best in Europe.

The Museum

Gagarin's beautiful reception rooms, with vaulted ceilings and double sets of Ionic columns stressing the axial composition of the huge space, are now used for displays devoted to the works of the revolutionary writer Maxim Gorky and his literary contemporaries. Of note are sketches and Gorky's portrait by Pavel Korin,* a painter whom Gorky patronized. Gorky's statue outside the museum was mounted in 1956.

Vorovskogo Street ends near the **Church of St Simeon** at **Kalinin Boulevard**, the former **Vozdvizhenkskaya Street** or **Vozdvizhenka**, now a modern, wide avenue lined with skyscrapers. Its construction in the 1960s

---

*The house where Korin lived is now a museum worth visiting on Malaya Pirogovskaya 16, inside the courtyard.

cost Moscow three old streets and most of the historic **Arbat Square**. Connecting the Kremlin's **Trinity Gates** with the **Kalinin Bridge**, it spans nearly 500 years of history in the course of its four kilometres.

For those who enjoy late-nineteenth-/early-twentieth-century architecture, particularly the *style moderne*, we suggest turning left at the New Zealand Embassy and walking around **Khlebnyi** and **Skaternyi Lanes** as well as **Paliashvili Street**. Where the Khlebnyi Pereulok runs into **Merzlyakovsky Lane**, note a well-preserved, well-restored eighteenth-century manor, now the **USA and Canada Institute** ⑩. Formerly it was the house of the Princes Volkonsky. From Merzlyakovskiy Lane, one can cut through the courtyard of the house where Gogol (see p. 258) wrote the second volume of *Dead Souls*, and which is still graced by a statue of the writer.

Excursion Plan 19
Theatre Lovers, Art
Collectors, and the
Social Lionesses of
Arbat

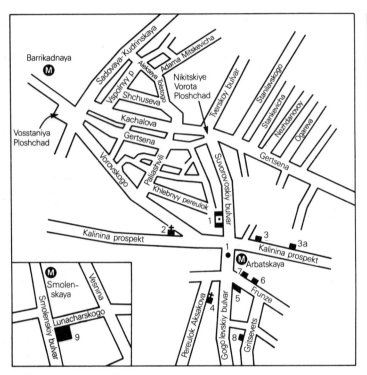

1. Gogol memorials
2. Church of St Simeon of the Pillar
3. House of Arseny Morozov (The House of Friendship)
3a. House of Avraam Morozov
4. Church of the Apostle Phillip
5. Apraksin Palace
6. Palace of Radion Vorontsov (Kutaisov's House)
7. House of the 'Composers'
8. House of Sergei Shchukin
9. House of Margarita Morozova

THEATRE LOVERS, ART COLLECTORS, AND THE SOCIAL LIONESSES OF ARBAT

The Church of St Simeon of the Pillar — Arbat Square — Gogol Memorials — The House of Avraam Avraamovich Morozov — The House of Arseny Avraamovich Morozov — Frunze Street — The Palace of the Apraksins — The House of Radion Vorontsov — The House of the Composers — The House of Sergei Shchukin — The Mansion of Margarita Morozova.

*A*rbat is the name of a square and of a small street which starts at the square and runs to the **Sadovoye Ring**: The area around the **'old Arbat'**, traditionally the citadel of Moscow high society and the stomping ground of Russian writers, artists, and musicians, is still Moscow's cultural heart. Despite the destruction of two monasteries and ten churches by Stalin's city planners, and the addition of **Kalinina Avenue,** which cuts through the centre of the charmed circle, old Arbat continues to attract Russian intellectuals and artists. Arbat's magic is not restricted to the street itself, but also envelops its neighbouring lanes.

The Church of St Simeon of the Pillar

(Tserkov Simeona Stolpnika)
Corner of Ulitsa Vorovskogo and Kalinina Prospekt
②

The multi-domed **Church of St Simeon**, perched at the junction of **Vorovskogo Street** with **Kalinina Prospekt**, looks like a miniature souvenir against the background of the new Arbat skyscrapers. It owes its survival — if not as a church, at least as a building — to its association with Prasokovia Zhemchugova-Kovaleva; the star actress of Count Nikolai Petrovich Sheremetiev's serf theatre (see 'Moscow of the Nobles', Excursion 14, Ostankino and Kuskovo, pp. 201–7), and later Countess Sheremetieva. In 1801, with only two witnesses, Count Sheremetiev married his beautiful Praskovia here in defiance of all social customs.

Educated in Germany and France, a friend of Denis Diderot and an accomplished musician in his own right, Sheremetiev owned a highly skilled troupe of serfs, trained by foreign instructors, rivaling the imperial theatres in St Petersburg in its repertoires. The theatre ceased to exist in 1803, the year Countess Sheremetieva died while giving birth to a son.

The Church of St Simeon was built between 1676 and 1679 by Tsar Fedor, the son of Alexis Romanov. The building presents a picturesque grouping of cubes and rectangles surmounted by drums with green onion-shaped cupolas.

Two rows of spade-shaped *kokoshniki* gables placed in alternating patterns, form a transition between the white walls and red coloured roof of the central church. Similarly shaped gables inscribed into the cornice of the smaller side chapel form a single tiered transition to the solitary dome. The church was built when the multi-cellular construction of the earlier seventeenth century was beginning to acquire vertical expansion and opulent Baroque decor.

Turning left and walking in the direction of the Kremlin we come to **Arbat Square**, the heart of literary and artistic Moscow.

(*Arbatskaya
Ploshchad*)

Arbat or Arbatskaya Square

The name of the square comes from the Tartar word *Orbat*, meaning suburb. In the fifteenth and sixteenth centuries, a suburb grew up here along the trade route to Novgorod. Later, another commercial route branched off in the direction of Smolensk, and the 'Orbat', or Arbat, Street became part of the **Smolenskaya Road**. The square was totally rebuilt at the same time as the Kalinina Prospekt, leaving nothing but memories* of its old buildings and the famous **Sobachya**, or 'Dog's' Square. The square's only notable architectural feature is the **Praga Restaurant**.

Until 1902, this late-eighteenth-century building with a semi-circular rotunda, housed only a bar, 'Praga', which the Moscow cab drivers nick-named 'Braga' or the 'home of the brew'. But in 1902, an enterprising merchant turned the bar into an expensive restaurant which immediately became popular with Moscow literary and artistic groups.

Later, a separate pavilion was added to Praga while the roof was transformed into an open-air restaurant, walled off by a graceful colonnade. Now radically rebuilt, Praga is still Moscow's favourite restaurant, and one of the few to serve good beer.

Gogol Memorials

Since 1924, the section of the boulevard linking Arbat to **Kropotkinskaya Square** has borne the name of **Nikolai Vasiliyevich Gogol** (1809–52), the Ukrainian-born prose writer, a self-conscious and introverted man, whose works first became known through Aleksandr Pushkin's encouragement and support.

An upright statue of Gogol (by N. V. Tomsky, 1952), known to Muscovites as 'the soldier' rises at the head of the **Gogol Boulevard**.† A second statue by sculptor N. A. Andreyev, which in 1909 graced this site, is now to be found in the **courtyard of No. 7, Suvorovskiy Boulevard**. Gogol spent the last months of his life here, working on the second volume of *Dead Souls* which he later burned, also in this house.

Andreyev depicts Gogol in a sitting position, his cloak draped around him in a characteristic mood of dejection and self-doubt. Bas-relief figures from Gogol's world circle the base of the pedestal: Taras Bulba, the Cossack hero of his native Ukraine and staunch protector of Russian Orthodoxy against the onslaught of the Roman Catholic Poles, the squalid clerk described in Gogol's *Overcoat* epitomizing the drabness of St Petersburg's bureaucracy, and the rascal Khlestakov, who terrozied a provincial town as the *Inspector General*,

Statue of Nikolai Gogol (1809–52) by N. A. Andreyev in the courtyard of Suvorovskiy bulvar, 7.

---

*In the eighteenth century the street was called Vozdvizhenka after the Krestovozdvizhensky Monastery located on this street near house No. 7. In 1935, having blown up the monastery, Stalin's city 'planners' renamed it the street of the Commintern, then Kalinina Street, and since 1963 it has merged into Kalinina Prospekt.

†Formerly Prechistensky Boulevard. One block down, then right and left, on **Aksakova Lane**, No. 5, is the **Church of St Phillip**, one of two working churches in central Moscow.

stand next to Chichikov, the anti-hero of Gogol's *Dead Souls*, and many other figures conceived in the tormented writer's brilliant mind.

On the other side of Arbat Square two buildings attract attention: a Moorish castle and, next to it, an emerald green mansion. Both belonged to the cousins of Savva Morozov, the Moscow Art Theatre patron.

Prospekt Kalinina, 14

The House of Avraam Avraamovich Morozov

Hidden behind a garden, the house of Avraam Avraamovich Morozov dates from 1886. It was built by the architect Roman Klein (1858–1924) who has sixty buildings in Moscow to his credit, including the **Pushkin Museum of Fine Arts**. Morozov's house dates from Klein's earlier period when the architect worked in the fashionable eclectic style. While making lavish use of Classical details, Klein also gave this Western-looking building features of a Russian country-style villa, in which numerous service buildings are scattered around the main manor house.

The prosperous textile merchant Morozov was not destined to enjoy his house for long. Shortly after moving to Moscow with his wife and three sons, he died. His young widow, Varvara Alekseyevna, daughter of the textile tycoon and art collector Khludov, took over the management of the Morozov's textile mills. A contemporary writer who modelled his heroine on Morozova, described her as a 'regal woman, a lively businesswoman and the elegant hostess of the most intellectual salon in Moscow'. She was also Moscow's leading benefactress, discreetly endowing the Turgenev Library, founding an old people's home, organizing schoools for factory workers and special courses for women.

Morozova's second husband was V. M. Sobolevsky, Professor at the Moscow University and manager of the *Russkiye Vedomosti*, Russia's most popular newspaper. Their literary salon brought together the prominent people of the time: the writers Chekhov and Korolenko, the poet Briusov and the theatre directors Stanislavsky and Nemirovich-Danchenko. An enthusiastic collector of old Russian manuscripts, a passion which she shared with her father, Morozova influenced the cultural interests of her son Ivan (see Excursion 12, p. 190), who went on to become a great collector of French art. He owned 250 works of Impressionists, Fauves, Cubists, and Futurists.

The second son Mikhail, known as the 'dandy' was more inclined towards gambling than art. He lost one million roubles to a tobacco merchant in a game of cards. Mikhail's wife, Margarita Kirillovna Morozova, the mystically inclined social lionness and musician (see pp. 264–5)* did her best to uphold the family traditions.

Prospekt Kalinina, 16

The House of Arseny Avraamovich Morozov

Arseny Morozov was no more comforting to his mother Varvara Alekseyevna

*Mme Morozova took piano lessons from the composer Alexandr Scriabin (1871–1915).

than was his older brother Mikhail. A staunch Old Believer, he married a Catholic and built the extraordinary Moorish castle which led his mother to exclaim 'I always knew you were crazy, now all of Moscow knows it, too'.

Baptized the 'Spanish Castle' Morozov's house embodies eclecticism. The inspiration for the building came from Portugal, where Arseny and his friend B. A. Mazyrin were travelling at that time. During their visit they came upon a sixteenth-century castle that combined Medieval and Renaissance architecture. Bewitched by the castle, Morozov immediately commissioned Mazyrin to recreate it for him in Moscow.

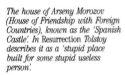

The house of Arseny Morozov (House of Friendship with Foreign Countries), known as the 'Spanish Castle'. In Resurrection *Tolstoy describes it as a 'stupid place built for some stupid useless person'.*

Mazyrin did his best: borrowing the massing and the two towers of the facade from the original, he dressed them up with lace-like bands and encrusted them with shell motifs. On either side of the entry Mazyrin placed stout columns made to look like twisted sea cables. His reliance on nautical motifs had less to do with architectural imagination than with the personal tragedy of the Portuguese owner of the castle, whose daughter had perished at sea. For the rest Mazyrin relied on the more typical features of *style moderne*.

The house can be visited, since it is now the **House of Friendship with Foreign Countries**. The **hallway** is decorated in a style reminiscent of English hunting lodges, with wooden beams ending in carved animal heads and a huge fireplace. The same rope motives are found above the entry, interwoven between animal and floral designs.

To the right is a **white hall** with golden bas-relief friezes. Adjoining the ballroom is a superb Greek **atrium**: its walls and floors are inlaid with rare marble from every part of the world and semi-precious stones, including malachite, in geometric designs. From the atrium a passage leads to the **music room** and Morozov's former dressing room: a splendid Renaissance hall which

The Morozov house: the atrium.

adjoined his private sauna. The house also includes an air-conditioned kitchen laid out with blue delphic tiles.

In his novel *Resurrection*, Tolstoy paints a wrathful portrait of this 'stupid place built for some stupid useless person'. Arseny died from blood poisoning after shooting himself in the leg during a billiard game to prove his manliness.

Arseny's mistress, a well-known actress from MKHAT, rather than his outraged wife, inherited the mansion in 1908 and lived in it until the Revolution. Afterwards she emigrated, the house was leased first to the Japanese, then to the British, and finally to the Indian embassies. In 1959 it was made the House of Friendship and is still used for staging receptions and exhibits from foreign countries.

Frunze Street

Leaving **Metro Arbatskaya** (1935) on our left, we turn into **Frunze Street**, the former **Znamenka**. This street, an ancient trade route to Novgorod, was a contemporary of the Kremlin. The name Znamenskaya Street or simply Znamenka dates from the seventeenth century when the Romanovs erected here the **Church of the Sign (Znamenie)**. By that time the trade route had already switched to the present day **Gertsena Street**.

Znamenka, like Gertsena, still boasts luxurious eighteenth-century palaces and distinguished coats of arms. The residents of this street were Moscow's greatest art collectors and theatre builders. Tolstoy, always sensitive to creating a proper background for his characters, chose Znamenka as the home of the Bolkonskys of *War and Peace* and the Oblonskys from *Anna Karenina*.

In 1925, the Znamenie Church of the Romanovs came down on Stalin's orders, and the street was renamed after Mikhail Vasilievich Frunze (1885–1925), an old Bolshevik and military leader who headed the Revolutionary Military Soviet, headquartered in the old Apraksin palace.

(Soviet Defence Ministry)
Ulitsa Frunze, 19

The Palace of Stepan Stepanovich Apraksin

Despite the Ministry of Defence's reconstructions of the 1940s, the gigantic, heavily guarded structure, displaying features of neo-Classicism, is many things to many people. Some associate it with Frunze, Budennyi, Voroshilov, and other Soviet military leaders who used the building as their headquarters. For others, it is still the prestigious tsarist **Aleksandrovskoye Military School**, where future White Russian officers were trained and where twenty-year-old cadets fought their last desperate battle against the Reds.

Yet others think of it as the home of Moscow cadets in the 1850s, and before that a state orphanage. But for lovers of old Moscow, the building concealed behind the Ministry's mammoth wall will always be the palace of General Stepan Stepanovich Apraksin (1756–1827), Moscow's grand seigneur and theatre lover.

The Apraksins were born under a lucky star. Their forebear Tartar Khan

Solokhmir married a Rurik princess in 1371. The nickname 'Opraksa' which he received from Oleg, the Prince of Riazan, whose sister he married, was passed on to his sons. The family prominence was further boosted in the seventeenth century, when Marfa 'Opraksa', or Apraksina, as the family was then called, married Tsar Fedor, Peter the Great's half-brother.

In Peter's time two Apraksin brothers were awarded the title of admiral: one for his skill as a naval commander, the other for creating the Russian fleet. Stepan Stepanovich's own father was the general who defeated Friedrick the Great's army at Gross-Jaegerndorf in 1757. To reward the general, Empress Elizabeth became godmother to his new born son Stepan, whom she showered with gifts as an infant, and later appointed to the élite Semenovsky regiment with a sergeant's rank.

Fortune continued to smile on the Empress's godson. He reached the rank of general before he turned 30, was beloved by women, and was as popular at St Petersburg as he was at other European courts. Even when he lost secret State documents during an escapade with a Polish adventuress he saved his career by marrying Princess Golitsyna, the sister of Moscow's military Governor General, whose haughty beauty earned her the sobriquet of 'Angry Venus'

His fortune repaired, the unruffled Apraksin retired from active service and settled down to a life of luxury in the palace which the architect Francesco Camporesi completed for him in 1792. The Apraksin balls and the theatrical performances, in which the host took part himself, became Moscow's most sought after social events. The performers were Apraksin's serf-actors, some trained in Italy, and their repertoire ranged from foreign operas to works by Russian musicians.

In 1814 when the Bolshoy Theatre was destroyed by fire, Apraksin offered them his stage, which the Bolshoy Company used until 1827.

The severe judgement of Apraksin's wife which ruled Moscow society did not apply to her husband. In gratitude for her overlooking his escapades, Apraksin commissioned a marbled likeness of his wife with the words 'Homage to Virtue' inscribed on it in gold.

Ulitsa Frunze, 10
⑥

The House of Radion Vorontsov (Kutaisov's House)

Diagonally across from Apraksin's former palace is the house which belonged to the powerful Count Radion Illarionovich Vorontsov, uncle of Princess Vorontsova-Dashkova and brother of the powerful Mikhail, chancellor under Empress Elizabeth and Catherine the Great. Built in the 1760s and remodelled in 1802, the classical decor of the house (which is said to have provided Leo Tolstoy with inspiration for the residence of Pierre Bezukhov in *War and Peace*) is well preserved.

It is also said that the house briefly belonged to Count Ivan Pavlovich Kutaisov, a Turkish hairdresser whose skilful handling of Emperor Paul's looks and moods won him the title of count, a Moscow estate, and an annual income of 300,000 roubles.

Voronstov's residence did provide refuge for Russia's first public theatre, the future Bolshoy which Prince Ouroussov (see p. 252) founded in 1776 and which remained there until 1780 while the Bolshoy Petrovsky Theatre was being built. The house is now a children's musical school honouring Elena Fabianovna Gnesina (1874–1967) a graduate of the Moscow Conservatory and a distinguished pianist, who, together with her two sisters, founded and directed the **Moscow School of Music**.

Ulitsa Frunze, 16
⑦

The House of the 'Composers'

Nikolai Rubinstein, the founder of the Moscow Conservatory of Music, and Peter Tchaikovsky, composer and teacher at the conservatory, rented their apartments here between 1868 and 1871. During their stay, this was the meeting place of the St Petersburg based 'Mighty Handful',* a group of five composers who, like the Mamantov group of artists, were developing music along national Russian lines.

While living at this apartment, Tchaikovsky composed the overture to *Romeo and Juliet*, his first quartet, and several lyrical songs.

Ulitsa Grivets, 8
⑧

The House of Sergei Ivanovich Shchukin

Until 1917, this mansion in **Grivets Street**, or **Krestoyozdvizhensky Lane**, as it was then called, belonged to Sergei Ivanovich Shchukin (1854–1936), textile industrialist and owner of the world's greatest collections of Impressionist art.

With his dark angular features and a speech defect, Shchukin was no match for the glamorous builder of the house, Stolypin, whose serf theatre rivalled Apraksin's. In 1806, Stolypin sold his seventy-four actors and the female lead, a Wagneresque, six-foot singer with a booming voice, to the Bolshoy Theatre Company for 42,000 roubles and the house to Prince Trubetskoy.

Ivan Vassiliyevich Shchukin, Sergei's father, who in 1878 had converted his family's textile shop into the leading Moscow textile firm of Shchukin and Sons purchased the house from Trubetskoy, four years later. His wife, the daughter of the merchant and art collector Botkin (see 'Moscow of the Nobles', Excursion 8, p. 135), bore him eleven children of whom six inherited the collector's fever.† Sergei, the third son, who took over the house from his father,

---

* 'The Mighty Handful' (*Moguchaya Kuchka*) consisted of Mili Balakirev (Glinka's successor who developed Russian music along national lines), Cesar Cui, Modest Mussorgsky (*Boris Godunov*), Nikolai Rimsky-Korsakov (*The Snow-Maiden*, *The Golden Cockerel*), and Alexander Borodin (*Prince Igor*).

† The eldest son, Peter (1853–1912) collected icons, Russian folk craft, Russian history books, and ancient manuscripts, which he willed to the Moscow Historical Museum on Red Square in 1905. In recognition of his services, Emperor Nicholas II granted Peter the title of general. Dmitry (1855–1932) owned a collection of old European masters which was nationalized in 1918 and turned over to the Pushkin Museum of Fine Arts.

was the most imaginative and influential of Moscow's collectors of foreign art.

At the turn of the twentieth century, Sergei and his friend Ivan Morozov (see Excursion 12, p. 190), another prosperous textile merchant, began to collect the works of French painters. Both were then in their mid-forties. When Ahchukin first took him to Matisse's studio in 1908, Morozov was uncertain about the painter's more recent works but Shchukin delighted in outraging the Moscow bourgeoisie.

By the start of the First World War, Shchukin had amassed over 200 paintings which included works by Monet, Van Gogh, Gauguin, Cezanne, Degas, Renoir, Picasso, and others.

To provide maximum light for his collection, Shchukin decided to remodel the house, dispensing with columns and other Classical trappings to make room for the huge windows of the second-floor gallery and to light the grand staircase, where he planned to hang two of Matisse's huge panels *Dance* and *Music* commissioned specifically for the spot.

Shchukin's taste in art was ahead of its time; he bought many artists' canvasses before they became famous and the prices of their works rose accordingly. None the less, he made his choice slowly and deliberately, asking the painters' permission to let the works hang in his gallery before finalizing the purchase.

Shchukin, justifiably proud of his collection, wanted to share his work with everyone. Like Prince Golitsyn (see 'Moscow of the Nobles', Excursion 7, p. 122), the first art collector to open his gallery to the public, Shchukin would act as a guide every Sunday to those who came to view his collection. The paintings drew many people from abroad and Sergei's eloquence, despite his stutter, won over sceptical viewers more than once.

Shchukin's collection broadened the horizons of an entire generation of young Russian artists, who could acquaint themselves with the latest trends and works of Western European artists in his mansion, without making the trip to Paris.

Sergei Shchukin left Russia after the Revolution of 1917. His collection was nationalized by the Soviet government and divided between the Pushkin Museum of Art and the Hermitage Museum in Leningrad. Shchukin, then living in Paris, refused to start a court case against the Soviet government for the return of his collection, saying that he had gathered it not for himself, but for his country and for his people.

The last house described in this tour is the famous literary salon of Mme Morozova. The mansion can be reached by taking the Metro at the Arbatskaya (Filievskaya line) station and riding one stop to Smolenskaya. The salon and its famous *habitués* provides an appropriate end to this chapter and presage the Bolshevik Revolution; it is located at the corner of **Smolenskiy Boulevard** and **Lunacharskogo Lane**. Ironically, the street bears the name of Anatoly Vasilievich Lunacharsky (1875–1933), Commissar of Education under Lenin and the first Bolshevik patron of arts.

The Mansion of Margarita Kirillovna Morozova

Margarita Kirillovna turned the stately mansion of her husband Mikhail Morozov into the gathering place of Russia's twentieth-century intelligentsia. Poets, writers, politicians, and philosophers heatedly debated their country's future in Mme Morozova's white drawing room and in the formal ballroom with its upraised platform. The prophetic words of Vladimir Solovyiev (1853–1900) hung over the *habitués* of Morozova's salon like snow-laden clouds: 'The end is near, the unexpected will soon be accomplished'. Prince Sergei Trubetskoi aired his liberal ideas, Sergei Bulgakov (1871–1944) preached romantic anarchy, Pavel Miliukov (1859–1943), historian and founder of the liberal Kadet party defended his views, and the Symbolist Andrei Belyi (1880–1934) recited his mystic verse there. (It was said that Belyi, enamoured of Morozova, sent her white roses and love poems anonymously.)

The undisputed idol of these fateful days was Aleksandr Blok (1880–1921), a disciple of philosopher Solovyev and a representative of the young generation of Symbolists. Blok, whose early poems (*Verses about a Beautiful Woman*) were full of mysticism, greeted the October Revolution as a cleansing storm. His controversial poem 'Twelve' gives an apocalyptical vision of the Revolution personified by revolutionaries as the apostles of the new world, headed by Christ crowned with a wreath of white roses.

Moscow merchant millionaires like the Morozovs financed their own downfall, realizing it too late, as did Blok, who spoke the words 'And poet dies because he can no longer breathe: life has lost its meaning', in an address commemorating Pushkin's birth a few months before his own death at the age of 41. The Revolution was yet to come and a whole generation of artists, writers, musicians, and thinkers would feverishly 'paint their hut their own colour', but for Mme Morozova's philosophing *habitués* and the merchant princes of Moscow, it was the end of an era.

Major contributors to Moscow's economic, philanthropic, and cultural life, the bourgeoisie never played a significant role in Russia's politics. While individual wealthy industrialists donated money to the Revolution, they did so for their personal satisfaction, and not as an organized activity. Instead, the businessmen created powerful associations for mining, oil, metallurgy, and textiles, which petitioned the government on specific problems of economic policy: enlightened self-interest genuinely was their *leitmotif*.

Lenin nationalized Russia's banks and businesses. A planned economy and five-year plans now contain Moscow's eclectic mercantile spirit, and the old trading capital has become the centre of the largest economic bureaucracy in the world.

ABRAMTSEVO

Open: 11:00 to 18:00, Tuesday, Thursday, Sunday.
Closed: Monday, Wednesday.
Across from the museum there is a good restaurant.
Vistors must request special permission through Intourist, since Ambramtsevo
is located 57 kilometres out of Moscow on the way to Zagorsk.

*I*f the takeover of the Moscow City Council by the merchants in the 1870s
(see 'Moscow of the Townspeople', Excursion 6, p. 73) symbolized the new
role the industrialists were to play in the administration of the city, the
acquisition of **Abramtsevo** by **Savva Ivanovich Mamantov** (1841–1918)
represented a similar takeover in the cultural domain. The railway tycoon
Mamantov purchased this small run-down wooden dacha, picking it over all
grand villas simply because of its literary association with the writer **Sergei
Timofeyevich Aksakov** (1791–1859). During Aksakov's ownership,
Abramtsevo became a literary mecca of Russian intellectual gentry.

It was in this early-eighteenth-century house that Aksakov's sons **Ivan** and
Konstantin, along with **Ivan Kireyevsky** and **Aleksei Khomiakov**
formulated the Slavophile ideology (see 'Moscow of the Nobles', Excursion 13,
page 191), to which Mamantov himself subscribed. Here **Nikolai Gogol** read
the first chapter of the second volume of *Dead Souls* to a selected audience
which included **Ivan Turgenev** and actor **Mikhail Shchepkin**. To Mamantov's
credit, after purchasing the dacha, he enlarged and improved it, while lovingly
preserving the relics of the 'men of the forties'.

Mamantov's own concepts of the type of cultural activity that he would
foster in Abramtsevo crystallized during a chance meeting at Rome's *Café el
Greco* in 1874. Over a cup of tea with sculptor **Mark Matveyevich Antokolsky**
(1843–1902) and painters **Vasily Dmitrievich Polenov** and **Ilia Efimovich
Repin** (1844–1930), Mamantov listened to them talk about the superficiality
of French art and the need to create a Russian national school. Inspired,
Mamantov returned to Abramtsevo, having secured, *en route*, the promise
of Serov's widow to send her eight-year-old son **Valentin Serov** to Abramtsevo,
where he would study art. The core of Mamantov's Art Workshop was thus
formed.

By 1879, the Abramtsevo circle also included the two **Vasnetsov brothers**,
Victor (1848–1926), a painter and stage designer, and Appolinarius (1856–1933),
a painter-archaeologist, **Elena Polenova**, a master embroiderer and designer,
Vasily Surikov (1848–1921), the creator of monumental historical paintings,
and **Maria Yakunchikova**, a painter who was related to Elizaveta Grigorievna,
Mamantov's wife. Picnics, boating on the river Vora, swimming, fishing,
hunting, and horseback riding alternated with serious painting and literary
discussions.

The Abramtsevo Museum

The old Aksakov house overlooking the Vora River, birch groves, and pond, along with Mamantov's additions, is now a museum run by the Ministry of Culture of the USSR. The exhibits inside the villa evoke memories of Aksakov's family, the Mamantovs, and Mamantov's protégés, whose sketches, paintings, and sculptures are displayed at the museum.

Among the carefully preserved rooms which belonged to Aksakov is the writer's **study**, containing the desk at which he wrote between 1844 and 1870 and the bookshelf with his favourite books and mementoes. The walls are hung with portraits of Aksakov's wife, his children, and friends. Another room to have kept its original decor is the family's **dining-room** with sculptures of the owner and his friends.

Mamantov's personal belongings, mixed in with bits and pieces of Aksakov's furniture, also contain art works of the painters who worked and lived at Abramtsevo. The former **bedroom of Aksakov's daughters** is hung with sketches by Elena's brother Vasily Dmitrievich Polenov (1844–1927), consisting mainly of landscapes depicting the beautiful countryside around Abramtsevo. The **study of Mme Mamantova** is decorated with canvases of the Vasnetsov brothers.

Another room honours Repin, the charter-member of the Mamantov's circle. Three of his works also occupy the place of honour in the **dining-room**, which Savva Mamantov added in 1887. Displayed above Aksakov's red wood living-room set are three of Repin's most famous works: the portraits of Savva and of his wife, and one of Repin's rare still-lifes, a bouquet of flowers. All three were finished at the villa in 1878.

Despite Repin's paintings, the dining-room none the less belongs to Valentin Aleksandrovich Serov (1856–1911) who arrived at Ambramtsevo as an eight-year-old boy. *The Girl with the Peaches* is among one of the artist's greatest works, which he created in Mamantov's studios in 1887. His model was the twelve-year-old Verusha Mamantova, who had the knack for dispelling the

Abramtsevo: the main house, former residence of Aksakov (eighteenth century).

EXCURSION 20

267

painter's morose moods. The painting of Verusha with sunlight casting luminous highlights on her hair, the pink blouse and the peaches, sparked Serov's career as Russia's leading portraitist. *The Girl with the Peaches*, acclaimed by art historian Igor Grabar as the masterpiece of Russian painting, won Serov the first prize and 200 roubles at the Exhibition of the Moscow Society for Art Lovers.

The dining-room was also the site of the annual Christmas show, which featured carefully prepared costumes and settings. The heart and soul of each performance was Savva himself, or, as his friends called this Russia Medici, 'Savva the Magnificent'.

Another of Mamantov's great contributions to Russian culture was the creation of his **private opera** in 1886. Until then, operas were only performed at the Bolshoy Theatre. At first Mamantov recruited foreigners for the leads, until he heard **Fedor Shaliapin** (1837–1938) sing at the annual Nizny Novgorod (Gorky) Fair. Mamantov's opera made the handsome Shaliapin an overnight star. His portrayal of Boris Godunov in Mussorgsky opera entered the annals of operatic history.

Work on the opera attracted fresh talent to Abramtsevo. Using the designs of Viktor Vasnetsov, **Isaac Levitan** (1860–1900) drew stage settings for the opera *The Mermaid* (*Rusalka*). Its success can be gauged by the fact that the audience broke out in a mass ovation for the stage designers, who were made to take a bow to thunderous applause. The opera also attracted the temperamental painter **Konstantin Korovin** (1861–1939), one of Serov's close friends who soon became the favourite of the Mamantov circle.

The Red Sitting-Room

It was this former reception room of Aksakov, where Gogol read excerpts from his *Dead Souls*, that became the centre for Mamantov's protégés. The oval table perched on a lyre-shaped pedestal still has a table cloth covered with the initials of Mamantov's painters and guests. Here they gathered in the evenings to read aloud, paint, or play theatrical pieces and charades beneath Serov's portraits of Mamantov's son Andrei and another of his daughter Vera (Verusha). Both children died young and were buried in the cemetery of the estate church.

Savva Mamantov, strongly influenced by the Slavophile ideology, set the tone for his circle. He believed that the future of Russia lay in the return to the native sources and that its art would be revitalized through Russian Orthodoxy and the traditions of Muscovy. The momentous decision to create a new Russian art by turning back to its sources was sparked inside this room.

The Saviour's Estate Chapel

The old Aksakov chapel had been washed away in a flood and needed to be replaced. Searching for inspiration, Mamantov's painters wandered from Novgorod to Rostov and Yaroslavl to study old church architecture, frescoes, wooden buildings, and ceramics. Elated by their findings they began work

...bramtsevo Church (twentieth ...ntury).

on the church in 1882.

The interior of the chapel was a collective undertaking of Repin, Viktor Vasnetsov, and Polenov which explains the diversity of styles between the frescoes, icons, and the building's exterior. Repin's *Saviour* was pronounced 'a martyred intellectual' and not a Christ. The main praise went to Polenov's *Annunciation* and Vasnetsov's icons, particularly his *St Sergius*.

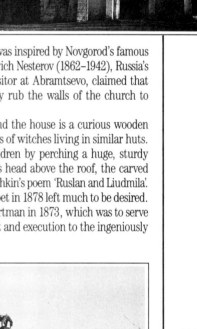

The exterior of the simple white church with a central onion-shaped dome was inspired by Novgorod's famous Church in Nereditsy. Painter Mikhail Vasilievich Nesterov (1862–1942), Russia's leading religious painter and a frequent visitor at Abramtsevo, claimed that Elizaveta Grigorievna would surreptitiously rub the walls of the church to give them that mouldy, antique look.

Located half-way between the church and the house is a curious wooden '*izba*', inspired by Russian fairytale accounts of witches living in similar huts. Vasnetsov created this **playhouse** for children by perching a huge, sturdy tree trunk atop craggy stumps. The horse's head above the roof, the carved figures of bats and mythical beasts recall Pushkin's poem 'Ruslan and Liudmila'.

The **Sauna** designed by architect I. P. Ropet in 1878 left much to be desired. The second building, conceived by V. A. Gartman in 1873, which was to serve as the painters **Studio**, came closer in spirit and execution to the ingeniously decorated peasant *izbas*.

...ramtsevo: the Studio (1873), ...igned by V. A. Hartman.

Woman in Kothornos, *pencil sketch (c.1890) by Mikhail Vrubel (1856–1910). Collection of Mr and Mrs Nikita D. Lobanov-Rostovsky.*

Under the direction of master craftswoman Elena Dmitrievna Polenova, the Studio became a veritable museum of old Russian crafts and a workshop for peasant arts such as carving, embroidery, and ceramics. Some of the best ceramic works of **Mikhail Aleksandrovich Vrubel** (1856–1910) were created here. The ceramic stoves which embellish Abramtsevo were also the works of Vrubel, the last and most brilliant of Mamantov's art fledglings.

Serov met Vrubel in Kiev and introduced him to the Mamantovs. Vrubel's religious painting influenced Serov's style and the development of the Russian 'Art for Art's Sake' movement. Drawing his inspiration from Byzantine frescoes, Vrubel employed ornamental rhythms and dark, brooding colours to great effect. The art of Theophanes the Greek (see 'Moscow of the Tsars', Excursion 1, Annunciation Cathedral, p. 25), with its emotional depth, found an ardent response in the tortured Vrubel, whom Serov found living in utter misery.

Serov eventually persuaded Vrubel to move to Abramtsevo in 1889. Even though the Mamantovs did not appreciate his work at first, he soon won them over: the portrait he painted of Savva Mamantov is an outstanding work of art.

No one was a better judge of Vrubel's genius than the artists themselves. When Serov and Korovin were preparing the sketches for the interior decoration of the Tretyakov* factory in Kostroma, their lack of experience with religious painting was obvious: *Christ Walking on the Waters* remained a mortal skimming over Mamantov's parquet floors. Vrubel, who was working on a stage set, finally could bear it no longer. Within half an hour he produced a superb watercolour and handed it over to his friends, saying that 'people born to paint frescoes never get the commissions'.

Vrubel's colourful **bench**, inlaid with tiles and christened '*Divan*', still ornaments Abramtsevo's park. The theme of Lermontov's poem 'The Demon' fascinated Vrubel, it became the subject of many of his canvases. To him, the Demon was not the evil Devil of the Old Testament, but the symbol of endless loneliness reflected in the poet's haunting lines:

> If you could only understand
> This nameless bitterness of living.

'The nameless bitterness of living' was Vrubel's own destiny. He died in a mental asylum in 1910. His work, more than anyone else's, served to bridge the realism of the nineteenth century with the 'Art for Art's Sake' movement of the twentieth.

*Founder of the Tretyakov Gallery of Art (see 'Modern Moscow', Museums and Theatres, p. 355).

PART V

MOSCOW OF
THE CLERGY

INTRODUCTION

*A*s an unknown Soviet writer once said: 'It is impossible to separate the Russian Orthodox Church from the history of the Russian people. It is equally impossible to speak or write about Moscow without mentioning its churches and monasteries. This is where it all began'.

In 988 **Prince Vladimir** converted Kievan Russia to Byzantine Christianity. His choice of faith was influenced as much by the aesthetics of the Byzantine liturgy as by the benefits of closer ties with Constantinople. Not the least of these benefits was the exposure of Russia to Byzantine religious tradition with its sacred texts couched in an understandable Church Slavonic, rites, arts, and architecture.

Three and a half centuries later, **Metropolitan Peter**, having witnessed the decline of Kiev and Vladimir, paved the way for the transfer of the Holy See to Moscow. Moscow thus became Russia's third religious capital and the bastion of Russian Orthodoxy. It has maintained this role ever since, despite foreign invasions, Peter the Great's secularization of the Church, and the Bolshevik Revolution. Today, even if the Patriarch of Moscow and All the Russias is allowed to live in Danilovsky Monastery and administer the Church, he must do so under the close supervision of the government's Atheistic Council for the Affairs of the Russian Orthodox Church.

The adoption of Orthodox Christianity from Byzantium was to have a lasting effect on the history of the Russian Church. The schism in 1054 between Rome and Constantinople served only to reinforce Russia's devotion to its newly adopted faith and added sanctity to Greek rituals, arts, and texts. Russia obediently accepted Greek metropolitans or dispatched its own appointees to Constantinople for confirmation by the Greek patriarch.

But in 1439 the relationship between Moscow and Byzantium was altered by the Council of Florence. The Patriarch of Constantinople recognized the Pope of Rome as the head of the church, hoping to find in him an ally against the Ottoman Turks. Horrified by the patriarch's betrayal of true Orthodoxy, a council of Russian bishops met in 1448 and declared the Russian Orthodox Church independent of its Greek parent. The same year, the Russian-born **Metropolitan Iov** was elected to head the autocephalous Russian Church.

The fall of Constantinople in 1453 confirmed Moscow's belief that divine retribution had struck Byzantium: Rome had lapsed into heresy and been captured by the barbarians. Constantinople, the second Rome, embraced Latinity and was overrun by the Turks. Now, wrote monk Filofei in 1510 to **Grand Prince Basil III**, 'The Third Rome had sprung up in thy sovereign kingdom. Moscow will stand . . . and Fourth Rome is not to be.' The Grand Duchy of Moscow came to regard itself as the guardian of unsullied Orthodoxy.

Hand in hand, the Church and the State transplanted the Byzantine concept of autocracy to Russian soil. The tsar, an autocrat by divine right, was to guard Orthodoxy and care for his subjects like a true father. The metropolitan was to provide religious guidance for the state, watch over the Moscow throne, and act as spiritual advisor to the tsar.

If, in the early days of the Moscow Grand Duchy, the partnership between

*he Church of St Clement (mid-ighteenth century). A rare *ample of Elizabeth I's Baroque 1 Moscow (see p. 314).

INTRODUCTION

the Church and the State had fostered Russian unity, by the sixteenth century the balance was to be disturbed by the rising authoritarianism of the tsars and the increased wealth of the Church.

The Church itself was divided on its role concerning its relationship to the State and its spiritual mission. The 'possessors' and 'nonpossessors', as they were called, engaged in a fierce debate.

In the late fifteenth century, **Abbot Joseph of Volokolamsk**, leader of the 'possessors', defended the close State–Church relationship and argued that independent wealth (the Church owned nearly one-third of the lands) permitted the monasteries to dispense charity and maintain centres of learning. Monk **Nil Sorsky** countered by criticizing the wealth of the Russian Orthodox Church and its collaboration with the State. Sorsky argued that monks should be poor and detached from matters of the State.

The church canonized leaders of both factions, but the argument was settled in the favour of the 'possessors', whose support was crucial to the Russian State even though the Church had courage to criticize the excesses of the tsars. In return for the support of the Church, the tsars were solicitous of its interests. In 1589, thanks largely to the diplomatic skills of **Regent Boris Godunov**, Constantinople agreed to the creation of the Russian Patriarchate and the elevation of metropolitan to the rank of patriarch.

During the Time of Troubles in the early 1600s which followed the death of Boris Godunov, the Russian Church demonstrated its patriotism and spiritual strength. **Patriarch Germogen** launched an appeal to repulse the Catholic Poles from Moscow's Kremlin and ordered the monasteries to turn their gold into arms. In 1612, the sacrifice and determination of the Church resulted in a Russian victory. **Tsar Michael Romanov** ascended the vacant throne, with his father, **Patriarch Filaret**, assuming the role of the co-ruler.

After fifteen years of war, the Russians laid down their arms with the monarchy restored and the Orthodox faith intact. The attempts of the Poles to catholicize the Russians had resulted in a strengthening of the people's devotion to the faith of their forebears. Miseries and the isolation from other Orthodox communities had added a new sanctity to the national Church, its religious practices, texts, and arts.

Ironically, it was the Church, in the person of **Patriarch Nikon**, that in the 1650s struck the final blow to this harmonious relationship. Nikon's determination to impose the supremacy of the Church over the State cost him the support of the devout **Tsar Alexis**, who had Nikon deposed. The patriarch's heavy-handed reforms also produced a schism between the main body of believers who accepted the reforms and the 'Old Believers' who rejected them and clung to their old faith.

The Russian Church paid dearly for Nikon's ambitions. **Peter the Great** took the strongest action of any Russian monarch to curb the power of the Church by making it dependent on the State. In 1721 he abolished the Patriarchate and replaced it with the Holy Synod, a commission of twelve members presided over by a secular chief procurator. **Catherine the Great**

increased still more the dependence of the Church on the crown by confiscating the bulk of its monastic landholdings.

The Church–State relationship entered a new stage. The tsar guaranteed Orthodoxy its predominance in the Russian State; in return the Church became a branch of the secular government obliged to defend 'unsparingly all the powers, right, and prerogatives' of the tsar-autocrat.

Having floundered under the impact of German pietism, freemasonry, Catholicism, and agnosticism among the nobility, the Russian Church experienced a new spiritual revival in the nineteenth century. A strong movement arose among the Russian monastic clergy to renounce the material world in favour of meditation and poverty. The image of the spiritual elder is portrayed by *starets* Zosima in Fedor Dostoevsky's *The Brothers Karamazov*.

Organized charity work, improved scholarship, and an emphasis on the value of prayer contributed to the growing prestige of the Church. The search for the true nature of Russian Orthodoxy had, by the early twentieth century, produced many outstanding religious philosophers in Russia.

In 1917, the office of the Chief Procurator of the Holy Synod was abolished. The 564 delegates to the Council of the Russian Orthodox Church, which convened in Moscow, restored the Russian Patriarchate. On 12 November 1917, **Metropolitan Tikhon** was invested at the Kremlin's Uspensky Cathedral as the eleventh Patriarch of Moscow and All the Russias. This was the last formal act of the church before **Lenin**'s decree of 23 January 1918, separating the Church from the State. Other measures were soon to follow. The first Soviet Constitution still allowed freedom of religious propaganda. But in May 1929 this clause was amended to read: 'Freedom of religious worship and freedom of anti-religious propaganda'. The Church was thus forbidden to engage in any public proselytizing activities or educational work, while the atheists were allowed to step up their numerous campaigns against it. The confiscation of Church property and possessions followed, reflecting the determination of the new government to undermine the Church both economically and morally.

Never before in the history of Russia had the Church found itself confronted by a government so hostile to religion. Lenin himself emphatically stressed that he shared the views of Marx on religion as the 'opium of the people' and advocated relentless atheistic propaganda and struggle.

Patriarch Tikhon was arrested on false charges in 1922, while more than 8,000 bishops, priests, monks, and nuns were tried, deported, or executed. Profiting from Tikhon's arrest, the government sought to bring about a schism by lending support to the **Living Church**, which repudiated the patriarch and professed loyalty to the State. Tikhon's integrity thwarted the reform movement and in June 1923, following his release from prison, the believers rallied around their patriarch. On 7 April 1925, Tikhon died and the patriarchal seat remained vacant until 1943.

Under **Stalin**, the antireligious campaign continued with renewed vigour. By 1941 the number of Russian Orthodox parishes in the USSR had been reduced to one-twentieth of their number during the 1920s.

INTRODUCTION

The Second World War however, changed Church–State relations. Stalin, remembering the patriotic value of the Russian Church, unsealed churches, returned bishops to their Sees, and permitted **Patriarch Sergius** to formally occupy the patriarchal throne. Today, the Russian Church still preserves the right of selecting the patriarch, subject to approval by the State.

Other concessions won by the Church during the Second World War disappeared when **Khrushchev** renewed the campaign against the Church. Not only were the clergy persecuted, but Khrushchev drastically reduced the number of those churches and monastic houses which had survived Stalin's excesses.

In pre-revolutionary days Moscow boasted 450 working Russian Orthodox churches, 15 monasteries, 9 convents, and 22 churches of other denominations; today only 65 religious houses of all denominations are open for worship although the population is seven times what it was in 1913.

The monasteries fared no better. Only two functioning monasteries remain in the Moscow area: **Danilovsky Monastery** in the city and **Trinity Sergius Monastery** in Zagorsk. Novodevichy Convent and Donskoy Monastery are museums with one working church each. The other five monastic institutions which escaped destruction have now been re-opened as architectural monuments and museums. The millennium of Christianity in Russia celebrated in 1988 and Mikhail Gorbachev's *perestroika* have — at least on the surface — improved the Church-State relationship. In preparation for the millennium festivities, a considerable number of churches were refurbished in Moscow, and other cities opened to tourists. Also of significance was the fact that Russia's oldest monastery, the **Pecherskaya Lavra** in Kiev, was reopened and foundations were laid for the construction of a new Church in Moscow — the first for seventy years — at **Orekhovo-Borisovo**, a modern suburb near the outer circular road.

Religious Services

None the less, religious life persists in Russia. The cultural, spiritual, and artistic heritage of the Church is as impressive to the modern-day Russian as it was to the envoys of the Kievan Prince Vladimir some thousand years ago. The person attending a Russian Orthodox service today may have difficulty in following it in the Old Church Slavonic language but will still respond emotionally to the beauty of the liturgy and delight in the sounds of the chants and the beauty of icons, frescoes, and vestments.

The Russian Church still adheres to the Julian calendar, which accounts for a thirteen-day difference between many Russian and Western Church holidays. The Christmas celebration in the Russian Church falls, therefore, on 7 January. The celebration of Russian Easter (*Paskha*), however, is controlled by special rules so that the Orthodox and Western Easter celebrations may occasionally coincide. The midnight Easter service is the highlight of the year for the Russian Church and is well worth attending. The Sunday liturgy, or mass, lasts approximately two hours, including a preparatory office. Otherwise,

the traditional order is similar to that of the Catholic mass, except that the priest officiates largely behind the iconostasis. Holy Communion is limited to the faithful who are fasting and have been through confession. Services on Church feasts often include a *moleben*, a brief service of celebration and supplication invoking intercession of the Virgin or favourite saint.

Since religious burials are forbidden at cemeteries, believers must bring the bodies of their deceased relatives to church for the priest to say a memorial mass. In recent years there has been an increased number of baptisms, which are also performed after the liturgy, usually for several children at once.

Icons and Frescoes

The purpose of representational art in the church is both to explain Christian teaching and to render visible the object of that teaching to the believer. The frescoes and icons illustrate texts from the Old and New Testaments in a coherent and systematic arrangement.

Some icons are mounted into an **iconostasis**, or icon screen, which separates the main part of the church from the sanctuary. Like the frescoes, the icons on the iconostasis narrate the history of the Christian Church, progressing from the representation of the Old Testament prophets in the upper tier through to the New Testament scenes in the lower registers.

The icons are devotional images painted on wooden panels with figures of Christ, the Virgin, the saints, or sacred events. The stress is on the saints' spiritual, rather than human, attributes, with each holy personage or event endowed with his or her own distinct characteristics.

The *Virgin Mary*, for example, is usually shown with the *Child*, her veil displaying the traditional symbols of her virginity: three stars, one on her forehead and one on each shoulder. The *martyrs* can be recognized by their red cloaks and the crosses they hold. *St George* is depicted most often as a knight on a white mount battling the dragon, while *St Trifon*, also on a white horse, has a falcon perched on his arm.

Several icons in Moscow are credited with miracle-working powers, some of which are renowned throughout Russia. The *Virgin of Vladimir*, which once hung at the Uspensky Cathedral in the Kremlin, is one such example. Other venerated and wonder-making icons of Moscow are:

1. *St Nicholas* (from the Kremlin's St Nicholas Gates) and the *Saviour* (from the Spassky, or Saviour's, Gates in the Kremlin), now at the Church of St John the Warrior.
2. *Our Lady, Joy of All the Afflicted*, at the Transfiguration Church.
3. *St Trifon*, at the Znamenskaya church.
4. *Our Lady of Bogoliubovo*, at the Church of SS. Peter and Paul.
5. *Our Lady of Three Hands*, at the Church of the Dormition in Gonchary.
6. *Our Lady, Joy to All Sinners*, at the Church of St Nicholas in Khamovniki.
7. *Our Lady of Kazan*, at the church of the same name in Kolomenskoye.
8. *Our Lady of Iberia*, at the Church of the Resurrection in Sokolniki.
9. *Our Lady, the Unexpected Joy*, at the Church of St Elias.

Excursion 25

Excursion 25
See p. 213
Excursion 15
Excursion 25
Excursion 25
Excursion 3
Metro: *Sokolniki*
ydenskiy Pereulok, 2

INTRODUCTION

Church Architecture

The churches commissioned by the tsars for the Kremlin, particularly the Uspensky Cathedral, had as their prototype the Byzantine stone architecture. This influence did not come to Moscow directly from Constantinople, or Kiev, since Kiev's St Sofia Cathedral (1037), a Russian adaptation of its Greek namesake, was ravaged by the Tartars in 1240. Rather, Byzantine architecture reached Moscow via the prism of Vladimir, Suzdal, and Novgorod builders who emulated the Kievan model while endowing their own churches with regional characteristics. The Italian builders of Uspensky Cathedral modified the Russo-Byzantine mould still more by adding to it features of the Renaissance.

Just as the **Kievan St Sofia** had served as the matrix for the earlier Russian churches, so the Kremlin's **Uspensky Cathedral** (1475–9) became the new architectural textbook for all major cathedrals built at the monasteries or on royal estates.

The stone churches built by the clergy had as their models the sparkling limestone churches of Vladimir-Suzdal. In Moscow, however, these cube-shaped, one-dome churches acquired a new look. Their walls, as in Vladimir churches, were divided by pilaster-like bands into three sections, each ending in a *zakomar* arch. Whereas the *zakomars* of Vladimir were semi-circular, in Moscow the arches and the deep-shadowed portals received ogee-shaped outlines. The purest examples of this early Moscow style are the **Trinity Church** (1422) at the **Trinity Sergius Monastery** (Excursion 21) and the **Saviour's Church** (1410–27) at the **Spaso-Andronikov Monastery** (Excursion 24) where the famous spade-shaped *kokoshniki* arches appeared for the first time.

Equally important to the architectural evolution of Moscow were the Church of **St Anne** in Kitai Gorod (Excursion 5) and the **Church of St Trifon** on Trifonovskaya Ulitsa 38, both built by private individuals. The Pskov masters summoned for the job chose to copy the sturdy merchant churches of their native town. As a result, the Moscow churches acquired an elevated basement and the three-fold division of the walls, the sides of which were lowered in relation to the main body of the church.

Gone were the internal piers which encumbered the Vladimir churches. The new corbelled arches now spanned the nave. The spade-shaped *kokoshniki* gables, which become the exterior expression of the tiered construction, appeared as a band at the base of St Trifon's thin drum.

Moscow, however, was a predominantly wooden city. While stone was scarce and required special building techniques, timber was plentiful and easy to handle. Over the centuries, Russian carpenters perfected the art of wood carving and turned eaves, staircases, and window surrounds into objects of rich ornamentation. Even the tsars preferred wooden palaces which offered greater scope for artistic expression and were easier to heat during the cold winter months.

Thus, for many years the timber and stone architecture developed side by side without noticeably affecting one another. Stone churches were commissioned almost exclusively by the tsars and churchmen, while the rank and file constructed their churches of wood, relying on the distinctive forms of Russian timber architecture. The only instance of masonry techniques affecting the wood was the adoption of the Byzantine dome which evolved into the typical onion-shaped cupola better adapted to the heavy Russian snowfalls.

In the seventeenth century, when stone began to displace wood as a safety measure against fires, the characteristic forms of the timber architecture were transferred to stone. The churches acquired turrets, barrel-shaped roofs, ornamental entries, and open staircases surmounted by roofed porches and covered terraces. The flamboyant **Church of the Holy Trinity** (1628–57) 'in Nikitniki' (Excursion 6) is an excellent example of the 'Moscow Ornamental' style in which timber forms were adapted to stone. Built by a rich merchant it served as a model for other merchant churches, rectangular in shape with five domes, three apses, and a bell tower at the western end.

No less dramatic was the soaring **Ascension Church** (1532) in Kolomenskoye (Excursion 3), an outgrowth of the wooden octagonal churches and defence towers. Even when the Patriarch Nikon banned this type of construction, the Moscow builders by-passed the churchmen's decree by transferring their love five domes, three apses, and a bell-tower at the western end.

It is the **Church of St Basil** (1555–61), however, which represents the sum total of all Russian and foreign building traditions. In it, Byzantine, Italian, and timber forms were fused together to create this unique monument in Red Square.

By the end of the seventeenth century, the western influences which reached Moscow via the Ukraine, gave rise to the so-called 'Moscow Baroque'. In some churches, which preserved the earlier rectangular plan and a five-dome covering, the Moscow Baroque manifested itself in the use of western order architecture in the outside decor. In others, particularly those commissioned by the Naryshkin relatives of the tsar, hence 'Naryshkin Baroque', the churches surged upwards in a series of superimposed cubic and octagonal shapes. The most famous example of the 'Naryshkin Baroque' is the circular and profusely decorated **Church of Pokrov** (1690–3) **in Fili**, placed on an elevated terrace served by four monumental staircases.

The 'Western Baroque' style, for which St Petersburg is famous, had little impact on Moscow, because of Peter the Great's ban on all stone construction outside of St Petersburg.

One of the few exceptions is the **Church of St John the Warrior** designed by Peter himself, which marks the transition from the purely Russian style to that of the West (Excursion 25).

INTRODUCTION

Excursion 21

TRINITY SERGIUS MONASTERY AT ZAGORSK

To tour the Trinity Sergius Monastery, all foreigners, except for accredited diplomats, need special permission to travel to Zagorsk, 72 kilometres from Moscow. Tourists must apply at Intourist as soon as they arrive in Moscow. There are organized bus tours, or Zagorsk can be reached by car or by train.

*E*ach country has a historic or religious landmark that throughout the centuries has served as a source of pride and inspiration to its people. For the Russians, it remains the Trinity Sergius Monastery. For more than five hundred years, pilgrims have come from all over Russia to pray at the grave of **St Sergius**, its founder.

One of Russia's most beloved saints, St Sergius formulated a religious philosophy which helped weld fourteenth-century Russia into a unified state. To bring about the reconciliation of feuding Russian princes, St Sergius used neither threats nor coercion. Bareheaded, he would walk long distances to plead the cause of Russian unity with the rebellious princes. In politics, as well as in his personal life, St Sergius was known for his humility and service to others.

Born of wealthy Rostov boyars who settled near Moscow after fleeing the Tartars, Sergius sought his salvation through prayer and meditation. Alone, but enjoying immense strength and robust health, St Sergius made a clearing in the forest — the present site of the Trinity Sergius Monastery. He built for himself a cell and a wooden chapel which he dedicated to the **Holy Trinity**. He also planted vegetables to sustain himself during his first winter. His sole companions were wild animals with whom he became friendly, particularly the legendary brown bear who appeared every evening at dinner time.

The world, however, did not accept St Sergius's wish to devote himself to solitary meditation; even the mighty came to his door in search of guidance.

When **Metropolitan Alexis** asked St Sergius to suceed him as metropolitan, the abbot refused but could not avoid being drawn into Russia's political life. In 1380, **Prince Dmitry Donskoy** of Moscow came to seek St Sergius's blessing before leading his army against the formidable Tartar Khan Mamai. St Sergius blessed the prince but only after Dmitry's reassurance that all peaceful negotiations had failed.

An astute judge of character, Sergius sensed the emotional crisis Dimitry would suffer on the eve of the attack. To prevent a change of heart, he dispatched into the Russian camp a messenger with a communion bread and encouragement for the grand prince. The battle of Kulikovo, the first major Russian victory against the Tartars, proved to the Russian people that united they could defeat their enemy.

As Russia rejoiced, St Sergius remained preoccupied with the monastery. He supervised the translation of Greek texts into Old Slavonic, established

Three of the Zagorsk churches. From left to right: St Sergius' Refectory, Holy Trinity, and Holy Spirit (with bells incorporated into the drum).

chronicles to record historic events, and laid foundations for one of the finest libraries in Russia.

Nor was St Sergius's influence limited to Moscow alone. Inspired by their teacher, the Trinity monks left to found new monasteries in other parts of Russia, as far as the White Sea and the Arctic Circle. Thus, in the end, St Sergius's followers created 150 monasteries, which also served as fortresses and cultural centres. One of them was the **Simonov Monastery** in Moscow. This fourteenth-century monastery was turned into a car factory but is being restored (**Vostochnaya Ulitsa, 4**).

In 1612, barely recovered from the sixteen-month siege by 30,000 Poles, the Trinity Sergius Monastery became the centre of Russian resistance to the Poles, who were then occupying the Kremlin. When two great Russian patriots, Prince **Dmitry Pozharsky** and burgher **Kuzma Minin**, succeeded in raising an army in Nizhny Novgorod, the monastery donated its gold to equip the new force.

Michael Romanov, who came to the Russian throne in 1613, showed his appreciation of the monastery's patriotism by donating money towards its reconstruction and embellishment. The slow and tedious process of restoration began with the monastery walls and towers. Of the seventeenth-century towers, the **Utichnaya**, or **Duck**, Tower deserves a special mention. Tallest of the twelve, it stands in the north-east corner of the enclosure, its red and white decorations giving it a cheerful appearance. According to an old monastery belief, **Peter the Great** used to shoot ducks in a nearby pond from this very tower, hence the figure of the duck crowning the three-tier turret, and its name.

With a wealth now rivalling that of the tsar, the monks also engaged in new construction. The seventeenth-century additions — the hospital buildings

EXCURSION 21

surmounted by the tent-shaped **Church of SS. Savvaty and Zosima** and the two palaces along the northern wall of the monastery — are large and abound in architectural embellishments as was then customary. The palaces house the **Seminary** and the **Theological Academy**, the latter one of the three left in the Soviet Union. The Theological Academy was originally built as the tsar's residence, but all that remains today is the design of multicoloured lozenges and the sculptured details around the windows.

Church of St John the Baptist

A rounded gateway leads to the cloister covered with frescoes depicting the life and miracles of St Sergius. The gates are topped by the Church of St John the Baptist, built in 1692–9.

Uspensky, or Dormition, Cathedral

Five blue domes, studded with golden stars, rise proudly above the snow-white Uspensky Cathedral, which in size and shape reminds one of its Kremlin predecessor. Its builder was Ivan the Terrible, one of the monastery's most generous patrons. In 1559, having triumphed over the Tartars of Kazan and Astrakhan, Ivan laid the foundations for the Uspensky Cathedral, which was finished in 1585 after Ivan's death, mostly with funds left by the tsar to atone for his sins.

The interior of Uspensky is luminous and ornate. The frescoes were executed in 1684 by local iconographers with the help of Yaroslavl masters. The large iconostasis includes the icon of the *Last Supper*, the work of the seventeenth-century artist Simon Ushakov.

St Sergius's Refectory Church

Another working church is the immense and ornate Church of St Sergius, the monastery's former refectory, to the left of Uspensky. In the days when the pilgrims gathered annually for the feast day of St Sergius, on 5 July, food was served here after the mass. Irrespective of wealth and rank, those pilgrims who had walked for more than three days were first to taste the freshly baked bread, savoury pies, marinated mushrooms, and other home-made delicacies.

The 600-foot-long gallery that circles the Church of St Sergius with its polychrome pillared and luxuriously decorated facade suggests a generous patron.

(Tserkov Sviatogo Dukha)

Church of the Holy Spirit

Between the refectory and the Uspensky Cathedral is the interior court — the spiritual core of the monastery. In the shadow of the 290-foot-high **bell-**

tower — an eighteenth-century masterpiece of narrowing octagons — stand the Church of the Holy Spirit and the Church of the Holy Trinity, the monastery's oldest. The blue onion-shaped dome encircled by a golden band is not the only unusual feature of the white stucco Church of the Holy Spirit, which was built in 1476. Equally remarkable is the arrangement of the lower cube with its three projecting altar apses and above it a pillared circular belfry. The ingenious Pskov masters added a final touch to their 'church-beneath-the-bells': they stressed the decorative value of the horizontal band that circles the walls by dressing it up with terracotta details.

(Troitsky Sobor)

Church of the Holy Trinity

Small, square, and unprepossessing, the Church of the Holy Trinity owes its charm to the dignity of its proportions and to the sparse use of ornamental detail. The Pskov masters marked the transition from the cubical mass of the church to its single dome by use of pointed gables. In the sixteenth century the building was extended by the addition of **St Nikon's Chapel** and a covered gateway with a tent-like roof.

The church was built above the **grave of St Sergius**, still visited by many pilgrims. His remains lie in a tomb encased in a silver shrine that was donated by Empress Anna in 1730. Above the grave sway numerous rows of icon lamps, which were gifts of tsars, emperors, noblemen, merchants, and commoners who had come to pay their respects to the saint. The lamps and the flickering candles provide the sole illumination of the church.

The **icons** were executed by the Trinity monks, among them Andrei Rublev and his contemporary, Daniil Chernyi, Russia's foremost iconographers.

Nowhere is the theme of dedicated service and Sergius' theological vision of the Trinity expressed more clearly than in the early-fifteenth-century icon which Rublev painted in honour of his teacher. The *Icon of the Old Testament Trinity*, Rublev's masterpiece, once occupied the niche to the right of the royal gates. As the original is now at the Tretyakov Gallery of Art, a copy of Rublev's famous composition is displayed.

Other icons attributed to Rublev are those in the iconostasis of the *Apostle Peter and Apostle Paul* and also *Archangel Gabriel*. Daniil Chernyi is considered the artist of the figures of *Saviour Enthroned*, *Archangel Michael*, and *David*.

n in Holy Trinity inspired story from Genesis of God ring in the form of three to Abraham and Sarah. Rublev, 1422-7.

Boris Godunov's Tomb and the Holy Well

Across the square from the Trinity Church and adjoining the southern entrance to Uspensky Cathedral is the tomb of Tsar Boris Godunov, his wife, and his two children.

Only a few steps away from the tomb is a small, gaily painted chapel which houses a well that, according to legend, sprang up during the Polish siege of the Monastery, which lasted for sixteen months in the early 1600s.

EXCURSION 21

Museums

For those who can secure special permission to visit the religious **Archaeological Office** by applying at the reception desk, there is a fine collections of **icons of the Virgin** to see, and a five-century-old tradition to observe. To this day, the seminary students rise in silence during their lunch in memory of the day when St Sergius stood up during his midday meal and bowed, apparently to no one in particular. The abbot was actually returning a greeting of a friend, St Stephen of Perm, the learned monk who converted the pagan Komi people some 750 miles east of Moscow. Not having time to visit St Sergius, Stephen simply stopped and bowed in the direction of the monastery as he passed by.

Besides the icon collection at the Archaeological Office there are two more State-run museums located in the monastery grounds. One houses **toys** and **wooden objects**; the other contains **royal** and **ecclesiastic jewels**, icons, and silver. The latter, located in the monastery's vestry behind the Trinity Church, is the oldest (fifteenth century) and one of the finest museums in Russia. Among its treasured possessions is an **incense burner** dated 1428. The cover of the receptacle copies the outline of the original dome of the Trinity Church.

Also of note at the vestry are the **embroideries** contributed by Russian women, many of them works of the tsaritsas themselves. They are embroidered with gold and silver thread on exquisitely dyed silk or wool cloth. Precious and semi-precious stones, as well as fresh-water pearls, are worked into the design. A fine example of fifteenth-century artistic sewing is the life-sized **portrait shroud of St Sergius** executed by women of the royal household.

Icons and **icon covers**, reflecting styles of different Russian masters, are also an important part of museum's treasures. An unusual icon which originated at the Trinity Sergius Monastery and is kept there is the *Visitation of St Sergius by the Virgin*. The icon depicts the Virgin reassuring the dying St Sergius that no harm would come to his domain.

Excursion 22

DANILOVSKY AND DONSKOY MONASTERIES
CHURCH OF THE DEPOSITION OF THE LORD'S ROBE

A tour of the Danilovsky and Donskoy monasteries includes the Church of the Deposition of the Lord's Robe, all within walking distance from Serpukhovskiy Val Square.

*D*anilovsky and Donskoy monasteries were built to safeguard the southern periphery of Moscow against the Tartars.

Danilovsky, the older of the two monasteries, was founded in 1282. Three centuries later **Tsar Fedor** commissioned the building of Donskoy north of Danilovsky to seal the vulnerable gap in Moscow's defences just upstream from the present-day Krymskiy Bridge. At this time Moscow was also encircled by an earthen rampart, which gave the suburb the name of Earthen City, known today as the **Sadovoye Koltso**, or Garden Ring. The rampart enclosed the Kremlin, the Kitai Gorod, the White City, and other suburbs, stopping at the fortified monasteries.

(Residence of the Moscow Patriarch)
Danilovsky Val Ulitsa, 22
③
Metro: *Tulskaya ML7 (Chekhovskaya–Novoslobodskaya)*

Danilovsky Monastery

Prince Daniel, who began his rule in 1276, was the first prince to settle permanently in Moscow and to fortify the city by commissioning three walled monasteries. Of the three, he favoured Danilovsky and showed his preference by dedicating the monastery to St Daniel of the Pillar, his own patron saint. As he grew older, Daniel spent most of his time at Danilovsky sharing the ascetic life of the monks. In 1303, shortly before he died, Prince Daniel asked to be buried among the friars' graves. The Russian Orthodox Church canonized Daniel.

print of the Danilovsky ...astery, one of three walled ...asteries commissiond by ...ce Daniel in the late ...eenth century. Soviet ...orities began restoration of ...onastery in 1983. It is now ...esidence of the Moscow ...arch.

EXCURSION 22

285

Excursion Plan 22
Danilovsky and
Donskoy

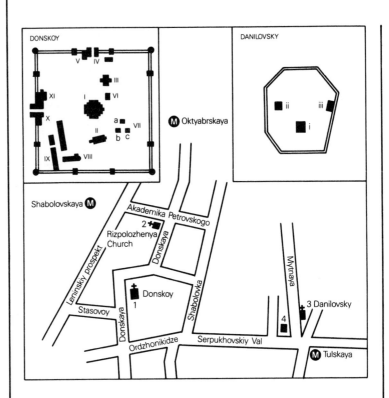

1. Donskoy Monastery
2. Church of the Deposition of the
   Lord's Robe (Rizpolozheniya)

3. Danilovsky Monastery
4. Kolkhoz (Danilovsky) Market

DONSKOY MONASTERY

I   'New' Cathedral of the
    Donskaya Virgin
II 'Old' Cathedral of the Donskaya
    Virgin
III Church of St John
    (Ioanna Zlatousta)
IV Gate Church
V   Guards' House

VI   Abbot's Residence
VII Memorial chapels
VIII Church of Archangel Michael
     (Arkhangela Mikhaila)
IX   Monks' quarters
X   Bell-tower
XI   Former Theological Academy

DANILOVSKY MONASTERY

i Church of the Seven
   Ecumenical Councils (Semi
   Vselenskikh Soborov)
ii Church of the Holy Trinity
   (Troitsy)

iii Gate Church of St Simeon of
    the Pillar (Simeona Stolpnika)

After Daniel's death, Danilovsky fell into disrepair. Its restoration in the sixteenth century gave rise to the following legend. One day, the legend claims, **Ivan the Terrible** and his retinue were riding past Danilovsky Monastery. A horse stumbled under one of Ivan's courtiers, dragging him down. When the rider rose, before him stood a monk, who, having identified himself as Prince Daniel, urged the courtier to ask Ivan the Terrible to honour his memory. Upon hearing the courtier's account, Ivan ordered Danilovsky restored to its former glory and erected in 1565 the **Cathedral of the Holy Fathers of the Seven Ecumenical Councils** on the site of the old St Daniel's church.

In 1662 this church was enlarged by Tsar **Alexis Romanov**, who had the relics of Prince Daniel placed in a golden sarcophagus near the right choir of the upper church. The fresco of *St Daniel*, the only interior decoration to survive, dates from that time. The very survival of the fresco on the altar wall of the lower church confirmed the belief of Muscovites that St Daniel watches over his beloved monastery. Indeed, after the Revolution of 1917, several churches were destroyed, others were converted into factories, while the monks quarters became detention centres. Only in 1983 after numerous petitions did Soviet authorities agree to relinquish the crumbling monastery to the patriarchate. The restoration was finished in time for the celebration of the thousandth anniversary of Christianity in Russia.

(i)

wer in the Danilovsky
wing the intricate brickwork.

Church of the Seven Ecumenical Councils

The two-storey-high brick cathedral occupying the southern part of the monastery remains an important architectural landmark of seventeenth-century Moscow. It combines the rectangular ship-shaped body with features of late seventeenth-century 'Moscow Baroque'. The carved entry, the octagonal tower of the central dome, and the pillared frames of the windows reflect influences of Russian timber architecture.

The interior of the church is made up of five separate chapels. Three are located on the ground level, of which the largest and best preserved is the Church of the Seven Ecumenical Councils. Above, a still larger church commemorates the **Feast of Pokrov** (Protection of the Virgin's Veil) and adjoins **St Daniel's Chapel**, where the relics of the monastery founder were once kept.

Both the upper and the lower church are surrounded by wide galleries. Broad stairways, starting on the right side of the vestibule, connect the churches. The brickwork is unusually attractive: note the imaginative designs of the windows opening into the gallery, the stout pillars with round pendants, and ornate entries. Some of the brickwork dates to the sixteenth century, as does the original floor at the lower level — rediscovered during the restoration.

The **Church of the Holy Trinity** ⓘⓘ (1838), a fine example of Osip Bove's classical style, is also fully restored and features a new iconostasis.

The entry to the cloister is through a multi-tiered red and white **Gate Church of St Simeon of the Pillar** ⓘⓘⓘ resting on stout pillars. Inside the spacious courtyard, which encircles the **abbot's residence** (1820), the **Hospital** (1890), remodelled churches and **monks' quarters**, there is also the **residence for the Patriarch** and a large contemporary structure with the image of the Saviour surmounting the entry. This is a **hotel** for important visitors to the monastery. Many icons in the churches, chapels, and buildings have been specially painted for the Danilovsky monastery, some have been brought from other churches.

Danilovsky, during many years a prison for junior delinquents, is once again a working monastery and the new seat of the Patriarch of Moscow and all the Russias.

(Division of the Shchusev Museum of Architecture)
Donskaya Ploshchad, 1
①
Metro: *Shabolovskaya*

Donskoy Monastery

This beautiful monastery was founded by Tsar Fedor in 1591, the year Khan Kaza Girei crossed the Moscow River and laid siege to the city. Surprised by the horde of invading Tartars at their walls, the Muscovites felt doomed. But the attack never came, for, according to the legend, the Blessed Virgin rescued the city.

The rescue of Moscow was attributed to the icon of the *Donskaya Virgin* which Prince Dmitry Donskoy carried with him into the battle against the Tartars in 1380. Since the battle took place near the River Don, the icon received its name, 'Donskaya'.

Two centuries later, on the eve of the battle against Kaza Girei, Tsar Fedor ordered his men to carry the icon to the place where the Tartar khan was expected to strike. The tsar's prayers were answered. The night before the attack, Kaza Girei dreamt that his tent was pitched in a dark forest. He could hear chants in the distance. Suddenly, the icon of the Donskaya Virgin arose and began to drift over the Tartar encampment. As it stopped over the tent occupied by the khan, thousands of burning

Donskoy: the bell-tower and western gates, dating from 1730–53.

288

arrows shot from the icon and fell upon the Tartars. The frightened khan awoke and ordered an immediate retreat.

Boris Godunov, Tsar Fedor's brother-in-law, also helped save Moscow. While Fedor prayed, Boris had bonfires lit on all of the Kremlin's towers; his soldiers fired into the air, blew their trumpets, and beat their drums to make the khan believe that fresh Russian troops were marching from the north. As soon as the Tartars retreated, Tsar Fedor began work on this monastery, which he dedicated to the miracle-working icon of the Donskaya Virgin.

Except for the small Old Cathedral, which is still a working church, all of Donskoy's churches and buildings constitute part of the **Shchusev Museum of Architecture**. The exhibits are devoted exclusively to Russian pre-revolutionary architecture and provide a valuable insight into Moscow's old building styles.

'Old' Cathedral of the Donskaya Virgin

The church honouring the *Donskaya Virgin* was built in 1591, the same year as the monastery. It is usually referred to as the 'Old' Cathedral, to distinguish it from the monastery's 'New' Cathedral, which rose a century later.

The cathedral is small but well proportioned. Diagonal stripes traverse the walls, while the white stone frames of the windows and pillars serve to relieve the sombre brick surfaces.

bstones near the Old hedral of Donskoy belong to rons of the church. The neplates of aristocratic patrons inside the church.

The oldest part of the building is cube shaped. Three rows of semi-circular arches form a stepped transition from the cube to the blue onion-shaped cupola. A golden cross of delicate design carries a half-moon symbolizing the Christian victory over Islam.

The church lost much of its original compactness in the 1670s, when two side chapels, a bell-tower, and a refectory were added to the original cube.

The architect's use of pendentive supports, rather than the cumbersome pillars commonly found in sixteenth-century churches, contributes to the interior's lightness.

The original **iconostasis** perished in the 1930s. The silver and gold icon screen seen today was brought in 1945 from another Moscow church. The only icon which still occupies its original place is a seventeenth-century copy of the *Donskaya Virgin* set between two Corinthian pillars of the iconostasis to the left of the royal gates.

A curved **metal vault** to the left of the iconostasis contains the remains of Archbishop Amvrosy, who was killed in 1771 outside the monastery walls.

EXCURSION 22

Next to the tomb is the chapel of Tsar Fedor's patron saint; opposite it, the southern chapel honours St Sergius, who blessed Prince Dmitry Donskoy on the eve of his departure for the battle against the Tartars.

The remains of Patriarch Tikhon, who was enthoned in November 1917 and who lived at the monastery, lie encased in a white **marble tomb** adjoining the southern wall of the refectory.

Other tombstones in the church commemorate Russian aristocratic families who patronized Donskoy. Those whose nameplates appear inside the church were particularly generous donors. Lesser patrons were buried in the monastery's graveyard.

① 'New' Cathedral of the Donskaya Virgin

This tall red church differs in spirit and appearance from the Old Cathedral, although it also honours the *Donskaya Virgin*.

Dating from 1684–93, the elongated building displays Ukrainian influences, best seen in the treatment of the facades and the placement of the drums on the corners of the roof. Its architecture heralds the advent of the 'Naryshkin Baroque', the final and most opulent expression of 'Moscow Baroque'.

The circular gallery of the cathedral houses such architectural displays as paintings and engravings illustrating the history of pre-revolutionary Moscow. There are also models of famous buildings, including Vasily Bazhenov's grandiose projected reconstruction of the Moscow Kremlin in the late eighteenth century.

Because of the gallery's width, the actual place for worship appears disproportionately small relative to the cathedral's great size. The crowded effect is further reinforced by the massive seven-tier **iconostasis**, a masterpiece of carved and gilded wood executed between 1695 and 1699.

This iconostasis is unique in two respects. The icons of the upper tiers, and particularly those depicting the *Sufferings of the Apostles*, are distinctly Western. Furthermore, the selection of icons for the bottom tier of the iconostasis provides an insight into the political ambitions of Regent Sofia, Peter the Great's half-sister.

To the right of the royal gates is the representation of the *Donskaya Virgin*, the symbol of Russian victories over the Muslim Tartars. When Sofia commissioned the cathedral in 1684 she hoped that her lover, Prince Vasily Golitsyn, would successfully defeat the Crimean Tartars. The other icons painted by the royal masters Zolotarev and Ivanov commemorate the patron saints of Sofia's immediate family. Next to the *Donskaya Virgin* stands the full-length figure of *St Catherine*, the patron saint of Sofia's sister. On the other side of the altar gates, *St Alexis*, patron saint of Sofia's father, Tsar Alexis, kneels at the feet of the Virgin. Next is a likeness of *St John*, patron of the feeble-minded Ivan, Sofia's younger brother.

The reason why the namesake of Sofia's half-brother Peter is excluded is easy to guess. Not only was Peter the child of Alexis Romanov's second marriage but he was also Sofia's rival for the throne.

The New Cathedral of Donskoy represents the earliest example of the 'Naryshkin Baroque' style, notable for the circular effect of its facade. The cathedral dates from 1684–94.

The **frescoes** decorating the cathedral have little relationship with either Sofia or the triumph of Orthodoxy. Executed between 1782 and 1785 by the Italian artist Antonio Claudio, they represent a departure from the traditional Russian religious painting. Claudio's treatment of biblical subjects is purely Western, with the accent placed on the dramatic value of the figures, an approach far removed from the schematic and symbolical frescoes of Russian masters.

⑧ Church of Archangel Michael (Museum of Monumental Sculpture)

The Church of Archangel Michael, occupying the south-western corner of Donskoy Monastery, was built between 1806 and 1809. This dignified Classical building served as a memorial chapel for the Golitsyn princes, who were obliged to seek a new gravesite for their dead after the outbreak of a cholera epidemic in 1771 (see Excursion 4 ⑨).

The sculptures and tombstones inside the church commemorate the more astute members of the Golitsyn clan who took Peter's side and prospered. Mikhail Golitsyn (1681–1764), whose marble tomb and profiled likeness are near the door, began his career as Peter's drummer and ended it as the tsar's admiral/general. Still closer to the door is the memorial to Mikhail's son, Dmitry, Catherine the Great's philanthropic ambassador. The memorial with Golitsyn's bust and sculptures of weeping women is the work of Fedor Gordeyev. It was moved from Golitsyn Hospital in Moscow.

The **graves** of the fourteen Golitsyns buried inside the church are marked by metal plates bearing their names. Among them is Dmitry Vasilievich Golitsyn, Moscow's favourite governor general, and his wife, Natalia, who inspired Pushkin's characterization of the enigmatic Queen of Spades.

Besides the Golitsyn memorials, a number of remarkable **sculptures** were collected here from other churches. Among them is the *Sitting Christ* of Mark Antokolsky and the *Kneeling Angels*, which Ivan Vitali had originally designed for the **Church of St Tatiana** at Moscow University. Ivan Martos, another celebrated Russian sculptor, designed the memorial for Princess Volkonskaya but is better known for his statue of Minin and Pozharsky on Red Square.

Today, Donskoy's cemetery is a depot for relocated statues. The bas-reliefs mounted into the eastern wall are the only remnants of the grandiose **Saviour's Cathedral**, destroyed in the 1930s. One bas-relief shows *St Sergius in the act of blessing Dmitry Donskoy* on the eve of the Kulikovo battle and is the work of sculptor P. P. Loganovsky.

Other Buildings

The **bell-tower** above the northern gates ⑩ was begun by Domenico Tressini in 1730 and completed in 1753. The handsome **Tikhvin Gate Church** built by architect Ivan Zarudny resembles a decorative pavilion.

EXCURSION 22

The **guard's house** (V), the former **burial chapels** (VII), and the **abbot's** eighteenth-century **residence** (VI) now house the museum's staff. Donskoy's early-twentieth-century **Church of St Seraphim**, located in the new section of the cemetery, is used as a crematorium.

From the gates of Donskoy monastery one can see the Church of Rizpolozheniya ②, a working church whose priests officiate at the Old Cathedral of Donskoy Monastery on Sundays and holidays.

(Tserkov
Rizpolozheniya)
Akademika Petrovskogo
Ulitsa
②
Metro: *Shabolovskaya*

Church of the Deposition of the Lord's Robe

The Church of the Deposition was built in 1701, although its architectural features suggest earlier origins. The architect, weary of the then prevailing multi-tiered construction, opted for the old-fashioned, rectangular plan. To amend for his structural conservatism, the builder faceted the five silver domes and bunched them closer together. He created scallop-like motives inside the rounded arches crowning the walls and added white stone pillars to the corners of the church and around the windows. To further accentuate the colour of the brick, he painted the church a deep red.

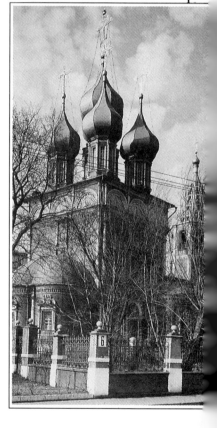

The interior of the church is opulent. Nowhere in Moscow are there so many cherubs as in this church. They perch on ceilings, embellish icon screens, and look down from the walls. Cherub motives also decorate the magnificent eighteenth-century iconostasis.

The royal gates of the main **iconostasis** and those of the two side chapels feature the *four Evangelists*, the scene of the *Last Supper*, and the *Annunication of the Virgin*.

The icon of the *Iberian Virgin* painted in the early eighteenth century is to the left of the royal gates in the main altar. Next, hidden by the choirs, is the icon of *All the Saints* venerated by the Russian Orthodox Church. A copy of the original icon of the *Deposition of the Lord's Robe* is located in the right-hand corner of the church, underneath a gilded canopy. The subject matter of this icon is

The Church of the Deposition of the Lord's Robe (1701) has silver domes and is built of brick painted deep red.

unique to Russia. In 1625 the Persian envoy of Shah Abbas I presented Tsar Michael Romanov and his father, Patriarch Filaret, with a golden coffret containing a fragment of Jesus' robe.

The Persian shah's gift was of major political and religious significance to Russia. Filaret summoned a congress of Russian and Greek Orthodox clergymen to assess the authenticity of the cloth, which was recognized as a genuine piece of Christ's vestment. Shortly thereafter the patriarch announced the creation of a new religious holiday and commissioned the original icon (now in Tretyakov Gallery) to be painted. In this icon, Patriarch Filaret and Tsar Michael, surrounded by noblemen and clergy, are placing the golden coffret containing the Lord's robe upon the alter of the Kremlin's Uspensky Cathedral. The border scenes depict the arrival of the Persian ambassador and the subsequent events.

The left side chapel honours *St Jacob*, whose relics are mounted into the icon. St Jacob's likeness is the fourth icon to the right of the altar gates. The revered icon of the Virgin, known as the *Unexpected Joy*, is displayed under a gold canopy.

The right-hand chapel is dedicated to *St Catherine*, one of the favourite patron saints of the Romanov tsars. Her icon, too, occupies the fourth place from the royal gates.

Excursion Plan 23
Novodevichiy Convent

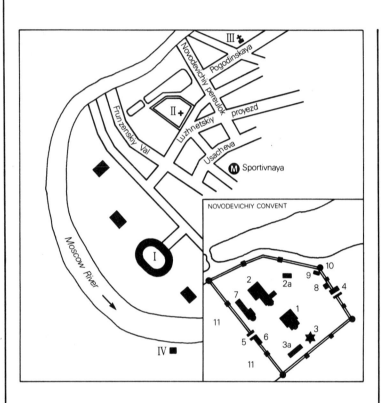

I Lenin Central Stadium
II Novodevichiy Convent
III Pogodin's Wooden Hut
IV Andreyevsky Monastery

NOVODEVICHIY CONVENT:

1. Smolensky Cathedral
2. Dormition (Uspenskaya) Refectory Church
2a. Choir building
3. Bell-Tower
3a. Guard House
4. Transfiguration (Preobrazhenskaya) Gate Church
5. Intercession of the Virgin (Pokrovskaya) Souther Gate Church
6. Miloslavsky Chambers
7. Godunova Chambers and the Church of St Amvrosy
8. Lopukhin Chambers
9. Sofia's Chamber-Prison (guard house)
10. Pond Tower
11. The New Novodevichiy Cemetery

Excursion 23
NOVODEVICHIY CONVENT

A tour to Novodevichiy Convent, now a division of the Russian Historical Museum, includes several churches and residences of royal nuns.

Pirogovskaya Bolshaya Ulitsa, 2
Ⓜ
Metro: *Sportivnaya*

General view of Novodevichiy Convent. Regent Sofia, Peter the Great's rival for the throne, lived a prisoner in one of the corner towers after being deposed.

West of the Kremlin, nestled in a bend of the Moscow River, is Novodevichiy, a convent of sixteen golden domes, white chiselled walls, and red-topped turrets. The convent was founded in 1524 by **Grand Prince Basil III** to celebrate the return of Smolensk to Russia after more than one hundred years of Lithuanian domination. By repossessing this 'jewel of Russian cities', Basil not only reclaimed part of the former Kievan Grand Duchy but also secured for Moscow a key fortress guarding the trade route to Poland and other points west.

Surrounded by stout walls and fortified towers, Novodevichiy was built to withstand enemy attacks. Its real purpose, however, was to provide a religious retreat for Russian noblewomen and members of royalty, even those who did not enter Novodevichiy voluntarily. The nunnery thus witnessed the rages of **Regent Sofia**, Peter the Great's half-sister and rival for the throne, who was banished to the convent; the tears of Sofia's sisters; and the laments of **Evdokia**, Peter's first wife — all of whom Peter forced to take the veil.

After Sofia's death, **Peter the Great** turned the convent into an orphanage. Deprived of its royal patronage, Novodevichiy continued to decline and almost disappeared altogether in 1812 during Napoleon's invasion of Moscow. Shortly before leaving the city, Napoleon ordered Novodevichiy blown up, but a heroic

EXCURSION 23

295

nun extinguished the fuses just before the fire reached the powderkegs.

Peter the Great's successors, particularly the empresses, restored the convent, although it never recovered its former glory.

Smolensky Cathedral

The first stone building to rise between 1524 and 1525 in the very centre of Novodevichiy was the large five-domed cathedral dedicated to the *Virgin of Smolensk*. This grandiose edifice resembles the Uspensky Cathedral in the Kremlin. A few changes were made, however, by the architects. They placed the building on a high terrace, making it appear taller than Uspensky, omitted all decorations, except for pilasters and rounded arches at the top of the walls, and bunched cupolas closer together. These modifications created a dynamic upward movement rare for churches of this type.

The eastern side of the Smolensky Cathedral is joined by three semi-spheres corresponding to the main altar and two side chapels which are connected by a covered passage circling the church. Inside, the gallery is decorated with nineteenth-century frescoes which repeat the original seventeenth-century motives but are executed in oil. The **western portal**, carved and painted as if it were wood, is particularly remarkable. To the left, a beautifully worked wrought-iron door leads to the **burial vault**, which includes among others the tomb of Ivan the Terrible's daughter Anna.

Art

Our Lady of Smolensk, to whom the church is dedicated, is represented by a large fresco above the altar screen. This particular representation of the Virgin with the Child evolved in Byzantium and is known as the *Virgin Hodigitria*. According to legends, the original Hodigitria icon of *Our Lady of Smolensk* was brought from Constantinople to Kiev but became known as *Our Lady of Smolensk* after it was moved to the city of Smolensk, where it was kept for 300 years.

In 1404, the citizens of Smolensk, fearing for the safety of their prized icon, moved it to the Moscow Kremlin. But fifty years later when they asked for the icon to be returned, the Moscow princes demurred. They had come to regard the icon as a palladium of Russian Orthodoxy

Novodevichiy: Smolensky Cathedral (1525), built to celebrate the return of Smolensk to Russia.

whose Byzantine origins and earlier links with Kiev made it a valuable political asset for the Moscow State. When the Muscovites finally agreed to part with the icon, a copy of the *Smolensk Virgin* was commissioned for the Kremlin and the original returned to Smolensk.

The tearful farewell to the icon of *Our Lady of Smolensk* took place on the Devichiy Field, on the very spot where in 1524 Prince Basil III laid the foundations for the Smolensk Cathedral. As soon as the cathedral was completed, the Kremlin copy of the *Smolenskaya Virgin* which accompanied the prince into the battle and to which he ascribed his victory in Smolensk was reverently placed inside.

The cathedral is covered with magnificent sixteenth-century **frescoes** which provide an insight into the life and aspirations of Basil III. They illustrate three main subjects which preoccupied the grand prince: (1) the transformation of Moscow into the 'Third Rome', (2) the repossession of the Kievan ancestral lands, including the city of Smolensk, and (3) the personal tragedy of the prince in failing to produce an heir.

The first of these themes — Moscow the 'Third Rome' — is illustrated by a series of frescoes relating to the history of the *Roman Virgin*, believed to be the earliest icon of the Hodigitria type. The narration begins on the western wall with the fresco of *St Luke Painting the Virgin* and continues on the northern and southern walls. By depicting the transfer of this military palladium of Orthodoxy from Rome to Constantinople and, finally, to Russian soil, the frescoes supported Moscow's claim to be the leader of Orthodoxy.

Below these frescoes are the **tombs** of Sofia and her two sisters. Nearby is the tomb of Evdokia, Peter's first wife.

The second and main theme of the cathedral focuses on the glorification of the *Virgin Hodigitria*, who helped the Orthodox armies overcome their foes. Highlighting the theme are the frescoes decorating the second and third tiers of the wall.

To show that the victory at Smolensk was not an isolated triumph but a step towards Russian unity, the artist depicted on the western facets of the pillars the canonized princes whose principalities were part of Kievan Russia. The positioning of the portraits on the pillars corresponds to the geographical locations of their principalities. The northern princes, *Andrei Bogoliubsky* of Vladimir and *Mikhail of Tver*, are painted on the northern pillars. The southern princes, *Boris and Gleb* of Kiev and *Mikhail of Chernigov*, are painted on the southern piers.

The third and last theme was the prince's despair over the lack of an heir. Attesting to his sorrow are the paintings on the vaults of the central nave devoted to the life of *St Anne*, who was also childless.

Nearly fifty years after Basil died, Tsar Boris Godunov became another famous contributor to the decorations of Smolensk Cathedral. Godunov's sister, Irina (widow of Tsar Fedor), refused the Russian throne upon Fedor's death. Instead she retreated to Novodevichiy, where she took the veil under the name of Nun Aleksandra. While Boris waited for the Russian National Assembly to elect him, he stayed at his sister's chambers in Novodevichiy. During these six weeks he began to renovate the cathedral, which he commemorated with the inscription circling the lower walls of the church:

> In accordance with the wishes and spiritual disposition of the Great Tsaritsa and Nun Aleksandra of Russia and her royal brother and Great Prince Boris Fedorovich, the ruler of all Russia [here follows the enumeration of the names of Boris's children] . . . we decorated the Smolensk Cathedral during the Patriarchy of Iov in the year 7106 [1598].

In 1598 Boris also commissioned new icons for the **iconostasis** of the church and a new frame for the icon of the *Virgin of Smolensk*. The frame is a remarkable work of art with finely engraved floral design incorporating river pearls, precious stones, and gold medallions. It is affixed to the sixteenth-century icon of the *Smolenskaya Virgin* mounted next to the royal gates.

Sofia, Peter's half-sister, succeeded Boris as the patron of the Novodevichiy Convent. Not suspecting that one day Novodevichiy would become her prison, Sofia used the convent as her second residence where, undisturbed, she could supervise the work on the cathedral.

During her regency, Sofia presented Smolensk Cathedral with the five-tier iconostasis, a masterpiece of eighty-four carved and guilded columns. Executed between 1683–1686 by Andreyev, Mikhailov, and Zinoviev, the icon screen is regarded as one of the best pictorial statements of Russian Orthodoxy.

Sofia also commissioned Ushakov and Zubov, the two great Kremlin artists, to paint several new icons for the enlarged iconostasis. When the icon screen was finished, the new icons, along with those painted for Boris Godunov, were mounted in their proper places. Most of the icons in the bottom tier of the iconostasis commemorate the patron saints of Russian tsars.

To the right of the royal gates is the *Enthroned Saviour* attended by *St John the Baptist* and *Apostle Peter.* Farther to the right, next to the *Virgin Portrayed as the Heavenly Queen*, is a family icon of Tsar Alexis Romanov. On the opposite side there is a full-length representation of *St John the Baptist*, a sixteenth-century contribution of Ivan the Terrible. Next, Boris Godunov's patron saints, *SS. Boris and Gleb*, are shown wearing fur-trimmed caps and coats with long sleeves.

The monumental icon screen is by no means the only treasure of the cathedral. Since the church was turned into a museum under the Soviets, it has become a repository of bibles, ecclesiastic vestments, silver, and embroideries made by the women who took the veil at Novodevichiy.

As well as commissioning art work, Sofia also proved to be a master builder. Under her watchful eye, the overall composition of the convent was conceived in the form of a cross. The cathedral became the point of intersection of the two axes, which were aligned north-south and east-west. Harmony of the new churches was achieved through the repeated use of Baroque motifs, the application of white stone ornaments to red brick walls, the presence of large windows set into carved frames, and the faceting of the church domes.

② Dormition (Uspenskaya) Refectory Church

Along the east-west axis is situated the Uspenskaya Refectory Church built in 1685-7. It was originally designed as a five-dome church surrounded by an open gallery. The gallery has since disappeared, but the covered staircase leading to the oblong refectory remains.

The windows of the refectory form an ornamental belt while the bunching of the columns at the corner and the narrowing of the pilasters toward the bottom break the monotony of the elongated lines. The interior of the dining hall is spacious and has no interior supports. While the frescoes and iconostasis are not outstanding, the church is worth visiting particularly while services are performed to hear the fine choir which sings there.

③ Bell-Tower

To the east of the cathedral on a direct line with the refectory stands the monastery's bell-tower, which was completed in 1690. The heavy mass of red octagons tapering toward the golden dome is punctuated by open arcades. A different detail was chosen for each of the five tiers: some repeat the curve of the arches; others, such as the elongated columns, accentuate the octagonal shape of the tower. The horizontal divisions are also marked by white stone balustrades with handsome balusters.

④ ⑤ Gate Churches

Two beautiful gate churches, one over the northern entry and the other at the southern, are advantageously set off by the white-washed walls of the convent. The five-domed **Transfiguration Gate Church** ④, at the northern entry, is somewhat reminiscent of Arkhangelsky Cathedral in the Kremlin because of its elongated form and its windows with scalloped-shaped niches. In 1687, when she commissioned the church, Sofia engaged the Kremlin masters to work on its seven-tier iconostasis, which no longer exists. The present iconostasis was moved from the destroyed church of Dormition.

The **Church of Pokrov** ⑤, dating from 1683-8, at the southern entry displays a clever arrangement of three towers whose narrowing octagons bear onion-shaped domes.

Novodevichiy: Preobrazhenskaya (Transfiguration) Gate Church (late seventeenth century).

Residences of the Royal Nuns

There are four royal residences at the convent.

The **Miloslavsky Chambers** ⑥, located in the southern part of Novodevichiy next to the Pokrov Gate Church, are named after Maria Miloslavskaya, one of Sofia's sisters who ended her life at the convent as a nun.

The **Chambers of Irina Godunova** ⑦ are located in the white oblong building between the Miloslavsky Chambers and the red Refectory Church. They were built in the sixteenth century as the residence of Irina Godunova, the widow of Tsar Fedor, who chose the seclusion of the nunnery in preference to becoming Russia's first lawfully elected queen. The building's barrel-shaped roof and covered porch are being restored, as is the **Church of St Ambrose** (Amvrosy) at the chambers' eastern end.

The **Lopukhin Chambers** ⑧, a red-brick building with constrasting white stone work adjoining the northern entry gates, once housed Yevdokia Lopukhina, the first wife of Peter the Great. Here, too, lived Ekaterina, another of Sofia's sisters, whom Peter also forced to become a nun. The Lopukhin Chambers, with their low vaulted rooms and tiled stoves, are the reception quarters of the metropolitan of Krutitsy and Kolomma.

Sofia's Chamber-Prison ⑨, the small building adjoining the Pond Tower ⑩, witnessed the demise of Sofia and served as her prison after Peter the Great deposed her in 1689.

Cemetery

Many illustrious Russians are buried at the **old Novodevichiy cemetery** on the museum premises. Located here are the grave of writer Anton Chekhov and the tomb of Aleksandr Scriabin, the pianist-composer who died in 1915.

The **new cemetery** to the south of Novodevichiy ⑪ is closed to the general public. Buried there is Nadezhda Allelueva, Stalin's first wife and the first Soviet 'tsaritsa' to rest in the cemetery of Russian royal women. There, too, is the tomb of Nikita Khrushchev, surmounted by the statue by Ernst Neizvestny. Nearby rest the remains of publisher Aleksandr Tvardovsky, whom the Nobel-prize winning writer Aleksandr Solzhenitsyn eulogized in his funeral oration shortly before he left the Soviet Union.

Excursion 24

SPASO-ANDRONIKOV AND NOVOSPASSKY MONASTERIES

A tour to the Spaso-Andronikov Monastery includes the Andrei Rublev Museum of Icons. The Novospassky Monastery features churches built by the Romanovs and their relatives.

Pryamikova Ploshchad,
10
(10)

letro: *Ploshchad Ilicha*

e Saviour's Cathedral is the
al point of the Spaso-
adronikov Monastery. Note the
rrowing tiers of the spade-
aped kokoshniki *gables, the*
ademark of Moscow churches.

*T*he monastery was founded in 1359 by the canonized **Metropolitan Alexis**, who governed the Moscow Grand Duchy during the minority of Prince Dmitry Donskoy.

In 1353, returning from Constantinople, where Alexis was confirmed by the Byzantine patriarch, the metropolitan's ship ran into a storm. Praying for deliverance, Alexis vowed to build a monastery named after the saint on whose day the ship reached port. The winds calmed down and Alexis's ship sailed into the harbour on 16 August, the day on which the Russian Orthodox Church commemorates the icon of the *Saviour* known as the '*Holy Face*', or *Vernicle*. Alexis interpreted his arrival date as a sign of God's grace, since during the consecration ceremony in Constantinople, the Greek patriarch bestowed on Alexis an icon of the *Vernicle* to take back.

EXCURSION 24

301

Excursion Plan 24
Spaso-Andronikov
Monastery and
Novospassky Monasteries

NOVOSPASSKY

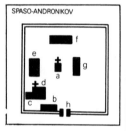

SPASO-ANDRONIKOV

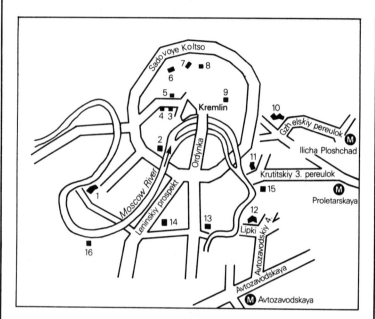

MONASTERIES:

1. Novodevichiy
2. Convent of the Immaculate
   Conception
3. Zaikonospassky (Monastery of the
   Saviour)
4. Nikolsky (Monastery of St
   Nicholas)
5. Bogoiavlensky (Pentecostal)
6. Vyssoko Petrovsky (St Peter on
   the Heights Monastery)
7. Rozhdestvensky (Nativity Convent)

8. Sretensky
9. Ivanovsky Convent
10. Spaso-Andronikov Monastery
    (Rublev Museum)
11. Novospassky
12. Simonov
13. Danilovsky
14. Donskoy
15. Krutitsky
16. Andreyevsky

NOVOSPASSKY MONASTERY:

I Transfiguration Cathedral
II Refectory Church of Pokrov and
   Baking Chamber
III Church of St Nicholas
IV Monks' cells
V Abbot's quarters
VI Mead (*kvas*) Chamber

VII Znamenskaya Church
VIII Walls
IX Bell-Tower (1786)
X Bell-Tower
XI Tarakanova's Memorial Chapel
XII Service Building

SPASO-ANDRONIKOV
MONASTERY:

a. Saviour's (Spassky) Cathedral
b. Office Building
c. Walls and Towers
d. Archangel Michael's
   (Arkhangelsky) Church

e. Monks' quarters
f. Exhibition Hall
g. Exhibition Hall (former
   Seminary)
h. Entry gates

Metropolitan Alexis was about to begin the construction of the Saviour's Monastery when he was urgently summoned to the Golden Horde, the headquarters of the fearful Tartars in the south of Russia. **Princess Taidula**, the favourite wife of Khan Dzhani Beck, had become blind and begged the khan to send for the metropolitan, whose spiritual and healing qualities were well known to the Tartars. Unable to refuse the khan, Alexis requested **Andronik**, a student of St Sergius of Radonezh, to oversee the construction of the monastery while he travelled to Sarai, the capital of the Golden Horde.

Arriving at Sarai, Alexis prayed for the sick princess and touched her eyes with holy water. Miraculously Taidula's sight returned. In gratitude, the princess slipped off a ring which bore the official insignia of the Khanate and gave it to the metropolitan. The khan made a gift to Alexis of some land in the Kremlin and promised to uphold the reign of the ten-year-old Prince Dmitry.

Having secured a peaceful interlude for Russia, the metropolitan returned to dedicate the new monastery, named after the *Saviour's Vernicle* and Andronik, the monastery's first abbot. Alexis then placed the icon of the *Saviour*, which had accompanied him on his stormy voyage, on the altar of the Saviour's Cathedral, completed in 1360.

The monastery, a virtual fortress with stout oak walls, became the last Christian outpost in hostile Tartar territory. The princes, who were required by the khans to visit and to pay tribute to them, would stop at the monastery for a chance to rest and to confer with Metropolitan Alexis before undertaking the final leg of their journey.

ⓐ Saviour's (Spassky) Cathedral

The monastery's focal point is the small, white Cathedral of the Saviour which was built between 1420 and 1427. It is one of the most admired and copied fifteenth-century buildings in Russia. The cathedral combines features of the churches of Suzdal and Vladimir, construction techniques developed by the builders from Pskov, as well as some of the innovations introduced by the fifteenth-century Moscow architects, namely the spade-shaped *kokoshniki* gables, the trademark of Moscow churches.

The interior decorations of the Saviour's Cathedral were executed by **Andrei Rublev**, Russia's foremost

...blev painting the Saviour's ...hedral at Spaso-Andronikov.

iconographer, who trained as a monk at the Trinity Sergius Monastery. Today only a floral fragment of a fresco survives in the arch of the altar window.

The cathedral is empty except for a recent statue of Rublev. The monastery is now the **Rublev Icon Museum** devoted to the Moscow School of Icon Painting, which Rublev founded.

Archangel Michael's Church

To the left of the Saviour's Cathedral, in the northern part of the pentagon formed by the white-washed seventeenth-century walls and green-capped towers, rises the grand Baroque Church of the Archangel Michael, built in 1694. The church encompasses the old monastery refectory, which provides the base for the elongated cube and the octagon constituting the three tiers of the one-domed St Michael's Church. It now houses an **icon restoration studio**.

Like many Moscow Baroque churches, each level has individual decorations, such as pillars, patterned cornices, and windows encased in carved stone frames. Note the Renaissance shell-like inserts in the arches of the octagonal tier.

The church was commissioned by Ustinia Lopukhina to celebrate the birth of Alexis in 1690, son of Peter the Great and Ustinia's daughter Yevdokia. The proud grandmother chose to patronize the monastery because of its association with the revered Metropolitan Alexis, her grandson's namesake. The **upper church** of the newly built cathedral, which she named after Metropolitan Alexis, occupies an area of approximately 200 square metres and has in its centre a massive pier supporting the vaulted hall.

Ustinia's dedication of the cathedral's **lower-level church** to Archangel Michael betrays her ambitious designs for the Lopukhins. She chose to name this church, which was to serve as the Lopukhins' burial chapel, after the Kremlin's **Arkhangelsky Cathedral**, the necropolis of the Russian tsars. Unfortunately, Ustinia's ambitious dreams were cut short by Peter the Great's decision to divorce Yevdokia and to banish the Lopukhins to Siberia.

Rublev Museum of Russian Icons

The museum's collection of icons is divided among three buildings.

The most valuable collection, containing the works of Rublev's students, is to be found in the former **Seminary Building**, built in a neo-classical style. Of special note are the icons of *St John the Baptist* (fifteenth century), *Dormition of the Virgin* (mid fifteenth century), the icon of *St Sergius* (early fifteenth century), and the two icons of the mounted *St George* (early sixteenth century).

The most recent discovery at the Rublev museum is that of a thirteenth-century icon of *The Saviour*, found in the 1960s under eighteenth- and nineteenth-century overlays. It now hangs in the Seminary Building.

More icons are to be found in the former **Monks Quarters** ⓔ to the left and behind the Saviour's Cathedral. Most of the icons in this collection date from late sixteenth and early seventeenth centuries and were painted primarily in Novgorod. The two finest icons are both of *St Nicholas* and are dated mid sixteenth century.

A third collection consisting of icons and iconostases rescued from churches destroyed during the Soviet period is located in the new **Exhibition Hall** ⓕ behind the Saviour's Cathedral. The seventeenth-century icon of *Our Lady of Tikhvin* is noteworthy both as a work of art and as a historical document. The twelve border scenes which surround the representation of the Virgin and the Child illustrate the construction of the Virgin Mary's Dormition Monastery near Tikhvin, where the icon was first discovered. The border scenes show how the monastery evolved from a small timber fortress into a large edifice with stone walls and churches.

Fedor Volkov's Memorial

The gravestone over the tomb of Fedor Volkov (1729–1763), the Yaroslavl-born founder of the Russian national theatre, is all that remains of the monastery's cemetery. The memorial is located between the Saviour's Cathedral and the new Exhibition Hall.

Novospassky Monastery

Krestynaskaya Ploshchad, 10
⑪
Metro: *Proletarskaya*

The mighty fortress in south-eastern Moscow stood originally in the Kremlin and was known as **Spassky** or **Saviour's Monastery**. But in the fifteenth century **Prince Ivan III**, needing more room for his new palaces and churches,

Novospassky (New Saviour's) Monastery: view from the east engraving, 1849, Shchusev Museum).

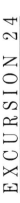

ordered the monastery transferred to the banks of the Moscow River. As well as providing a more spiritual surrounding, he argued, Moscow would also gain a much needed fortification. To mollify the monks, the Grand Prince generously endowed what now became the **Novospassky** or the **New Saviour's Monastery**. He then dismissed it from his mind.

The neglected monastery might have disappeared altogether, were it not for the Romanovs, who chose the monastery as their place of burial. When, in 1613, **Michael Romanov** was elected tsar, the monastery's prestige received an immediate boost. To honour the graves of his mother, his grandparents, uncles, and other numerous Romanov relatives, Michael undertook to build a memorial church over their tombs, but the project was abandoned for lack of funds until 1649 when his son **Alexis** completed the cathedral.

The Transfiguration Cathedral

(Spaso-Preobrazhensky Sobor) Ⓘ

The Transfiguration Cathedral, like the Dormition or Uspensky Cathedral in the Kremlin, is built on a cruciform plan. It has the same tri-sectional division of the walls and a five-dome covering. The reason for imitating the Kremlin prototype, the very citadel of Russian Orthodoxy, was to stress the role of the Romanov tsars as protectors and champions of the Russian Orthodox faith.

Located in the very centre of the monastery, the cathedral is the tallest building in the cluster of interlinked structures: the three-domed **Refectory Church of Pokrov** Ⓘ (1675) which adjoins the cathedral from the north, as does the **Khlebodarnaya Palata** (1778), a sturdy white building with small windows which served as the monastery's bakery, and the **Znamenskaya Church**, Ⓥ placed south of the cathedral.

Frescoes and Icons

The interior decorations of the cathedral are an elaboration of the theme embedded in the building's architecture. Beyond the heavy portals surmounted by a mosaic of the *Saviour*, the first frescoes of the enclosed gallery inside the church are the portraits of the *Hellenic philosophers* who forsaw the coming of the Lord. Next we see the representations of *St Fedor of Yaroslavl* and *St Michael of Chernigov*, patron saints of Tsar Fedor (r. 1584–98) and Tsar Michael Romanov. The reason for including *St*

Fresco in the gallery of the Transfiguration Cathedral, 1688, depicting a philosopher (Historical Museum).

Fedor, the patron of the last Rurik rulers, was to stress the link between the Rurik and Romanov dynasties. This link was provided by Anastasia Romanova, wife of Ivan the Terrible and mother of Tsar Fedor.

The frescoes on the pillars of the parvis tell the story of Christianity coming to Russia. The theme is introduced by the fresco of *Apostle Andrew* who allegedly visited the future site of Kiev and foretold its emergence as a Christian capital. Next are the representations of the Scandinavian Princes *Askold* and *Dir* who captured Kiev in 862. They are astounded that the Bible thrown into the fire by the Greek Bishop Michael remains intact. The scene is followed by the *Baptism of Princess Olga* and of her grandson *Prince Vladimir of Kiev* (978–1015), who converted his people to Christianity. The series ends with the *Wedding of Vladimir and Princess Anne*, sister of the Byzantine Emperor Basil II.

A *group of monks* copying the books nearby serve to remind that the enlightenment was also introduced to Russia from Byzantium. Between the pillars there are seven large sequences depicting the *Seven Ecumenical Councils*, starting with the seventh by the entrance and ending with the first around the bend of the gallery's wall.

The painting of the *genealogical tree of the Rurik tsars* inside the church proper summarizes the theme underlying the decorations and is one of the cathedral's curiosities. The trunk of the tree follows the camber vault and spreads its branches into the vault's spandrels. At the bottom of the tree Princess Olga and Prince Vladimir, the planters of Christianity on Russian soil, water the roots of the tree. The branches bear the names of the royal princes, the last of which was Tsar Fedor. The care which Olga and Vladimir lavish on the tree emphasizes the close relationship between the Church and the State.

The **portraits** of Tsar Michael Romanov and his son Alexis behind the right choir of the cathedral were painted by the monks in appreciation of the generous support of the Romanovs.

The **iconostasis** of the Transfiguration Cathedral, completed in 1649, was the gift of Tsar Alexis Romanov. Among the notable icons is that of the *Transfiguration*, encased in a silver frame with medallions of twelve Church holidays. Another famous icon is that of the *Saviour*, which Prince Dolgoruky carried with him during his campaign against the river pirate Stenka Razin.

(VII) Znamenskaya or the Church of the Sign

Znamenskaya Church was built originally as the necropolis of the Princes Cherkassky (see Excursion 14), a noble family related by marriage to Michael Romanov. When, in 1743, Varvara, the last of the Cherkassky line, married Count Petr Borisovich Sheremetiev, the Znamenskaya Church became Sheremetiev's property. Their son Nikolai commissioned the architect Elizvoy Semenovich Nazarov to rebuild it as the Sheremetiev's memorial chapel (1791–5).

Nazarov created a classical church in which the white columns stress the simplicity of the green walls. Western influences also mark the wide Pantheon-type dome and the iconostasis with a triangular pediment.

In 1803 Praskovya Zhemchugova-Kovaleva (see pp. 203, 257), the beautiful young wife of Nikolai Sheremetiev, and the former star of his serf theatre, died. The grief-stricken Count buried his wife with regal honours and placed her body in the Znamenskaya Church next to the noble Cherkasskys.

Ironically, a serf girl achieved honours denied to a princess of royal blood whose body lies buried nearby. The slim black **memorial chapel** ⓧ adjoining the monastery's bell-tower is a modest tribute to Princess Elizaveta Alekseyena Tarakanova, daughter of Empress Elizabeth I and her morganatic husband Count Aleksei Razumovsky (see p. 155). Until the chapel was built in 1900, the site of Tarakanova's grave was marked only by a tombstone giving her name as Sister Dosifeya. In 1768, six years after her mother's death, Tarakanova was forced by Empress Catherine the Great into the **Ivanovsky Nunnery** (see p. 136). For the next thirty-two years, until her death the royal nun was not allowed any visitors save the Mother Superior.

The mammoth eighteenth-century **bell-tower** ⓘⓧ over the monastery's entrance is the work of Ivan Zherebtsov, who worked on it for thirty years. On the opposite side of the monastery are the former **Monks cells** ⓘⓥ, extending from either side of the **Church of St Nicholas** ⓘⓘⓘ (1652). At one point Patriarch Filaret (1619–33), father of Tsar Michael Romanov, lived here.

Today the well-restored cells of the monks, with their unusual recessed windows, serve as restoration studios. Here young Russians are being taught old crafts such as metal working, embroidery, and weaving.

THE CHURCH BUILDERS OF BOLSHAYA ORDYNKA STREET

A tour of Zamoskvorechie which includes the Church of the Resurrection — Church of SS. Mikhail and Fedor — Church of St John the Baptist — the Church of the Transfiguration — St Clement's Church — the Church of St Nicholas 'v Pyzhakh' — the Church of St Catherine — SS. Martha and Mary Sisterhood — the Church of St John the Warrior and the guild churches of St Nicholas 'in Khamovnikakh', the Dormition 'in Goncharakh', and St Nicholas 'na Bolvanke'.

*M*uscovites were enthusiastic church builders. Tsars, churchmen, nobles, and merchants alike prided themselves on their houses of worship and embellished them with equal zeal.

A pleasant way to savour the rich variety of Moscow church architecture is to start in **Red Square**, below the **Church of St Basil** and then cross the **Moskvoretskiy Bridge** to **Bolshaya Ordynka Street**. The bridge which spans the right and left banks of the Moscow River also provides a link between the building styles favoured by the tsars and clergy and those developed by the artisans and merchants who settled in **Zamoskvorechie**.

Zamoskvorechie, literally the 'area beyond the Moscow River', was the home of the Moscow guilds which catered to the needs of the royal court. Least affected by Stalin's reconstruction, this former artisan suburb retains the panorama of onion-shaped domes rising above open yards and small old-fashioned houses.

Bolshava Ordynka is Zamoskvorechie's largest and most important street. Until the sixteenth century it was the main road to the Tartar headquarters in the south of Russia, known as the 'Orda' or the Golden Horde.

The first lane that veers off to the right is **Kadashevskiy 2. Pereulok**, the former territory of the Kadashi barrel makers and cloth weavers. The Kadashi guild made *kadi* or barrels which the tsar's household used for pickling and packaging fruits and vegetables. When the barrel makers left, the weavers moved in, though the area preserved the original name 'Kadashi'. The weavers' guild was the birthplace of Moscow's textile industry and remained a production centre for centuries.

Providing the tsar with an annual quota of 4,000 yards of linens and table cloth, the weavers also sold their textiles on the open market. With profits of their trade, they built four churches. The most famous of them, the **Church of the Resurrection**, dominated the landscape of Zamoskvorechie, just as the weavers guild dominated the textile trade.

Church of the Resurrection in Kadashakh

(Tserkov Voskreseniia 'v Kadashakh')
Kadashevskiy, 2-oi, Pereulok

The vertical alignment of shapes and the skill with which an unknown architect combined different geometrical forms into a harmonious entity make the Church of the Resurrection unique. Its crowning glory is the octagonal bell-tower whose narrowing tiers inspired its nickname of 'the candle'. The church represents

Excursion Plan 25
The Church Builders
of Bolshaya
Ordynka Street

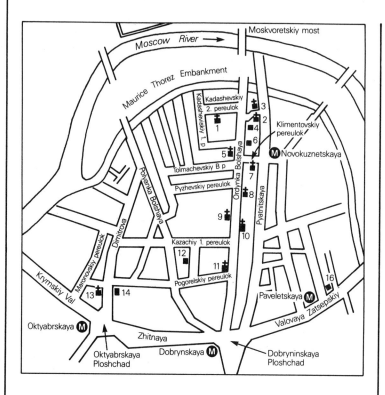

1. Church of the Resurrection 'in Kadashakh'
2. Church of SS. Mikhail and Fedor of Chernigov
3. Church of St John the Baptist 'pod Borom'
4. Kozitskaya School for Girls
5. Church of the Transfiguration
6. House of the Merchant Dolgov
7. Church of St Clement
8. Church of St Nicholas 'in Pyzhakh'
9. The Sisterhood of SS. Martha and Mary
10. Church of Our Lady of Iberia
11. Church of St Catherine
12. Tropinin Museum (see 'Modern Moscow' p. 355)
13. Church of St John the Warrior
14. House of Igumnov (French Embassy)

one of the earliest and finest example of 'Moscow Baroque'. Unlike European Baroque, which manifested itself later in the palaces of St Petersburg, it was an elaboration of the ornamental ship-shaped plan which became popular in the first half of the seventeenth century. Characterized by the graduation of geometrical shapes progressing upward from a broad, square base to narrowing octagonal sections, the 'Moscow Baroque' includes features of both Classical order architecture and native timber-inspired detailing: the Church of the Resurrection, for example, has rows of hollow pediments, christened 'cockscombs' and widely copied by the Muscovites, instead of the popular semi-circular gables. The beading of the narrow geometrical shapes and the intricate carving seen in this church reached their full development in a later style known as the Naryshkin Baroque.

he Church of the Resurrection 'in dashakh' (1687–1713) oresents one of the earliest and est examples of 'Moscow roque'.

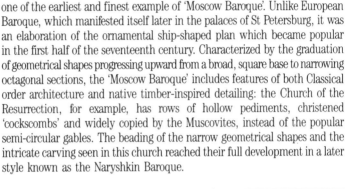

The Kadashevskiy Lane makes a U-turn and winds back to Bolshaya Ordynka, just below the western-style **Transfiguration Church**. Before visiting it, however, we suggest a quick detour to see the former **St John Monastery**. Walk back on **Bolshaya Ordynka** and turn right into **Chernigovskiy Pereulok**, which links Bolshaya Ordynka to **Pyatnitskaya Street**. The lane widens into a lovely square with an eighteenth-century mansion, two churches and a green bell-tower whose silhouette dominates Zamoskvorechie.

(Tserkov Chernigovskikh Muchenikov)
Pyatnikskaya Ulitsa, 4
②

The Church of the Martyred Saints Mikhail and Fedor of Chernigov

The white cube-shaped church, whose five bulbous domes are scaled like pine cones, commemorates Prince Mikhail and his faithful companion Fedor. In 1245, because they refused to worship heathen gods, Khan Baty ordered wooden planks placed over Mikhail and Fedor and his Tartar guards to jump on the boards until the two Russians were trampled to death. In the sixteenth century the martyrs were canonized and in 1675 a memorial church rose over their tombs.

The bell-tower of the Church of St John the Baptist 'pod Borom' is a prominent Zamoskvorechie landmark.

(Tserkov Ioanna Predtechi 'pod Borom')
③

The Church of St John the Baptist 'Pod Borom'

The second whitewashed church with horizontally banded walls and a single dome, directly opposite that of Chernigov martyrs, honours St John the Baptist, the patron of the former St John's Monastery, whose origins go back to the fourteenth century.

In the eighteenth century, St John's Church was extended by the addition of a red refectory and the famous green tower (1753) executed in the classical style.

On the other side of the square the **Mansion**, with a six-column portico and bas-reliefs of angels, was the residence of the monastery's bishop, prior to becoming the fashionable Kozitskaya School for girls. ④

Church of St John the Baptist (1675) showing the octagonal drum and the horizontal bands of patterned brick.

The former Kozitskaya School, once the residence of the Monastery bishops.

Back on Bolshaya Ordynka, we now proceed to the **Transfiguration Church** on our right.

(Vsekh Skorbiashchikh Radost)
Bolshaya Ordynka, 20
(5)

Church of the Transfiguration (Our Lady, Joy of all the Afflicted)

The large yellow Church of the Transfiguration looks like a proud, tall ship with a rounded bow and stern and is considered one of the finest examples of Moscow Empire style.

Of the original church, only the round bell-tower built by Vasily Bazhenov between 1783 and 1791 survived the fire in 1812. Osip Bove rebuilt the rest of the church between 1828 and 1833, adding the rotunda with its Western-looking dome and sculptured bands in which the heads of cherubs are woven into a complicated floral pattern, and porticos with Ionic columns. The interior of the building carries motifs from Western Classicism further still, with a curving marble colonnade in the refectory and an iconostasis that looks more like a triumphal arch than a traditional icon screen.

Because of a famous miracle-making icon which is kept in the Transfiguration Church, the Muscovites refer to it as the **Church of Our Lady, Joy of all the Afflicted**. The icon of the Virgin by the same name is sheathed in a golden cover and displayed in the left aisle of the refectory.

The miracle of *Our Lady, Joy of all the Afflicted*, occurred in the seventeenth century. When the icon was brought to the sister of Patriarch Joachim and she was cured of a crippling disease, believers thronged to the Transfiguration

EXCURSION 25

313

Church to venerate the icon. The close association with the wonder-working Madonna and the church's marvellous choir still attract Muscovites to this church. The choir sings two special services each year commemorating the deaths of their composers: Sergei Rachmaninov's 'Vespers' on the Saturday nearest 28 March, and Tchaikovsky's 'Liturgy' on 25 October.

The House of Merchant Dolgov

(Institute for Latin America)
Bolshaya Ordynka, 21
⑥

The Transfiguration Church and the yellow mansion across the street from the Church form an architectural unit. Both were built by the merchant Dolgov who engaged two of Moscow's foremost architects for the task.

The first architect was Vasily Ivanovich Bazhenov (1738–99), whom Catherine the Great nearly drove to suicide by rejecting everything he designed for her. Nevertheless, the Moscow nobles lionized the snobbish French-trained architect who was elected vice-president of the St Petersburg Academy of Arts. Bazhenov agreed to design the church and the house for the merchant Dolgov, only because he had married the merchant's daughter.

Bazhenov's exposure to French Classicism and his stay in Italy influenced his love for grandeur in architecture. Even his small buildings are known for their elegant proportions, Corinthian order architecture with fluted columns, plastic moulding in bas-relief, and decorative friezes. A few of Bazhenov's touches remain on the garden facade of the mansion. The street facade was disfigured by the fire of 1812, which also destroyed the church.

The Dolgov house and the Transfiguration Church, reconstructed by Osip Bove in the 1830s, now feature a 'Bazhenov' back and a 'Bove' front. Both retained Bazhenov's architectural concept, though the decorative statement, including the six Ionic pilasters and sophisticated sculptured friezes, is closer to the Empire style which Bove also used for the Transfiguration Church.

Another quick detour along Klimentovsky Pereulok is a must for lovers of Baroque architecture. Their reward will be the flamboyant red **Church of St Clement**, one of the few such monuments surviving in Moscow from the reign of Empress Elizabeth I.

The Church of St Clement I

(Tserkov Klimenta, Papy Rimskogo)
Pyatnitskaya Ulitsa, 26
⑦

The Church of St Clement, which evokes the gaiety and lightness of Rastrelli's palaces in Leningrad, is ascribed to Pietro Antonio Tressini. He started it in 1742, but because of his departure from Russia an unknown architect finished the church between 1762 and 1774.

Despite the traditional religious design, the Church of St Clement differs considerably from most Moscow churches. One is struck by the absence of the projecting altar apses and the secular character of the building. The elongated body of the penta-cupolar church resembles a palace more than a house of prayer. This impression is reinforced by the division of the facade

large yellow Church of the
nsfiguration shows clear
stern influences. The refectory
a curving marble colonnade
the iconostasis looks more like
iumphal arch than a
itional icon screen.

into lofty stories and the richness of white decorations which serve to heighten the red background. The well-preserved baroque iconostasis inside the church can only be seen by special arrangement.

The dedication of the church to St Clement, the third pope, had more to do with Empress Elizabeth's accession to the throne than the Muscovites' devotion to this pope. On 23 November 1741, the feast day of St Clement, Elizabeth and her favourite, Alexis Bestuzhev-Riumin, plotted a *coup d'etat* and seized the throne from Ivan IV on the 25th. To commemorate Elizabeth's accession, Bestuzhev-Riumin commissioned the church honouring St Clement on his estate in Zamoskvorechie.

(Tserkov Nikoly
'v Pyzhakh')
shaya Ordynka, 27a
⑧

The Church of St Nicholas 'in Pyzhakh'

The musketeers of Colonel Bogdan Pyzhev's regiment were justifiably proud of their Church of St Nicholas which took them thirteen years (1657–70) to complete. The cube-shape building which resembles a sugar-dusted confection is an excellent example of the 'Moscow ornamental style' which made its brilliant debut with the Church of the Holy Trinity built by Merchant Nikitnikov (see Excursion 5, p. 95).

The church and the bell-tower are lavishly decorated with row upon row of horizontal belts, featuring every known design from ribs and dentals to squares and circles. The columns are round, beaded, and sculptured. The window frames are topped with triangular, rounded, and pointed pediments. The superb *kokoshniki* gables form a pyramid-like transition to the five drums which swell into powerful silver domes. Of particular note is the recessed portal of carved stone and the bell-tower with its handsome tiered steeple.

In spite of its exterior, St Nicholas's Church does not evoke happy memories. Its builders, the regiment of Colonel Pyzhov, were executed in Red Square on 10 October 1698. Peter the Great, who had nearly perished during the riots, had them put to death for their participation in the rebellions instigated by the Regent Sofia. On that day in October, the musketeers (*streltsy*) ceased to exist as a privileged social class.

rfo-Mariinskaya
Obitel)
haya Ordynka, 34a
⑨

The Sisterhood of SS. Martha and Mary

The short distance which separates the Church of St Nicholas from the Church of the Intercession of the Virgin of SS. Martha and Mary's Sisterhood represents, in architectural terms, a leap of nearly two centuries. The striking Church

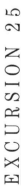

EXCURSION 25

of the Intercession built between 1908 and 1912 by the architect A. V. Shchusev, incidentally the builder of Lenin's Mausoleum, is one of Russia's most remarkable examples of the Art Nouveau style.

Shaped like a cube and surmounted with a large onion dome, the Intercession Church represents a novel and ingenious interpretation of the solid earth-bound churches of Russia's north-west. The walls are divided into three equal sections and end in triangular arches not found elsewhere in Moscow. The refectory is marked by a slim drum with a small blue dome and, like the rest of the church, displays sculptured ornaments of geometrical design. Because of Shchusev's tendency to enlarge each detail, the diminutive church appears monumental. Thus, the rounded tri-fold apse seems out of proportion with the main cubic volume. The central dome covered with dark sheets of iron brings to mind a brown-capped mushroom sitting on a stout white stem.

The **frescoes** and **icons** inside the church are the work of painter Mikhail Nesterov, a protégé of the railway tycoon Savva Mamontov. Nesterov's works are noted for their lyrical colours, beautiful design and the accessible saintliness of the personages he depicts on his icons and frescoes.

The sisterhood of SS. Martha and Mary was founded in 1905 by the Grand Princess Elizaveta Fedorovna, the sister-in-law of Emperor Nicholas II. When her husband Grand Prince Sergei was killed by a terrorist bomb, the widowed Grand Princess organized the semi-monastic order called the Sisters of Charity and devoted the rest of her life to aiding the sick and the wounded. In July 1918 she died in the iron quarry near Alapaevsk, where she and other members of the Romanov family were beaten by the Red Guards and left to die.

The Church of Our Lady of Iberia

(Tserkov Iverskoi Bozhey Materi)
Bolshaya Ordynka, 39
(10)

This large church with four powerful columns dating from 1802 was designed by the famous architect I. V. Egotov in the then prevailing Classical style. The disfigured building illustrates the sad fate suffered by many of Moscow's churches. In 1932 the building was vandalized and turned into a factory club.

The Church of Saint Catherine

(Tserkov Ekateriny Muchenitsy)
Bolshaya Ordynka, 60
(11)

The original builders of the church were most likely the members of the cosmetics guild who once lived in Zamoskvorechie. The rouges and skin whiteners they produced were used in abundance by the merchants' plump belles. In the eighteenth century the wooden Church of St Catherine burned to the ground. To honour her patron saint, Catherine the Great had the church rebuilt in 1767, entrusting the task to Karl Blank.

The church recalls the Baroque garden pavilions popular in eighteenth-century Russia. Blank achieved the octagonal effect by inscribing a cross into the cube and rounding off the pillared projections. He completed the church by adding an octagonal drum with an elongated cupola. The bell-tower and a second church were built in 1869.

(Sadovoye Koltso)

Sadovoye Ring

Bolshaya Ordynka ends at **Dobryninskaya Square** which marks the boundary of Zamoskvorechie. **Valovaya** and **Zhitnaya Streets** located on either side of the square are now part of the Sadovoye or Garden Ring which circles Moscow. In days past there stood the fortifications known as the **Earthern Rampart**.

(Tserkov Ioanna Voina)
Dimitrova Ulitsa, 46
⑬

Church of St John the Warrior

To reach the Church of St John the Warrior, turn right on Dobryninskaya Square, and walk along Zhitnaya Street to the next large square, called **Oktyabrskaya Square** or **Ploshchad**; make another right turn into **Dimitrova Ulitsa** which runs parallel to Bolshaya Ordynka.

Still a working church, the Church of St John the Warrior was constructed between 1709 and 1713 according to the plans drawn up by Peter the Great. When he first saw its parishioners trying to salvage the flood-damaged foundations of the church built by musketeers in 1657, he was prepared to ignore the efforts since the riots of the musketeers and their support of Sofia's regency were still fresh in his mind. However, he realized that his soldiers frequently invoked the name of the saint before doing battle and decided that he wanted St John's support for his last contest with Sweden's invincible Charles XII. After his victory over the Swedes at Poltava on 27 June 1709,

Church of St John the
—rior (1709–13), designed by
—r the Great, was one of the
— churches to combine elements
—he old order, seen in the
—gonal bell-tower, faceted
—de, and tiered construction,
—n features of Western Baroque.

Peter presented 300 roubles to the priest of the crumbling church. Architect Ivan Zarudny, hired to renovate the church, finished it in 1713.

This monument marks a new page in the history of Russian architecture. Even as reliance on seventeenth-century tradition can be seen in the graduation of the superimposed cubes toward a slender octagon and the octahedral shape of the bell-tower, new Classical shapes brought from the West appear as well. Broken pediments replace the spade-shaped gables, and geometrical pyramids appear instead of whimsical 'cockscombs'. Other details gain in significance. Traditionally minute windows evolve into large lucarnes with carved ornaments, flat masonry strips get capitals, and scrolls become more pronounced in the decorative statement of the church. The silhouette itself, with its elongated nave and single cupola, constitutes a break with the five-dome format prescribed by Patriarch Nikon in the middle of the seventeenth century.

From the moment of its dedication in 1712, the Church of St John enjoyed a privileged status. Its new parishioners, rich merchants whose houses replaced those of the coachmen on **Yakimanka Street**, contributed generously to the church and chose its clergymen carefully. Toward the end of the eighteenth century, the merchants found the incarnation of their ideal in the person of the Father Matvei, whose thoughtful sermons drew large crowds from all over Moscow.

On 30 July 1796, the feast day of St John the Warrior, people flocked to the church. The size of the crowd aroused the curiosity of Emperor Paul I, who was in Moscow celebrating his coronation, so he went to the church to hear what the renowned priest would say on the subject of military valour. Unaware of the tsar's presence, Father Matvei drew from St John's life to suggest that one should always be ready to sacrifice one's life to defend the faith and the tsar, and that the sovereign, in turn, was under a solemn obligation to care for his subjects' welfare.

Paul liked the sermon so much that he asked Father Matvei to write it down for him and kept a copy of the sermon by his bed as a reminder of his duties as a monarch.

The magnificent five-tier **iconostasis** is a masterpiece of Russian seventeenth-century workmanship. The gilded columns are carved from entire hollowed logs so that the interwined grape clusters resemble translucent lace patterns. Painted by members of the tsar's workshops, the icons of the bottom row of the altar screen depict left to right: *The Virgin* (Annunciation of the Virgin), *Evangelist John*, *St Maxim* (Fool for God's Sake) *with St Peter of Athos*, *St John the Baptist*, and the *Virgin Portrayed as the Heavenly Queen*.

To the right of the royal gates appear the icon of the *Enthroned Saviour*, a group icon of the *Three Ecumenical Doctors of the Greek Orthodox Church* (St Gregory of Nazianzus, St Basil, and St John Chrysostom), the icon of the *Resurrection*, the icon of *St George*, and finally the icon of *Patriarch Germogen*, who was starved by the Poles during their occupation of the Kremlin in 1612.

In the fourth tier of the iconostasis, note that, instead of the Crucifixion, Jesus is shown carrying his cross and is surrounded by angels.

The image of *St John the Warrior* is mounted beneath a gold canopy to the right of the main iconostasis. The icon is sheathed in a gold cover and surrounded by sequences from the life of the fourth-century Roman officer who was martyred for his refusal to deny Christ. The streamlined design of the eighteenth-century altar screens of the two chapels in the refectory indicates that, unlike the main iconostasis, they were designed specifically for this church. The southern chapel honours St Dmitry, Bishop of Rostov, who founded the Yakovlevsky Monastery in Rostov and wrote the *History of the Russian Orthodox Church* as well as compiling the *Lives of the Saints*. The nineteenth-century icon of *St Dmitry*, clad in the traditional white headgear of the bishops, is to the right of the *Saviour*.

A large icon of *Our Lady of Kazan* and that of *St Triphon with the Falcon* are to the right of this side chapel.

The northern side chapel is dedicated to *SS. Gurias, Samonas, and Abibus,* whom Russians venerate as patron saints of family life. This group icon is in its traditional place adjoining the icon of the *Saviour.*

Also preserved in the church are the icons of the *Saviour* and *St Nicholas,* removed from the **Kremlin's Saviour**'s (Spassky) and **St Nicholas Gates** (see Excursion 2, p. 57).

(Residence of the French Ambassador)

Dimitrova Ulitsa, 43

The House of Igumnov

Directly across from the Church of St John the Warrior stands an opulent red-brick mansion, a typical example of neo-Russian revival architecture, patterned on a seventeenth-century Russian timber palace. Like many buildings of its type, the house looks morose despite its extravagant ornamentation. The facade is weighed down by the richly carved sandstone and bulky proportions of the second-storey balcony. Neither the peaked and barrel-shaped roofs, nor the colourful ceramic insets fully offset the voluminous mass of the house.

The individual details, however, warrant attention. The pendentives, which look like pineapples, decorate the arches of the porch and are integrated into the carving above the windows and the cornice. The balcony posts are pleasingly stout and are carved no less elaborately than their wooden prototypes. Equally attractive are the brightly painted, glazed tiles, mounted on the walls of the house or affixed to the gates.

The building has a curious history. After completing the house in 1893, architect Nikolai Ivanovich Pozdeyev presented its owner, Igumnov, with a bill which exceeded the original estimate. When the merchant refused to pay the difference, Pozdeyev hung himself inside the house. Igumnov never moved in and the mansion stood empty until 1918 when it was first used as a factory club and later occupied by a Medical Research Institute. Lenin's brain was supposedly examined there after his death. At the end of the Second World War the building was placed at the disposal of the French Embassy.

It is also said that the house is haunted by the ghost of Igumnov's mistress whose likeness appears in the medallions decorating the residence's drawing room. When the lass took a new lover, or so the legend goes, the spurned merchant had her cemented into the thick wall between the living room and vestibule, burying with her the jewellery he had given her during the courtship.

The walk through **Zamoskvorechie** hardly exhausts the artistic treasury left behind by the Moscow guilds. Remarkable for their colouring and wealth of ornamentation, the churches were the guilds' houses of worship and also their status symbols. The weavers who built the **Church of St Nicholas** and the ceramists who constructed the **Church of Dormition** succeeded in imparting the trademark of their profession to their churches.

(*Tserkov Sviatitelia
Nikolaia 'v
Khamovnikakh'*)
*Timura Frunze
Ulitsa, 1*
**(Excursion
Plan 13 ⑨)**

Church of St Nicholas 'in Khamovnikakh'

The *khamovniki*, or weavers, took as much pride in their church as they did in the fine linens which their guild wove and embroidered. In 1679, they instructed their architect to design a church that could rival the Church of the Resurrection of the barrel makers. The result was a large, rectangular building, with a low refectory, an ornamental bell-tower, and five onion-shaped domes. It is still a working church.

Grand as it is, the Church of St Nicholas would differ little from other churches were it not for the architect's use of multicoloured tiles and the tinting of architectural details in bright shades of orange and green. The inspiration for this design came from the weavers themselves: the architect transposed a pattern of their exquisite embroidery on to the walls of the church. The

Church of St Nicholas 'v Khamovnikakh' (1679–82). The decorations of the church were inspired by the fine embroideries produced by its builders.

combination of glazed tiles with orange and green details and stripes makes St Nicholas one of the most colourful churches in Moscow.

Apart from its festive exterior, the Church of St Nicholas prides itself on its **icons**, particularly the miracle-working icon of the Virgin, known as the *Helper of all Sinners.*

A copy of this icon is affixed above the entry to the church. The original, which came from the Nikolaevsky-Odrin Monastery near Orel, is displayed in a glass case beneath a golden canopy, to the left of the entrance. When one Dmitry Boncheskul, who lived behind the church, heard about a woman being cured while praying in front of the icon in 1844, he commissioned a copy of this icon for himself.

One day, as he prayed in front of the icon, Boncheskul noticed beads of moisture on the shiny surface of the wooden board. The priest, having also witnesses the wet drops, asked Boncheskul to move the icon to the church. Since then, several more miracles have been reported at St Nicholas at the site of the icon.

A larger copy of the miracle-working icon of the Virgins appears in the main **iconostasis** of the church. Next to it, also to the left of the royal gates, is a copy of the *Iberian Virgin.* The likeness of *St Nicholas*, patron saint of the church and the favourite saint of the merchants, is to the right of the *Saviour.* This large seventeenth-century icon is encased in a gilded silver frame. Scenes from the life of *St Nicholas* are painted on the walls of the main church. In one of them, St Nichlas is shown deflecting the sword about to strike an innocent man; on the opposite wall, he deposits a sack with golden coins on the window of a poor merchant's house, enabling the man's daughter to get married.

The side chapels commemorate *St Alexis* and the *Virgin, Helper of all Sinners.* Also note the icon of the *Virgin of the Three Hands* (see p. 332) displayed on the pillar between the two auxiliary chapels.

Church of the Dormition 'in Goncharakh'

(Tserkov Uspeniia 'v Goncharakh')
lodarkogo Ulitsa, 29
Excursion Plan 15,
⑪)

The diminutive Dormition Church 'in Goncharakh' near **Taganskaya Square** is still a working church and is one of Moscow's architectural gems. Built in 1654, the rectangular five-dome construction of the pillarless church represents a fine example of the 'ornamental style' of Moscow architectur which preceded the 'Moscow Baroque'. The interplay of red walls and white stone details and the contrast between the mellow green of the roof and the cobalt blue of the five bulbous domes decorated with exquisite gold crosses are further enhanced by ceramic insets. One such band of multicoloured tiles runs the length of the refectory adjoining the cube of the church itself. The tiles are decorated with a design of interwoven fruits and flowers. A tile-inlaid frame also surrounds the image of the *Virgin of Three Hands* which is affixed to the wall of the eighteenth-century bell-tower. The original of the icon is kept inside the church.

EXCURSION 25

The ceramists also used tiles to build a cupola above the **side chapel** dedicated to Bishop Tikhon Amafuntsky, which dates from 1702. The cupola is one of a kind: against the ochre green surface of the dome, figures of the four Evangelists are mounted in relief. The cupola is best seen from inside the courtyard.

More tiles are displayed against the red stuccoed wall of the refectory which faces into the courtyard. These tiles were made, coloured, and glazed by Stepan Polubes, the seventeenth-century master ceramist of the *Goncharnaya* guild. When he died, his family selected Stepan's best tiles and donated them to the Dormition Church, where they serve as a memorial to the man whose craftmanship was prized by tsars and patriarchs.

Tile making became a flourishing business in the 1600s, and the ceramist guild prospered. The tile makers used their ample financial resources to build and decorate the Domition Church, for which they commissioned many fine icons. The most famous icon at the Dormition Church of the Gonchary is the miracle-working icon of the *Virgin with Three Hands*, which is said to have three hands because of the hand painted at the bottom corner of the icon. This icon is located to the right of the main iconostasis in a glass case beneath a golden canopy.

Legend has it that the third hand commemorated St John Damascene's miraculous recovery of his hand. St John was the grand vizier of the caliph of Damascus. When Leo the Isaurian began his campaign against holy images, John defended their veneration, only to lose his post and have his hand chopped off. St John picked up the severed hand and held it up to his bleeding arm, praying to the Virgin for her intercession. The arm miraculously healed, and St John passed the rest of his life praising the Virgin.

As an expression of gratitude, he commissioned an icon of the Virgin to be painted with three hands, which he later presented to St Savva of Serbia. The icon remained in Serbia until the fourteenth century, when a Serbian monk carried it on the back of a donkey to Mt Athos to preserve it from the rampaging Turks. The prototype of the *Virgin with Three Hands* still hangs at the Serbian monastery of Hilander on Athos, while the icon at the Dormition Church is a seventeenth-century copy and, like the original, is believed to be endowed with curing powers.

The icon of the *Dormition of the Virgin*, to which the church is dedicated, occupies the place of honour in the main iconostasis. It depicts the *Death of the Mother of God* and her *Assumption*. The Virgin's soul is represented as a swaddled baby in the arms of Jesus, who is carrying his mother's body to heaven.

A superb seventeenth-century biographical icon of *St Nicholas* hangs on the refectory's left wall between two windows.

The right-handed altar, added in 1702, honours the Bishop Tikhon Amafuntsky, whose icon is to the right of the Saviour's. The icon located opposite the *Virgin with Three Hands* depicts *St Alexis, St Barbara,* and *St Basil the Blessed*. The saint who is depicted without clothes is St Basil, the fool for

Christ's sake whom the Church of St Basil in Red Square commemorates.

(Tserkov Nikoly 'na Bolvanke')
Verkhnyaya
Radishchevskaya
Ulitsa, 20
(Excursion Plan 15, ⑫)

Church of St Nicholas 'na Bolvanke'

It took the members of the *Bolvanka* (Hat-form makers) guild sixty-five years longer than the ceramists to raise enough money to replace their old wooden Church of St Nicholas with a new stone church, which was finished in 1712. Compared with other contemporary churches of the period it looks outdated and archaic. The adherence of hat-form makers to the mid-seventeenth-century architectural forms may have reflected the artisans' antagonism towards Peter the Great's reforms and innovations.

The church forms a tall rectangle in which the transition from the flat roof to the five drums is accomplished by rows of gables devoid of any structural role. The main attraction of the church is its bright colouring (vivid pink, white and green) and the unusual **bell-tower**, whose wide linear body is divided horizontally by flat strips of white masonry. Above the triangular roof rises an old-fashioned tent-shaped belfry with dormer windows.

The church is restored on the outside, but it is used as a gas pumping station.

EXCURSION 25

GUIDE TO MOSCOW'S WORKING CHURCHES

References to metro lines are indicated as **ML** *with the appropriate number.* Inactive monasteries and convents are listed in the general index.

I. Monastery, Convent, and Cemetery Churches

The Armenian Cemetery Church
Makeyeva Sergeya, Ulitsa
Metro: *Ulitsa 1905 Goda ML6*

Danilovsky Monastery: Residence of the Moscow Patriarch
Danilovsky Val. Ulitsa, 22 (Excursion 22)
Metro: *Tulskaya ML7 (Chekhovskaya-Novoslobodskaya)*
   Holy Trinity, Church of (*Tserkov Troitsy*)
   Seven Ecumenical Councils (*Tserkov Semi Vselenskikh Soborov*)
   St Simeon of the Pillar (*Simeona Stolpnika*)

Donskoy Monastery
Donskaya Ploshchad, 1 (Excursion 22)
Metro: *Shabolovskaya ML1*
   Our Lady of the Don (the 'Old' Cathedral)

Novodevichiy Convent
Pirogovskaya Bolshaya Ulitsa, 2 (Excursion 23)
Metro: *Sportivnaya ML1*
   Dormition Refectory Church (*Trapeznaya Uspenskaya Tserkov*)

Pyatnitskoe Cemetery
Droboliteynyy Pereulok, 5
Metro: *Rizhskaya ML5*
   Holy Trinity (*Tserkov Troitsy*)

Preobrazhenskoye Cemetery (Old Believers)
Preobrazhenskiy Val, Ulitsa, 18
Metro: *Preobrazhenskaya Ploshchad ML1*
   St Nicholas (*Tserkov Nikoly*)
   Raising of the Cross (*Tserkov Vozdvizhenya Kresta*)
   Transfiguration (*Tserkov Preobrazheniya*)

Rogozhskoye Cemetery (Old Believers)
Voytovicha, Ulitsa, 29 (Excursion 16)
Metro: *Ilicha Ploshchad ML6–A*
   Intercession of the Virgin (*Tserkov Pokrova*)
   St Nicholas (*Tserkov Nikoly*)
   Resurrection (*Tserkov Voskreseniya*)

Trinity Sergius Monastery
Zagorsk (Excursion 21)

Holy Spirit (*Tserkov Sviatogo Dukha*)
Holy Trinity (*Tserkov Troitsy*)
St Sergius Refectory Church
Uspensky or Dormition Cathedral

II. Churches in Central Moscow (within the Sadovoye Ring)

1. **Dormition 'in Goncharakh'** (*Tserkov Uspensia 'v Goncharakh'*, 1654)
   Volodarskogo, Ulitsa, 29 (Excursion 25)
   Metro: *Taganskaya ML4*

2. **St Elias** (*Tserkov Ilyi Proroka Obydennaya*, 18th–19th century)
   Obydenskiy Pereulok, 2
   Metro: *Kropotkinskaya ML1*

3. **Archangel Gabriel** (*Tserkov Arkhangela Gavriila*, 1704–7)
   See St Theodore, below
   (Excursion 8, 16)

4. **St John the Warrior** (*Tserkov Ioanna Voina 'on Yakimanka'*, 1709–13)
   Dimitrova, Ulitsa, 46 (Excursion 25)
   Metro: *Oktyabrskaya ML4*

5. **Joy of all the Afflicted (Church of the Transfiguration)** (*Tserkov Vsekh Skorbiashchikh Radost*, 1783–91; 1828–33)
   Ordynka Bolshaya, Ulitsa, 20 (Excursion 25)
   Metro: *Novokuznetskaya ML2*

6. **St Nicholas** (*Tserkov Nikoly 'v Kuznetsakh'*, 1805)
   Vishnyakovskiy Pereulok, 15
   Metro: *Novokuznetskaya ML2*

7. **SS. Peter and Paul** (*Tserkov Petra i Pavla*, 1700)
   Petropavlovskiy Pereulok, 4 (Excursion 15 (5))
   Metro: *Nogina Ploshchad ML5*

8. **Apostle Philip** (*Tserkov Apostola Philippa*, 1688)
   Aksakova, Pereulok, 5
   Metro: *Arbatskaya ML3-A*

9. **Resurrection** (*Tserkov Voskreseniya na 'Uspenskom Vrazhke'*, 1620–9)
   Nezhdanovoy, Ulitsa, 15 (Excursion 6 (11))
   Metro: *Puskinskaya ML6*

10. **St Theodore** (*Tserkov Fedora Stratilata*, 1806)
    Telegrafniy Pereulok, 15 (Excursion 8 (16))
    Metro: *Kirovskaya ML1*

III. Churches Between Sadovoye and the Moscow Ring Road

11. **Adrian and Natalia** (*Tserkov Adriana i Natalii*, 1911)
Yaroslavskoye Shosse, 95 (Babushkin village)
Metro: *VDNKh ML5*

12. **All Saints** (*Tserkov Vsekhsviatykh*, 1733) **in Verkhosviatskoye**
Leningradskiy Pereulok, 73
Metro: *Sokol ML2*

13. **Armenian Church**
See Armenian Cemetery, above.

14. **Deposition of the Lord's Robes** (*Tserkov Rizpolozheniya*, 1701)
Petrovskogo Akademika, Ulitsa (Excursion 22)
Metro: *Shabolovskaya ML5*

15. **Dormition Refectory Church** (1685–7)
See Novodevichiy Convent, above (Excursion 23)

16. **Dormition of the Virgin** (*Tserkov Uspenia 'v Veshnyakakh'*, 1644)
Yunosti Ulitsa, 2
Metro: *Zhdanovskaya ML6*

17. **St Eliah** (*Tserkov Ilyi Proroka*, 1644) **in Cherkizovo**
Shtatnaya Gorka, 17
Metro: *Preobrazhenskaya ML1*

18. **Epiphany Cathedral** (*Sobor Bogoiavlenia 'v Yelokhove'*, 1835–45)
Baumanskaya Ploshchad, 15 (Excursion 11)
Metro: *Baumanskaya ML3*

19. **Intercession of the Virgin** (*Tserkov Pokrova*, 17th century) **in Medvedkovo**
(Excursion 14)
Metro: *Sviblovo ML5*

20. **Intercession of the Virgin** (*Tserkov Pokrova*)
See Rogozhskoye Cemetery, above

21. **St John the Baptist** (*Tserkov Ionna Predtechi*, early 19th century) **in Ivanovskoye**
Stalevarov Ulitsa, 6
Metro:*Novogireyevo ML6-A* (or car/taxi)

22. **St John the Baptist** (*Tserkov Ionna Bogoslova 'na Presne'*, 1730)
Predtechenskiy, Malyy Pereulok
Metro: *Krasnopresnenskaya ML4*

23. **Our Lady of the Don, the 'Old' Cathedral** (*'Staryi' Donskoy Sobor*, 1591)
See Donskoy Monastery, above (Excursion 22)

24. **Our Lady of Kazan in Kolomenskoye** (*Tserkov Kazanskoi Bogomateri*)
(Excursion 3)
Metro: *Kolomenskaya ML2*

25. **Our Lady of Tikhvin** (*Tserkov Tikhvinskoi Bogomateri*, 1680-2) **in Alekseyevskoye**
Tserkovnaya Gorka, Ulitsa, 26a
Metro: *VDNKh ML5*

26. **Our Lady of the Sign** (*Tserkov Znamenia*, 1765)
Krestovskiy 2. Pereulok
Metro: *Rizhskaya ML5*

27. **Laying of the Lord's Robes** (*Tserkov Rizpolozheniya*, 1722) **in Leonovo**
Dokukina, Ulitsa, 10 (Leonovo village)
Metro: *Botanicheskiy Sad ML5*

28. **Nativity** (*Tserkov Rozhdestva Khristova*, 1676-8) **in Izmaylovo**
Nikitinskaya Ulitsa
Metro: *Izmaylovskaya ML3*

29. **Nativity of the Virgin** (*Tserkov Rozhdestva Bogoroditsy*, 17th century) **in Vladykino**
Altufyevskoye Shosse, 16
Train: *Okruzhnaya Station*

30. **St Nicholas of the Weavers** (*Tserkov Nikoly 'v Khamovnikakh'*, 1679- 82)
Timura Frunze, Ulitsa, 1 (Excursion 25)
Metro: *Park Kultury ML1*

31. **St Nicholas** (*Tserkov Nikoly*, 1790)
See Preobrazhenskoye Cemetery, above

32. **St Nicholas** (*Tserkov Nikoly*, 1776; 1864)
See Rogozhskoye Cemetery, above

33. **St Nicholas** (*Tserkov Nikoly*, 19th century) **in Biryulevo**
Medynskaya Ulitsa and Kharkovskiy Proyezd
Train: *Biryulevo-Pass Station* (from *Yaroslavl Station*)

34. **SS. Peter and Paul** (*Tserkov Petra i Pavla 'v Soldatskoi Slobode'*, 1711)
Krasnokurantskiy 1. Proyezd and Soldatskaya Ulitsa (Excursion 9 ⑥)
Metro: *Baumanskaya ML3*

35. **Raising of the Cross** (*Tserkov Vosdvizhenya Kresta*, 1771)
See Preobrazhenskoye Cemetery, above

36. **Resurrection** (*Tserkov Voskresenya*, 1912)
See Rogozhskoye Cemetery, above

37. **Resurrection** (*Tserkov Voskresenya*, 1909-13)
Sokolnicheskaya Slobodka, Ulitsa
Metro: *Sokolniki ML1*

ORTHODOX CHURCHES

38. **Transfiguration** (*Tserkov Preobrazhenya*, 1781)
See Preobrazhenskoye Cemetery, above

39. **Transfiguration** (*Tserkov Preobrazhenya*, 1880) **in Bogorodskoye**
Krasnobogartyrskaya Ulitsa, 25
Metro: *Preobrazhenskaya Ploshchad ML1*

40. **Trinity** (*Tserkov Troitsy*, 1811) **in Vorobyevo**
Vorobyevskoye Shosse, 3
Metro: *Leninskiye Gory ML1*

41. **Trinity** (*Tserkov Troitsy*)
See Pyatnitskoye Cemetery, above

42. **Unexpected Joy** (*Tserkov Nechaiannoi Radosti*, 1904) **in Marina Roshcha**
Sheremetyevskaya Ulitsa, 73
Metro: *Shcherbakovskaya ML5*

IV. Other Religious Denominations

43. **Evangelist (Reform) Church** (Baptist)
Vuzovskiy Malyy Pereulok, 3
Metro: *Nogina Ploshchad ML5*

44. **Jewish Choral Synagogue** (19th century)
Arkhipova, Ulitsa, 8
Metro: *Nogina Ploshchad ML5*

45. **St Louis** (Roman Catholic, 1830–2)
Lubyanka Malaya, Ulitsa, 12
Metro: *Dzerzhinskaya ML1*

46. **Mosque**
Vypolzov Pereulok, 7
Metro: *Prospekt Mira ML4*

Regular religious services are also held at the **United States Embassy** (tel. 252-2451-59) and at the **British Embassy** (tel. 231-8511-12). Call for further information.

PART VI

MODERN MOSCOW

INTRODUCTION

*T*he symbols and symptoms of the modern age visibly affected Moscow as it entered the twentieth century. Factory smoke stacks and large apartment buildings rose to disrupt the harmony of the city's onion-domed skyline. The growing proletariat also made its presence felt as blocks of workers' dwellings crept into Moscow's pastoral outskirts. Moscow's *Belle Epoque* was coming to an end amidst pre-war tensions and the attacks of the revolutionary-minded avant-garde.

Rejecting all traditional concepts, the avant-garde groped for new forms of expression that could serve them as weapons against the institutions of the State. Possibly because of Moscow's inherently conservative character, and possibly because of the timing of the attack, the avant-garde's offensive in 1913 had the resounding effect of a 'slap' at the public taste.

The year 1913 was the 300th anniversary of the ruling Romanov dynasty, which came to poer in 1613 with the coronation of **Tsar Michael Romanov**. To celebrate the occasion, **Emperor Nicholas II** (1894–1917) made a triumphant entry into Moscow to the ovation of a crowd waiting in Red Square. The year 1913 also witnessed an exhibition of icons displayed for the first time in their full beauty. Just when it seemed that Premier Stolypin's land reforms (giving peasants full ownership of communal land) were bearing fruit, and political equilibrium was being established in Russia, the avant-garde struck.

At the 1913 Target Exhibition **Mikhail Larionov** and **Natalia Goncharova** (see 'Moscow of the Art Patrons', Excursion 19 ㉚), both in their early thirties, unveiled their rayonnist paintings. In the manifesto which accompanied the show, Larionov explained that his abstract style was inspired by the crossing of rays emanating from various objects. Larinov went on to condemn the West for 'vulgarizing our oriental forms' and decreed the genius of the day to be: 'trousers, jackets, buses and airplanes'.

Kazimir Malevich (1878–1935) followed closely in the footsteps of Larionov and Goncharova. A student of icon painting and Russian folk-art, he proclaimed his 'supremacy of pure perception' by drawing a *Black Circle* and *Black Square*. His Suprematist theory was to have a profound effect on Russian abstract painting.

The third pictorial 'slap' was delivered by **Vladimir Tatlin** (1885–1953), the father of Russian **constructivism**. Intentionally or not, Tatlin's three-dimensional relief constructions also coincided with the Romanovs' tercentary celebration. His spatial compositions, assembled from industrial materials, combined Picasso's cubist concepts with those of three-dimensional design.

On the literary front, the primary attack came from a group of poets who called themselves the '**futurists**'. Futurism in Russia became the banner of the revolutionary avant-garde. Its goal was to liberate art from bourgeois traditions and bring it into the streets. In March 1913, **Vladimir Mayakovsky** (1893–1930) formally vocalized the 'slap [the ultimate confrontation] to the public taste' in his lecture entitled 'Having Come Myself'. Characteristic of Mayakovsky and other futurist manifestoes, was the use of irreverent associations, coarse street language, distorted words, eroticism, and hostile dada-like rejections of reality.

MODERN MOSCOW

Futurism united the world of art and literature but for the first time in Russian history, painting was the dominant force. The futuristic opera *Victory over the Sun*, performed in December of 1913, featured songs written by the poet **Aleksei Khruchenikh** set to the quarter-tone music of **Mikhail Matiushin**, with backdrops and costumes designed by **Kazimir Malevich**. Larionov and Goncharova illustrated the early publications of futurist poets and designed costumes for Diaghilev's Ballet Russe in Paris. Mayakovsky's first play had stage settings by **Pavel Filonov**, illustrator of children's books and a forerunner of surrealist painting in Russia.

Come the revolution

The 'Feast of the Coming Years',* so ardently desired by Mayakovsky and **Maxim Gorky** (1868–1936), the two self-appointed bards of the proletariat, came eight months after the revolution of March 1917. That same year, Nicholas II abdicated and a democratic provisional government was established in Petrograd (Leningrad). This government was overthrown by **Lenin** on 7 November. The elections to the Constituent Assembly were still held on 25 November, giving Lenin's Bolshevik Party only twenty-five per cent of the popular vote. Disregarding the outcome of the ballot, Lenin disbanded the Constituent Assembly on 18 January 1918, thus negating Russia's only democratic election. Two months later, Lenin moved the seat of the revolutionary government from Petrograd to Moscow. By the mid 1920s, the flower of the Russian intelligentsia,† including many advocates of the Revolution, emigrated to the West.

The artists and writers who stayed in Russia threw themselves wholeheartedly into the building of the Communist society. It hardly mattered to them that the new Russian society was famine-stricken and chaotic. They themselves sustained intense hardships and privations, elated by their mission of fusing art with life.

By 1918 Malevich and Tatlin occupied key positions at the **Department of Visual Arts** (IZO) created under the auspices of the Commissariat for People's Education, headed by **Lunacharsky**. IZO allowed the radical artists to develop their innovative ideas, organize pedagogical programmes, create museums of abstract art, stage exhibits, and, above all, to engage in debates about the rôle of art in life.

Two new art schools **SOMAS** and the **Institute of Artistic Culture in Moscow** (INKHUK) brought together the Russian avant-garde, many of whom had returned from exile, as for example **Marc Chagall** (1887–1985), **Naum Gabo** (1890–1978), **Vasily Kandinsky** (1886–1944), **Aleksandr Rodchenko** (1891–1956), and others. Many of these artists are today better known in the West than in the Soviet Union.

*The 'Feast of the Coming Years' was the Bolshevik Revolution of November 1917 in which Mayakovsky vowed to: 'lend my sonorous voice of a poet/to you the attacking class'.

†Writers Bunin, Andreyev, Kuprin, Merezhkovsky, Remizov, Gorky, A. Tolstoy, Ehrenburg (the last three returned); artists Repin, Benois, Somov, Korovin; musicians Stravinsky, Kusevitsky, etc.

As time went by the constructivist concepts advocated by Tatlin and his followers won over the suprematist camp presided over by Malevich. In 1919, after the Fifth State Exhibition, Malyevich announced the end of the suprematist movement in painting. The State now had no use for non-inspirational art, nor for the abstract art patronized by the new wave of art patrons created as a result of Lenin's New Economic Policy. By 1921, rejected and repulsed, the suprematists ceded their place to the constructivists.

Precious little remains of Tatlin's work, yet with the economic revival of the late 1920s, the constructivists finally had the opportunity to start building. The architects **Vesnin** and **Ginsburg**, who in 1925 founded the **Society of Contemporary Artists** (OSA), were among the first to apply their functional method to life. Their style called for a rejection of all historical precedents and the adaptation of forms derived from abstract art. The big, simple geometric forms they erected were based on functionalism and rational use of construction materials. Developed in the relative isolation of the Soviet Communist State, the constructivist style was to influence greatly the later international functional style of architecture and design. The outgrowth of the OSA was the **Union of Architects**, formalized in 1928, which focused its attention on the problems of urban construction.

Constructivists vs Traditionalists

During the same period, which extends roughly from the 1920s to 1932, a heated debate arose between the constructivists and a group of more traditionally oriented architects who favoured the study of Classical precedents. The best-known representative of the latter group was **Alexei Viktorovich Shchusev*** (1873–1949), who had achieved fame in pre-revolutionary times and whose best-known contemporary project is the **Lenin Mausoleum** on Red Square. Shchusev headed the **MAO** (Moscow Architectural Society) which continued to function for a number of years.

e Convent of SS. Martha and ry (1908–12) by A. V. Schusev, o combined the techniques of Nouveau with the medieval ms of Pskov and Novgorod.

Another school based on the study of ancient Classical architecture was founded by **Ivan Vladislavovich Zholtovsky** (1867–1959) whose architectural concepts won favour under Stalin. Between 1918 and 1924, Zholtovsky was entrusted with the Moscow reconstruction project. His blueprints outlined a plan to shift the load from the central city centre to the suburbs. The idea was realized in the 1950s and 1970s, when most of the new residential complexes rose in Moscow's peripheral regions.

*See Kazan Railway Station (p. 175), Pokrov Cathedral at the Convent of SS. Martha and Mary (pp. 315, 346, 353).

Konstantin Stepanovich Melnikov (1890–1974) was another important contributor to the early period of Soviet architecture. In 1923 his 'Makhorka' Pavilion won immediate acclaim for its roofs cut on the diagonal, with triangular faces and light constructions shooting upwards. Melnikov's next work, the USSR Pavilion at the International Exhibition in Paris in 1925, drew worldwide attention. He was later accused for formalism and drifted into obscurity.

Constructivist Buildings of the 1920s and 1930s

An impressive number of buildings designed by constructivist architects are still to be seen in Moscow. Since they are scattered throughout the city (precluding the possibility of being visited in the course of one excursion) eleven have been selected as most characteristic.

1. **Izvestia Building**, 1925–7, by Grigory Barkhin. Pushkinskaya Square 5. (Also see Moscow of the Townspeople, Excursion 6.)
2. **Klub Imeni Zueva** (Workers' Club), 1928, by Ilya Golosov. Lesnaya Ulitsa 18.
3. **Planitary** (The Moscow Planetarium), 1929, by Mikhail Barshch and M. Siniavsky. Mikhail Barshch, member of the OSA, was also one of the authors of *Obelisque Dedicated to the Conquerors of Space*, 1964, at the VDNKh.
4. **Communal Housing**, 1926, By Moisei Ginsburg: Bronnaya Malaya Ulitsa, 21; also at Chaykovskogo Ulitsa, 25, built between 1928 and 1930.
5. **The Pravda Building**, 1931–7, by Panteleimon Golosov. Pravdy Ulitsa, 24.
6. **The House of the architect Konstantin Melnikov**, 1927–9. Krivoarbatsky Pereulok, 4.
7. **The Zil Palace of Culture**, 1930–7, by the brothers Vesnin, Vostochnaya Ulitsa, 4.
8. **The Ministry of Agriculture**, 1928–33, by Alexei Shchusev. Orlikov Pereulok, 1/11 and Sadovaya Samotechnaya.
9. **Office Building**, 1928–36, by Le Corbusier. Ulitsa Kirova, 39. See also, 'Moscow of the Nobles', Excursion 10.

Two buildings which are not representative of this modern architectural movement, but which none the less were significant as examples of their time are: The **Lenin Library**, built between 1928 and 1958 on Prospekt Marksa, and the **Frunze Military Academy**, which engulfed an earlier building in 1936, Frunze Ulitsa, 19.

THE MAYAKOVSKY HOUSE-MUSEUM

The Mayakovsky House-Museum

*Open: 12:00 to 20:00, Monday, Tuesday, Friday
10:00 to 18:00, Wednesday, Saturday, Sunday
Closed: Thursday*

*A*part from the buildings designed by the constructivist architects, the House Museum of **Vladimir Vladimirovich Mayakovsky** (1893–1930) is perhaps the only tangible* vestige of Moscow's avant-garde of the 1920s. The two-room apartment, located on the second floor of the museum, where the poet spent the last few years of his life, served as a meeting place for the rebellious group of artists, writers, and musicians. Co-founder of the futurist movement and political activist, the poet Mayakovsky was a member of the Communist party from the age of fifteen. He remained its official bard until his suicide in 1930.

The Museum

The Mayakovsky Museum is a simple two-storey stucco building. The lower floors contain all of Mayakovsky's works, in Russian and in translation. Among them are: *Mystery Buffo*, a verse play which appeared in 1918, prophesying the victory of the Revolution, *The Bedbug* (1928) and *The Bathhouse* — both satires on the bureaucracy of Soviet life.

There are two rooms upstairs: the poet's dining-room and study. In the **dining room** is a collection of posters and photographs which recall Mayakovsky's work and numerous trips to Paris. In the adjoining **study** (where Mayakovsky worked) is a collection of personal photographs and memorabilia, as well as the original draft of *At The Top of My Voice*.

In 1913, Mayakovsky, a brazen and muscular youth, announced his arrival upon the literary scene with the following words: 'Twenty-two and beautiful/Here I come'. Mayakovsky's arrival did not go unnoticed. By 1914, he had already won the admiration of Boris Pasternak and other members of the futurist movement. He captivated them with his iron-will and determination which Pasternak so aptly summarized in his memoirs: 'Before me sat a handsome youth of gloomy aspect with the bass voice of a deacon and the fist of a pugilist, inexhaustible, deadly, witty, something between a mythical hero of Alexander Grim and a Spanish torreador.†

Mayakovsky's multi-faceted career inspired a generation of artists, writers, poets, and musicians. His literary achievements as well as his political activities are eulogized today by the Soviet régime and his memory preserved in the two Mayakovsky Museums.††

*A few costume and stage designs are on display at the **Bakhrushin Theatrical Museum**, Bakhrushina Ulitsa, 31/12.

†Boris Pasternak, *I Remember*, (Milan, 1959), pp. 91–3.

††The second Mayakovsky Museum is located at Serova Proezd, 3/6. It was opened in 1974. Mayakovsky's statue (1958) is on Mayakovskogo Square.

EPILOGUE

The Artists and the Revolution

The Revolution came and went. 'Every artist, and everyone who regards himself as one', wrote Vladimir Lenin, 'claims as his proper right the liberty to work freely according to his ideal whether good or not . . . Nevertheless we must try to guide this development consciously, clearly and to shape and determine its results.'* Dating from this period is the magazine *LEF* (Left Front of Literature), a publication which Mayakovsky founded in 1923. It drew its support from the futurists and some theatrical producers, including Stanislavsky's wayward student **Vsevolod Emilyievich Meyerhold** (1874–1942). *LEF* urged the 'army of arts to glorify life and the joy to be found along the road . . . to Communism'.

In 1927, the year *LEF* folded, Mayakovsky denounced futurism. His attempt to breach the gap with social realism coincided with the end of the *New Economic Policy* which provided partial respite from State interference in the arts. Three years later, Mayakovsky committed suicide in the house which has since become the **Mayakovsky Museum**. 'It seems to me' wrote Boris Pasternak, 'that Mayakovsky shot himself out of pride because he had condemned something in himself or around himself with which his self-respect could not be reconciled'.† In Mayakovsky's own words he and the rest of the Silver Age poets 'stepped on the throat of their own song'.

Akhmatova was silenced in 1923 and did not publish another book of poems until 1940. **Gumilev** was shot in 1921 for allegedly participating in White Guard activities. **Boris Pasternak** turned to translations. His great novel, *Doctor Zhivago*, appeared in the West in 1957 after a gap of 25 years. Mayakovsky's rival in literature, poet **Sergei Yesenin** (see 'Moscow of the Nobles', Excursion 12) committed suicide in 1925 after having written a last poem in his own blood:

> My poems are no longer needed here
> And I too, by your leave, I am no longer needed.

Stalin's Era: Repressions

Stalin's coming to power put an end to the token creativity and liberalization which had survived Lenin's *New Economic Policy*. By 1932, the independent artistic and literary associations were re-organized into State-run Unions of Artists, Writers, Musicians and Architects. All that was written, painted or built had to be approved by the State and conform to the formula of 'socialist realism': that Soviet culture was to be 'national in form, but socialist in content'.

The restrictions which Stalin imposed on the arts, paled, in comparison with his other repressive measures. In agriculture, for example, the forced collectivization was accompanied by famine and the deaths of independent *kulak* farmers sentenced to concentration camps for resisting State controls. An estimated 51 million died as a result of these measures.

*Quoted in Donald W. Treagold, *Twentieth Century Russia* (Chicago, 1959), p. 242.

†Boris Pasternak, *I Remember* (Milan, 1959), p. 89.

Building dating from Stalin's period.

One seemingly innocent memorial tucked away in a children's park* recalls to this day Stalin's ruthlessness. This is the **Statue of Pavlik Morozov** (1918–32) whom the sculptor A. I. Rabinovich depicted as a young pioneer (the equivalent of a boy scout) carrying a flag. Pavlik was immortalized for denouncing his parents as *kulaks* and sending them to their deaths in a labour camp.

Moscow's architectural losses were severe. Nearly half of Moscow's artistic and historical landmarks perished as a result of Stalin's 1935 *Reconstruction Plan*. The principal aim of this plan, according to the *Resolution of April 1934*, was that the reconstruction of the city must reflect the grandeur and beauty of the new socialist epoch. The driving spirit of this plan, the academician **Strumilin**, announced that Moscow's architecture must depict its role as capital of the USSR as well as the world headquarters of the 'Communist International'.

The Destruction of the Saviour's Cathedral

The marble and gold inlaid **Saviour's Cathedral**, a memorial to the Russian victory over Napoleon, was one of the first victims of Stalin's reconstruction plan. It had taken 46 years (1837–83) and 16 million roubles to build this 103-metre-tall cathedral which occupied 6,700 square metres and was capable of accommodating 10,000 people. It took six days and two explosions to reduce the cathedral to a heap of rubble and twisted steel.

While the demolition experts were busy at work, Stalin's architects were putting the finishing touches to their entries for the '**Palace of the Soviets**' contest. Stalin, meanwhile, intended the palace to occupy the site of the dismantled cathedral and to use the marble from it to decorate Metro stations.

Two architects, Krasnin and Kutsaev, submitted a design for the competition in which the cupola of the Saviour's Cathedral would be placed on the Palace of Soviets while the cross on top would be replaced with a sculpture of a proletarian worker carrying a red banner. Iofan's design for a stepped building crowned with a sculpture of Lenin, eventually won the competition.

The construction of the palace begain in 1933. The rubble from the church was cleared away, a hole was excavated for the foundations, and the nearby metro station on **Kropotkinskaya Square** was named 'Palace of the Soviets'.

*Pavlika Morozova Pereulok in the Children's Park of the Krasnopresnenskiy District, where the first fighting broke out during the October Revolution of 1905.

The Saviour's Cathedral, a memorial to the defeat of Napoleon built in the Russo-Byzantine style between 1837 and 1883, demolished under Stalin.

However, the unforeseen occurred: the hole filled up with water. The construction group soon realized that the swampy soil would not support Iofan's grandiose project. The engineers now understood why it took Thon and his assistants forty-six years to build the Saviour's Cathedral. The construction of this mammoth church on swampy grounds represented a feat of engineering they could not match. Defeated, Stalin abandoned his project. Twenty years later, **Khrushchev** had the hole transformed into the 'Moskva' swimming pool, the vapours from which are slowly destroying the art collection at the **Pushkin Art Museum** across the street.

Stalin's 'Ornate Monumentality'

The **Intourist Building** (see 'Moscow of the Tsars', Excursion 2, ⑩ₐ) created by Ivan Vasilievich Zholtovsky in 1933, represents a turning-point from constructivist-oriented architecture to the pomposity and grandiosity, which became mandatory under Stalin. The monumental and ornate style was meant to impress the population with the power of the State and, at the same time, maintain some connections with historical traditions.

A high-rise development erected under Stalin on Kotelnicheskaya Naberezhnaya (embankment).

Despite the halt on building construction during the Second World War, the Plan for the Reconstruction of Moscow was carried out as Stalin's pompous creations mushroomed around the city. The most notable of these works were the **Moscow Subway** (see pp. 341–50), whose first line was opened in 1935, the **bridges** over the Moscow River and the eight famous '**Stalin's wedding cakes**', the skyscrapers which appeared in the mid 1950s. These include the **Moscow University** on Lenin Hills, by L. V. Rudnev *et al.* (1949–1953), **The Ministry of Foreign Affairs** (1948–1952) on Smolenskaya Ploshchad, by V. G.

Gelfreich *et al*, hotels **Leningradskaya** (1953: architects L. M. Poliakov and A. B. Boretsky) and **Ukraina** by Mordvinov (1957),[*] and the **Apartment House** on Vosstaniya Ploshchad (square) (1950-4) by the architects Ashot Ashotovich Mndoiants and Mikhail Vasilevich Posokhin, both born in 1910 and subsequent collaborators on the **SEV building** which Mndoiants never saw completed.

Those who know Russian architecture superficially see in Stalin's towers a direct continuation of old building traditions in their whimsical shapes and asymmetry. Upon closer examination, however, the observer will realize that borrowed forms, if deprived of their original architectural concept, are as alien to their sources as Mussolini's creations were alien to the masterpieces of ancient Rome.

The Khrushchev Period

When Nikita Sergeyevich Khrushchev came to power in 1956, the direction of Soviet architecture changed dramatically. The period of the 'Thaw' which had brought some relaxation of controls over science, literature, and the arts, ushered in an era of hastily created pre-fabs, known in Moscow as *khrushchoby*. This term was coined by combining the word *trushchoby*, meaning slums, with the name of Khrushchev, the originator of mass housing. The pre-fabricated residential quarters which rose on the periphery of the old city, contributed little to Moscow's aesthetics, though the housing they provided was desperately needed.

~ushcheby apartment ~elopment in Khimki. ~ushcheby is derived from ~ushchev's name and ~shcheby, meaning slums.

The **Lenin Stadium**, built between 1955 and 1956 and reconstructed later in the 1970s by the architect Aleksandr Vasilyevich Vlasov (1900-62) at Luzhniki on the Moscow river, represented the first timid departure from the Stalinesque style.

Simultaneously, the reconstruction of the old city continued, again at the expense of pre-revolutionary churches and mansions. But there were no architectural masterpieces, no repeat of the 1920s. **The Palace of Congresses** in the Kremlin was probably Khrushchev's most notable architectural achievement. The Muscovites, with their unfailing sense of humour, compared Khrushchev's glass and concrete structures to a proletarian amongst the boyars, the venerable old Kremlin aristocrats (see Excursion 1 ㊱).

The Post-Khrushchev Period

Under Leonid Ilyich Brezhnev, the Secretary General of the Communist Party and President, who died in 1983, an effort was made to create more attractive

[*]Leningradskaya Hotel is in **Kalanchevskaya Ulitsa. 21/40**, Ukraina Hotel, **Kutuzovsky Prospekt, 21**.

and contemporary buildings. A few examples of such structures — often built with the help of Western architects — are the **International Hotel (Gostinitsa Mezhdunarodnaia)** the luxury hotel **Cosmos** designed by the French, and the German-built **Sheremetievo Airport II**.

The tall white building of the **SEV** (Socialist Economic Co-operation), overlooking the Moscow River, and many of the new apartment buildings sprouting throughout Moscow, show a marked effort to improve the aesthetics and quality of construction.

SEV (Socialist Economic Co-operation) building overlooking the Moscow River. In the foreground is the American-built International Hotel.

During the entire post-war period Moscow continued to expand; its latest boundary is marked by a circular by-pass approximately twenty-five kilometres from the city's centre. There is presently an attempt by the authorities to control the spread of the city beyond the **Ring Road**. Even so, much of the area on the outside of the Ring Road has been turned into housing developments or industrial parks.

Today this city of 8 million is the sixth largest in the world. The sheer size of the USSR, with its wealth of natural resources, and highly developed industry, technology, and educational system, demonstrates its status as a major political and nuclear superpower.

Modern Moscow represents a dichotomy between old and new. Much of its historical identity has been threatened not only by reconstruction projects, but also through careless negligence. Only a dedicated campaign by Moscow's residents, and the interest of tourists can preserve what still remains of old Moscow.

The coming to power of **Mikhail Gorbachev** has brought with it better chances for the survival of old Moscow. A ban was issued on the destruction of historical buildings in the city and elsewhere. The era of *glasnost* also bene-fited the beleaguered Russian Church. Aside from the **Danilovsky Monastery**, which is now the seat of the Patriarch, Optina Pustyn and the Pecherskaya Lavra, Kiev's oldest monastery, will once again be functioning monasteries. On the occasion of the millennium of Russian Orthodoxy, government funds were allocated for the refurbishing of religious buildings and the construction of a new church was approved in **Borisovo-Glebovo**, New Moscow. This new church, to be modelled on the destroyed Saviour's Cathedral, will help to celebrate part of the second millennium of Christianity in the year 2000. One can only hope that the new thinking of Soviet leaders will include putting a permanent end to the senseless destruction of Moscow's architecture, visual testimony to the travails and triumphs of the Muscovites and their ancient city.

THE MOSCOW METRO

*G*randiose and extensive, the Moscow Metro was originally built to provide each Soviet citizen with a palace of his own.

In 1931, under Stalin's rule, the construction was begun. The marble, mosaic, gold-studded, stained glass, stucco edifices served as a camouflage for what doubled as air-raid shelters during the Second World War. Hence you will find the subway stations very deep underground.

The Moscow Metro lines are open from 6 a.m. to 12:30 a.m. The trains are frequent and rapid, travelling at an average rate of 80 kilometres an hour. In addition, the Moscow Metro costs only 5 kopeks, which when dropped into a turnstile allows one to travel continuously. Change machines are available in all subway stations.

The Moscow Metro is well worth seeing. The marble stations, with sculptures and panelled ceilings, put most Western stations to shame. For a complete tour, contact Intourist. There are tours daily.

Note: the numbers appearing after churches refer to the Church Guide (CG), pp. 324–8.

ML1   **Line 1 Kirovsko-Frunzenskaya:** north-east, south-west. Constructed in 1932–5; 22.4 kilometres long, 17 stations; bridges over the Moscow and the Yauza rivers.

Preobrazhenskaya Ploshchad
Preobrazhenskaya, former site of a royal estate where Peter the Great trained his mock regiment (*see* p. 143), and **Preobrazhenskoye Cemetery** (CG: 1)

Sokolniki
International exhibition park
19th-century **Church of the Resurrection** with a copy of the famous icon of the *Iberian Virgin* (CG: 37)

Krasnoselskaya
Former Alekseyevsky Convent and Cemetery (Krasnoprudnyy Pereulok, 1)

Komsomolskaya
Three railway stations: Leningradskaya, Kazan, Yaroslavl (Excursion 11)
Hotel Leningradskaya

Lermontovskaya
SS. Peter and Paul, commissioned by Peter the Great (Excursion 11)

Kirovskaya
Central station

Church of the Archangel Gabriel, 17th-century seat of the Patriarch of Antioch
Church of St Theodore (Excursion 8)

Dzerzhinskaya
Polytechnical Museum (p. 357)
Myakovsky Museum (p. 335)
Museum of the History and Reconstruction of Moscow (p. 351)
Hotel Berlin
Detsky Mir department store for children
Church of St Louis (Roman Catholic) (CG: 45)

Prospekt Marksa
Heart of Moscow: Red Square (Excursion 4)

Biblioteka Imeni Lenina
Entrance to Kremlin museums (Excursions 1 & 2)
Kremlin cathedrals
Lenin Library
Alexander's Garden
Concert rooms of the Moscow Conservatory (Excursion 17, p. 238)

Kropotkinskaya
Pushkin Museum of Fine Arts (Excursion 7)
Moscow swimming pool
Kropotkinskaya Ulitsa: Tolstoy and Pushkin Museums (Excursion 12)
Excursions 11, 12
Church of St Elias (CG: 2)

Park Kultury
Gorky Park
Church of St Nicholas of the Weavers (Excursion 25, CG: 30)

Frunzenskaya

Sportivnaya
Novodevichiy Convent (Excursion 23)
Pavel Korin Museum (p. 353)
Beriozka store (p. 366)

Leninskiye Gory
Lenin Central Stadium
Palace of Pioneers
Panoramic view of Moscow from the Lenin Hills
Church of the Trinity (CG: 40)

Universitet
Lomonosov University, built by Lenin in the 1950s
New Circus of Moscow (*see* p. 361)

Yugo-Zapadnaya
Two stations built for the 1980 Olympics

ML2 | **Line 2 Gorkovsko-Zamoskvoretskaya**: north-west, south-east. Conceived in 1935 and constructed in several stages; 30 kilometres long; 17 stations. The design for the Mayakovskaya station won the grand prize at the International Exposition in New York of 1938.

Rechnoy Vokzal
North river station
Church of Our Lady of the Sign (Znamenia), a working church (CG: 26)
Festivalnaya Ulitsa

Voykovskaya
Water sports stadium

Sokol
Ancient village
All Saints Church (CG: 12)

Aeroport
Moscow Airport

Dinamo
Dinamo Stadium
Hotel Sovietskaya
Petrovsky Palace (*see* p. 67)

Belorusskaya

Mayakovskaya
Tchaikovsky Concert Hall (*see* p. 361)
Stanilavsky Theatre
Theatre of Satire

Gorkovskaya
Sofia Restaurant
Central Museum of the Revolution (Excursion 6)
Moscow Art Theatre (MKHAT) (*see* p. 359)
Rossiya Film Theatre (*see* p. 103)
Church of the Nativity of the Virgin (Excursion 6 ④)
Minsk and Zentralnaya hotels

Sverdlova Ploshchad
Red Square (Excursion 4); Bolshoy Theatre (*see* p. 355)

Novokuznetskaya
Tretyakov Art Gallery (*see* p. 355)
Joy of all the Afflicted Church (Excursion 25 ⑤)

Paveletskaya
Bakrushin Theatre Museum (*see* p. 361)

MOSCOW METRO

Avtozavodskaya
This and the following two stations were constructed in 1941–5 and the decor reflects the suffering and heroism of the Russian people.

Kolomenskaya
Former summer estate of the tsars (Excursion 3), now a museum and park. Within the park is **Our Lady of Kazan** church, open for worship. Moscow Centre for Cancer Studies

Kashirskaya

Varshavskaya

Kakhovskaya
SS. Boris and Gleb in Zyzino. Former estate of the Old Believer Boyarina Morozova (*see* p. 230).

ML3   **Line 3 Arbatsko-Pokrovskaya**: 19 kilometres long, 12 stations; opened in 1944.

Shchelkovskaya

Pervomayskaya

Izmaylovskaya
Nativity Church (CG: 28)

Izmaylovskiy Park
Izmaylovo, former summer estate of the tsars, now a park (Excursion 3)

Semenovskaya

Elektrozvodskaya

Baumanskaya
Lefort's Palace (Excursion 9 ①)
Epiphany Cathedral in Yelokhovo, (Excursion 11)
Rubtsevo: Cathedral of Pokrov (Excursion 9)

Kurskaya
Decor of this station and the next three reflects the history of Russia during the Second World War
Excursions 11 and 12

Revolutsii Ploshchad
Red Square, St Basil's (Excursion 4)
Gorky Street (Excursion 6)

Arbatskaya
Kalinina Prospekt, the old Arbat district (Excursion 19)
House of Friendship (Excursion 19 ③)
House of Books store (p. 365)
Praga Restaurant (p. 258)

Smolenskaya
Ministry of Foreign Affairs (MID) building
American Embassy
Vakhtangov Theatre
House of M. K. Morozova (Excursion 19 ⑨)

Kiyevskaya
Kiyevskaya (Kiev) railway station
Hotel Ukraina, containing a Beriozka store for souvenirs and toys
Embarkation point for tour boats

ML3-A **Line 3a Filevskaya**: From the Lenin Library to the end of Kalinina Prospekt via Arbatskaya, Smolenskaya, and Kiyevska stations; an extension toward Fili Park; 14 kilometres in length, 12 stations; almost entirely above ground.

Kalininskaya
Linin Library (Excursion 7 ⑬)
Kremlin (Excursion 1)

Arbatskaya
Apostle Phillip's Church, Aksakova Pereulok (CG: 8)

Smolenskaya (*see* **ML3**)

Kiyevskaya (*see* **ML3**)

Studencheskaya

Kutuzovskaya
Borodino Panoramic Museum (*see* p. 351)
Arch of Triumph
Kutuzov's Hut Museum

Fili
Church of the **Intercession of the Virgin in Fili**, example of the circular Naryshkin Baroque (Novozavodskaya Ulitsa, 47)

Bagrationovskaya

Filevskiy Park
Fili Park

Pionerskaya
Kuntsevo Estate and Park, Voroshilovsky Park, 5 (Excursion 10)

Kuntsevskaya
Academy of Veterinary Sciences

Molodezhnaya
Krylatskoye Sports Centre and Rowing Club

MOSCOW METRO

ML4

Line 4 Koltsevaya: circular line. This line, partially opened in 1954, has the most monumental and impressive station. The line circles the old town within the major boulevards; 19.3 kilometres in length, 12 stations; 10 of which are on two levels. The circular line joins all of Moscow in a unified system and connects 7 of the 9 train stations of the city.

Park Kultury (see also **ML1**)

Oktyabrskaya
Donskoy Monastery (Excursion 22)
Museum of Architecture
Church of St John the Warrior (Excursion 25 ⑬)

Dobryninskaya
New metro line to Dnepropetrovskaya

Paveletskaya
Railway station where Lenin's coffin arrived from Gorki in 1924

Taganskaya
Taganka Theatre (*see* p. 360 and Excursion 15)
Church of the Dormition 'in Gonchary' (Excursion 25)
Mayakovsky Museum (*see* p. 335)

Kurskaya (*see* **ML3**)
Kursk railway station

Komsomolskaya
Leningradksya, Kazan, and Yaroslvl railway stations (Excursion 11)
Komsomolskaya station won the grand prize at the International Exposition in 1958. It is inlaid with mosaics by Pavel Korin depicting heroes of Russian victories, including Dmitry Donskoy and Alexandr Nevsky.

Prospekt Mira
New Olympic complex
Mosque (CG: 46)

Novoslobodskaya
Dostoevsky Museum (p. 356)

Belorusskaya (*also see* **ML2**)
European railway station

Krasnopresenskaya
International Park of Expositions and new International Centre of Commerce
Hotel Ukraina
St John the Baptist 'na Presne' (CG: 22)

Kiyevskaya (*see also* **ML3, ML3-A**)
Kiev railway station

ML5 | **Line 5 Kaluzhsko-Rizhskaya**: north-south. Formerly the southern part extended to the Moscow River, but in 1970 the northern end was extended and in 1978 reached the suburbs; 32 kilometres in length, 20 stations.

Medvedkovo

Babushkinskaya

Sviblovo
  Church of the Intercession of the Virgin (Pokrov) in Medvedkovo (Excursion 14)

Botanicheskiy Sad
  Botanical gardens

VDNKh
  Park of Soviet Economic Achievements (*see* p. 357)
  Palace of Ostankino (Excursion 14)
  Hotel Cosmos
  Church of Our Lady of Tikhvin in Alekseyevskoe (CG: 25)

Shcherbakovskaya
  Church of Unexpected Joy (CG: 42)

Rizhskaya
  Church of St Trifon (Trifonovskaya Ulitsa, 38) (*see* p. 213)
  Riga railway station
  Church of the Holy Trinity (CG: 41)
  Church of the Sign (CG: 26)

Prospekt Mira (*also see* **ML4**)

Kolkhoznaya

Turgenevskaya (*see* **ML1**)

Nogina Ploshchad (*also see* **ML6**)
  Jewish Choral Synagogue (CG; 44)
  Hotel Rossiya
  Embarkation for tour boats
  Razina Ulitsa and Church of the **Holy Trinity 'in Nikitniki'**
  Polytechnical Museum
  Evangelist Church (CG: 43)

Novokuznetskaya (*also see* **ML2**)

Oktyabrskaya (*also see* **ML4**)

Shabolovskaya
  Donskoy Monastery (Excursion 22)

MOSCOW METRO

Leninskiy Prospekt

Akademicheskaya
Deposition of the Lord's Robe (Excursion 22)

Profsoyuznaya

Novyye Cheremushki

Kaluzhskaya

Belyayevo

ML6   **Line 6 Zhdanovsko — Krasnopresnenskaya**: north-west, south-east. This line connects to the bathing spots on the Moscow River in the summer (cross country ski trails in winter); 37 kilometres long, 19 stations.

Planernaya

Skhodnenskaya

Tushinskaya
Serebriannyi Bor (beach)
Bathing spot

Shchukinskaya

Oktyabrskoye Pole

Polezhayevskaya

Begovaya
Hippodrome (p. 371)

Ulitsa 1905 Goda
Armenian Cemetery (CG: I)

Barrikadnaya
Zoo

Puskinskaya
Church of the Resurrection (CG: 9)
Nativity of the Virgin 'v Putinkakh' (Excursion 6 ④)
Monastery of St Peter in the Heights (*Vyssoko-Petrovsky*), superbly restored 17th-century ensemble (Petrovka, Ulitsa, 28)

Kuznetsky Most (*also see* **ML1**)

Nogina Ploshchad (Excursions 5, 15; *also see* **ML5**)
Rozhdestvensky Convent, Zhdanaova Ulitsa, 20

Taganskaya

Proletarskaya
Old Believers' (Rogozhskoye) Cemetery (Excursion 16): three churches open for worship

Mayakovsky Museum (*see* p. 335)

Volgogradskiy Prospekt

Tekstilshchiki
Moskvitch Stadium

Kuzminki

Ryazanskiy Prospekt
Kuskovo Palace (Excursion 14)

Zhdanovskaya
Church of the Dormition of the Virgin 'in Veshniakakh' (CG: 16)

ML6-A   **Line 6a Kalininskaya**: leaving north from Taganskaya toward Novogireyevo; 6 stations.

Marksistskaya (*see* Taganskaya **ML4**)

Ilicha Ploshchad
Rogozhskoye (Old Believers' Cemetery) (Excursion 16. CG: 1)
Rublev Museum of Icons (Excursion 24)

Aviamotornaya

Shosse Entuziastov

Perovo

Novogireyevo
Church of St John the Baptist (CG: 21)

ML7   **Line ML7: Serpukhovskaya Line**

Savelovskiy Vokzal

Novoslobodskaya

Chekovskaya
See Gorkovskaya (**ML2**) and Pushkinskaya (**ML6**)

Borovitskaya
Lenin Library (Excursion 7 ⑬)
House of Pashkov (Excursion 7 ⑩)

Polyanka
Church of St Gregory of New Caesarea (Bolshaya Polyanka Ulitsa, 29), 1662–9

Serpukhovskaya

Tulskaya
Danilovsky Monastery (Excursion 22)

Nagatinskaya

Nagornaya

Nakhimovskiy Prospekt

Sevastopolskaya

Chertanovskaya

Yuzhnaya

Prazhskaya

Krasnyy Stroitel

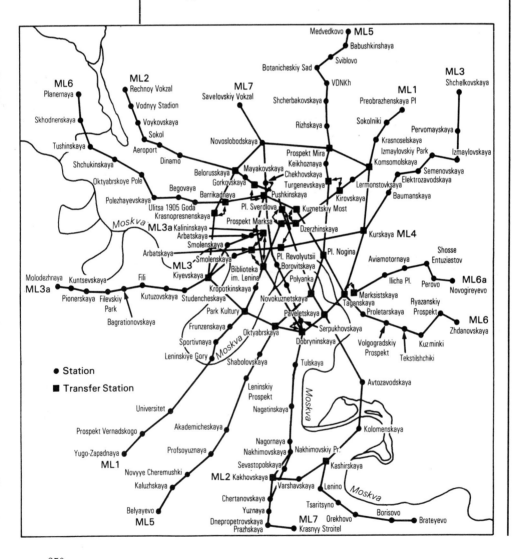

MUSEUMS AND THEATRES

Historical and Architectural Museums

Metro:
Novoslobodskaya
ML4

Central Museum of the Armed Forces of the USSR
Sovetskoy Armii Ulitsa, 2
Open: 10–7 Tuesday and Friday, 12–8 Wednesday and Thursday; closed Monday.
The permanent building for this museum was opened in 1965, with more than 600,000 items dedicated to the history of the armed forces of the Soviet Union.

Metro: *Ploshchad Revolyutsii*
ML3, 2 or 1

Church of St Basil (Pokrovsky Cathedral Museum)
Krasnaya Ploshchad (Red Square)
Open: 10:30–5 Wednesday–Sunday; closed: Tuesday and first day of month.
See Moscow of the Townspeople, Excursion 4

Metro: *Kutuzovskaya*
ML3-A

Battle of Borodino Panorama Museum and Kutuzov's Hut
Kutuzovskiy Prospekt, 38
Open: Panorama 9–8, Hut 10–5; closed: Friday.
The museum commemorates the battle that took place between the Russian army, under Field Marshal Mikhail Kutuzov, and Napoleon's Grand Army on 26 August 1812, at the Borodino battlefield, 124 kilometres from Moscow. Napoleon had 135,000 men; Kutuzov had 132,000. In this 14-hour-long combat, the French lost 58,000 men, the Russians 44,000. Both sides claimed victory. The French won by causing the Russians to retreat. The Russians gained an upper hand by inflicting losses from which Napoleon's army would never again recover.

In 1912 the Russian painter, Franz Rouband, produced a giant panorama of the Borodino battle (115 metres in circumference and 15 metres high).

Nearby is the wooden hut where Kutuzov met with his staff and made the decision to retreat from Moscow. The Muscovites who abandoned Moscow started a fire which destroyed two-thirds of the city.

Metro: *Shabolovskaya*
ML4, 5

Donskoy Monastery
Donskaya Ploshchad, 1
Open: 10–3 Tuesday, Wednesday, Thursday, Saturday and Sunday; closed: Monday and Friday.
See 'Moscow of the Clergy', Excursion 22

Metro: *Ploshchad Revolyutsii*
ML3, 2, or 1

Historical Museum
Krasnaya Ploshchad, 1–2 (Red Square)
Open: 10–6 Monday, Thursday, Saturday, and Sunday; 11–7 Wednesday and Friday; closed: Tuesday and first Monday of month.
See 'Moscow of the Townspeople', Excursion 4

Metro: *Dzershinskaya*
ML1, 6

Museum of History and Reconstruction of Moscow
Novaya Ploshchad, 12
Open: 10–13 Monday, 2–9 Wednesday and Friday, 10–5 Thursday and

Sunday, 10–6 Saturday; closed: Tuesday and last day of month.
The Museum of History and Reconstruction of Moscow, founded in 1896, was transferred in 1954 from the destroyed Sukhareva Tower to the former Church of St John the Baptist. It contains maps, photographs, engravings, and models describing the historical development of Moscow. Also on display are Moscow's plans for the future, some of which entail major reconstructions of central Moscow.

Metro: *Kolomenskaya ML2*

Kolomenskoye Estate Museum
Kashirskoye Shosse
Open: 11–5 Wednesday, Thursday, Friday, Saturday and Sunday; closed: Monday and Tuesday.
See 'Moscow of the Tsars', Excursion 3

Metro: *Revolyutsii Ploshchad ML1, 2 or 4*

Central Lenin Museum
Revolyutsii Ploshchad, 2
Open: 11–7:30 Tuesday, Wednesday, Thursday; 9–6:30 Friday, Saturday and Sunday; closed: Monday.
See 'Moscow of the Townspeople', Excursion 6
The Central Lenin Museum is housed in the former Moscow City Council (*Duma*) building. Over 12,000 items, displayed in 34 rooms, are devoted to the life and work of Lenin. On exhibit are first editions of his writings, manuscripts, and letters as well as the first issue of the underground newspaper *Iskra* (The Spark) published while Lenin was living. The furnishings of Lenin's house where he lived while exiled in Siberia, the coat with bullet holes from an assassination attempt in 1918, and a replica of his study and office in the Kremlin are also on display.

Metro: *Kropotkinskaya*
ML1

Marx and Engels Museum
Marksa i Engelsa Ulitsa, 5
Open: 12–7 Tuesday, Wednesday, and Friday; 11–6 Thursday and Saturday;
closed: Monday and last day of month.

Metro: *Sportivnaya*
ML1

Novodevichiy Convent
Pirogovskaya Bolshaya Ulitsa, 2
Open: 11–5 May–October; 11–4:30 November–April; closed: Tuesday and first
Monday of the month.
See 'Moscow of the Clergy', Excursion 23

Metro: *Revolyutsii*
Ploshchad
ML1, 2 or 3

Central Museum of the Revolution of the USSR
Gorkogo Ulitsa, 21
Open: 10–6 Tuesday; 12–8 Wednesday; 11–7 Friday; closed Monday,
Thursday and Saturday.
See 'Moscow of the Townspeople', Excursion 6 ①

Metro: *Nogina*
Ploshchad
ML5, 6-A

House of the Boyars Romanov (Museum of 17th-Century Boyardom)
Razina Ulitsa, 10
Open: 10–5 Monday, Wednesday, Thursday to Sunday; closed: Tuesday.
See 'Moscow of the Townspeople', Excursion 5

Metro: *Ilicha Ploshchad*
ML6-A

Rublev Museum of Russian Religious Art
Pryamikovo Ploshchad, 10
Open: 11–6 Monday, Tuesday, Thursday to Sunday; closed: Wednesday.
See 'Moscow of the Clergy', Excursion 24.

Metro: *Biblioteka Imeni*
Lenina
ML1, 3, or 3-A

Shchusev Museum of Architecture
Kalinina Prospekt, 5
Open: 10–6 Wednesday; closed: Tuesday.

Art Museums

Armoury Museum (Oruzheinaya Palata)
Kremlin
Open: 9:30–5 Monday to Wednesday, Friday to Sunday; closed: Thursdays.
See 'Moscow of the Tsars', Excursion 1

Metro: *Revolyutsii*
Ploshchad
ML1, 2 or 3

Museum of Folk Art
Stanislavskogo Ulitsa, 7
Open: 11–5 Wednesday, Friday to Sunday; 2–8 Tuesday and Thursday;
closed: Monday and last day of month.

Metro: *Nogina*
Ploshchad

State Museum of Oriental Art
Obukha Ulitsa, 16
Open: 11–7 Tuesday to Sunday; closed: Monday.

MUSEUMS AND THEATRES

The Pushkin Museum has a substantial collection of Greek treasures as well as French sculptures, including works by Rodin.

Pushkin Museum of Fine Arts (1898–1912), best known for its collection of French Impressionist art.

Pushkin Museum of Fine Arts (Museum of Western Art)
Volkhonka Ulitsa, 12
Open: 10–8 Tuesday to Sunday; closed: Monday.
The Pushkin Museum of Fine Arts, designed in neo-classical style by architect Roman Klein, opened in 1912 and is best known for its collection of French impressionist art. It was originally conceived as a museum for plaster casts of famous sculptures so that Moscow art students could familiarize themselves with the masterpieces of Western sculpture without having to leave Russia. Gradually, the museum's holdings expanded with private collections, such as the Golenishchev collection of ancient Egyptian art, a prized exhibit. Following the 1917 Revolution, during which Lenin nationalized all private collections (including Rumiantsev's, Shchukin's, and Morozov's), some of the finest paintings, including masterpieces of impressionists and post-impressionist art, moved to the Pushkin Museum. The French collection includes works by Corot, Monet, Matisse, Manet, Picasso, Cezanne, Gauguin, Van Gogh, and Degas. Spanish, Italian, Dutch, and Flemish art is also represented.

The museum has a substantial collection of Greek treasures as well as an important collection of French nineteenth- and twentieth-century sculptures, including statues by Rodin.

Metro:
Novokuznetskaya
ML5, 2

Tretyakov Gallery of Art
Lavrushinskiy Pereulok, 10
Open: 10–7 Tuesday to Sunday; closed: Monday.
The Tretyakov Gallery, with its collection of almost fifty thousand paintings, is devoted exclusively to Russian art and serves as a guide to Russian art history beginning with Kievan icons from the eleventh century. A collection of icons representing Vladimir-Suzdal, Novgorod, and Pskov artists is on display as well as the famous *Trinity* and other icons by Rublev, Theophanes the Greek, and Dionysius. Other halls are devoted to portraits, sketches, landscapes, and other works by Russian artists dating from the eighteenth to the twentieth centuries.

Metro:
Novokuznetskaya
ML5, 2

Tropinin Museum of 18th- and 19th-Century Russian Painting
Shchetininskiy Pereulok, 10
Open: Monday, Thursday, and Friday 12–9; Saturday and Sunday 10–7; closed: Tuesday and Wednesday. (Excursion Plan 25 ⑫)

Metro: *Prospekt Mira*
ML3, 4

Vasnetsov House Museum
Vasnetsova Pereulok, 13
Open: 11–5 Tuesday; 1–9 Thursday and Saturday; 11–7 Sunday; closed: Monday, Wednesday and Friday.
This picturesque wood and plaster house modelled after the old Russian wooden houses with a *terem* (turret) garret was designed by architect/artist Viktor Vasnetsov as his home. It was built between 1893 and 1894 by carpenters

House museum of the painter Viktor Vasnetsov (1848–1926).

from the city of Vladimir renowned for their skilled carpentry and for their wooden churches and houses.

The living room is perhaps the most impressive with a large beautifully carved table and chairs. The buffets in this room were built according to Vasnetsov's plans by his brother, Apollinary. A circular staircase leads to the upper level occupied by Vasnetsov's studio. On display are the painter's canvases, mainly scenes from Russian fairy tales, his favourite theme.

Literary Museums

Metro:
Krasnopresnenskaya
ML4, 6

Chekhov House Museum

Sadovaya-Kudrinskaya Ulitsa, 6

Open: 11–5 Tuesday, Thursday, Saturday, Sunday; closed: Monday, Wednesday and Friday.

The Anton Chekhov Museum opened in 1954, the date coinciding with the fiftieth anniversary of the writer's death. While living here between 1896 and 1900, Chekhov decided to abandon his medical profession and become a writer. *Ivanov* and nearly one hundred short stories, including *The Fires*, *The Birthday Party*, *The Fit*, and *The Marriage*, were written in this house. Chekhov's study contains his ink set, candelabra, and letter opener. Photographs of scenes from his stage plays and scenes from films based on his writings are kept on the second floor.

Metro:
Novoslobodskaya
ML4

Dostoevsky Museum

Dostoyevskogo Ulitsa, 2

Open: 11–6 Thursday, Saturday, and Sunday; 10–4 Monday; 1–9 Wednesday and Friday; closed: Tuesday.

This house, where Fedor Dostoevsky was born in 1821 and raised, was converted into a museum in 1928; a monument to him was placed in the adjoining garden.

Metro: *Arbatskaya*
ML1, 3 or 3-A

Maxim Gorky's House

Kachalova Ulitsa, 6/2

Open: 8–5 Wednesday, Thursday, and Friday; 8–8 Saturday and Sunday; closed: Monday and Tuesday.

Maxim Gorky lived here during the later period of his life from 1931–6. More than just a residence, it served as the headquarters for meetings leading to the First Congress of Soviet Writers. Gorky was elected by the Congress to be the chairman of the first Union of Soviet Writers.

Metro: *Arbatskaya*
ML1, 3 or 3-A

Maxim Gorky Literary Museum

Vorovskogo Ulitsa, 25a (Excursion 18 ⑨)

Open: 8–8 Tuesday and Friday: 10–5 Wednesday, Thursday and Sunday: closed: Monday and Saturday.

The museum, opened in 1937, has books, letters, manuscripts, and photographs relating to the life and work of the father of Soviet literature, Maxim Gorky (real name, Alexei Peshkov). Of particular importance is a first edition of his book, *Mother* (1906), partly written while he was in the United States.

Pushkin Museum

Kropotkinskaya Ulitsa, 12/2

Open: 1–7:30 Saturday; 11–5:30 Sunday; closed: Monday–Friday.

The museum contains letters, first editions, and paintings relating to the life and work of Russia's greatest poet, Aleksandr Pushkin. Of particular interest is the authentic furniture, china, and other household items which belonged to the poet, his family, and close friends. (Excursion 12.)

Leo Tolstoy House

Lva Tolstogo Ulitsa, 21

Open: 10–3 Tuesday to Sunday; closed: Monday.

This museum is located in the former residence of Leo Tolstoy where sixteen rooms are preserved as they were when Tolstoy lived here with his family from 1882 to 1901. In his study he wrote *The Living Corpse* and *The Power of Darkness*. (Excursion 13.)

Leo Tolstoy Museum

Kropotkinskaya Ulitsa, 11

Open: 10–3:30 Tuesday to Sunday; closed: Monday.

This museum, founded in 1911, contains the best documentation on the work of Leo Tolstoy. (Excursion 12.)

Other Museums

Polytechnical Museum

Novaya Ploshchad, 3/4

Open: 10–5 Wednesday, Friday, and Sunday; 1–8 Tuesday and Thursday; closed: Monday and Saturday.

This building designed in 1887 by architects I. A. Monighetti, N. A. Shokhin, and P. A. Voeikov, is one of Moscow's oldest museums. It houses collections of natural history, anthropology, and ethnography. The original collection is based on materials from the first polytechnical exhibit of 1872.

Timiriazev Biological Museum

Gruzinskaya Malaya Ulitsa, 15

Open: 12–7 Tuesday–Sunday; closed: Monday.

The museum was opened in 1922 and named after the naturalist Kliment Timiriazev (1843–1920). Exhibits in seventeen halls display materials connected with the lives and work of such Russian life scientists as Timiriazev and I. V. Michurin. Included is a unique collection of sculptures of prehistoric man.

USSR Exhibition of Economic Achievements (VDNKh) Proskpekt Mira

Open: 9:30–10 Monday–Friday; 9:30–11 Saturday and Sunday.

Included in this 553-acre park are pavilions built in the architectural styles of the different Soviet republics and others devoted to different branches of agriculture, industry and science.

MUSEUMS AND THEATRES

Theatres, Concert Halls, and Theatrical Museums (Visitors should request tickets through their hotels via Intourist)

Metro: *Sverdlova Ploshchad, Prospekt Marksa, or Revolyutsii Ploshchad ML1, 2 or 3*

Bolshoy Theatre

Sverdlova Ploshchad

The Bolshoy Theatre, Moscow's oldest and most famous opera and ballet house, has existed on this site since 1780, except that is was then known as the Bolshoy (Big) Petrovsky Theatre. After burning down in 1805, it was rebuilt in 1824 by architect Osip Bove. In 1853 after it burned down for the second time, the Imperial Theatrical Society acquired the site and commissioned architect A. K. Cavos to design the present structure incorporating the walls and the colonnade of the earlier buildings. The eight Ionic columns and the bronze sculpture of *Phoebus in the Chariot of the Sun* are distinct and unique in Moscow (Excursion 18 ④)

The Bolshoy Theatre, Osip Bove (1824) and A. K. Cavos (1853).

Since its first performance in 1776, which predated the building, the Bolshoy developed an impressive repertoire of Russian operas and ballets in addition to programmes of Western music and dance. The Russian opera repertoire includes: *Ruslan and Ludmila* (Glinka), *Boris Godunov* (Musorgsky), *The Queen of Spades* (Tchaikovsky), *Prince Igor* (Borodin), *Eugene Onegin (Tchaikovsky), Sadko* (Rimsky-Korsakov). *Khovanshchina* (Mussorgsky), and *The Legend of the Invisible City of Kitezh* (Rimsky-Korsakov).

Beginning with 1778, the Bolshoy was known for its ballet performances, choreographed by M. Petipa, M. Fokine, L. Ivanov, and others. Don't miss: *Giselle, Swan Lake, Ivan the Terrible, Spartacus, Anna Karenina, Fountains of Bakhchiserai,* and *The Nutcracker.*

Metro: Sverdlova Ploshchad, Prospekt Marksa, or Revolyutsii Ploshchad ML1, 2 or 3

Malyi Theatre
Sverdlova Ploshchad, 1/6
The Malyi (Little) Theatre, Moscow's first dramatic theatre, was designed by the architect Osip Bove between 1821 and 1824 and subsequently rebuilt by Konstantin Thon in 1840. It played a major role in the development of Russian national theatre and is famous for staging Russian classical plays, particularly those of the playwright Aleksandr N. Ostrovsky, whose statue is outside Malyi. Its present repertoire includes Russian classics, plays by Soviet dramatists, and those translated from foreign languages.

etro: Prospekt Marksa ML1, 2 or 3

Moscow Arts Theatre (MKHAT)
Khudozhestvennogo Teatra Proyezd, 2
The Moscow Art Theatre, better known by its initials MKHAT (Moscow Art Acedemic Theatre), was founded in 1898 by two famous actors and directors, K. S. Stanislavsky and V. I. Nemirovich-Danchenko. The theatre is sometimes called the House of Chekhov because it owes its fame to the plays of dramatist Anton P. Chekhov, particularly the *Chaika*, or *The Sea Gull*, the theatre's emblem. (Excursion 5 ⑥).

Metro: Pushkinskaya ML2, 6

Moscow Arts Theatre, New Building
Tverskoy Bulvar, 24
This theatre, an extension of MKHAT, opened in 1973.

tro: Biblioteka Imeni Lenina ML1, 3 or 3-A

Kremlin Palace of Congresses
Entrance through the Trinity Gate leading to the Kremlin
See 'Moscow of the Tsars', Excursion 1 ㊱.
The Kremlin Palace of Congresses was designed as a convention hall, but when not in use by the government, it serves as a second stage for the Bolshoy Theatre.

tro: Prospekt Marksa or Arbatskaya ML1, 3

Moscow Conservatory of Music
Gertsena Ulitsa, 13 (Excursion 5 ⑥)
Bolshoy Zal is used for symphony concerts; Malyi Zal is used for recitals.

Metro: Sverdlova ~shchad ML1, 2 or 3

Stanislavsky and Nemirovich-Danchenko Musical Theatre
Pushkinskaya Ulitsa, 17

MUSEUMS AND THEATRES

Founded in 1941 as the result of a merger between the Stanislavsky Opera Theatre and the Nemirovich-Danchenko Musical Theatre. The repertoire includes operas and ballets and the quality of performances often matches those of the Bolshoy.

Metro: *Pushikinskaya*

Stanislavsky House Museum
Stanislavskogo Ulitsa, 7
Open: 2–7 Wednesday and Friday: 11–6 Thursday, Saturday, and Sunday; closed: Monday and Tuesday.

Metro: *Prospekt Mira*

Yermolova Drama Theatre
Gorkogo Ulitsa, 5
Founded in 1937 and named after the famous Russian actress Maria Yermolova (1853–1928). It has a varied repertoire which includes both Russian and Western classics as well as modern plays.

Metro: *Taganskaya*

Taganka Theatre of Drama and Comedy
Ulitsa Chkalova, 76
Considered to be Moscow's avant-garde theatre, it features plays by contemporary Soviet writers and Western playwrights. The performances are often controversial. Taganka was the home of the popular singer-composer Vladimir Vyssotsky, whose premature death and rebellious writing made him a legendary hero.

The actress M. N. Yermolova.

Metro: *Belorusskaya*

Roman Gypsy Theatre
Leningradskiy Prospekt, 32–2, in the concert hall of the Hotel Sovetskaya. Started in 1931 by a group of Moscow singers, dancers, and playwrights determined to preserve the gypsy folk traditions, it is today the only gypsy theatre in the world.

Metro. *Universitet*

Children's Musical Theatre
Vernadskogo Prospekt, 5
The repertoire of the Children's Musical Theatre, which opened in 1965 under the directorship of Natalia Sats, was designed to captivate young audiences and educate them. A particular attraction for children, besides the programme, is the bird atrium on the second floor.

Metro: *Mayakovskaya*

Central Puppet Theatre
Sadovaya-Samotechnaya Ulitsa, 3
The Central Puppet Theatre in Moscow is as entertaining for adults as it is

for children. The theatre dates from 1931 and bears the name of Sergei I. Obraztsov, who took over as director in 1945. The repertoire is outstanding, and some plays like *Don Juan* do not even require knowledge of the Russian language to enjoy. Note: Evening performances are closed to children under the age of 18.

Metro: *Kolkhoznaya*
Metro: *Universitet*

Moscow State Circus
Tsvetnoy Bulvar, 13
Vernadskogo Prospekt, 17
The old, or the original, theatre on Tsvetnoy Bulvar is cosier; the new one, more modern. The performances at both are well worth seeing by children as well as adults.

Metro: *Smolenskaya*

Scriabin Museum
Vakhtangova Ulitsa, 11
This museum, honouring pianist and composer Aleksandr Scriabin (1871–1915), is located in the house where the musician lived and worked during his life.

Metro: *Dzerzhinskaya*

Mayakovsky Museum
Serova Proyezd, 3/6

Metro: *Paveletskaya*

Bakhrushin Central Theatre Museum
Bakhrushina Ulitsa, 31/12

Metro: *Prospekt Marksa*

Operetta Theatre
Pushkinskaya Ulitsa, 6

Metro: *Prospekt Marksa*

Kolonnyi Zal
Pushkinskaya Ulitsa

Metro: *Prospekt Marksa or Nogina Ploshchad*

Sovetskaya Hotel Concert Hall
Hotel Rossiya

Metro: *Mayakovskaya*

Tchaikovsky Concert Hall
Ploshchad Mayakovskogo
Sadovaya Bolshaya Ulitsa, 20
The large circular auditorium of the Tchaikovsky Hall, named after Petr I. Tchaikovsky (1840–93), was designed as a concert hall. Its giant pipe organ (7,800 pipes and weighing 20 tons) is Czechoslovakian made and was installed in 1959. This is where the famous Tchaikovsky music competitions are held.

MUSEUMS AND THEATRES

RESTAURANTS

*E*ating out in Moscow can be a pleasant experience, especially if several rules are observed. One, since Russians seldom go to restaurants, eating out is a special occasion, and fast service is not to be expected. Two, reservations should be made at least one day in advance. When making reservations, mention whether you want *Zakuski* (appetizers), otherwise you may find the table laden with cold hors d'oeuvres which can be expensive. Some large restaurants often have live bands and dance floors, so you may wish to request a table away from the music. If you do not speak Russian, ask your hotel to make reservations for you.

The following are a few specialities which are usually worth trying:

Note: Since telephone numbers change in Moscow, check first with your hotel.

	Phonetic Pronunciation
Black caviar (with bread and butter)	*Ikra chornaia*
Cucumbers with sour cream	*Ogoortsy so smetanoy*
Beet soup	*Borshch*
Meat and cabbage soup	*Solyanka*
Bouillon with meat patties	*Boullion c pirozhkom*
Beef Stroganoff	*Bif Stroganov*
Chicken Kiev	*Kotleta po Kievski*
Pancakes	*Bliny*
Meat on a skewer	*Shashlik*
Ice cream	*Morozhenoye*

Perestroika has brought many changes, including the appearance of numerous private restaurants throughout Moscow. Check with your hotel for any recommendations, reservations, and prices since most of these restaurants tend to be very expensive. Listed below are some of Moscow's best restaurants:

Krasnopresnenskaya Naberezhnaya, 12; tel.: 253-2383

International Hotel and Trade Centre (Gostinitsa Mezhdunarodnaya)
Hotel International has the following four restaurants:

The Russian Restaurant (Russky or Rus) is decorated in the old Russian style with velvet upholstered chairs and rugs. The food is fairly good, especially *Chicken Kiev* and the consomme with a Russian variety of ravioli, known as *pelemeni* (*soop s pelemeniami*). A gypsy band with singers and dancers provides live entertainment on Tuesday, Thursday, and Saturday nights. Reserve in advance.

Sakura (Japanese) is Moscow's most expensive restaurant payable in hard currency or with a charge card. The food and decor are Japanese.

Continental is cosy and comfortable with good service. A pianist and violinist provide soft background music for evening dining.

Business Club features a nightly floor show, has a dance band, and serves a limited dinner menu. Food is often served cold. There is a steep entrance fee payable in hard currency ahead of time. There is an extra charge for drinks and dinner, also in hard currency. Reserve in advance.

Gorkogo Ulitsa, 1, in the National Hotel; tel.: 203-55-50	**National Restaurant (Natsional)** The atmosphere is pleasant and the restaurant has a scenic view of the Kremlin. The main restaurant has a band and a menu payable in roubles. There is also a hard currency restaurant which is less crowded. Note, however, in the hard currency restaurant a portion of caviar costs 15 roubles while the same caviar in the rouble restaurant is 6 roubles a portion! There are also private banquet rooms suitable for private business parties or dinners. (See p. 56.)

Gorkogo Ulitsa, 1, in the National Hotel; tel.: 203-55-50

National Restaurant (Natsional)

The atmosphere is pleasant and the restaurant has a scenic view of the Kremlin. The main restaurant has a band and a menu payable in roubles. There is also a hard currency restaurant which is less crowded. Note, however, in the hard currency restaurant a portion of caviar costs 15 roubles while the same caviar in the rouble restaurant is 6 roubles a portion! There are also private banquet rooms suitable for private business parties or dinners. (See p. 56.)

Arbat Ulitsa, 2; tel.: 291-4185

Praga Restaurant

One of Moscow's favourite restaurants with several dining rooms of which the best are the Czech (*Cheshkiy Zal*), decorated with Czech motives; the Winter (*Zimniy Zal*), with fountains and greenery; the Terrace Restaurant, an open-air summer restaurant. Upstairs there is also the Mirror (*Zerkalnyi*) Banquet Hall, an attractive room for a reception (up to 100 people). The food is excellent, the prices reasonable, and one can frequently find good Czech beer there. Reserve in advance. (See p. 258.)

Neglinnaya, Ulitsa 29; tel.: 924-6053

Uzbekistan

The food and decor are characteristic of the Central Asian Republic of Uzbekistan. It is now somewhat run down, but the garden restaurant is still pleasant in the summer. Specialties include *shashlik*, *liulia kebab* (ground lamb), and very good soups.

Dvadtsat Pyatogo Oktyabrya Ulitsa, 13; tel.: 921-1872 (October 25 Street, No. 13)

Slaviansky Bazar

This is Moscow's oldest and most colourful restaurant. Located near GUM, it has a band on weekends and a lively atmosphere. The *bliny* (pancakes) and *miaso v Gorshechke* (stewed beef in clay pots served piping hot with potatoes and vegetables) are considered the best in Moscow. No smoking is allowed. (See Excursion 5 ⑥.)

Gorkogo Ulitsa, 24; tel.: 299-94-20 or 299-85-06

Baku

The food, decor, and music are characteristic of the Azerbaydzhan Republic near the Caspian Sea. Specialities include soup Azerbayzhdansky (a rice soup), a variety of *shashliks*, rice (pilaf) dishes, and a wide selection of hors d'oeuvres, which are a meal in themselves. (Don't hesitate to try the pickled garlic. It's excellent.)

Ostankino Television Tower; tel.: 282-12-38

Sedmoe Nebo (Seventh Heaven)

This restaurant should be seen during the day, preferably a clear one, after visiting the observation deck which offers a panoramic view of Moscow from 1,200 feet. The dining room revolves, allowing a full view of the city. There is one fixed menu with a set price.

Gorkogo Ulitsa 6; tel.: 229-37-62

Aragvi

Serves Georgian specialities and has a Georgian decor. The service is slow.

RESTAURANTS

Zhdanova Ulitsa, 3, in the Berlin Hotel; tel.: 923-3581

Berlin Restaurant

Once the dining-room of a fashionable hotel, it still preserves the gilded Baroque decor of the belle epoque. As one of the few restaurants accessible to Russians, it is always crowded and lively.

An out-of-town restaurant on the road to Uspenskoye, a 25-minute drive out of Moscow; tel.: 561-42-44

Russkaya Izba (The Russian Hut)

This is a colourful restaurant built in the style of old Russian peasant homes, with carved wooden beams and painted lintels. The hors d'oeuvres are locally prepared and often feature such delicacies as marinated mushrooms, herring, cranberry sauce, fruit preserves, etc. The soups are hearty and a meal in themselves. Try *solianka* or *borshch*. The restaurant overlooks a river where one can swim in summertime or ski in the winter.

Across the road from the Arkhangelskoye Estate-Museum; tel.: 562-0328

Arkhangelskoye

Located 30 kilometres outside Moscow, the restaurant provides a welcome rest after a visit to the museum, the former estate of Prince Yussupov (see Excursion 3). The restaurant is located in a picturesque birch grove and is particularly pleasant in the summer when the tables are set out on the terrace. Occasionally one can find game dishes such as *zharkoe po okhotnichi* (hunter's stew) or bear meat on the menu.

SHOPPING

*S*hopping in Moscow can be a challenging experience, depending on one's particular interests. There are some stores specializing in Russian souvenir goods (for Western currencies) called *Beriozkas*, as well as antique stores known as *Kommissioniy* (Commission Shops). We suggest shopping at *Beriozkas* for souvenirs and browsing through department stores such as GUM (Red Square) for local flavour. Of particular interest to the Westerner would be the **poster store** on Ulitsa Arbat, around the corner from Praga Restaurant, and the **military shop**.

The following shops have been divided into two categories: Those where payment is made in roubles, and those which accept only hard currency or international charge cards.

Rouble Stores

Items to look for in the local stores are fancy carved wooden boxes, ceramic vases and bowls, colourful peasant-style figurines, red and black lacquered dishes and china, posters and framed prints of Russian fairy tales. Compare prices before buying. You may find hard currency stores offer the best prices.

Department Stores

GUM (Gosudarstvennyi Universalnyi Magazin — State Department Store), Krasnaya Ploshchad, 3 (Red Square)

Detsky Mir (Children's World; more than just a childen's department store), Prospekt Marksa, 2

Dom Igrushki (House of Toys; playthings, some clothing), Kutuzovskiy Prospekt, 8

Souvenir Shops

Russian Souvenir, Kutuzovskiy Prospekt, 9

Handicrafts, Ukrainskiy Bulvar, 6

Bread Store,
Kalinina Prospekt, 46

The largest bread and pastry shop in Moscow with a wide variety of freshly baked bread and rolls.

Old Books

Bukinist (secondhand books). Many such stores are located throughout Moscow. Two of the better-stocked are at Ulitsa Dimitrova, 18 and Leninskiy Prospekt, 69.

Antikvar (antique books and prints), Prospekt Marksa, 1 (next to the Hotel Metropol)

New Books

Dom Knigi, Kalinina Prospekt, 26. Moscow's largest bookstore with a good collection of art books, prints, and books in Western languages.

Book World, Kirova Ulitsa, 6

Crystal, Glass, Ceramics, China

Dom Farfora (House of Porcelain), Leninskiy Prospekt, 36. Moscow's largest and nicest store for china, crystal, ceramics, and glassware.

Kristal, Gorkogo Ulitsa, 4

Theatrical and Ballet Supplies,
Gertsena Ulitsa, 49

Records

Melodiya, Kalinina Prospekt, 40. Moscow's largest and most complete collection of classical and popular records.

Antique Shops

It is possible to find attractive antiques in Moscow, but they are usually overpriced. Remember that antiques can be taxed at 100 per cent upon leaving, so keep all receipts of purchase.

Commission Shops

It is best to shop at commission shops when they first open for better selections — at 11 a.m. and after lunch at 3 p.m.
Ulitsa Arbat, 32. The speciality here is china and crystal.
Ulitsa Dimitrova, 54/58. This is one of the largest commission shops. It has a varied collection of samovars, porcelain, crystal, brass, and art.
Frunzenskaya Naberezhnaya, 54. This store has antique furniture, clocks, mirrors, and old boxes.

Hard Currency Stores (*Beriozka Stores*)

Items to buy from Beriozkas are black caviar, enamelled and filigreed *podstakanniki* (metal tea-glass holders), and other such enamelled items as tiny forks and spoons, hand-painted flowered trays and boxes, tea cosy dolls dressed in native Russian peasant clothing, flowered wool shawls, and old books. Russian fur hats, amber jewellery, and wooden *Matryoshka* dolls used to be popular items, but they are now enormously overpriced.

All Intourist hotels have Beriozka stores that sell gift items as well as cigarettes, alcohol, chocolate, and imported goods. The Beriozka in the Rossiya Hotel is the largest. The following are Beriozka stores not located in hotels:

Ulitsa Kropotkinskaya, 31

This bookstore is the best source in town for English and other language books and also has a good collection of books in Russian, especially classical literature. The art books are well written and make excellent gifts.

Kutuzovskiy Prospekt, 7

This Beriozka, a branch of the Rossiya Hotel Beriozka, is similar to the ones found in the hotels. The lower level has a selection of crystal, porcelain, and small souvenirs. On the second level are fur hats and coats, jewellery, perfumes, and a limited selection of imported clothes.

Pirogovskaya Bolshaya Ulitsa (across the street from the Novodevichiy Monastery)

This is the largest gift/souvenir store, but it offers only the usual Beriozka items.

Vneshtorg Gold Shop
(Pushkinskaya Ulitsa, 9)

This store specialists in gold coins, medals, diamonds, and other precious and semiprecious stones and jewellery.

In general, stores, except for hotel Beriozkas and some food stores, are closed on Sunday. Food and bread stores are closed between 1 and 2 p.m. All others are closed between 2 and 3 p.m. Nearly all stores stay open until 7 or 8 p.m.

SHOPPING

HOTELS

*T*he tourist arriving in Moscow usually does not have a choice of hotels. This decision is made by Intourist, the Soviet government agency in charge of 'International Tourists'. Most Intourist hotels have at least one restaurant, a barber shop, hairdresser, laundry service, and a special bureau (open from 9 a.m. to 9 p.m.) which arranges for excursions, transportation, and theatre, circus, and concert tickets. In addition, some of the hotels have excellent health facilities, particularly saunas. For the women, we recommend the cosmeticians. Most of them make their own creams and astringents. Facials, manicures, and pedicures are priced very reasonably.

Mantulinskaya Ulitsa, 5: tel.: 253-77-29 or 253-2378

International Hotel and Trade Centre (Mezhdunarodnaya)
Barber, hairdresser, cosmetician, swimming pool, Beriozka shop, bar, cafe

The International Hotel, a joint Soviet-American venture, opened in 1978. It has a modern interior with glass elevators and a water fountain in the main lobby. Of interest is a Russified clock with a gold rooster which crows and flaps its wings on the hour. There are three restaurants (the Russ, Continental, and Sakura). The Business Club has a floor show.

Gorkogo Ulitsa (across from Red Square); tel.: 203-65-39 or 203-55-66

The Natsional
Hairdresser, cosmetician

The National is one of Moscow's grand old hotels, decorated in the European tradition. It has a pleasant restaurant overlooking Red Square which also serves good food.

Prospekt Marksa, 1/4; tel.: 255-66-77 228-41-67, or 225-67-73

The Metropol
Barber, Hairdresser, hard currency bar

The Metropol is an attractive building located near Red Square. The hard currency bar, which stays open at night, is a convenient place to go after the Bolshoy Theatre or Palace of Congresses. The attractive hard currency tea room (*Chainaya*) on the fourth floor serves excellent bliny as well as other Russian specialities until midnight. There is currently a cover charge per person after 7 p.m.

Ulitsa Razina, 6 (behind Red Square); tel.: 298-5400

The Rossiya
Barber, hairdresser, cosmetician

The Rossiya which overlooks Red Square, is one of the world's largest hotels. It has the best hard currency Beriozka in Moscow with the largest selection of Russian souvenirs. The restaurant on the twenty-first floor has mediocre food but offers a sensational view of the Kremlin.

Gorkogo Ulitsa, 3/5; tel.: 203-40-08 or 203-40-07

The Intourist
Barber, hairdresser, hard currency bar, cosmetician

The Intourist is centrally located near Red Square and is the point from which most excursions begin. There is a restaurant on the third floor which accepts only hard currency and a lunchtime buffet which accepts roubles. Of interest is a nightclub in the basement which attracts a diverse group of Russians and foreigners.

The Cosmos

Prospekt Mira, 150;
tel.: 217-07-86 or
217-0786

Barber, hairdresser, pool, sauna, bowling alley

The French-built Cosmos (circa 1970) has several bars and three large restaurants (Le Lunaire, La Terrasse, and the Dubrava). The bars accept hard currency only, but restaurant bills are payable in roubles.

RECREATIONAL ACTIVITIES

*S*ince the Moscow winter is long, cold weather sports, such as ice skating and cross country skiing, are popular with everyone. Listed below are some of Moscow's most popular recreational activities for both winter and summer.

Ice Skating

Moscow's most popular ice skating rink is at **Gorky Park**. With the onset of winter, this pleasant park with an amusement area is turned into one large rink. Music is piped through loud speakers and lights go on at night to transform the park into a fairylike scene of colourfully clothed ice skaters.

In addition to frozen paths throughout the park, there are two large rinks, each with its own music system. Skating on the paths is free, but there is a small charge for the rinks.

The park is open every day from 10 a.m. to 10 p.m. (winter hours). Tickets for the rink can be purchased at the cashier's box outside the entrance to the main gate. Ice skates can be rented at **Sokolniki Park**.

Cross-Country Skiing

Cross-country skiing in and around Moscow allows one to enjoy the Russian landscape at its scenic best. Often the trails lead right up to small farming villages, with their brightly painted wooden houses and carved window frames, little changed from tsarist days. Two of the most picturesque areas for skiing are:

Peredelkino: Drive straight out Kutuzovskiy Prospekt, away from the centre of the city and park your car a few kilometres beyond the outer ring road.

Warsaw Pact Lake Area: Drive straight out Leninskiy Prospekt and stop several hundred yards beyond the outer ring road on the right hand side. Good skiing is also available on the left side of the road where, from your car, you can see several villages in the distance.

Cross-country skiis can be rented at **Sokolniki Park**.

Troika Rides

For a few weeks each year around the New Year, troika rides can be arranged at the **Park of Soviet Economic Achievement** (VDNKh) on **Prospekt Mira**. The troika, a sleigh pulled by three horses (*Troika* means 'a group of three' in Russian), was the traditional form of winter transportation in the days before the train and automobiles. Though the ride is only about fifteen minutes long and the cost is rather high, it is a memorable experience. After the ride, vodka, tea, sandwiches, and pastries are served in one of the nearby pavilions. Arrangements must be made through Intourist.

Swimming

Year-round swimming is possible in several places throughout the city. The most interesting, perhaps, is the heated open-air pool at **Kropotkinskaya Naberezhnaya, 37**. Other more conventional places to swim in winter are at the **Intourist** hotel pools at the **International** and the **Cosmos**. Bring your own soap and towel.

During the summer, a number of river beaches outside Moscow are open for swimming. These include **Khimki**, **Serebryanniy Bor**, **Uspenskoye**, and **Bukhta Radosti** (Bay of Joy). Swimming is not recommended in the rivers inside the city, but sunbathing is popular on the banks of the Moscow River. Ask your local Intourist Service Bureau for directions to the swimming areas mentioned above.

Tennis

There are special outdoor courts reserved for foreigners at **Luzhniki Park** in Lenin Hills, beginning around 1 March, weather permitting.

Horseriding

Horseriding is available to foreigners at the **Hippodrome**, **Ulitsa Begovaya**, **22**. Reservations for lessons or riding must be arranged through Intourist.

Boat Cruises

Boat cruises along the Moscow River last an hour and a half and are available during the summer from June until September or October, depending on the weather. The cruise begins at the wharf near the **Kiev Train Station** (Metro: Kiyevskaya). The fare is inexpensive. A pleasant way to relax in the summertime.

Spectator Sports

Tickets for soccer matches, ice hockey games, figure skating, and other athletic events may be purchased at many kiosks (newstands) throughout the city. An easier way, however, is through the Intourist Service Bureau at your hotel.

Parks

There are several parks in the Moscow area where one can go for pleasant walks. The most popular of these parks are:

Gorky Park, near Oktyabrskaya and **Park Kultury Metro stations**. In the summer the park is open from 9 a.m. to midnight. In addition to the many wooded paths, the park has an amusement area, a boating lake, a restaurant, and several small cafes.

Sokolniki Park, Sokolniki Metro station. This park is the site of most Soviet international trade exhibitions. In winter, paths are flooded for skating, and the park's broad expanses and birch groves are also favourite places for cross country skiing. Skates and cross country skis can be rented in the large pavilion at the entrance to the skating area. In addition to skating and skiing, the park has an amusement park, a place to rent bicycles, a sports arena, and several restaurants and cafes.

Izmaylovo Park, Izmaylovskaya Metro station. This park was once the estate of the Romanov family and was often visited by the tsars. It is one of the largest parks (2,950 acres) and contains an amusement park, open-air theatre, and several cafes. (See Excursion 3.)

Zoo, Gruzinskaya Bolshaya Ulitsa, 1; **Krasnopresnenskaya Metro station (ML4 or 6)**. Walking through this zoo is a pleasant way to spend a few hours, with or without your children. The smaller animals (birds, monkeys, etc.) are on the main entrance side of the street. Across the street are the larger animals. Several lakes adorn the park, and there are many cafes and ice cream stands for refreshment.

EMBASSIES AND EMERGENCY TELEPHONE NUMBERS

American	252-2451-59
Australian	246-5011-16; 241-203536
Austrian	201-7137; 201-7379
Belgium	203-6566; 290-6734
Canada	241-5882; 241-5070
Finland	246-4027-33
France	236-0003; 231-8501
Federal Republic of Germany	252-5521
Greece	290-2274; 291-8900 (day & night)
Ireland (Eire)	288-4101; 288-4192
Italy	241-1533-34
Japan	291-8500-01
Netherlands	291-2999; 291-2948
New Zealand	290-3485; 290-1277
Norway	290-3872; 290-3874 (day & night)
Spain	202-2161; 202-2180
Sweden	147-9009
Switzerland	925-5322; 925-5289
United Kingdom	231-8511-12
Emergency Numbers	
Diplomatic Polyclinic	237-5933; 237-8338
Embassy Doctors	ring Embassies
Tourists' Clinic	254-4396
24-Hour Chemists	925-1846; 221-4942
First Aid, Ambulance	03
Fire	01
Police	02
Emergency Gas Service	04
Information (Moscow telephone numbers)	09
Lost Property	
Metro	222-2085
Taxi	923-8753
Tram, trolley bus, bus	233-4225 Ex. 139
Lost Children	02
Tracing people in hospital	924-3152
Veterinary Services	212-8076

EMBASSIES and EMERGENCIES

RUSSIAN RULERS IN WORLD HISTORY

862 Rurik, Viking Prince of Novgorod

879–912 Oleg makes Kiev the capital of (Kievan) Russia

978–1015 Vladimir I (St Vladimir)

988 Vladimir's baptism. Russia adopts Christianity along with the religious and cultural traditions of Byzanitium

r. 1019–54 Iaroslav the Wise

1113–25 Vladimir Monomach

1147 Yuriy Dolgoruky (first mention of Moscow)

r. 1276–1303 Daniel, First Prince of Moscow

r. 1325–41 Ivan Kalita (The rise of Moscow)

r. 1359–89 Prince Dmitry Donskoy

r. 1389–1425 Basil I

r. 1425–62 Basil II

r. 1462–1505 Ivan III

r. 1505–53 Basil III

b. 1533 Ivan IV (The Terrible) 1547 (crowned Tsar)

r. 1584–98 Fedor Ivanovich (I)

r.1598–1605 Boris Godunov

1605–13 Time of Troubles

r. 1613–45 Michael Romanov

r. 1645–76 Alexis Romanov

700 *Beowulf*
678–814 Charlemagne

814–40 Louis le Debonnair
395–1455 Byzantine Empire
858–867 Pope Nicholas I

r. 962–73 Otto I, Holy Roman Emperor

1031–60 Henri I (married to Yaroslav's daughter Anne)

1071 First Crusade

1200 *Nibelungenlied*
1265-1321 Dante

1270 Louis IX (St) of France dies
1216?–94 Kublai Khan

1328 Black Death

1364–1380 Charles V (the Wise) of France

1400 Chaucer's *Canterbury Tales* completed

1453 Fall of Constantinople
1461–83 Louis XI of France

1479–1516 Ferdinand and Isabella
1492 Christopher Columbus discovers America

r. 1520–66 Suleiman the Magnificent

r. 1558–1603 Queen Elizabeth I
Reformation
1572 Massacre of St Bartholomew

1598 Phillip II King of Spain dies

1606–69 Rembrandt

1610–43 Louis XIII

1618–48 The Thirty Years War

1625–49 Charles I beheaded in 1649.

r. 1676–82 Fedor Alekseyevich III

1682–89 Regent Sofia (daughter of Alexis from his first marriage, sister of Fedor)

r. 1697–1718 Charles XII of Sweden

r. 1689–1725 Peter the Great (son of Alexis from his second marriage)

1701–14 War of the Spanish Succession

r. 1725–27 Catherine I (wife of Peter)

r. 1715–74 Louis XV

r. 1727–30 Peter II (Peter I's grandson)

r. 1730–40 Anna Ivanova (Peter I's niece)

1733–38 War of the Polish Succession

r. 1740–1 Anna Leopoldovna (Ivan V's granddaughter)

r. 1740–86 Frederick II, King of Prussia

r. 1741–61/2 Elizabeth I (daughter of Peter I)

1740–80 Maria Theresa of Austria

r. 1761–62 Peter III (Peter I's grandson)

1774–92 Louis XVI

r. 1762–96 Catherine II, Great (wife of Peter III)

1776 American Revolution
1789–95 French Revolution

r. 1796–1801 Paul I

r. 1801–25 Alexander I

1804–15 Napoleon Bonaparte

r. 1825–55 Nicholas I

1824–30 Charles X of France

r. 1855–81 Alexander II Liberation of serfs

r. 1837–1901 Queen Victoria

1861–5 Abraham Lincoln

r. 1881–94 Alexander III

1871 Unification of Germany

1894–1917 Nicholas II

1901 Discovery of X-rays

March–Nov 1917 Provisional Government

1914 First World War

7 Nov. 1917 Soviets take power

1917–20 Civil War

1922 USSR officially declared

1922 Mussolini

RUSSIAN RULERS

SELECT BIBLIOGRAPHY

Antonova, V. I. and Mneva, N. E. *Gosudarstvennaya Tretyakovskaya Gallereya. Katalog Drevnerusskoy Zhivopisi,* 12 vols (Moscow: Iskusstvo, 1963).

Baedeker, K. *A Handbook for Travellers* (Arno Press/Random House, 1914).

Berton, Kathleen. *Moscow, an Architectural History* (Macmillan, 1977).

Dobson, G. *Moscow* (London: A. & C. Black).

Egorova, M. V. *Zolotoe Koltso* (Moscow: Sovietskaya Rossiya, 1978).

Felber, J. E. (comp.). *The American's Tourist Manual for the USSR* (New Jersey: International Intertrade Index, 1973).

Florinsky, M. *Russia. A History and an Interpretation* (New York: The Macmillan Company, 1953).

Geyneke, N. A. *et al.* (eds.). *Po Moskve* (Moscow: Sabashnikov, 1917).

Gray, C. *The Russian Experiment in Art: 1863-1922* (New York: Harry N. Abrams Inc., 1962).

Hingley, R. A. *Concise History of Russia* (New York: The Viking Press, 1972).

Ikonnikov, A. V. *Kamennaya Letopis Moskvy* (Moscow: Moskovskiy Rabochiy, 1978).

Ilin, M. A. *Moscow. Monuments of Architecture of the 14th-17th Centuries* (Moscow: Iskusstvo, 1973).

——. *Moscow. Monuments of Architecture of the 18th-First Third of the 19th Centuries* (Moscow: Iskusstvo, 1975).

Iswolskiy, H. *Christ in Russia* (Milwaukee: Bruce Publishing Company, 1960).

Kirichenko, E. I. *Architectural Monuments of the 1830s-1910s Moscow:* Iskusstvo, 1977).

Kluichevsky, V. *Istoriya sosloviy v Rossii* (Moscow: 1913).

Louis, V. and Louis, J. *The Complete Guide to the Soviet Union* (London: Michael Joseph, 1976).

Mashkov, I. P. (ed.). *Putevoditel po Moskve* (Moscow: M. A. O. 1913).

Massie, R. K. *Peter the Great* (New York: Alfred Knopf, 1980).

Massie, S. *Land of the Firebird* (New York: Simon & Schuster, 1980).

Mazour, A. G. *Russia, Tsarist and Communist* (New Jersey: D. Van Nostrand Company Inc., 1962).

Moskvich, G. *Illyustrirovanniy Prakticheskiy Putevoditel po Moskve* (Vladikavkaz: Kazbek, 1907).

Owsjannikov, Ju. M. *Moskauer Kloster* (Dresden: VEB Verlag Der Kunst, 1975).

Pushkarev, S. *The Emergence of Modern Russia. 1801-1917* (New York: Rinehart and Winston, 1963).

Simon, S. *Moscou* (Paris: Fayard, 1964).

Sytin, P. V. *Iz istorii moskovskikh ulitis* (Moscow: Moskovskiy rabochiy, 1958).

Talbot Rice, T. *A Concise History of Russian Art* (London: Thames and Hudson, 1963).

Tolstaya, T. V. *The Assumption Cathedral of the Moscow Kremlin* (Moscow: Iskusstvo, 1979).

Voyce, A. *Moscow and the Roots of Russian Culture* (University of Oklahoma Press: 1964).

Vyurkov, A. I. *Rasskazy o staroy Moskve* (Moscow: Moskovskiy rabochiy, 1958).

Zabelin, I. *Domashniy byt Russkikh Tsarey v XVI i XVII st* (Moscow: A. A. Stupina, 1918).

Around the Kremlin (Moscow: Progress Publishers, 1967).

Guide to the Great Kremlin Palace (Moscow: Synod Press, 1914).

Istoriya Moskvy v 6 Tomakh (Moscow: Akademiya nauk SSSR, 1952-7).

Moskva v eye proshlom i nastoyaschem (Moscow: Obrazovanie, 19-).

Nagel's USSR Travel Guide (Geneva: Nagel, 1965).

Pamyatniki Arkhitektury Moskvy. Kreml, Kitay-gorod, Tsentralnye ploshchadi (Moscow: Iskusstvo, 1982).

SELECT BIBLIOGRAPHY

INDEX

Names: *personal names*, patronymics have not been listed, unless to distinguish persons of the same name; *family names*, wives, and daughters are suffixed 'a'/'aya', e.g. Lopukhin, Lopukhina; *Tsars (Emperors)* and *Empresses* are indexed under forename, e.g. Alexis Romanov, Peter I. Some index entries will be found under general headings: Bridges, Cathedrals, Churches, Convents, Hotels, Houses, Monasteries, Museums, Palaces, Squares, Streets, Theatres, Towers.